£4.50p

11/1/74

# THE LITURGY OF COMPREHENSION 1689

ALCUIN CLUB COLLECTIONS
No. 54

# The Liturgy of Comprehension
# 1689

—

*An abortive attempt to revise*

*The Book of Common Prayer*

—

TIMOTHY J. FAWCETT, B.D., Ph.D.

THE ALCUIN CLUB

MAYHEW-McCRIMMON
Southend-on-Sea

First published in Great Britain in 1973
on behalf of the Alcuin Club by

MAYHEW-McCRIMMON LTD
57 London Road
Southend-on-Sea SS1 1PF
England

Printed in Great Britain by
Silver End Press,
Letterpress Division of E. T. Heron & Co Ltd, Essex and London

1SBN 0 85597 031 6

To

My Parents

# CONTENTS

I am greatly indebted to
His Grace the Archbishop of Canterbury
and the Trustees of Lambeth Palace Library,
For permission to reproduce
MSS. No. 886, 2173, and Secker MS 24/6
and to quote from MSS 1774, and
other Manuscripts.

# PREFACE

The primary aim of this book, is to make available an accurate working text of the Proposals of the Commissioners who sat in the Jerusalem Chamber in 1689, on the revision of the Book of Common Prayer.

For many years this Revision has been neglected, and copies of the alterations which were envisaged are become scarce, the only editions printed being those of 1854 and 1855. The most important of these was that of 1854, edited by Henry Black a retired keeper of the Public Records for the Honourable House of Commons, and published on their authority. The edition was however limited in a number of ways; no account was taken of the different hands which were at work in the manuscript; nor was account taken of previous readings of the text, which were subsequently deleted by the Commissioners. Furthermore Black only listed the alterations, so that his edition had to be read in conjunction with a Prayer Book. This edition by providing the complete final text as envisaged by the Commissioners, attempts to alleviate this problem.

The Discovery of the text of the previous revision of the Prayer Book in 1688, which was initiated by the talks between Churchmen and Dissenters while the Bishops were incarcerated in the Tower under James II, has considerably advanced our knowledge of what was intended by the Commissioners, who undoubtedly used the revision as one of their primary sources. These alterations, together with the previous readings of the 1689 Revision, have been included in the notes.

The text and notes have been printed following the model advanced by Dr G. J. Cuming in his work *The Durham Book* (Oxford, 1961). The texts, and writings of the period have, wherever possible, been allowed to speak for themselves, thereby making available a large number of writings which are difficult to obtain. In following Dr Cuming's method the intention has also been to provide a book, which used side by side with it, will complete the picture of Anglican thought on Prayer Book revision between 1660 and 1700.

This book is therefore limited in its scope. It makes no attempt to follow the politics which surrounded the setting up of the Commission, except where they impinge upon it; nor does it deal with the worship of the Church in practice, the definitive study of which has already been made by J. Wickham Legg in *English Church Life from the Restoration to the Tractarian Movement* (1914) which should be read in conjunction with this book. Dr P. F. Bradshaw's excellent work on the *Anglican Ordinal* (1971) has likewise rendered any detailed study of it unnecessary.

Some account has, however, been necessary of the growth of interest and the problems connected with, the Comprehension schemes since 1660. There is much need of a detailed study, not only of these talks but also of the relationships of the leading Dissenters with the Clergy of the Anglican Church. There is evidence that they not only met in the conference hall, but over the dinner table as well, as friends. The account here is necessarily brief, as the schemes do not form an integral part of the revision of the Liturgy per se.

Finally, I would like to express my gratitude to all those who have helped in the preparation of this book, with useful advice and criticism. My thanks particularly are due to the Reverend Canon R. C. D. Jasper, who has guided my studies for many years, as an undergraduate, post-graduate, and now author; and for the wealth of experience he has put at my disposal, without which this book would never have been written: also to Dr G. J. Cuming who felt the need of this book, and pressed for its completion; and to the Alcuin club for publishing it. My thanks are also due to the Right Reverend Charles Claxton and the Venerable Geoffrey Gower-Jones who allowed me the time to do the research for my thesis at the University of London from which this book was born; also to the Cleaver Trustees for their financial help during this period. Thanks are also due to Mr Geoffrey Bill and his staff of Lambeth Palace Library, for their patience and help during the preparation of the text; and to the staff of Dr Williams Library, especially Mr John Creasey whose knowledge of early non-conformity and its literature was put at my disposal. Last, but not least, my thanks are due to my wife whose constant encouragement and long-sufferance has been indispensable.

# INTRODUCTION

The Commonwealth was over. Dilapidated churches were being inspected again; people were hunting for the chalices which had lay hidden for years; there were no surplices, no fonts, few Communion tables. The horses' dung was being cleared out of St Paul's and St Asaph's Cathedrals. It was 1660, and the religious question was in the forefront of men's minds. For the past decade, the Prayer Book had been banned, and was now almost totally unavailable; even the Westminster Directory which was designed to replace it, had soon faded into oblivion. Many churchmen had been forced to suffer exile, their places taken by Independent or Presbyterian ministers; others had been forced to celebrate, confirm, and ordain clandestinely, continually fearful of exposure.

But now the situation was reversed. Charles II was returning to his own again, accompanied by the triumphant exiled clergy, who bore little love for those that had ejected them. But for the moment, both trod carefully.

Shortly before his return, Charles made the Declaration of Breda on 4 April, hoping to allay the fears of the Presbyterians in power. He promised:

> A liberty of tender consciences and that no man shall be disquieted or called in question for differences of opinion in the matter of religion, which do not disturb the peace of the Kingdom; and that we shall be ready to consent to such an act of Parliament as upon mature deliberation shall be offered to us for that granting that indulgence.

The Presbyterians, however, hoped for more than this; toleration was important, but it implied that the Laudian Church of England, with its Prayer Book and Ceremonies would also be tolerated. It was therefore decided to approach Charles before he returned, while they still held the whip hand. And so a month later, on 4 May, Reynolds, Calamy, Case, Manton and other eminent Presbyterians, presented a petition to the king at the Hague. In a series of private audiences they put their case before him: As the Prayer Book had been long discontinued it should not be resurrected; they were looking to the king for support in this, and would be grateful if he would not use it in his own chapel. They had thrown down the gauntlet before the exiled clergy; and they received their first rebuff. The king replied that it was the best form of service in the world, and that he would continue to use it.

Charles returned to England on 25 May 1660 amid great rejoicing. At his insistence, Reynolds, Worth, and Calamy drew up a long address on behalf of the Presbyterians, covering their views on Church Government and Liturgy. In the preamble they took it for granted that there was:

1

A Firm agreement between our brethren (churchmen) and us in the doctrinal truths of the reformed religion, and in the substantial parts of divine worship, and that the differences are only in some various conceptions about the ancient form of church government, and some particulars about liturgy and ceremonies.

The ideal liturgy which they suggested, was highly critical of the Prayer Book, and they could not have misjudged the situation more.

We are satisfied in our judgments concerning the lawfulness or form of Public Worship, provided that it be for the matter agreable unto the Word of God, fitly suited to the nature of the several ordinances and necessities of the Church; neither too tedious in the whole, nor composed of too short prayers, unmeet repititions or responsals; not to be dissonant from the Liturgies of other reformed Churches; nor too rigorously imposed; nor the minister so confined thereunto, but that he may also make use of those gifts for prayer and exhortation which Christ hath given him for their service and edification of the Church. . . .

That inasmuch as the Book of Common Prayer hath in it many things that are justly offensive and need amendment, hath been discontinued, and very many, both ministers and people, persons of pious, loyal, and peaceable minds, are therein greatly dissatisfied; whereupon if it be again imposed will inevitably follow sad divisions, and widening of the breaches which your Majesty is now endevouring to heal: we do most humbly offer to your Majesty's wisdom, that for preventing so great evil, and for settling the Church in unity and peace, some learned, godly and moderate divines of both persuasions indifferently chosen, may be employed to compile such a form as is before described, as much as may be in Scripture words; or at least to revise and effectually reform the old, together with addition or insertion of some other varying forms of scripture phrase, to be used at the minister's choice; of which variety and liberty there be instances in the Book of Common Prayer.[1]

They likewise ask that Kneeling to receive the Sacrament, the Cross in Baptism and Bowing at the name of Jesus, might not be imposed on those who scrupled to use them.

The Bishops replied to this at length, but agreed that the Liturgy should be ' revised by such discreet persons as his Majesty shall think fit to employ therein '.

The two sides had to face each other officially. Something had to be decided. There must be a compromise, or someone must win; Presbyterians and churchmen could not be reconciled within the existing system. And so, on 25 October The King issued his ' Declaration to all his loving Subjects of his Kingdom of England

and Dominion of Wales, concerning Ecclesiastical affairs'. In some ways it was a temporizing move; the Church was gaining control, but needed more time; and the Presbyterians were losing ground. The main work of drafting was done by Clarendon, who was seriously concerned with the threat of the Dissenters to the Church. The Declaration promised to appoint some 'learned divines of different persuasions to review (the liturgy) and to make such alterations as shall be thought most necessary, and some additional forms (in the scripture phrase as near as may be) suited unto the nature of the several parts of worship, and that it be left to the minister's choice to use one or other at his discretion'. Until the revision had been undertaken no one would be punished for not using the book, or the nocent ceremonies: Kneeling to receive the Sacrament, the Cross in Baptism, Bowing at the name of Jesus, and the use of the Surplice. The Presbyterian demands had been temporarily allowed.

## THE SAVOY CONFERENCE

The Promised Commission[2] was set up on 25 March 1661, to meet at the Savoy for a period of four months. It was authorized to, advise upon and review the said Book of Common Prayer, comparing the same with the most ancient Liturgies which have been used in the Church, in the primitive and purest times: . . . . And if occasion be, to make such reasonable and necessary alterations, corrections and amendments therein, as by and between you . . . shall be agreed upon to be needful or expedient for the giving satisfaction unto tender consciences, and the restoring of peace and unity, . . but avoiding, as much as may be, all unnecessary alterations of the forms and Liturgy wherewith the people are already acquainted, and have so long received in the Church of England.

How far Charles had moved from the Declaration of Breda! Breda had promised ' A liberty of tender consciences', the commission of the Savoy asks for alterations which will give them satisfaction. Toleration in itself implies no alteration of the Liturgy, since while it fully acknowledges the *status quo* of the Anglican Church, it also permits other systems of belief to co-exist with the establishment, suffering no disabilities for their dissent from it. Comprehension on the other hand, necessarily involves a revision of the Liturgy, since it is an attempt to bring Dissenters within the body of the national Church. As many Dissenters objected to the rites and ceremonies of the Church (particularly those which had been stressed by Laud) a revision was necessary before they would even consider worshipping in Unity. Which the better policy was, became a moot point among Churchmen, for the next hundred years.

Charles himself was known to be in favour of Toleration, but the Commission for the Savoy Conference, had opted for Comprehension. It was, however, only part of the question: far more had to be done than alter the liturgy, to achieve the desired ends. Baxter in his autobiography, gives seven main points of controversy, without the

3

alteration of which there was no chance of reunion. These in brief are: (1) acceptance of the English Diocesan frame of Government; (2) the oath which caused them to repudiate the Solemn League and Covenant (Corporation Act; 13 Car. II Stat. 2 c. 1); (3) the oath that it was illegal under all circumstances to take up arms against the King; (4) the oath of Canonical Obedience; (5) the reordination of those not Episcopally Ordained; (6) the unfeigned Consent and Assent to the Book of Common Prayer (Act of Uniformity 14 Car. II c. 4); (7) the matter of discipline in ' actual administration according to the Common Prayer and canons '. While some of these post-date the Savoy Conference itself (e.g. No. 6), they were relevant to the discussions nevertheless. The seven points are all interrelated, most of them referring to the taking of oaths (a tender point), and the others turning on a particular interpretation of Episcopacy.

But why should the Bishops at the Savoy yield all this, which would entail a radical alteration of the whole structure and theology of the Church as they knew it? They were in the ascendancy, their position consolidated, and felt no need to make this sort of concession to the Presbyterians. The Presbyterians themselves had no leaders, and were all from the lower middle class of Society, with the exception of Baxter who alone could speak to the Bishops as an equal. The Bishops had been displaced by the Presbyterians, and their Church had lain neglected for ten years; and now that fortunes were reversed, they were unwilling to forget that the Presbyterians had shown them little sympathy.

This does not mean that the Conference was a complete sham.[3] The Bishops were endeavouring to win over the moderate Presbyterians by minor concessions, and were in fact able to effect a partial Comprehension in that many Presbyterians conformed at once, and one out of five who did not conform at once, did so later. Minor concessions alone could be given, because the Bishops were determined not to alter the Church to any major degree; their concern was to preserve their Catholic heritage, and to work in such a way as would be ' acceptable and approved by all sober, peaceable and truly conscientious sons of the Church of England '. In this vein Sparrow, one of the Commissioners, writes in his *Rationale of the Book of Common Prayer*:

> The poor liturgy suffers from two extremes, one sort says, it is old superstitious Roman dotage, the other, it is schismatically new. This book endevours to show particularly, what Bishop Jewel says in general, that 1. it is agreable to primitive usage, and so not novel, 2. that it is reasonable and so not superstitious.[4]

The Savoy Conference almost inevitably failed, and the Anglicans continued the Revision of the Prayer Book alone, making about 600 alterations, which were ratified by the Act of Uniformity in 1662. All these changes were minor ones, and none referred to any characteristic

4

points in the debate between the Presbyterians and the Church. There were no alterations of the Apocryphal lessons, the expressions complained of in the liturgy, the cross in Baptism, the objections to the marriage and Burial Services, the vestment rubric, the absolution, or kneeling to receive the Sacrament. Some of the things conceded by the Bishops at the Savoy Conference in their reply to the ' Exceptions ', were also forgotten. Many of these things had been conceded by the committee of 1641, and had been virtually withdrawn by the Royal Declaration of October 1660; some had been abandoned at the Savoy Conference. But all were retained and confirmed by the Act of Uniformity on 19 May 1662; and for the next few years, there would be lean times for many Presbyterian ministers.

In Parliament,[5] voting on all amendments to the Bill had been close; the Prayer Book had been accepted on a majority of only six votes. This showed a considerable sympathy for those who would have to leave their parishes, and there lot was eased in a number of Amendments; Parliament itself was more protestant than the Bishops. But go they must if they could not accept the Act of Uniformity. 2,447 ministers were ejected from livings or offices, between 1660 and 1662, 1,873 being ejected in 1662 alone. Of these, 254 conformed later. These numbers were large, yet the policy of the Bishops was successful, for about 7,000 ministers conformed in 1662. Of those who did not conform, some, like Richard Baxter, still received Communion in the parish Churches, and many went there to hear the Sermons. It was the custom in some parishes to ring the Church Bell after the Nicene Creed to call the Dissenters to the Sermon which concluded the Ante-communion service, so that they would not be forced to sit through the Prayers before it.

On 26 Dec. 1662 Charles attempted to ease the lot of those who had been expelled from the Church by issuing a Declaration which referred to the promises he made at Breda, and suggested that the Parliament might accept legislation which would sanction the use of his royal Dispensing power. The following February, however, the speaker replied that the Declaration of Breda, ' was not a promise in itself, but only a gracious declaration of your Majesty's intentions to do what in you lay, and what a parliament should advise you to do '. Such a declaration would establish schism by law, and chaos would ensue.

It was a valiant attempt by Charles, but Parliament was determined to secure the Church. The Corporation Act of 1661 had removed the Presbyterians from holding offices, where they could support the Nonconformists after the Act of Uniformity had been passed. In 1664 the first Conventicle Act was passed, and this was followed in 1665 by the Five Mile Act, which forced ministers to reside in sparsely populated parts of the country, where often they found it difficult to make a living.

# COMPREHENSION AND TOLERATION SCHEMES
## 1667 - 1685

There was, however, a large body of opinion in the Anglican Church which was willing to compromise with the Dissenters, hoping thereby to strengthen themselves against the common enemy of Popery. Charles II's known wishes were for a toleration, as is evidenced by the Declaration of Indulgence; but it was a toleration which was to include Roman Catholics. Many moderate churchmen reacted against this, and joined the ' Comprehension party ' within the Church. Their chance came in 1667 with the fall of Clarendon, and his replacement by Sir Orlando Bridgeman as Lord Keeper. The Dissenters were elated at the change of Government, and Pepys records that, ' the Nonconformists are mighty high, and their meetings frequented and connived at; and they do expect to have their day now soon; for my Lord Buckingham is a declared friend of them, and even of the Quakers.[6] '

A bill for Comprehension was soon after drawn up by Sir Robert Atkins, for the October Session of Parliament. It stated:

> That all ministers already ordained whether under episcopal ordination or presbyterian in the late times, and any other hereafter episcopally ordained, being above the age of 23 years, of good life and conversation, and able to answer and render to the Ordinary an account of their faith in Latin, who shall within three months next after publication hereof in the presence of the Bishop of the diocese, or Guardian of the Spiritualities, wherein such person now resides, declare their assent and subscribe to all the Articles of Religion which only concern the confession of the true Christian faith and the doctrine of the Sacraments mentioned in an Act of Parliament made in 13 Elizabeth (c. 12) . . . .

These men would be capable of preaching and administering the Sacraments and holding benefices with cure of souls, providing that the Prayer Book service should be read before the sermon either by the person concerned, or a deacon. The cross in Baptism and the wearing of the surplice by the minister were to be optional, and the sacrament could be received in a posture other than kneeling. The significance of 13 Elizabeth c. 12, was that it was held to waive Articles 34, 34, 36 and part of 20, which dealt with Ordination, the Tradition of the Church, and Homilies. The bill stood or fell, by the exclusion of Article 36, since it implied that all those who had not been ordained by the Prayer Book Ordinal, should not be regarded as ' rightly, orderly, and lawfully consecrated and ordered '.

This was in fact the weakness of the bill; it attempted to solve the problem of ' valid ' Orders, by acknowledging the validity of Presbyterian Orders. Such an approach would have left the Church in a very difficult position, and even within the Comprehension party, it was felt that some sort of re-ordination, was necessary. Opposition was so strong on this point, that the bill was quietly dropped, and was never presented to Parliament.

Another attempt was made the following year, and a conference was arranged between Dr John Wilkins (who had married Cromwell's sister, and was soon to become Bishop of Chester) and Hezekiah Burton on the Anglican side, and Baxter, Manton, and Bates on the Presbyterian. The basis of discussion was the Declaration of Breda, which it was hoped to implement. However, to strike a balance between the wishes of the King and the Church, was no easy matter.

Wilkins began by dividing the Dissenters into two parties, dealing with each separately; the Presbyterians were to be comprehended into the Church, and the Independents were to receive Toleration. The Independents, as represented by Dr John Owen, were thus drawn into the discussions, and they proceeded to negotiate on their own.

Wilkins proposed that non-episcopally ordained ministers should be admitted into the Church after the laying on of hands, with the words ' Take thou authority to preach the Word of God and to administer the Sacraments in any congregation of the Church of England where thou shalt be lawfully appointed thereto '. Subscription would also be softened; after the Oaths of Allegiance and Supremacy had been taken, it would only be necessary to subscribe to ' the doctrine, worship and government established in the Church of England, as containing all things necessary to salvation ', co-joined with a promise not to disturb the Church's peace. The nocent ceremonies were to be optional, and a revision of the liturgy should be undertaken which might include the abolition of the Apocryphal lessons, references to Baptismal regeneration, and repetitions and responses. The Burial service would be revised, and the custom of Godparents in Baptism was not to be insisted on.

These were very reasonable terms, but Baxter felt that they were not good enough, and drew up his own list of proposals. The laying on of hands, and prayer at reception smacked too much of re-ordination, and he contended that any reception should be regarded as the ministers taking ' the magistrates licence and confirmation ' of his Orders, and suggested it might be phrased ' Take thou legal authority to preach the Word of God . . . . ' Furthermore Assent should be given only to the Articles required by 13 Elizabeth c. 12, which negated Numbers 34-6.

The proposals when eventually debated, were taken to Sir Matthew Hale, who drew up the first draft of the Bill to be presented to Parliament. As with all the Comprehension schemes nothing came of it.

The Commons were still very suspicious of Roman Catholicism on the one hand, and the Dissenters on the other, fearing that if either party grew too strong there would be a repetition of the Civil War. They were equally conscious of the strong tie between the

Church and State, and believed that any alteration in the establishment and its liturgy would upset the political equilibrium. The Dissenters were regarded as regicides, and were often subjected to the rigorous enforcement of the disability laws by those who had suffered at their hands during the Commonwealth. This happened in the Parliament of 1668; the Commons demanded that the ' laws against the non-conformists be put into execution '. The house also passed a second Conventicle Bill to replace that of 1664 which had just expired, but it did not become law as Parliament was prorogued before the bill had passed through the Lords. This was no time to introduce a comprehension scheme, and Baxter believed that Hale burnt the draft of the bill as it had ceased to have any material use or value.

Hopes for Comprehension waned, and the Dissenters turned instead to the Royal prerogative and Toleration, despite the sharp blow it had received in the Parliament of 1662, when the speaker said that the Declaration of Breda was ' not a promise in itself, but only a gracious declaration of your Majesty's intention to do what in you lay, and what a Parliament should advise you to do '. In 1670, Charles became independent of Parliament by the Secret Treaty of Dover, and in March 1672, he was able to issue A Declaration of Indulgence. This suspended all the penal laws against the Dissenters, including the Roman Catholics, and announced his intention of issuing licences to preach and conduct worship in public for Dissenting ministers, and their places of worship. Catholics were allowed to continue their own form of worship in private houses.

This was a tactical error, for it revealed as never before the strength of the nonconformists in the country. In 1669 Episcopal returns showed 1,138 nonconformist preachers in England and Wales, and 1,234 Conventicles with 70,875 people attending them. These are known to be conservative figures; Calamy gives the numbers of licences issued in 1672, in England only as 854 Presbyterians, 385 Congregationalists, and 202 Baptists. These figures were frightening for the Church, but far worse was the inclusion of Papists in the Declaration, of whom there were over 12,000 in the country. Parliament was also alarmed, and questioned the legality of the Declaration itself. The Parliament of 1673, petitioned the King on 14 Feb., that 'penal statutes in matters ecclesiastical cannot be suspended but by Act of Parliament', requesting that 'the said laws may have their free course until it shall be otherwise provided for by Act of Parliament'. Eventually after sustained pressure from Parliament, Charles cancelled the Declaration on 7 March, and on 3 Feb. 1675 an Order in Council recalled all the licences issued under it. Parliament in 1673 also passed the Test Act, excluding the King's brother (later James II) from holding office. The test was sacramental, and this held few terrors for the protestant Dissenters, but many for the Papists, to whom it was a constant source of worry.

There was, however, a new mood of Toleration in Parliament. providing such a toleration did not include the Catholics, and a bill was brought in for the 'easing his Majesty's Protestant subjects'. But a Toleration, was not the policy of the Bishops, who led by Sheldon and Morley succeeded in defeating the bill. The scheme for a Comprehension thus came to the fore once more, and this resulted in Morley himself introducing a bill in the Lords on 13 Feb. 1674. It was confined to the repeal of two clauses in the Act of Uniformity; those requiring 'Assent and Consent' and the renunciation of the Solemn League and Covenant. Once more, it was lost in the prorogation.

Later in the year Tillotson, Dean of Canterbury, and Stillingfleet, a prebendary of St Pauls continued the talks with Baxter, though with little success. Some proposals were drawn up but were rejected almost immediately by the Bishops, and Tillotson grew despondent. He wrote to Baxter on 11 April 1675:

I took the first opportunity after you were with us to speak to the Bishop of Sal————— who promised to keep the matter private, and only to acquaint the bishop of Ch————— with it, in order to a meeting. But upon some general discourse, I plainly perceived several things could not be obtained. However he promised to appoint a time of meeting; but I have not heard from him since. I am unwilling my name should be used in this matter; not but that I do most heartily desire an accommodation, and shall always endeavour it. But I am sure it will be a prejudice to me, and signify nothing to the effecting of the thing; which, as circumstances are, cannot pass in either house, without the concurrence of a considerable part of the bishops and the countenance of his Majesty: which at present I see little reason to expect.

Tillotson, however, continued to keep in touch with the Dissenting interest, so that by 1680, he was inviting both John Howe and Bishop Lloyd of St Asaph to dinner to discuss things.

In 1679 hopes began to rise again, when, on 6 Nov., the Commons voted unanimously against abuses in the prosecutions under the Recusancy Acts when applied to Quakers and Anabaptists. On 3 Nov. 1680, Sir Edward Dering suggested a bill for the 'better uniting of his Majesty's Protestant subjects' and a committee was set up under Daniel Finch to review it.[7] This eventually took the form of a Toleration and a Comprehension Act, on much the same lines as the previous ones. The two bills were necessary as the Presbyterians refused to accept a Comprehension, which would leave the Independents and other Dissenters to take the full brunt of the Anti-Dissenter Laws. Both bills were however lost in the prorogation of Parliament on 10 Jan. 1681, which was due in a large part to the anger of the King, at the attitude of Parliament during the Exclusion crisis.

9

Stillingfleet about this time, was becoming enigmatic. In 1659 he had written his *Irenicum; or A Weapon Salve for the Church's Wounds,* and supported the Comprehension schemes; but in 1680 he became Dean of St Pauls, and seemed to turn with the preferment. In December he published *The Unreasonableness of Separation* as a reply to Baxter's *Nonconformist's Plea for Peace* (1679). And yet the following year he seems to have indulged in discussions again. Thomas Long wrote in 1690:

> In the year 1681, when Dr Stillingfleet, now Bishop of Worcester, made large Overtures to gratifie the Dissenters, (viz) That the Cross in Baptism might be either taken off, or confin'd to publick Baptism, and left to the choice of the Parents: That such as could not Kneel might be permitted to stand at the reception of the Sacrament of the Lord's Supper: That the Surplice should be taken away: That at Baptism the Fathers should be permitted to joyn with the Sponsors in offering the Child to Baptism, or desire them publickly to present their Child, and the Charge be given to the both: That they should be required to Subscribe only to thirty six of the Articles: That there should be a new Translation of the Psalms for Parish Churches: That the Apocryphal Lessons should be exchanged for Scriptural: That the Rubrick should be Corrected, with many other Condescentions. They were all thrown, as it were, with spite in his teeth, by those that Answered his Sermon and Proposals, with a Habeat sibi & suis.[8]

## ANGLICANS UNDER A ROMAN CATHOLIC KING 1685

With the accession of James II on 6 February 1685, the religious situation changed rapidly. An avowed Roman Catholic, both privately, and publicly after the Exclusion crisis, he lacked the political acumen of Charles in his dealings with the established Church. From the very beginning of his reign, the clergy feared that James would act in a way that would be prejudicial to the Church, and reacted, despite the King's displeasure, by publishing an ever-increasing volume of tracts and sermons against popery.[9] James' attempts to silence them failed lamentably.[10]

The new King was unwilling to enforce discrimination against those of his own religion, but realized at the same time that he could do nothing to alleviate their condition without pursuing a policy of Toleration for all the nonconformist denominations. Many churchmen and parliamentarians were willing to accept such a toleration for the protestant ministers and their congregations, but were suspicious of terms which included the Roman Catholics. The fear of popery was still an ever-present one: the reign of Mary had not been forgotten and the plight of the French Hugenots after the Revocation of the Edict of Nantes served as a salutary reminder of the tribulations of protestant subjects under a catholic King; the deliberate insult to the established Church in the consecration of Count Ferdinand d' Adda as Archbishop of Amasia in St James' Chapel in 1687, the attempt to give Roman Catholics key army posts, the attack on the Universities—this Romanization of England which alarmed even Innocent XI, together with the obvious threat to the Church by the elevated position of Priests like Fr Petre, served only to accentuate the Anti-Catholic feeling in both Parliament and the country in general.

Finding himself unable to achieve his ends through Parliament, James appealed to the theory of Divine Right and to his Royal Prerogative, by publishing the Declaration of Indulgence in May 1687 and renewing it the following year.

Many Dissenters accepted it without hesitation, the Baptists, Quakers, and Independents all presenting loyal addresses of thanks to the King. The Presbyterians, and Calvinists, however, were more reticent, and 'began to conform to the Church of England' in the face of the common enemy of popery. Baxter refused to be party to any address to the King, in case such an action would prejudice his standing with the conformists. Many English Presbyterians followed his lead; they had long accepted the principle of a national Church under a modified form of Episcopacy, and not infrequently participated in the worship of their local parish churches. These men 'had a growing respect . . . for the national church as the great pillar of the protestant faith', and had been in conference with her for many years regarding the possible terms for reunion; all they now required was a reform of Ecclesiastical courts, some measure of recognition of their orders, and some allowance for the scruples of both minister and people in regard to the nocent ceremonies. They had too much to lose by hasty action.

The Stuart MSS. testifies to this move of the Presbyterians towards the Church of England:

> The Kingdom and the court were filled with incendiaries, whose constant endeavours were to scatter fears and jealousies, and draw suspicions from every step his Majesty made, and above all to pervert that royal and Christian one of granting liberty of conscience, and to insinuate a belief that it was only in order to supplant religion and then destroy it. And now the Dissenters too did not only concur in this, but valued themselves upon the strength and penetration of their judgments, that they could forsee and discover that to have been the original motive and end of it; and that all the mitigations to them was only for the sake of the Papists; by that means making the throne dreadful even when it was the seat of mercy. They soon therefore joined hands and voices with the Church of England party, so far at least as to rail against the Church of Rome . . .[11]

A letter to Archbishop Sancroft[12] from the Presbyterians of Scotland which he received after his acquittal from the tower, shows this same spirit of reconciliation:

May it please your grace,

It will doubtless be strange news to hear that the Bishops of England are in great veneration among the Presbyterians of Scotland; and I am glad that reason has retained so much of its old empire among men. But I hope that it will be no news to your grace, to hear that no one was more concerned in the safety of your conscience and persons than . . .

Geo Mackensie.[13]

The Declaration of Indulgence had passed by peaceably enough although there were rumblings beneath the surface. The churchmen had not reacted, positively or negatively; so, counselled by Stephen Lobb a Congregationalist minister, and William Penn the Quaker, the King decided to force their hand. The Declaration was reissued in April 1688, and was followed on 4 May by a proclamation ordering it to be read in the Churches of London and Westminster on 20 and 27 May, and throughout the rest of the country on 3 and 10 June. The proclamation continued, 'it is hereby farther ordered that the Rt Revd the Bishops cause the said declaration to be sent and distributed throughout their several and respective dioceses to be read accordingly'.[14]

## THE BISHOPS' PETITION 1688

Herein lay James' mistake. The Indulgence of Charles had been read in Churches because a command had been issued to the clergy as a whole; but in laying the onus on the Bishops, James was forcing them to repudiate all their attacks on popery in their own churches, and to eat 'humble pie'. Harried on the one side by the Roman Catholics, and on the other by a fear that the Dissenters would accept the toleration, the Bishops and the London clergy felt that the time had come to act. Symon Patrick, records the violence of their reaction:

We were in great perplexity about the reading the declaration for liberty of conscience which all my acquaintance seemed to abhor. We had many meetings about it; twice at Ely house with the bishop (London), and on the 11th of May at the Temple, where at the master's house (Dean Sherlock) we came to this resolution, that the bishops should be desired to address to the king, but not upon any address of ours to them. For we judged it best that they should lead the way, and we follow them.[15]

Thomas Tenison[16] seems to have been the leader of the London clergy, and he acted accordingly as their spokesman to the Bishops.[17] The following evening he went to Lambeth, and dined with the Archbishop, whose other guests included the Earl of Clarendon, and the Bishops of London, Ely, Peterborough, Chester and St Davids. 'The last two', wrote Clarendon, 'discomposed the company, nobody

12

caring to speak before them'. Cartwright and Watson were known friends of the King, and the subject of discussion was, as events showed, a dangerous one. The two bishops left immediately after dinner, and after Tenison had reported the discussions of the clergy, the company discussed the matter in detail, resolving not to read the declaration. They accepted the resolution of the previous evening, and promised to petition the King provided the rest of the London clergy were as committed in the matter as those who had met at Sherlock's house. To lend more weight to the petition they proceeded to get in touch with as many bishops as possible, and summon them to London; accordingly the Bishops of Winchester, Norwich, Gloucester, St Asaph, Bath and Wells, Bristol and Chichester were notified.

The following day, Sunday 13 May, the London clergy met again at Sherlock's house, and having reaffirmed their determination not to read the declaration, received Tenison's account of the Bishops' proviso. It was decided that they should 'feel the pulse of the ministers in London', and twenty of those present were detailed to respective areas of the city. As soon as the results of this became known, they were communicated to the Archbishop who was able to tell Lloyd of St Asaph and Turner of Ely on the Wednesday afternoon, that 'most of the city clergy had resolved not to read the declaration'.

The next day, Thursday, saw the consummation of their plans; but first, they had to be precise. The London clergy met again, this time in 'a house in St Pauls church yard', and collated their findings. A list was eventually arrived at of seventy people who were committed to not reading the declaration, and Symon Patrick made a fair copy of it for the Archbishop. He immediately took it to Mr Clavel's house where Bishop White of Peterborough was staying, with instructions that he should take it to the Archbishop. Tenison and he still had more work to do.

Having delivered the sealed list, the two set out for Clarendon's house, where they dined with Lloyd and Turner, discussing the finer points of policy. The Bishops were assembling. Lloyd and Turner had arrived on Wednesday, and now Ken of Bath and Wells, and Trelawney of Bristol had come. Winchester was ill.

After lunch the party left for Lambeth, and began discussions with Archbishop Sancroft, in the midst of which White arrived with the list of ministers Patrick had left him earlier in the day. Having received this confirmation, Sancroft began to act; all the Bishops in town were instructed to come to Lambeth the next morning, and Tenison was told that 'it was fit we should keep it as a day of fasting and prayer to beg God's direction on what was intended', from which it may presumed that a definite course of action had been decided upon that afternoon.

13

The events of Friday 18 May, are recorded by Patrick:

I gave notice of it to some others, and between 10 and 11 Dr. Tenison, Dr. Grove and I went over to Lambeth where we found 5 Bishops and Dr. Stillingfleet and Dr. Tillotson. After Morning Prayer we entered into consultation about an address to the King, and at last it was agreed it should be by way of petition from his Grace, the Bishops present with him, and in behalf of their brethren and the clergy of their dioceses. About 2 o'clock came another Bishop, so there were St. Asaph, Ely, Chichester, Bath and Wells, Peterborough, Bristol and also the Bishop of London. The matter of the petition after some debate was agreed, and all but the Bishop of London set their hands to it. Then it was considered how it should be delivered, and at last resolved they should all go in a body. So when even prayer was done, we went to dinner, and after that they went over to Whitehall, a little after 6 o'clock. Dr. Tenison, Dr. Grove and I stayed with the Archbishop till 8 o'clock, to hear what the success would be. But then we came away hearing nothing till the next morning, for it was 9 o'clock before they could have an audience, the king being abroad and not returning till that time.

The reception of the petition by James, which was hardly cordial, is well known. After a very disagreeable interview the Bishops returned to Lambeth by water, only to find that the petition they had just presented was on sale in the Streets. Compton, under suspension, had not gone to Whitehall with them; the leak probably came from him.

The petition which they presented is of profound importance, not only historically, but also liturgically, because it was frequently referred to (with varying interpretations) in the literary controversy of 1689-90 and later into the eighteenth century.

"To the King's Most Excellent Majesty,

The humble Petition of William Archbishop of Canterbury, and of divers of the suffragan Bishops of that Province (now present with him), in behalf of themselves and others of their absent brethren and of the Clergy of their respective Dioceses.

Humbly showeth;
That the great averseness they find in themselves to the distributing and publishing in all their churches your majesty's late Declaration for Liberty of Conscience, proceedeth neither from any want of duty and obedience to your majesty (our holy mother the Church of England being both in her principles and in her constant practice unquestionably loyal; and having, to her great honour, been more than once publicly acknowledged to be so by your gracious majesty), nor yet from any want of due tenderness to Dissenters, in relation to whom they are willing to come to

14

such a temper, as shall be thought fit, when that matter shall be considered and settled in Parliament and Convocation; but amongst many other considerations, from this especially, because that Declaration is founded upon such a Dispensing power, as hath been often declared illegal in parliament, and in particular in the years 1662, and 1672, and the beginning of your majesty's reign; and is a matter of so great moment and consequence to the whole nation, both in Church and State, that your Petitioners cannot in prudence, honour or conscience so far make themselves parties to it, as the distribution of it all over the nation, the solemn publication of it once and again, even in God's house, and in the time of divine service, must amount to, in common and reasonably construction.

Your Petitioners therefore most humbly and earnestly beseech your Majesty that you will be graciously pleased not to insist upon their distributing and reading your Majesty's said Declaration . . .

| W. Cant. (Sancroft) | Tho. Bath & Wells (Ken) |
| W. Asaph. (Lloyd) | Tho. Petriburgens (White) |
| Fran. Ely. (Turner) | Jon. Bristol (Trelawney)[18] |
| Jo. Cicestr (Lake) | |

The petition was later signed and approved by several Bishops who were not present at the meeting, viz. London (who had been under suspension), Norwich, Glocester, Sarum, Winchester, and Exeter.

The phrasing of the petition was agreed by the committee on the May 18 at Lambeth; a committee which included Tillotson, Stillingfleet, Patrick, Tenison, and Grove—men whom the events of the past fortnight had welded into a pressure group which was not to be broken in the ensuing months. It cannot, therefore, be cited as being representative of the view which either the Archbishop or the Bishops held at this time as regards the Comprehension schemes which were afoot. On the contrary, it would seem that the London clergy were continually forcing the hands of the Bishops in presenting the petition, and therefore the content must owe a great deal to their influence.

In this context, the phrase 'no want of due tenderness to Dissenters, in relation to whom they are willing to come to such a tempter as shall be thought fit, when that matter shall be considered and settled in parliament and convocation', is often quoted with an emphasis on the 'due tenderness', as an indication that the Bishops were willing to participate in a Comprehension scheme. This interpretation is due, however, to the later use that was made of the words in the following literary controversy, and indeed the way Tillotson was to use them. The emphasis, however, should be placed on the latter half

15

of the quotation. They were willing to accept something 'considered and settled in parliament and convocation', i.e. in what was a legal manner; they could not accept anything under the King's Dispensing power which had been declared illegal in the first Parliaments of both Charles II and James himself. The 'due tenderness' simply refers to the subject of the legal issue, and is no indication of the views of those concerned: it is a protest about the illegality of the King's proceedings, on legal ground.

James wanted the Bishops to protest about the liberty of conscience given to the dissenters by his Declaration; it would drive a wedge between them, which could only advance his own policies. To attack the Declaration on legal grounds, was unexpected; It was the Bishop's trump, to his ace.

The people involved in this protest fall into two distinct groups:
(1) The pressure group; This consisted of the London clergy in conjunction with Bishop Lloyd of St Asaph. They were all deeply committed to the cause of Comprehension; Tillotson[19] and Stillingfleet had been involved in the attempts of 1673-74, and even after the rejection of Morley's bill, continued the discussions with Baxter, Stillingfleet initiating further talks in 1681. Tenison, Patrick and Grove were in favour of it, and were to commit themselves irretrievably in the ensuing months. Lloyd had also participated in talks with the dissenters, having become especially friendly with the Quaker Richard Davies, and Philip Henry—to such an extent that in 1683 at the discovery of the Ryehouse plot, he found it necessary to clear himself from the suspicions which attached themselves to him.[20] All the members of this party were Latitudinarians, who subsequently took the oaths; and all were to become members of the Ecclesiastical Commission of 1689 to review the Liturgy.

The leaders of the group were Tenison and Lloyd, and it was under the latter's leadership that the Comprehension scheme was continued after the deprivation of the non-juring Bishops in August 1689. Both seem to have been chosen by the state to represent the King (William) in its dealings with the deprived Bishops, and Clarendon frequently refers to Tenison's presence at Lambeth during this time, implying that he was there to exercise pressure on the ageing Sancroft.[21] Lloyd had been in touch with the Hague during his imprisonment in the tower, and it has been suggested that he carried on a protracted correspondence with William, through the agency of his brother-in-law, Jonathan Blagrave.[22] In accordance with this he managed to persuade all the prelates except Sancroft to wait upon William when he arrived in London for the first time, and perhaps by way of thanks for services rendered, was chosen to perform the primate's part in the Coronation of presenting the queen to the people.[23]

Lloyd's influence seems to have been substantial at this time, and Clarendon testifies to this when he writes 'It is strange to see how many good men have their jealousies of St Asaph, as if he were not right'. In Clarendon's words also, he was 'deep in that comprehending project'. His influence was also felt in the election of new Bishops, the case of Burnet's elevation to Salisbury being a notorious example, and in the general political dealings with the deprived Bishops.[24]

(2) The high churchmen on the Episcopal bench. All these men became non-jurors, and all were against any revision of the Liturgy and the Comprehension scheme. The group centred on Turner of Ely and Lloyd of Norwich who exerted a considerable influence on Sancroft; so much so that when Wharton the Archbishop's Chaplain, read the prayers for William and Mary in the chapel at Lambeth, and was severely rebuked by Sancroft for doing so, he attributed it to their suggestion, 'to the great misfortune of the Church'.[25]

Sancroft himself seems to have been against a Comprehension, but was continually pressurized by the Latitudinarians to accept one, and found himself forced to give them their head. This accounts for the seeming 'inconsistences' in Sancroft's attitude to the events which followed.

The petition had been presented. The Declaration of Indulgence itself was read in four churches in London, and Westminster Abbey where Sprat of Rochester (who had dissented from the petition) was Dean; and even here it was read quickly, to a congregation that walked out as the first words were spoken.

The King was not prepared to let matters rest here though, and discussed the case with his advisors. Sunderland suggested that the affair should be quietly dropped, but James was not prepared to do so. The notorious Judge Jeffreys, who quailed at the idea of presenting them before the Ecclesiastical Commission in view of the emotions aroused by Compton's 'trial' suggested a prosecution for publishing a seditious libel before the King's Bench. This meant, trial by jury.

The Bishops were summoned before the King in Council on 8 June, where they were asked to enter into recognizances; this, as peers of the realm they refused to do, and were, for their rights and pains, lodged in the Tower. There they remained until the 15 June, when they allowed the court to take their recognizances (£200 for the Archbishop, £100 for the other Bishops), and their trial was set for that day in a fortnight. The facts of the trial are well known; suffice it to say, that on 30 June 1688, the foreman of the jury, Sir Robert Langley, gave the verdict 'not guilty', and on that same day, the Admiral of the Fleet, Arthur Herbert, took ship for Holland, disguised as a common sailor, with the letter that was to depose James, and bring William of Orange to England.

# THE INITIATION OF FURTHER DISCUSSIONS

While the Bishops were in the Tower, they were visited by ten nonconformist ministers, with whom they began some preliminary talks;[26] a visit 'which the king took so heinously, that he sent for four of them to reprimand them; but their answer was, "that they could not but adhere to the prisoners, as men constant and firm to the protestant faith".' These discussions were continued by the London clergy after the release of the Bishops from the Tower. On 21 July, one of the King's supporters wrote to John Ellis in Dublin, that:

> The Archbishop and the clergy of London are said to have had several conferences with the chiefs of the Dissenting ministers, in order to agree such points of ceremonies as are indifferent between them, and to take such measures for what is to be proposed about religion in the next parliament.[3]

Brother George Every has identified the results of these initial conversations, as a paper published in Francis Lee's *Life of Mr John Kettlewell* (1718). Of these 'minutes' a number are of importance:

> I. That the Church of England under the Government of Bishops, and Profession of the Protestant Religion, be the Publick Establishment.
>
> II. That the Terms of Communion in the Established Religion, be as large as is consistent with the Constitution of a National Episcopacy, a Liturgy, and Articles of Religion, in Substance at least, the same with those by law already established.
>
> III. That there be for the Clergy One subscription instead of all, to this purpose: I AB do approve the Articles and Liturgy, and Government, of the Church of England as by Law Established; and will conform myself thereto.
>
> IV. That the present Liturgy be Reviewed, and such Alterations and Abatements of Communion made, as may probably bring in Dissenters into (it) as the Publick Establishment.
>
> XVI: That a New Book of Canons Ecclesiastical be made, suitable to the present State and Circumstances.
>
> XVIII: A more Effectual Way for the Punishing and Depriving of Scandalous Ministers.[28]

These heads of agreement seem to reflect the discussions of the London clergy rather than those of any official body presided over by the Archbishop. Indeed, the letter to Ellis, makes the specific point that the discussions were held by the ' Archbishop and the clergy of London ' and does not mention any other Bishops. That Sancroft was not deeply involved may be implied in the last of the Eleven

Articles which he sent to the clergy of his diocese dated 27 July 1688. It reads:

> That they (clergy) also walk in wisdom towards those that are not of our communion; and if there be in their parishes any such, that they neglect not to confer with them in a spirit of meekness, seeking by all good ways and means to gain and win them over to our communion; more especially that they have a very tender regard to our brethren the protestant Dissenters; that upon occasion offered they visit them at their own homes, and receive them kindly at their own, and treat them fairly wherever they meet them; persuading them (if it may be) to a full compliance with our church, or at least whereto we have already attained, we may all walk by the same rule and mind the same thing. And in order hereunto that they take all opportunities of assuring and convincing them, that the Bishops of this church are really and sincerely irreconcilable enemies to the errors . . . of the Church of Rome . . . and that they warmly and most affectionately exhort them to join with us in daily fervent prayer to the God of peace, for the universal union of all reformed Churches both at home and abroad against our common enemies; that all they who do confess thy Holy Name of our Dear Lord, and do agree in the truth of his holy word, may also meet in one communion, and live in perfect unity and peace together.[29]

These are not the words of one contemplating a bill of Comprehension! Although Sancroft does speak of a ' tenderness ' towards the Dissenters, he nevertheless is advocating a wholesale proselytizing, without the promise of any further concessions at all. He wants them brought into the Church ' whereto we have already attained ', the means being consistent with such an interpretation. It seemed to Sancroft, in view of the popularity of the Bishops and churchmen, that the *status quo* was all that was necessary to bring the Dissenters into the Church.

## THE REVISION OF THE PRAYER BOOK 1688

The pressure group were persistent. In pursuance of the fourth head of the agreement, a revision of the Liturgy was begun in 1688. Wake testified in the Sacheverall trial in the house of Lords in 1710, that:

> The time was towards the end of that unhappy reign . . . . The scheme was laid out and the several parts of it were committed, not only with the approbation, but by the direction of that great prelate, to such of out divines as were thought the most proper to be intrusted with it. His Grace took one part to himself: another was committed to a then pious and Reverend Dean, afterwards a bishop, of our Church. The reviewing of the daily service of our

Liturgy, and the Communion-Book, was referr'd to a select number of excellent persons, two of which are at this time upon our bench; and I am sure will bear witness to the truth of my relation. The design was, in short, this: To improve, and if possible, to inforce discipline; to review and enlarge our liturgy; by correcting of some things, by adding of others: and if it should be thought advisable by authority, when this matter should come to be legally considered, first in Convocation, then in Parliament, by leaving some few ceremonies, confess'd to be indifferent in their usage, so as not to be necessarily observed by those who made a scruple of them; till they should be able to overcome either their weaknesses or prejudices, and be willing to comply with them.[30]

Thus the 1688 Committee for revising the Prayer Book had been set up. Sancroft took a part himself. Other members of the committee included ' the Reverend Dean ' Symon Patrick, and the two Bishops mentioned above, Thomas Sharp and John Moore, then Rectors of St Giles-in-the-Fields, and St Austin's respectively. Thomas Tenison acted as either the secretary of the leader, and it is argued elsewhere (notes on the Collects) that Stillingfleet, Burnet, and Tillotson were also part of the committee.

The results of the committee's deliberations may be found in MS 886 in Lambeth Palace Library, in a Folio Prayer Book which is undated. Internal evidence shows, however, that the book must have been compiled between 1684 and 1688, for the Table of Moveable feasts is that of 1681-1720, and the state prayers, except for those of the Communion Service which mention Charles, all refer to James as the sovereign.[31]

The book was probably therefore compiled specially to receive interleaved, blank pages which would be necessary for the work of the revisers. This method of recording revisions was also used in 1689. Most of the interleaved pages have been torn out of the text, but the few that remain contain suggested revisions in the hand of Thomas Tenison. That this was not simply a book belonging to him, is shown by the fact that in a number of places, several hands can been seen at work, though due to the mutilation of the book their contribution is graphically small. It is probable, that as in the following year Tenison acted as the Committee's secretary, or leader.

There are, however, a number of marginal notes and alterations remaining in the text. Whoever tore the interleaved pages out (Tenison?) also attempted to obliterate all these comments. Much of the text is, however, decipherable, and has been included in the notes on the 1689 text. There are also a number of words underlined or put in parentheses in the text of the Prayer Book which referred to alterations on the missing interleaves. These cannot tell us what the revisers wished to substitute in their place, but they do give a general idea of what words and phrases they wished to alter.

This assumes a great deal of importance when compared with the revision of 1689, for many of the alterations envisaged in 1688 were added to that revision, so the Commissioners must have used the book as a primary source.

The alterations are obviously intended to effect a comprehension. At the beginning of the book there are a number of notes in different hands, and a long section by Tenison, states the principles on which the revision was undertaken. These are based on the Exceptions to the Prayer Book drawn up by the Presbyterians before the Savoy Conference, and reflect the second article of the agreement mentioned above, that the terms of communion ' should be as wide as possible '.

On a remaining interleaf beside the beginning of the Ordinal is a note:

For ye promoting union betwixt the Protestant Churches. Episcopacy (is held as an opinion to be judicious by many) should not, however, be urg'd as a poynt necessary to be had by all that take orders. It may suffice that it be looked upon as the Antient Form in ye Churche, & as ye best where it may be had.

Such an approach would pave the way for a Comprehension, by dealing effectively with the problem of Presbyterial Orders, which all Dissenters held to be perfectly valid. Whether such a retrenchment from the Anglican position would be accepted by churchmen, is a different matter. The Alterations in the Promise of Canonical obedience in the Office of Priests reflects this post-tower situation, with its qualifications designed to allow liberty of conscience should such a situation re-occur.

It would also seem that some alterations were to be made in the nocent ceremonies, for in the rubric after the Consecration in the Communion Service, the word ' meekly ' in the phrase ' meekly kneeling ' is underlined. Similarly in Baptism, ' We receive this child &c ' and the phrase ' sign of the Cross ' is underlined; in Matrimony the prayer ' with this ring I thee wed ' is deleted, although the rubric is left intact. In many cases throughout the revision, it is evident that underlined words are often intended to be deleted, for in certain cases the word ' omitt ' is added in the margin beside them. In these cases, however, such a solution would be unacceptable to churchmen, so it may presumed that they were to be regarded either as optional ceremonies, or in the case of the Ring in Marriage, a suitable rubric was to be constructed explaining why they were to be done.

In accordance with Article 17 of the Agreement, there is a note that services of silencing, degredation, and suspension, as well as admonition, should be drawn up. Yet this revision is not simply one that was intended to ' reduce the Dissenters to our Communion '; it is much more than that. It bears more resemblance to the compilation of the Durham Book than to negotiations for a Comprehension. The text is thoroughly revised; new Collects were in the process of being drawn up under Patrick, and it is possible that Kidder had begun his new translation of the Prayer Book Psalms; A new form of the Articles of Religion was drawn up, and all services with perhaps the exception of the Ordinal, were improved.

The alterations are not simply of a low Church tenor. It was, for example, intended to draw up some new services, the most important being one for Maundy Thursday to help people to understand the ' pascale solemnitie ', and a ' Service for Passion Week '. Other high Church additions can be seen in the recommendation that each Church should have its own ' little cups & patins very portable ' for use in giving Communion to the Sick, as well as in the use of such terms as ' viaticum ', which in practice tended to imply that the Sacrament had been reserved.

This revision which has been dealt with so scantily here, is considered more fully in the notes on the 1689 revision, to which it bears more than a superficial resemblance in many aspects. It seems to have been another attempt at a ' Savoy Conference ', an attempt which, while prevented from coming to fruition by Archbishop Sancroft, nevertheless paved the way for the 1689 Revision. It is most unlikely that the Commission of 1689 could have produced such an important document, had not much of the work been done in these previous talks and alterations. In a sense, more in fact had been done in 1688; not only was the Prayer Book revised, but the talks initiated a Comprehension and a Toleration bill—a situation which was pre-empted by the time the Commissioners of 1689 sat.

## THE BLOODLESS REVOLUTION: FURTHER RECONCILIATION EFFORTS

Time, however, was not on the side of the London Divines,[32] and as early as 7 August 1688, Tenison was warning Symon Patrick of the impending invasion of William of Orange.[33] The Comprehension scheme was going ahead, despite the antipathy of the Bishops, under the auspices of the London clergy, as well as the liturgical reforms, in accordance with their previous agreements with the Dissenters.

The Bishops were not, however, idle. On 3 September, Turner of Ely wrote to Archbishop Sancroft, stressing his disapproval of the scheme, in such a tone as to suggest that he would be in complete acquiescence with his views, and which implies that neither was privy to these dealings.

One reason of my labouring so much on this point to introduce frequent communions and make them more numerous is really this; it grows everyday plainer to me that many of our divines, men of name and note [The London Clergy?]—I pray God there be not some bishops with them in the design [Lloyd?]—intend upon any overture for comprehension (when time shall serve) to offer all our ceremonies in sacrifice to the dissenters, kneeling at the sacrament and all. This makes it necessary for us to increase as much as possible the number of those who, as true lovers of devotion and decency in it, may contend even for multitude and interest in the nation with those that would strip this poor church of all her ornaments. It is a point of offence taken at them that will be most insisted upon one day. Let it appear them, that it will give great offence to innumerable better Christians, if we part with them.[34]

Turner was more prepared to set up a ' defence party ' against the pressure group than Sancroft was. The Archbishop was treading carefully, and while he was not at all convinced of the necessity of a Comprehension, there was so much pressure exerted on him that even if he refused to participate, he had to give the clergy the ' go-ahead '. Having done this, it was difficult to withdraw it. Poor Sancroft, now seventy-one, was confused; he was party to a little of what was going on in Church and state, but not enough. He was an ill man, often confined to his palace: how could he lead as a prince of the Church?

The pressure group on the other hand, was decided and united. Their point of view was expressed a little later by Humphrey Prideaux, a supporter:

The Church of England . . . hath to the utmost resisted all alterations from them (the Dissenters), hoping by less dangerous methods to cure the distraction and heal the divisions that are among us . . . but they have all proved ineffectual . . . so that now we are brought to that pass, that without abating something on our side for the sake of peace and union with them, we cannot have that prospect as formerly of supporting the Church of God and maintaining the Honour of his Worship with success among us. I think now to make such alterations as are proposed a thing so absolutely necessary as ought not any longer to be deferr'd.[35]

With the flight of James II on 11 December and again on 23 December, the London clergy were faced with the ruination of their plans. William was a Calvinist, and while the Presbyterians were prepared to join with the Church to put up a united front against popery and a Comprehension was viable, they were sure of a Toleration without the Papists now. The Presbyterians in Scotland were already beginning their campaign to overthrow the Episcopalians, and establish a Presbyterian government there; a campaign which came to fruition on 14 March 1689. The London clergy were alarmed; it looked as though their comprehension scheme would be redundant before it had even been proposed, for why should the dissenters negotiate for a union, when they were certain of recognition as they were?

On 3 January 1689, therefore, Tenison went to see the Archbishop at Lambeth, and tried to persuade him to take the lead in formulating the preparatory work which had been done over the past few months, to lay before the convocation. Clarendon was present at the interview:

> We spoke to him of the approaching Convention, and whether he would not think of preparing something against that time on behalf of the Dissenters. Dr Tenison added, it would be expected something should be offered in pursuance of the petition which the seven bishops had presented to the King; for which they had been put in the tower. The Archbishop said . . . he believed every bishop in England intended to make it good, when there was an opportunity to debate these matters in Convocation, but until then, or without a commission from the King, it was highly penal to enter upon Church matters; but, however, he would bear it in mind, and would be willing to discourse to the bishops or other clergy thereupon, if they came to him; he believed the Dissenters would never agree among themselves, with what conditions would satisfy them. To which Dr Tenison replied, he believed so too, that he had not discoursed with any of them on the subject, and the way to do good was, not to discourse with them, but for the bishops to endevour to get such concessions settled in Parliament, the granting whereof (whether accepted or not by the Dissenters) should be good for the Church.[36]

Tenison the politician! Tenison, of course, had recently been having a series of talks with the Dissenters, but in dealing with Sancroft he knows the arguments which will appeal to the aged primate.

Soon after, accepting Sancroft's invitation to discuss things with him, Lloyd of St Asaph pressed the matter. On 14 January the pressure group met again at Stillingfleet's house where Lloyd was able to tell them that he had the Archbishop's 'leave' if not his approval, to consult about concessions that might bring in the dissenters. Patrick, Tillotson, Tenison, and Sharp were present, and the six of them ' agreed that a bill should be prepared to be offered by the Bishops, and we drew up the matter of it, in 10 or 11 heads '.[37] This shows their strength. Five divines and one Bishop, draw up a bill ' to be presented by the Bishops '.

This was followed by six meetings of the ' bishops ' and Lord Nottingham who discussed the matter further. The original form of the Bill of Comprehension has been reconstructed by Brother George Every.[38] It allowed ministers in presbyterial orders at their own desire to be ' admitted to the ministry of this Church by the imposition of the Bishop's hand in this forme: Take thou Authority to Preach the Word of God and administer the Sacraments and perform all other Ministerial Offices in the Church of England '. Other concessions included the nocent ceremonies, and it was suggested that the Liturgy and Canons should be revised by a Royal Commission consisting of the two archibshops and eighteen other bishops and clergy.

The results of the debate between Comprehension, and Toleration, and the political aspects which surrounded them are well known, and have been dealt with in detail elsewhere. The Toleration Act became law in May 1689, and the Comprehension scheme was indefinitely put on the table where it remained unheeded. The effects of the Toleration Act were disastrous for the Comprehension party. The Dissenters as was foreseen, lost a great deal of interest in the scheme, as it was now possible for them to worship in their own way, unmolested. Also, they now had a legal basis to their existence, and were virtually on an equal footing with the established Church. Thus they refused to be content with small alterations in the Liturgy and canons, and became more demanding in their terms of reconciliation. The clergy of the Church of England were alarmed, not only by the abolition of Episcopacy in Scotland, but also by the rapid growth in the licencing of dissenting houses. They were unwilling to alter the establishment at all radically, and although a number were willing to concede a great deal to the Dissenters if a union could be effected, even more were chary of any rebuff they might receive for their intended alterations from them, and the general feeling rapidly became one of resentment towards them.

Despite this the London clergy continued their attempts at reconciliation. Tillotson became more and more involved, and as late as 13 September, he drew up a list of ' concessions which will probably be made by the Church of England for the Union of Protestants ', a copy of which is in Lambeth Palace Library (MS 954, f. 31)

1. that the ceremonies enjoined or recommended by the Liturgy or the ecclesiastical canons, be for the future left indifferent.

2. that the Liturgy be carefully review'd & such amendments & alterations made therein as may supply the defects of it; as by leaving out the Apocryphal lessons, by correcting the translation of the Psalmes now in use in the publicqe service, where there is a need of it; and in many other particulars.

3. that instead of all former declarations & subscriptions, to be made by the clergy, it shall be sufficient to subscribe one general declaration & promise to this purpose, that they do submit to the doctrine, discipline & worship, as they are established by law in the Church of England, and do promise to preach & practice accordingly.

4. that a new body of Ecclesiastical canons be compiled, principally with regard to a more effectual provision for the Reformation of manners both in ministers & people.

5. that there be an effectual regulation of the Ecclesiastical courts to remedy the great abuses & inconveniences which by degrees & length of time have crept into them; & particularly that the power of excommunication be taken out of the hands of lay officers & placed in the Bishop, and not to be exercised for trivial matters, but upon great & weighty occasions.

6. that for the future those who have been ordained in any of the foreign reformed churches be not required to be re-ordained here to render them capable of preferment in this church.

7. that for the future none be capable of any ecclesiastical benefice or promotion in the Church of England that shall be ordained in England otherwise than by Bishops: and that those who have been ordained onely by presbyters shall not be compelled to renounce their former ordination, but because many have, & do still make a doubt of the validity of such ordination, where episcopal ordination may be had & is required by law, it shall be sufficient for such persons to receive ordination from a Bishop in this or the like forms, If thou art not ordained, I ordain thee &c as in case of a doubt be made of any ones Baptism, it is appointed by our Liturgy that he be baptised in this forme, If thou art not baptized, I baptize thee &c.

## THE COMMISSION TO REFORM
## THE PRAYER BOOK 1689

Tillotson had long been pressing the King to set up the Ecclesiastical Commission to deal with all these points, and four days later, on 17 September 1689, that commission was signed and dated. After the list of names of those who were to take part in the revision, it continues:

WHEREAS the particular formes of Divine Worship and the Rites and Ceremonyes appointed to be used therein, being things in theire owne nature indifferent and alterable and soe acknowledged it is but reasonable that upon Weighty and Important Consideracons according to the various Exegency of tymes and occasions such changes and alteracons should be made therein as to those that are in place and Authority should from tyme to tyme seeme either necessary or expedient AND WHEREAS the Booke of Canons is fitt to be reviewed and made more suitable to the state of the Church And Whereas there are defects and abuses in the Ecclesiastical Courts and Jurisdiccons and particularly there is not sufficient Provision made for the removing of scandalous Ministers and for the reformacon of manners either in Ministers or people AND WHEREAS it is most fitt that there should be a strict method prescribed for the Examinacon of such persons as desire to be admitted into Holy Orders, both as to theire Learning and Manners Wee therefore out of Our pious and Princely Care for the good Order Edification and Unity of the Church of England comitted to Our Charge and for the reconciling as much as possible of all differences among Our good Subjects and to take away all occasions of the like for the future have thought fitt to Authorise Empower and Require You . . . or any nyne or more of you whereof three to be Bishopps to meet from tyme to tyme as often as shall be needful and to prepare such Alteracons and Amendments of the Liturgy and Canons and such proposalls for the Reformacon of Ecclesiasticall Courts and to Consider of such other matters as in your Judgment may most conduce to the ends above menconed soe that the Things by you soe considered and prepared may be in readinesse to be offered to the Convacacon at theire next meeting and when approved by them may be presented to Us and Our two houses of Parliament that if it shall be Judged fitt they may be establisht in due forme of law.

The members of the Commission were:

*Bishops:* Thomas Lamplugh of York, Henry Compton of London, Peter Mew of Winchester, William Lloyd of St Asaph, Thomas Sprat of Rochester, Thomas Smith of Carlisle, Jonathan Trelawney of Exeter, Gilbert Burnet of Sarum, Humphrey Humphreys of Bangor, and Nicholas Stratford of Chester.

*Deans:* Edward Stillingfleet (late Dean of St Paul's, but elevated to Worcester), Symon Patrick (late Dean of Peterborough, but elevated to Chichester), John Tillotson (Canterbury), Richard Meggot (Winchester), John Sharp (Norwich), Henry Aldrich (sometimes spelt ' Aldridge ' (Christ Church, Oxford), Richard Kidder (Dean-elect of Peterborough).

*Academics:* William Jane (Regius Professor of Divinity, Oxford, and also Dean of Gloucester), John Hall (Lady Margaret Professor, Oxford), Joseph Beaumont (Regius Professor of Divinity, Cambridge), John Montague (Master of Trinity College, Cambridge).

*Canons:* John Scott (Prebendary St Pauls), Edward Fowler (Gloucester), Robert Grove (St Pauls), John Williams (St Pauls).

*Archdeacons:* John Goodman (Middlesex), William Beveridge (Colchester), John Battley (Canterbury), Charles Alston (Essex), Thomas Tenison (London).

These Commissioners fall into four well defined groups:

(1) The pressure group led by Lloyd, Tillotson, Stillingfleet, Patrick and Tenison, and including Grove, Williams, Alston, Fowler, Kidder (and possibly Humphrey and Stratford, if they can be classed with anyone). The leaders and Grove and Fowler had all been involved in previous Comprehension schemes, and had played a part in the Bishop's petition to King James. Tenison, Patrick, Tillotson, and Stillingfleet (and perhaps Kidder) had all taken part in the previous revision of the liturgy in 1688.

This was a 'Latitudinarian' Body, which had the ear of the King through both Lloyd and Tillotson; indeed, William once said of Tillotson, whom he was soon to make Archbishop of Canterbury, that 'he was the best man whom he ever had, and the best friend whom he ever had'.[39] With the exception of Alston all these men were elevated to the bench; Lloyd was translated to Winchester, Tillotson and Tenison both became Archbishops of Canterbury, Tenison going first to Lincoln; Grove and Williams[40] both became Bishops of Chichester, and Stillingfleet went to Worcester; Patrick immediately went to Chichester through the patronage of Lloyd,[41] Kidder to Bath and Wells, and Fowler to Gloucester.

It is evident where the King's sympathies lay, if only from these subsequent appointments. Most of the work in the Commission was done by this group, as we learn from John Williams' Diary, which is printed fully in Appendix 1 (p. 160f.).

(2) The second group is a miscellaneous one, consisting of high churchmen who were deeply involved in the revolution and the Comprehension scheme, and so were in favour of a revision of the Liturgy; these men worked throughout with the pressure group. This comprises Compton, Burnet,[42] Sharp, Beveridge, and Scott. Compton was already a Bishop, but the others all received episcopal dignity from the King, except Scott[42] who died in 1695. Nevertheless, he received promotion for in 1691 his Majesty presented him with the living of St Giles in the Fields, in possession of which he died. Sharp later became Archbishop of York, Burnet received Sarum through the auspices of his friend Lloyd, while Beveridge was offered Ken's Bishopric, but refused it.

There was tension within this group. Burnet, of course, was committed to working with the pressure group, through his associations with Lloyd, and so was Sharp, who for many years had been a friend of Lord Nottingham who was now Secretary of State. Compton, however, had had reason to suspect Burnet since 1686 of undermining his influence with William, and had done his best to have him sent home from the Hague where William had invited him to stay. Furthermore, Compton had expected, after his services to William, the Archbishopric of Canterbury, and it was becoming painfully obvious that he was to be passed over in favour of Tillotson. Compton's dissatisfaction grew as time went on, but he was firmly behind the Comprehension scheme and concerned to strengthen the protestant interest, and so co-operated with the pressure group throughout the sittings of the Commission. In Convocation a battle was fought for his soul, and the pressure group lost; Compton helped the scheme miscarry.[43]

(3) The high Church group, whose members were Lamplugh, Mew, Sprat, Trelawney, Meggot, Aldrich, Jane, Battley and Smith. These men were all Tories who were against any revision of the Prayer Book in principle. Thus Lamplugh, Trelawney, Battley, and Smith, never attended a single meeting of the Commission; Mew and Sprat only attended twice, and Jane, Meggot, and Aldrich only three times. Those who were not already bishops received no further promotion, Aldrich remaining dean of Christ Church, and Jane dean of Gloucester.

(4) The four academics must be treated as a separate group. Beaumont and Montague cancelled each other out, and never attended the commission; Jane has been mentioned already, and Hall who attended nine times and later became Bishop of Bristol, was a puritan of the old school, and seems to have worked with the pressure group when he did attend the commission.

The Commission sat for the first time on 3 October, and for a second time on 16 October. In the latter, trouble began to brew between the two sides. Williams records that:

The Bp. of Rochester spoke to this purpose, That He questioned the Authority of this Comissn; and whether it was not pmunire to meet according to it . . . . that he shou'd not think himself safe unless He had it under the hands of the 12 Judges, having in his former Case[45] had Judges on his Side, That if it was legal, yet however He questioned whether this was not dissolved, and that there needed a new Commission and that 1. Because the quality of some of the Persons therein was altered; Such as He a few days ago had the Honour to lay his hands upon; and 2. because there were but 7 at the last meeting that Adjourned the Court; and that the Comiss: made 9 at least of the Quorum. He urged further that He could not see how We could enter upon such matters having given Assent and Consent to Them: That it was to accuse the Church, and condemn it as if it needed; That this was to prevent the Convocation, and that it could not be taken well by them to be called together to Confirm that which They had no hand in: That this wou'd provoke the Parliament.

Against such a barrage little could be done; Compton and Patrick argued against each point, but it was evident that the high Church party was going to make these arguments their excuse for not attending the Commission. Dr Jane said that Sprat had convinced him. Sprat never attended the commission again, and at the next meeting, Jane and Aldrich walked out ' and came no more '.

It was thus left to the pressure group and its good wishers to bear the whole burden. A glance at the following table will show to what extent the parties intermingled, and where the work of drafting was done.

## OCTOBER — NOVEMBER

Attendance table († signifies presence; * signifies a committee, or no quorum)

| | Oct 3 | 16 | *16 | *17 | 18 | 21 | *22 | 23 | 24 | 25 | 28 | 30 | 31 | Nov 1 | 3 | 6 | 8 | 11 | 13 | 15 | *18 | 18 | No. Times attended |
|---|---|---|---|---|---|---|---|---|---|---|---|---|---|---|---|---|---|---|---|---|---|---|---|
| **PRESSURE GROUP** | | | | | | | | | | | | | | | | | | | | | | | |
| Lloyd | | | | | | | | | | | | | | | | | | | | | | | 18 |
| Stillingfleet | | | | | | | | | | | | | | | | | | | | | | | 13 |
| Patrick | | | | | | | | | | | | | | | | | | | | | | | 18 |
| Tillotson | | | | | | | | | | | | | | | | | | | | | | | 14 |
| Tenison | | | | | | | | | | | | | | | | | | | | | | | 20 |
| Grove | | | | | | | | | | | | | | | | | | | | | | | 18 |
| Williams | | | | | | | | | | | | | | | | | | | | | | | 21 |
| Kidder | | | | | | | | | | | | | | | | | | | | | | | 11 |
| Alston | | | | | | | | | | | | | | | | | | | | | | | 17 |
| Humphrey | | | | | | | | | | | | | | | | | | | | | | | 7 |
| Stratford | | | | | | | | | | | | | | | | | | | | | | | 10 |
| Fowler | | | | | | | | | | | | | | | | | | | | | | | 8 |
| **MISCELLANEOUS** | | | | | | | | | | | | | | | | | | | | | | | |
| Compton | | | | | | | | | | | | | | | | | | | | | | | 20 |
| Burnet | | | | | | | | | | | | | | | | | | | | | | | 18 |
| Sharp | | | | | | | | | | | | | | | | | | | | | | | 15 |
| Beveridge | | | | | | | | | | | | | | | | | | | | | | | 13 |
| Scott | | | | | | | | | | | | | | | | | | | | | | | 18 |
| **HIGH CHURCH** | | | | | | | | | | | | | | | | | | | | | | | |
| Lamplugh | | | | | | | | | | | | | | | | | | | | | | | — |
| Mew | | | | | | | | | | | | | | | | | | | | | | | 2 |
| Sprat | | | | | | | | | | | | | | | | | | | | | | | 2 |
| Trelawney | | | | | | | | | | | | | | | | | | | | | | | — |
| Meggot | | | | | | | | | | | | | | | | | | | | | | | 3 |
| Aldrich | | | | | | | | | | | | | | | | | | | | | | | 3 |
| Jane | | | | | | | | | | | | | | | | | | | | | | | 3 |
| Battley | | | | | | | | | | | | | | | | | | | | | | | — |
| Smith | | | | | | | | | | | | | | | | | | | | | | | — |
| **ACADEMICS** | | | | | | | | | | | | | | | | | | | | | | | |
| Hall | | | | | | | | | | | | | | | | | | | | | | | 9 |
| Beaumont | | | | | | | | | | | | | | | | | | | | | | | — |
| Montague | | | | | | | | | | | | | | | | | | | | | | | — |
| (Goodman) | | | | | | | | | | | | | | | | | | | | | | | 3 |
| *Meeting attendance:* | 17 | 18 | *7 | *6 | 19 | 15 | *13 | 14 | 13 | 15 | 12 | 15 | 9 | 13 | 16 | 13 | 13 | 10 | 15 | 14 | *8 | 9 | |

*signifies a committee, or no quorum.

†signifies presence.

30

The final deliberations of the Commission may be found in Lambeth MS 2173, which is an interleaved folio Prayer Book. Like the Prayer Book which was used in 1688, it has been specially 'constructed' to receive the interleaves: thus the first title page bears the date MDCLXXXVI, the second '1683', and the state prayers refer to William and Mary as the Monarchs!

This was not the only copy of the Commission's work, for Calamy said that he had 'an exact copy' which he 'unhappily and irrecoverably lost by lending out'. This has been untraceable. The copy in Lambeth Palace Library, however, is obviously the one which was used by the Commissioners themselves.

Most of the alterations are in Tenison's hand, and he seems to have acted as secretary to the Commission. There are, however, a number of other hands at work throughout the book, and Tillotson's and Patrick's hands are easily recognizable, and there are a number of places where a hand which may possibly be Burnet's is at work. These additions are, however, small ones. By far the greatest part of the additions which is not that of Tenison, is in the copper plate hand of an Emanuensis.

Williams mentions that they 'took their parts', and it seems that the work of revision was divided up amongst members of the Commission, each having a service or part of a service to revise in the form of a first draft for purposes of discussion. Quite a lot of the work had been done already; by the first meeting of the Commission on 3 October, Kidder and Lloyd had completed the retranslation of the Psalter, and it was debated whether to accept it or not. Tenison had collected together all the exceptions made against the Liturgy in past years, and Patrick had compiled a large part of the new Collects. Furthermore, there had been a revision in 1688. Tenison used his Emanuensis to copy much of this previous material into the book, using him particularly on the new Collects.

At the beginning of their sessions, it would seem that each member of the Commission produced revisions on pieces of paper. Some of these were obviously accepted without alteration, and these have been added to the book by the Emanuensis; some when he had time, were added by Tenison. Thus Lambeth MSS 933-43 is the previous draft of the alterations to the Sunday and Holy day Lessons. In a number of cases therefore Tenison has begun to write a rubric or prayer, and the Emanuensis has completed it from a previous draft. This is particularly evident at the beginning of the Confirmation, where by a quirk of fate, the Emanuensis' previous draft, in Tenison's hand, still remains in the book.

What sources were used by the Commissioners is difficult to determine. They certainly had the Book of 1688 before them, for there are a large number of alterations taken from that book and embodied in their own report. They also had Tenison's collection of objections, and whether the Presbyterian Exceptions of 1661 were embodied within this or not, a great deal of notice was taken of them. Williams also records that ' that They might do them (Dissenters) Justice there were several of their Books laid before the Commee, that They might consult if there be occasion '. The very fact that ' they took their parts ', however, makes it impossible to analyse the modern literature used, for each man had the use of his whole library, and well as perhaps the libraries of others, in constructing his first draft.

The Commission obviously went out of its way to gratify the Dissenters, and about sixty per cent of the Exceptions of 1661 have been conceded. The Apocrypha has been expunged, the Ring in Marriage is duly qualified, the Surplice and the Cross in Baptism have been made optional, and so has kneeling at Communion.

It would be tautologous, when the full text follows this introduction with notes analyzing it in detail, to repeat those findings here. Instead, the Introduction must be allowed to ' introduce ', and we must turn to the pamphlet controversy which surrounded the setting up of the Commission.

## THE SURROUNDING LITERARY CONTROVERSY

There is one pamphlet which itself needs introduction, if only for the reason that its authorship must be argued. This is *A Letter from a Minister in the Country to a Member of the Convocation* (London, 1689) which is dated 20 November 1689 and signed N.L. It has previously been attributed to several people, and particularly to William Bassett. However, it would seem that this is a work put out by the Commission to test the reaction of people to the actual proposals which they had completed only two days earlier. The similarity to the debates as recorded in Williams' diary are too close to permit coincidence, and the phraseology and arguments are always those of one person on the Commission: Gilbert Burnet, Bishop of Sarum. The most material of these have been contrasted in the notes, one of the most important being the arguments concerning re-ordination (cf. p. 274f.). The contemporary pamphlets seem to imply a similar attribution. The ' *Remarks from the Country* ' by Henry Maurice, ascribes it to a ' director ' (i.e. Bishop) on the Commission.

. . . it is no wonder if the Company at Harry the Seventh's Chappel resented the affront, and cryed out a Libel, and carry'd their Complaints as far as Jerusalem-Chamber there to be decently buried in Oblivion. It is doubtless out of pure condescension, that one of these Directors is pleased to style himself a Minister in the Countrey; the undertaking does not agree very well with his

32

Character; and it is seldom that Persons of that Rank take upon them to direct and Catechise synods. (p. 2).

*Vox Cleri* also singles out Burnet:

But this clamor the present Bishop of Sarum with some others have silenced, proving undeniably that the Church of England had neither the temper nor the power to be of a Persecuting spirit. (Author's Protestation)

If in fact this has been written by Burnet, and there seems to be no others who could have undertaken it, it becomes a very important document in connection with what was intended by the Commission.

There was a great deal of distrust of the Commission mainly for the reasons which were given by Sprat for not attending the Commission. The first shots were in fact fired from his guns, in a pamphlet by Dr Jane, called '*A letter to a friend containing some Quaeries about the New Commission for making alterations in the Liturgy*'. This pamphlet proved to be the starting point of a controversy, in which many churchmen participated; the points which Jane raised were to be debated throughout that controversy.

He began by asking what the necessity of the alterations were. If they were to be made for the sake of the Church, why had the Church in her Convocations not been consulted? ' Or is it for the Peace and Unity and Edification of the Church, for some few assuming men to alter the Established worship to make it comply with their own private conceits or to serve their own private ends?' To remove the ceremonies would be to remove that which preserved decency and solemnity in worship, and to replace the primitive worship and discipline of the Apostolic churches with modern inventions.

Furthermore, there was no point in altering the Liturgy for the sake of the dissenters, for they would not accept any alterations except those which would destroy the ' fundamental Constitution of the Church of England '. ' Can any alterations in our Collects and Prayers (while we retain a Form) satisfie those who declare against all forms of Prayer as a quenching of the Spirit? and then it is not altering the Liturgy but taking it away, that must satisfie dissenters '. If the Presbyterians did not submit to episcopal ordination, there would be no union; the people would not desert them and join the Church. If the commissioners accepted the orders of Presbyterians, churchmen would not ' own such Presbyters '.

Any alterations would be bound to offend large numbers of the Church, and many might feel that they had to depart from any Church which so disregarded primitive practice. The Church of England was the best constituted Church in the world, and this was to be ' transformed by Nine men, who may have tenderness and moderation enough to part with any thing but their Church preferments ', and it was these men that would check all debate on the alterations in Convocation. Jane then brought up a subject which was to become a deadlock in Convocation:

Can it be thought a convenient time for such alterations as these, when the A.B. the Metropolitan of all England, and the head of the Convocation, and several other Bishops (not to mention those of the inferior clergy) who are as eminent for a prudent and well tempered zeal for the Church of England, as for their constant loyalty, are now under suspension? Will not some be apt to question the Ecclesiastical Authority of such proceedings . . .? Will not others be apt to suspect that this time is chosen on purpose, because the A.B. and those other bishops are now suspended, whose presence and authority in the Convocation they were afraid of, as sure and fast friends to the Church? and if they are afraid of those reverend Persons who had before declared their readiness to come to such a temper with reference to dissenters, as shall be thought fit by parliament and convocation, it is very suspicious that they intend something very unreasonable which they feared would not pass a free convocation, when those reverend and judicious Prelates were present.

Such an opening burst was unwelcome to the commissioners. They had not even finished their deliberations, and Jane had little knowledge of what they would recommend. This was not an attack on the alterations in detail, but an assault on the very existence of the Commission, which at one blow intended to invalidate all their proceedings. It was therefore felt that something ought to be undertaken in reply, and on 29 October, Tenison published his ' Discourse concerning the Ecclesiastical Commission opened in the Jerusalem Chamber October the 10th 1689 '. He began by stating the heads he proposed to discuss:

Though I have never entertained a good opinion of the late commission for Ecclesiastical affairs; yet concerning this . . . . I stand thus persuaded (1) It is agreable to the laws of the land. (2) It is not prejudicial, but useful to the convocation. (3) It tendeth to the well being of the Church. (4) This is a fit juncture for putting the design of it into execution.[46]

He is concerned throughout to show that the commission has no independent authority, and is only preparing material to be submitted to the convocation for their discussion. Greater things had been done, he pointed out, by way of commission without causing offence in the church, ' than giving MEER ADVICE concerning such things as are fit and proper to be laid before a Convocation; which is the present Case . . . That which the Commissioners do is only by way of preparation, which saveth time and labour, and provideth something ready for the Convocation to go on . . .[47] ' Such alterations were only honouring the obligations laid on the Church by the Bishop's petition to King James. This does not as Jane suggests, mean that everything that is essential in the Church is to be discarded; on the contrary. The Church of England like every other sound Church, is constant in the Substantials of her faith, and in the general frame of her forms of worship, but still the liturgy contains things which are acknowledged by all to be of an alterable nature. The Prayer Book has been reviewed before and 'yet notwithstanding that review is capable of another'. The Alterations and Additions which were intended, would conduce greatly to the good of the Church, despite the fact that ' it is the best constituted Church in the World ', for the ' great business as to the liturgy is the adding to some Offices, and preparing new ones which are wanting, and the amending of Rubricks '.

> An attempt is to be made towards an Union among Protestants, and I humbly offer those Reasons to the Consideration of better Judges, which move me to believe that This is the Time for It. Their Majesties have declared their desires of it. The House of Lords have given us their Sense of it in the Bill of Union . . . . Toleration is already granted by Statute: the Nature of which requires our utmost Application in order to the preserving our own People, and the bringing in of Dissenters, for the good of Both.'[48]

These two pamphlets dealt with little in detail, but threw out the main points of argument between them. Others were not reticent in filling the gaps which they had left. On the whole two questions were debated; whether there should be any Comprehension scheme put forward at all; and if a revision of the Prayer Book was necessary, what words and ceremonies should be altered, and why? The Second of these questions is dealt with fully in the notes on the text.

At the very beginning of the literary debate, Dr Jane was elected prolocutor of the Lower House of Convocation, in a straight fight with Dr Tillotson: an event which caused Thomas Long to cry:

> The Intelligence you were pleased to give me of the Election of Dr Jane to be Prolocutor of the Convocation, gives great satisfaction to the Clergy of these Parts; and that he was Chosen by much the major part of your Members, is lookt on as a good Omen of Success in your Proceedings for the good of the Church, as by Law established.[49]

It was a triumph for those against the revision of the Prayer Book. Fuel was almost immediately added to the flames, by the publication of a number of pamphlets which added little to the debate, but were of a provocative nature. The ' *Healing Attempt* ' with its demand for an Episcopacy of the type propounded by Usher, helped to antagonize churchmen against any concessions regarding re-ordination; while the ' *Vanity, Mischief, and Danger of Continuing Ceremonies* ' was so radical that a reaction was bound to occur. The ' *Conformists Sayings* ' were also published, which listed the comments of Divines through the ages on the Liturgy, and was designed as a hand book of authorities for revision. A number of books from previous controversies were also re-published, including L'Estrange's *Alliance of the Divine Offices,* and John Owen's *Discourse concerning Liturgies.* The *Judgment of Foreign Divines* was a re-publication of the Letters from Zanchy, the Genevan and Scottish Churches, and Calvin concerning the Liturgy dated between 1555 and 1571.[50]

Most of these pamphlets were completely ignored in the controversy, and their only effect was to harden the opposition against the Commission.

## 1 THE NECESSITY OF A COMPREHENSION

The supporters of the Commission had to show that a Comprehension was necessary, not only for the benefit of Dissenters, but for the good of the individual members of the Church of England. They argued therefore, that a Comprehension was necessary for:

(a) the security of the Church: Over the past few years, and especially since the granting of Licences under the Declaration of Indulgence, it had become evident that the Church was growing still ' weaker and weaker, and those that dissent from it, still stronger and stronger ' despite the efforts that have been made to unite them. There lies an ' indispensible obligation ' upon the Church to remove the schism which is dividing the Body of Christ, to the advantage of popery and atheism. Prideaux sums up:

> And for this the late act of Toleration hath added a very pressing necessity. For when our divisions ran so high, and our animosities against each other so far increased as that Dissenters were driven by them to take shelter from us in the Camp of our Common Enemy, and join with the Papists against us to the endangering both of Church and State to utter ruin. The Parliament then thought time to provide for the publick Safety by reconciling those men thereto by an Act of Toleration and Indulgence, whereby they being now put upon as good a bottom of legal right and protection as we our selves, there is no way left us of coming to a union with them . . . but by condescension and abatement to reconcile those men unto us . . . are a few excepted passages in our Liturgy and two or three ceremonies in our Worship things of so great value that we must for the sake of them still maintain those discords and divisions both in Church and State which have so long harassed both almost to utter ruine?[51]

(b) A Comprehension is necessary for the Security of the State: James that ' formidable Enemy ', had begun to make war to regain the throne, and his strength lay in ' divisions among our selves at home which enfeeble both our hearts and hands for the battel, and make us unable to resist him with that success which formerly used to attend most of our other expeditions against Enemies altogether as potent '. Against the combined weight of France and Rome, only the comprehension of protestants could secure the country.

Our love of our Countrey, and to the present peace and settlement of it, which nothing can endanger but our present divisions, which tend to throw us back into the miseries we have just escaped . . . should strongly engage us to a fair union and accord with one another.

The leading dissenters will come in for a few alterations, and will bring their congregations with them; the whole protestant interest would be strengthened, for by joining with the Church, those who were its enemies become its friends, owning its communion and submitting to its authority.[52]

(c) Such an approach would greatly strengthen the Churches relationship with the foreign reformed Churches, who are waiting and expecting something to be done for the sake of union and peace. The problem of re-ordination of those who come from those Churches to England, had to be solved, and this could only be done through a Comprehension scheme.[53]

The problems were not regarded as being as great as opponents of the scheme envisaged. There was a great deal in common, and this should be stressed more than the differences; both the Church and Dissenters believed the Creeds, used the same translation of the English Bible, and if there had not been so much misunderstanding in the past would agree in the same ceremonies. But a strict uniformity of Rites and Ceremonies is unnecessary 'provided there be an Agreement in all the Essentials of her Doctrine and Worship'. It is the imposition of these things which causes schism.[54]

The opponents of the scheme found a champion in Thomas Long a prebendary of Exeter, whose pamphlet, *Vox Cleri*, was the watershed of many other authors. He pointed out that there could be no 'necessity' for a Comprehension, because that was an absolute term:

The Acts For Uniformity were much more effectual than any Alterations that the Church can justly make will be, seeing the Dissenters have declared they will not be satisfied with the Alterations of our Ceremonies &c. but expect greater matters than the Church can grant. (2) Experience shews, that they will not acquiesce in such Alterations as may be granted. (3) Because it was not for want of success, that Toleration was granted against the Act for Uniformity; but because it was too successful, and the Common Enemies of our Church perceiving the good effects of that Act, which had well nigh reduced the whole Nation to an Uniformity, with their joynt Interest procured a Toleration; and it needs no proof, That if the Act for Uniformity hath made one Dissenter, Toleration and Alterations have made hundreds; so that as there is No Necessitas praecepti, neither is there Necessitas medii, to obtain the Ends which this Author proposeth.[55]

It was also pointed out, that a Comprehension would only bring into the Church Presbyterians and Independents; Toleration implied freedom for all sorts of sects from Muggletonians to Anabaptists. Any policy of Comprehension therefore only solved part of the problem, and still left people in Schism who had yet to be reconciled.[56]

Furthermore, the policy of Comprehension at the present time was placing the cart before the horse; toleration was already granted, and there was no reason to think that the Dissenters would unite with the Church when their separation was allowed.

> Nothing that you can do will promote their Union with Us, but that which makes it their Interest, and that can be only done by rewards and punishments; and therefore the taking off the Sanctions of the Laws, and making the Separation easie, was beginning at the wrong end, and a certain way to make a Comprehension ineffectual.[57]

The onus lies heavily with the dissenters; they are the people who have caused the schism, and combined against the Church. To Comprehend would be to put 'A secret enemy within the Walls of a well Fortified City' which was 'more dangerous than an open Foe in the Field'. As the matter stands, all the protagonists are doing is giving them fuel for their attacks on the Church; Anglicans are now licking up 'the Venome of the Dissenters, to spit it in the face of their own Church'. Any new reformation undertaken like this, only serves to disparage the old; it condemns great divines who have defended it and approved it; it shows the dissenters that they were right to dissent, from a house which had not yet been properly put in order. It simply exposes the Church to reproach.[58]

## 2 CONCESSIONS IN THE LITURGY

### SHOULD BE MADE FOR THE DISSENTERS

A Comprehension would aid the Church; but more than this, it was necessary to undertake a revision of the Prayer Book for the dissenters' sake, in fulfilment of the promise which the Bishops made in the tower. The clergy of the land approved that petition, when they refused to read the Declaration of Indulgence in their Churches, and now that there is a 'legal bottom' to their proceedings they should honour those promises which raised the expectations of not only the dissenters but the entire nation. If the Church fails to honour these commitments, which were made in her hour of need, it will reflect badly upon her; her clergy will be regarded as 'a base and false sort of men, who can promise fair in times of adversity, and forget all performances when they are over.'[59]

Such concessions would not have to be far reaching. Payne averred that:

'I doubt not, nay I have moral Assurance that a great many of the best and wisest Dissenters would come in upon some few alterations, such as I think no wise and good Church-man would refuse to them, for that end, such as altering the Subscription, and the like proposals made by that great man, the present Bishop of Worcester.'

Many of the Dissenters are forward in their desires to join with the Church, and apart from some ministers who find their present jobs lucrative and pleasant, most of the people will 'in large numbers come in to us as soon as those alterations shall be in our Churches; and when they are once come off, it will not be long ere their ministers also will be forced to follow'.[60]

But even if there was no dissenter in the country, the Church would still be bound by her promise. This would give satisfaction to the nation and raise the Church in their estimation. As it is most people are indifferent to both sides, and ready to join with either side which is dominant. If the Church does abate its rigour, and the dissenters do not come in, the people will condemn them as 'obstinate and unreasonable people' and the Church herself will be justified with the people on its side. If the Church does not do it, the parliament will, and it will be taken out of the clergy's hands.[61]

The initiative lies not with the Dissenters therefore but with the Church. The dissenters have put their objections in writing for many years now, and are waiting for some response from the Church. It is more to the honour of the Church that it should give terms to the dissenters rather than the other way round. 'No rather let the Parent wisely and by fair means bring the stubborn Child off from its disobedience if it be possible, without the Childs offering terms whether reasonable or unreasonable'.[62]

Their opponents pointed out that few would come in on slight alterations which were made by the Church without consulting them first. If the Convocation has the authority to make these alterations and not the Commission, as Tenison had pointed out, the Dissenters should apply to the Convocation. For the Church itself to propose terms was 'a condescension that renders authority cheap and contemptible, to stoop to its adversaries, and court them to accept of such terms as may be the cause of the churche's ruin . . .' Yet none had applied.[63]

The reason they have not applied to the Convocation is, that 'it is not their Cannot, but their Will Not that keeps them from our Communion; and when their Interest and Advantage requires it they can conform'. All members of the foreign reformed Churches who have come to this country, have universally joined with the Church of England rather than the dissenters for worship; they received communion kneeling, allowed their children to be baptised with the sign of the Cross and so on. How can it be therefore that all protestants find that they can worship with the Church of England except the English Dissenters? It is not a reflection of the Church, but on the Dissenters whose charity is very cold.[64]

The 'end' should be discussed before the 'means'. The end, it is acknowledged, is to give the Dissenter's consciences satisfaction; but what alterations will do that which has not been proposed with any moderation. Any alterations which are made will hurt the Church far more than they will benefit it:

> And we think we have a moral assurance, that whatever Concessions the Convocation can make with safety to themselves, will not only be despised, but cast back as filth in our faces; not only with a Quis requisivit, but with a Pudet haec Opprobria vobis; as if our manner of publick Worship were so corrupt, that we were ashamed of it, and convinced of a necessity to purge it.

There had been many previous attempts to win them over, and all had failed. If changes are made, they will find objections to them to support yet further dissent.[64] The situation is summed up in the biting words of Henry Maurice.

> Now Sirs, it is all done as you have ordered: Call the Dissenters in, that the Church may be full: Go to the Quakers, for they are a numerous and compact party; and let them know that there is now neither Apocrypha, nor obsolete translations, nothing but Scripture in the Lessons; . . . . what answer think ye, the Foreman of a Quaker Assembly would probably return to such an invitation? . . . . Friend, go to thy Steeple-house and thy dead letter again, thou mightest have kept thy old Lessons, and thy Prayers for us, and forbear tempting and troubling our Spirit any further . . . . Carry your reformed Liturgy to the Baptists . . . the sign of the Cross, in Baptism, that great Stumbling-block, is removed, and the Surplice that offended tender Eyes, is turned into Aprons for the Church-warden's Wife: . . . the Pastor . . . would gravely tell you, you were much mistaken if you intended to gain them by your alterations. For you could not but know, that their Exceptions were not against this or that passage in the Common-Prayer, but against the whole; All Forms of Prayer in their opinion tending to suppress the free motions of the Spirit: . . . . Go to your Independents, for they are civil Men; and tell your story to the best advantage . . . Parish-Churches and national Churches, reply the Independents . . . . You know we are in Covenant with God, and with our Pastors, from which we cannot recede, though all the World be destroyed: Those mixed Companies and Parish Assemblies our Souls hate, and therefore do not urge us. We have Liberty now to meet in our own way,

and for ought I know this Disturbance you have given us, may fall within the Compass of the Act: . . . . Send for T.F. and the Socinians; he perhaps may owe you a Visit, and will be glad of an opportunity to shew his coach . . . A Man of less Pertness than T.F. would return upon you, That you cannot expect any compliance from them, so long as the Nicene Creed, the Spring of all the Doctrin which makes up your Mystery, and their Abomination, does remain; and they will do the civility to hear you preach, provided you confine your selves to Morality, and forbear the Doxology at the Conclusion. (Go to) . . . . the good Presbyterians . . . . Methinks I see Mr A draw his mouth, and put this Question, And must this new Book be imposed? Why, you will say, it is so absolute and so perfect that it were to be wished that it were imposed upon the whole world. Nay, saith Mr A. do you not know the mischief of impositions? . . . To be brief, it is our Fervent pouring out, is the very Brandy of Devotion; those that are once accustomed to it, can never leave it."

Maurice concludes by agreeing, however, that the Moderate Presbyterians, if there are any, would gladly come in . . . . for a little preferment![66]

Alterations would satisfy no one; and therefore the peace of the Church must be considered first. Worship must be done decently and in order, and those who will not conform must be judged as contentious persons. 'As long as those Forms of Prayer used in our Church, and those Rites and Constitutions which are received, do answer the Ends of their first establishment, viz. The Honour of God, and Edification of the People, they ought with constancy alway to be retained.'

### 3 ALTERATIONS TO THE LITURGY ARE NECESSARY
#### FOR THE GOOD OF THE CHURCH

Liturgies are in their very nature alterable, simply because they are composed by human beings. While Christ prescribed what man should do in general terms, worship God and celebrate the Sacraments, he left the form and manner in which it should be done to the Church, who could alter these things as they became less relevant to her members. 'And that may be, by taking away what may be spared, and that sometime is superfluous. By supplying what is wanting, by clearing what is doubtful, by amending what's amiss, and improving what is tolerable and well, so as to make it yet more beneficial and solemn'.[67]

But more than this, a liturgy is a transitory thing, which relates strictly to the mood, intelligence and era of the worshippers. Prideaux explains this in detail:

As to the Liturgy of our Church I freely acknowledge, and I think no man can contradict me herein, that it is the best which was ever yet used in any Christian Church, but that it therefore be so perfect as not to be capable of amendments or alterations for the better doth by no means follow. For nothing of humane composure can be such, especially in a thing of this nature, where process of time and alteration of circumstances frequently produce a necessity for correction, as most certainly in our Liturgy they very often doe. For the language in which it is wrote being constantly in fluxu, as all other living languages are, in every age some words that were in use in the former grow obsolete, and some phrases and expressions formerly in grace and fashion through disuse become uncouth and ridiculous, and always to continue these in our Liturgy without correction would be to bring a disparagement upon the whole, and expose to contempt the worship of God among us. Besides there are several things which in one age may conduce to devotion, which through variation of times and circumstances may not be born in another; several things which may be proper of Prayer at one time which may not be so in another, and all those things call for alterations and amendments whenever they happen. And therefore I am so far from assenting with some of our brethren in this particular, that our Liturgy ought not to be altered, and I think it absolutely necessary from the above-mentioned particulars that it be always at least once in 30 years brought to a review for this purpose. And I am sure that this hath been the judgment of the whole Christian Church from the beginning till this time.[68]

There are ample precedents for this in the history of the Church of England. The Liturgy was first revised under Edward VI, and since then there have been a large number of alterations, the last being in 1662, when 600 alterations were made. It is not the fact that the Anglican liturgy is the best in the world that matters, but how far it comes up to the greater purity and simplicity of the Gospel. To lead the world, does not imply perfection; it only implies less error than other Churches and their liturgies.

Yet even within the liturgy as it stands there are certain things which unalterable:

Which Rule supposes the Alterations such as are consistent with the Being and Security of our Church. With the Being, whereby are excluded all such as will not allow a National Church, Episcopacy, and a Liturgy. With the Security, and so are excluded such alterations as will do more mischief by dividing us among our selves, than good by uniting others to us.[69]

Only what is just and fitting should therefore be altered, and there is no necessity to throw out the baby with the bathwater. The externals in religion can be altered, but not the essentials, and when the latter

42

are in danger that is the time to resist change. Outward ceremonies, however, cannot justify themselves if they are guilty of rending the Body of Christ.

Such alterations would benefit the Church, for they would help worshippers to grow in faith. Outmoded expressions only confused the uneducated, and the fact that so many churchmen had to write explanations, paraphrases, and commentaries on the Prayer Book confirmed this; was it preferable therefore to bind these in with the Prayer Book, rather than alter a few phrases, so that people could continually refer from one to the other?[70]

Against these arguments, their antagonists had little answer. The points they stressed instead, was that any alteration would divide the Church, and the way in which the alterations were being undertaken was suspect.

Should the Commission alter any of the substantials of the Church's worship, it would be as permissable for members of the Church to walk out as it was for the members of the Commission who disapproved. The making of alterations might indeed drive many good sons of the Church out, on the sheer hypothesis that others will come in. It is a very dangerous way of acting. Constant change and alteration will make many people suppose that there is nothing certain in the Church, and from the Liturgy they will begin to question the articles. These men will go to the Church of Rome, where the constancy that is needed in worship and principles is evident.

The Dissenters will not come into the Church whatever the concessions which are made. If things are left indifferent to use them or not, they will be a divisive influence in the church, with people doing one thing, and clergy the other; people vying against people, clergy arguing against clergy. This then is not the way to achieve peace and union.[71]

Those who are members of the Commission are suspect in their views. They are 'Latitudinarians', who while they have so far lived in conformity with the Church, may make alterations which will make the same course difficult for others.

Now although I dare not say, there was any partiality used in naming the Commissioners; yet when I consider that many of those that were named did not appear, and some very considerable persons that did appear, perceiving that some such things, as might in their judgment prove prejudicial to the Church, were proposed, did dissent and withdrawn; it was not altogether unlikely that Nine of those who remained might prepare such things, as the Convocation would not approve of, as the Event will shew.

There is evidence also that these men have attempted to pack the Convocation, and that the *Letter from a Minister,* and *a Letter to a Friend,* were written either by the Commissioners themselves or those employed by them. These pamphlets as well as the acting of the Commission itself, is to prevent the Convocation, which is bombarded with advice. Has the Liturgy and constitution of the Church grown worse from the time that the commissioners and their friends last gave their assent and consent to them? [72]

It is perhaps fitting that this brief analysis of the arguments put forward in the literary debate, should close with the words of Henry Maurice, who sums up the arguments against any revision of the Prayer Book in such a masterly way, that it has never been equalled.

I have almost filled up my sheet though I write in short hand, and therefore cannot now give you my reasons at length, why I think this is an unfit Time for alterations, if any at all were to be thought of: I will only hint them to you in the first place; the Dissenters do not seem to be in any Disposition to an Accommodation, having never made any Proposals either to the Commissioners or Convocation. (2) The Condition they are in at present by the Act of Toleration raises their expectations too high to be satisfied with any reasonable Terms. (3) The abolishing of Episcopacy by their Brethren of Scotland, may encourage them here to think of such matters as can never be the fruits of a Treaty, and perhaps to dream of a second Conquest. (4) Their insolence in all places since this Revolution declares them to be above the humble Dispensation of an amicable Composure. (5) The great men that influence them, will always think it their interest to keep them separate from the Church, for so they will be most for their turn, and therefore will never suffer them to joyn with us; or should they come in, will always keep them as a separate Party within the Church. (6) Several of the most considerable among them have declared, they will never think of treating, unless their Orders are allowed, and then too they will insist upon the Point of Episcopacy. (7) The Church of England Men do not seem to be in a Disposition for altering at this Time; for they find themselves insulted and oppressed in all parts of the kingdom, where the moderate Men are got in Power and Commission. (8) The Clergy are alarmed with the Destruction of Episcopacy in Scotland, and think they have reason to be jealous, that now the Presbyterians of England hold intelligence with the Scots; because they have always corresponded. (9) Our Lay-men find Dissenters even in this State of Separation to have the Preferrence; and upon a new Model they may have reason to suspect, that the Proselites may pass for the only Church-men, and then Veteres migrare Coloni. (10) There seems to want a Plenitude of Authority in the Convocation to enact these Alterations; the A.B. of Canterbury, and Five of his Suffragans, Persons of great Consideration and credit in the Church, lying at present under an incapacity . . . .

The Kingdom is yet in such a ferment, and many things so unsetled, that to change now in the Church, is like altering Military Exercise in the midst of a Battle, or carining a Ship in a Storm. The most proper time for Alterations in Religion, is that which is most calm, when the Spirits of Men run low, when there is a mutual confidence between parties, when they all conspire in one desire of accommodation, and when the Ecclesiastical Authority that is to Enact them, is entire, not only in respect of the Law, but of Common Opinion: And whether these circumstances belong to the present time, you will easily discern.[73]

## THE FATE OF THE REVISION

While all this was being written, both sides had been active in canvassing for support. Compton, already jealous of Tillotson's probable advancement to Canterbury, had joined with Dr Jane and Dr Aldrich in Oxford, to plan out their campaign. To what extent he was involved is uncertain; on the one hand he earnestly desired a comprehension and the union of all protestants in England, and on the other there was Tillotson.

When the Convocation sat on 21 November 1689, Compton was determined that Tillotson should not receive even more accolades, and when the election for prolocutor was between Jane and Tillotson, he threw his weight on the side of Jane. If the Comprehension scheme was to go through, and the liturgy be revised, a sympathetic prolocutor was essential. From the Commission's point of view Tillotson was the obvious man. But when it came to the vote, Jane was elected by a two-thirds majority.

Jane's Latin speech on 25 November, showed where his sympathies lay; and this was followed soon after by another speech by Aldrich,[74] which concluded with the words 'Nolumus leges Angliae mutari', the words which had adorned Compton's banner as he had ridden through Oxford to welcome William to the throne. It represented the antagonism to change which had centred on Oxford, and was at first attributed to Jane; but soon, when it became commonly realized that Aldrich had said it, it became a motto of the whole party.

The Convocation had no desire to sit at all. There were innumerable problems of procedure brought about by the absence and suspension of the Archbishop, and the members had little knowledge of procedure or precedent. Comprehension and Liturgical revision was never even discussed, the main debating point being the address to the crown, which became the battle ground between the higher and lower clergy. When that debate had concluded, instead of turning to comprehension, the fate of the non-jurors was discussed—could they sit in Convocation despite suspension, when no ecclesiastical censures had been laid on them? They were more important than the Dissenters. Realizing that nothing could be achieved, William prorogued the Convocation on 25 June.

The Revision of the Liturgy had been defeated, undiscussed. It died of neglect. The Book in which all the alterations were made was committed to Tenison, who kept it secret. 'If they became public', he later said, 'they would give no satisfaction to either side, but be rather a handle for mutual reproaches, for one side would upbraid their brethren for having given up so much; while the other would justify their nonconformity, because those concessions were too little, or, however little, not yet pass'd into a law'.[75] After Tenison's death, it passed to Edmund Gibson, Bishop of London, who likewise kept it secret; and after his death it passed into the safe keeping of Lambeth Palace Library.

Throughout the eighteenth century, however, those who felt that the Prayer Book stood in need of revision, attempted to obtain sight of the book, and in 1748, John Jones launched a public appeal for access to it. It was all of no avail. Instead would-be revisers, had to content themselves with garbled versions of the Commissions findings which were passed on by Nicholls and Calamy. And yet they did not give up, for in 1854 the House of Commons ordered the Book to be published, a work which was undertaken by Henry Black, a retired keeper of the Public Records. This edition however only produced the final alterations of the Commission, taking no note of differences of handwriting and previous readings which were subsequently deleted. Of course, it contained a few mistakes, but these were not important ones—that is no reflection on the editor; the production of the whole Book of Common Prayer from MS is no easy undertaking.

Black, however, had simply listed the alterations which were made, and it was not a particularly easy text to follow as it had to be read in conjunction with a Prayer Book. A need for fuller editions was therefore felt, and two were published in 1855. One was published by 'Seeley, Jackson and Halliday, Fleet Street' but contained none of the material before Morning Prayer, no Collects and no Ordinal. Another Edition was that edited by John Taylor, printed by 'Samuel Bagster and Sons', and this likewise contains no Ordinal. Both these editions were based on Black's text.

## M S 2173

*This Book is to be deposited in Lambeth Library, together with the Papers which belong'd to Archb. Tenison, and remain now, digested under their proper heads, in my Closet at Fulham, at the end of my Study.*

E. L.[1]

--------------------

### Directions.[2]

*The Original book of Alterations wch were intended to have been made in ye book of Comon Prayer in ye year 1689, & the Bundles of Papers wch were left by Archbishop Tenison to be delivered to ye Arch Bishop of Canterbury for ye time being, to be kept & pserv'd in ye Library at Lambeth; but ye Book to be kept secret, & under ye immediate custody of ye Archbishop, according to ye intention of Archbishop Tenison, and the same caution will be judg'd necessary as to some few of ye Papers when inspected and perus'd.*

+ 1. *Papers relating to Court affairs in ye Reigns of K. James ye 1st & K. Char. 1st.*

+ 2. *Miscellaneous Tracts & Papers in French &c.*

+ 3. *Printed papers & Pamphlets concerning Matters Ecclesiastical & Religious.*

+ 4. —————————————— *concerning Temporal matters of some value.*

+ 5. *Another Bundle of ye same.*

+ 6. *Miscellaneous tracts &c relating to Religion & ye Church, but of small value.*

+ 7. —————————————— *relating to Temporal matters of small value.*

+ 8. *Letters, chiefly to and from Lord Bacon.*

+ 9. *French papers relating to ye Swiss Cantons.*

+ 10. *An Essay towards reforming Newgate & other Prisons.*

+ 11. *Letters from Bp. Gauden & his wife to ye Earl of Bristol.*

*N.B. All these Papers were recd by me agreably to ye Bp. of Londons Directions. Oct 21. 1748. T.C.*

47

*From the Dean of the Arches*

*All the abovemention'd Papers were deliver'd to me & put into the Library at Lambeth by His Grace's order.*

23rd February 1748.                    Henry Hall, Librarian.

---

*After the Kalendar &c just before Catechism[9] &c in ye Preces privatae set forth by Author: of Q. Eliz. in 1573. in 16⁰. See Admon: ad Lectore.*

*Ubi in Calendario, singulis fere diebus uniuscujusq3 mensis, Sanctorum (quos vocant) nomina apposuimus: Id eo fecimus amice Lector, non quod eos omnes pro divis habeamus, quorum aliquos ne in bonis quidem ducimus: Aut quod alioqui (si Sanctissimi sint) ijs divinum Cultum atq3 Honorem tribuendum censeamus: Sed ut certarum quarundam rerum, quarum stata tempora nosse plurimum refert, quarumq3 ignoratio nostris hominibus obesse possit, quasi Notae quaedam sint atq3 indicia. Atq3 hac quidem hujus facti et instituti nostri ratio esto. Vale.*[3]

# THE BOOK[(1)]

of

## COMMON-PRAYER

And Administration

Of the

## SACRAMENTS,

and other

## RITES & CEREMONIES

Of the CHURCH,

According to the Use

Of the

## CHURCH OF ENGLAND,

Together with the

## PSALTER or PSALMS

## OF DAVID,

Pointed as they are to be Sung

or Said in Churches:

And the

Form & Manner

of

Making, Ordaining & Consecrating

of

Bishops, *Presbyters, Q.*[(2)] and Deacons.


London

Printed by His Maties Printers

Cum Privilegio


## MDCLXXXVI

P: Williamson scu.

# THE BOOK OF
# COMMON PRAYER,

And Other

Rites and Ceremonies of the Church,

According to the Use of the

# CHURCH OF ENGLAND;

Together with the

Psalter or Psalms

of

# DAVID,

Pointed as they are to be Sung or Said in Churches:

And the

# FORM and MANNER

Of

Making, Ordaining, and Consecrating of

BISHOPS, *PRESBYTERS,* & DEACONS.[3]

# The Contents of this Book.

The Acts for the Uniformity of Common Prayer.
The Preface.
Concerning the Service of the Church.
Concerning Ceremonies.
The Order how the Psalter is appointed to be read.
The Order how the rest of the holy Scripture is appointed to be read.
A Table of Proper Lessons and Psalms.
The Kalendar, with the Table of Lessons.
Tables and Rules for the Feasts and Fasts throughout the whole year.
The Order for Morning Prayer.
The Order for Evening Prayer.
The Creed of Saint Athanasius.
The Litany.
Prayers and Thanksgivings upon several occasions.
The Collects, Epistles and Gospels to be used at the Ministration
of the holy Communion throughout the year.
The Order for the Ministration of the holy Communion.
The Order of Baptism, both Publick and Private.
The Order of Baptism for those of riper years.
The Catechism, with the Order for Confirmation of Children.
The Form of Solemnization of Matrimony.
Visitation of the Sick, and Communion of the Sick.
The Order for the Burial of the Dead.
Thanksgiving for Women after Child-bearing.
A Commination, or Denouncing of Gods anger and judgements
against Sinners. [4]
The Psalter.
The Order of Prayers to be used at Sea.
The Form and Manner of Ordaining Bishops, Priests, and Deacons.

An Act for the Uniformity of Common Prayer, and Service in the
Church, And Administration of the Sacraments, Primo Eliz.

Where at the death of our late Sovereign Lord King Edward the
Sixth. . . .

An Act for the Uniformity of Public Prayers and Administration of
Sacraments, and other Rites and Ceremonies: And for Establishing
the Form of Making, Ordaining, and Consecrating Bishops, Priests,
and Deacons in the Church of England.

## XIV. Carol. II

Whereas in the first year of the late Queen Elizabeth. . . .

*A NEW Preface.*

## CONCERNING THE SERVICE OF THE CHURCH.

There was never any thing by the wit of man so well devised, or so sure established, which in continuance of time. . . .

Though it be appointed, That all things shall be read and sung in the Church in the English tongue, to the end that the Congregation may be thereby edified; yet it is not meant, but that when men say Morning and Evening Prayer privately, they may say the same in any language that they themselves do understand.

*And all Priests & Deacons that have Cure of souls[6] shall exhort ye People of their Congregations to come frequently to Prayers on Weekdaies, especially in the great Towns, & more particularly on Wednesdaies & Fridays, at least for ye reading of ye Litany. And where a Congregation can be brought together, the Ministers shall give their Attendance for saying of morning and Evening Prayr.*

## OF CEREMONIES, WHY SOME BE ABOLISHED AND SOME RETAINED.

Of such ceremonies as be used in the Church. . . .

## THE ORDER HOW THE PSALTER IS APPOINTED TO BE READ

The Psalter shall[7] be read through once every Month, as it is there appointed, both for Morning and Evening Prayer. But in February it shall be read onely to the Twenty eighth, or Twenty ninth day of the Month.

And whereas January, March, May, July, August, October and December have One and thirty days apiece; It is ordered, that the same Psalms shall be read the last day of the said Months, which were read the day before: So that the Psalter may begin again the first day of the next Month ensuing.

And whereas the cxix Psalm is divided into xxii portions, and is over long to be read at one time; it is so ordered that at one time shall not be read above four or five of the said portions.

And at the end of *ye Psalms for ye Morning & Evening Service shall be repeated this Hymn,* [8]

Glory be to the Father, and to the Son: and to the Holy Ghost;

As it was in the beginning, is now, and ever shall be: world without end. Amen.

Note, that the Psalter followeth the Division of the Hebrews, and the Translation of the great English Bible set forth and used in the time of King Henry the Eighth and Edward the Sixth.

*Nothing is to be sung or chaunted in the Church but Psalms, Hymns, or Anthems.* [9]

## THE ORDER HOW THE REST OF HOLY SCRIPTURE IS APPOINTED TO BE READ

The Old Testament is appointed for the first Lessons at Morning and Evening Prayer, and shall be read over orderly every year thrice, besides the Epistles and Gospels; Except the Apocalyps, out of which there are onely certain proper Lessons appointed on divers Feasts.

And to know what Lessons shall be read every day, look for the day of the Month in the Kalendar following, and there ye shall find the Chapters that shall be read for the Lessons both at Morning and Evening prayer; Except onely the Moveable Feasts, which are not in the Kalendar, and the Immoveable, where there is a Blank left in the Column of Lessons; the proper Lessons for all which days are to be found in the Table of proper Lessons.

And note, that whensoever proper Psalms or Lessons are appointed; then the Psalms and Lessons of ordinary course appointed in the Psalter and Kalendar (if they be different) shall be omitted for that time.

Note also, [10] that the Collect, Epistle and Gospel appointed for the *Lord's day*, shall serve all the week after, *(if there be occasion)* where it is not in this Book otherwise ordered.

# PROPER[11] LESSONS TO BE READ
## AT MORNING AND EVENING PRAYER ON
### *LORDS DAIES*[12] AND OTHER HOLY DAYS
## THROUGHOUT THE YEAR

### LESSONS PROPER FOR *LORDS DAYS*.

| Sundays of | | Matins | | Evensong. | |
|---|---|---|---|---|---|
| Advent | 1 | Isaiah | 1 | Isaiah | 2 |
| | 2 | ———— | 5 | ———— | 24 |
| | 3 | ———— | 25 | ———— | 26 |
| | 4 | ———— | 30 | ———— | 32 |
| After | | | | | |
| Christmas | 1 | ———— | 37 | ———— | 38 |
| | 2 | ———— | 41 | ———— | 43 |
| After | | | | | |
| Epiphany | 1 | ———— | 44 | ———— | 46 |
| | 2 | ———— | 51 | ———— | 53 |
| | 3 | ———— | 55 | ———— | 56 |
| | 4 | ———— | 57 | ———— | 58 |
| | 5 | ———— | 59 | ———— | 64 |
| | 6 | ———— | 65 | ———— | 66 |
| Septuagesima | | Genesis | 1 | Genesis | 2 |
| Sexagesima | | ———— | 3 | ———— | 6 |
| Quinquagesima | | —— 9, to v 20 | | ———— | 12 |
| [13]Lent | 1 | — 19, to v 30 | | ———— | 22 |
| | 2 | ———— | 27 | ———— | *37* |
| | 3 | —— *39, 40* | | ———— | 42 |
| | 4 | ———— | 43 | —*45, 46 to v 8*[14] | |
| | 5 | Exodus | 3 | Exodus | 5 |
| | 6 | 1 Lesson ———— | 9 | ———— | 10 |
| | | 2 Lesson Matthew 26 | | Heb 5 to v 11 | |
| Easter | | 1 Lesson Exodus 12 | | Exodus | 14 |
| | | [Remainder stands unaltered] | | | |

### PROPER PSALMS ON CERTAIN DAYS.

| | Matins | Evensong |
|---|---|---|
| Christmas Day | 19, 45, 85 | 89, 110, 132 |
| Ash Wednesday | 6, 32, 38 | 102, 130, 143 |
| Good Friday | 22, 40, 54 | 69, 88 |
| Easter Day | 2, 57, 111 | 113, 114, 118 |
| Ascension Day | 8, 15, 21 | 24, 47, 108 |
| Whit Sunday | 48, 68 | 104, 145 |

# (15)LESSONS PROPER FOR HOLY DAYS*

**\* When a Saints day falls on a Lords day, both Collects being used, the Lessons for the Lords daies are to be used, those of Christmas excepted.**

|  |  | Matins |  | Evensong |  |
|---|---|---|---|---|---|
| St Andrew |  | Proverbs | 20 | Proverbs | 21 |
| St Thomas Apost |  | ———— | 23 | ———— | 24 |
| Nativity | 1 Lesson | Isaiah 9, to v 8 |  | Isaiah 7 v 10 to v 17 |  |
|  | 2 Lesson | Luke 2 to v 15 |  | Titus 3 v 4 to v 9 |  |
| St Stephen | 1 Lesson | Proverbs | 28 | Eccles. | 4 |
|  | 2 Lesson | Acts 6 v 8, 7, to v 30 |  | Acts 7 v 30 to v 55 |  |
| St John | 1 Lesson | Eccles. | 5 | Eccles. | 6 |
|  | 2 Lesson | Revel. | 1 | Revel. | 22 |
| Innocents day |  | Jeremiah 31, to v 18 |  | *Prov* | *4* |
| Circumc. | 1 Lesson | Genesis | 17 | Deuteron 10 v 12 |  |
|  | 2 Lesson | Romans | 2 | Coloss. | 2 |
| Epiphany | 1 Lesson | Isaiah | 60 | Isaiah | 49 |
|  | 2 Lesson | Luke 3 to v 23 |  | John 2, to v 12 |  |
| Conv of St Paul | 1 Lesson | *Prov* | *5* | *Prov* | *6* |
|  | 2 Lesson | Acts 22 to v 22 |  | Acts | 26 |
| Purification |  | *Prov* | *7* | *Prov* | *8* |
| St Matthias |  | *Pr* | *9* | *P* | *10* |
| Annunciation |  | *Pr* | *18* | *Pr* | *22* |
| Before Easter — |  |  |  |  |  |
| Wednesday | 1 Lesson | Hosea | 13 | Hosea | 14 |
|  | 2 Lesson | John 11 v 45 |  |  |  |
| Thursday | 1 Lesson | Daniel | 9 | Jeremiah | 31 |
|  | 2 Lesson | John | 13 |  |  |
| Good Friday | 1 Lesson | Genesis 22 to v 20 |  | Isaiah | 53 |
|  | 2 Lesson | John | 18 | I Peter | 2 |
| Easter Even | 1 Lesson | Zechariah | 9 | Exodus | 13 |
|  | 2 Lesson | Luke 23 to v 50 |  | Hebrews | 4 |
| Easter Week — |  |  |  |  |  |
| Monday | 1 Lesson | Exodus | 16 | Exodus | 17 |
|  | 2 Lesson | Matthew | 28 | Acts | 3 |
| Tuesday | 1 Lesson | Exodus | 20 | Exodus | 32 |
|  | 2 Lesson | Luke 24 to v 18 |  | I Corin. | 15 |
| St Mark |  | *Pr* | *25* | *Pr* | *26* |
| St Philip & |  | *Pr* | *27* | *Pr* | *29* |
| St James | 2 Lesson | John 1 to v 43 |  |  |  |
| Ascension Day | 1 Lesson | Deuteron | 10 | 2 Kings | 2 |
|  | 2 Lesson | Luke 24 v 44 |  | Ephesians 4 to v 17 |  |
| Whitsun Week — |  |  |  |  |  |
| Monday | 1 Lesson | Genesis 11 to v 10 |  | Numbers 11, v 16 to 30 |  |
|  | 2 Lesson | I Cor | 12 | I Cor 14 to v 26 |  |
| Tuesday | 1 Lesson | I Samuel 19 to v 18 |  | Deuteron | 30 |
|  | 2 Lesson | I Thess 5, v 12 to v 24 |  | I John 4 to v 14 |  |
| St Barnabas | 1 Lesson | *Pr* | *30* | *Pr* | *31* |
|  | 2 Lesson | Acts | 14 | Acts 15 to v 36 |  |
| St John Baptist | 1 Lesson | Malachi | 3 | Malachi | 4 |
|  | 2 Lesson | Matthew | 3 | Matth 14 to v 13 |  |
| St Peter | 1 Lesson | *Eccles* | *1* | *Eccles* | *2* |
|  | 2 Lesson | Acts | 3 | Acts | 4 |
| St James |  | *Eccles* | *3* | *Eccles* | *5* |
| St Bartholemew |  | *Eccles* | *7* | *Eccles* | *8* |
| St Matthew |  | *E* | *9* | *E* | *10* |
| St Michael | 1 Lesson | Genesis | 32 | Daniel 10 v 5 |  |
|  | 2 Lesson | Acts 12 to v 20 |  | Jude, v 6 to v 16 |  |
| St Luke |  | *Eccles* | *11* | *Eccles* | *12* |
| St Simon & St Jude |  | Job 24, 25 |  | Job | 42 |
| All Saints | 1 Lesson | *Isai* 63 *at* 7 |  | *Joel* 2 *to* 28 |  |
|  | 2 Lesson | Heb. 11 v 36 to 12, v 7 |  | Revel 19 to v 17 |  |

55

# THE KALENDAR[16]

[No alterations, except that many Saints days are deleted, those which remain are . . .]

| January | 1 | Circumcision of Christ |
| | 6 | Epiphany |
| | 25 | Conversion of St Paul |
| | 30 | King Charles, Martyr |
| February | 2 | Purification of the Virgin Mary |
| | 3 | Blasius, Bishop and Martyr |
| | 24 | St Matthew, Apostle & Martyr |
| March | 25 | Annunciation of the Virgin Mary |
| April | 25 | St Mark, Evangelist & Martyr |
| May | 1 | St Philip & St James |
| | 29 | King Charles II Nativity & restitution |
| June | 11 | St Barnabas Apostle |
| | 24 | St John Baptist |
| | 29 | St Peter Apostle |
| July | 25 | St James, Apostle & Martyr |
| August | 24 | St Bartholemew |
| September | 20 | Fast |
| | 21 | St Matthew, Apostle |
| | 29 | St Michael |
| October | 18 | St Luke, Evangelist |
| | 28 | St Simon & St Jude |
| November* | 1 | All Saints Day |
| | 5 | Papists Conspiracy |
| | 30 | St Andrew, Apostle |
| December | 21 | St Thomas, Apostle |
| | 25 | Christmas Day |
| | 26 | St Stephen, the first martyr |
| | 27 | St John, Apostle & Evangelist |
| | 28 | Innocents-day. |

*[the following footnote to the text is deleted]

Note, that (a) Ecclus 25. is to be read onely to vers. 13 and (b) Ecclus 30. onely to vers. 18. and (c) Ecclus 46 onely to vers. 20.[17]

## TABLES AND RULES FOR THE
## MOVEABLE AND IMMOVEABLE FEASTS; TOGETHER
## WITH THE DAYS OF FASTING AND ABSTINENCE
## THROUGH THE WHOLE YEAR.

Rules: to know when the moveable Feasts and Holy Days begin.

*Easter-day (upon wch the rest depend)*[18] *shall be allwaies the first Lords day after ye Full Moon wch happens upon or next after the 21st Day of March, according to ye Kalendar.*

Advent Sunday is always the nearest Sunday to the Feast of Saint Andrew, whether before or after.

| Septuagesima | Sunday is Nine | |
|---|---|---|
| Sexagesima | Sunday is Eight | Weeks before Easter |
| Quinquagesima | Sunday is Seven | |
| Quadragesima | Sunday is Six | |

Rogation Sunday is Five weeks
Ascension Day is Forty Days      after Easter.
Whit Sunday is Seven weeks
Trinity Sunday is Eight weeks

*A Table of all the Feasts to be observed in the Public Reading of divine Service.*

*All Lords days in ye year comonly call'd Sundays.*[19]

|  |  |
|---|---|
| | The Circumcision of our Lord Jesus Christ |
| | The Epiphany |
| The Days | The Conversion of Saint Paul |
| of the | The Purification of the Blessed Virgin |
| Feasts | Saint Mark the Evangelist |
| of | Saint Philip and Saint James the Apostles |
| | The Ascension of our Lord Jesus Christ[20] |
| | Saint Barnabas |

Monday and Tuesday in Easter week

|  |  |
|---|---|
| | The Nativity of Saint John Baptist |
| | Saint Peter the Apostle |
| | Saint James the Apostle |
| | Saint Bartholemew the Apostle |
| | Saint Matthew the Apostle |
| The Days | Saint Michael and all Angels |
| of the | Saint Luke the Evangelist |
| Feasts | Saint Simon and Saint Jude Apostles |
| of | All Saints |
| | Saint Andrew the Apostle |
| | Saint Thomas the Apostle |
| | The Nativity of our Lord |
| | Saint Stephen the Martyr |
| | Saint John the Evangelist |
| | The Holy Innocents. |

Monday and Tuesday in Whitsun week.[21]

Certain Solemn days, for which Particular Services are appointed.

1    The Fifth Day of November, being the day kept in Memory of the Papists Conspiracy.

11   The Thirtieth Day of January, being the day kept in Memory of the Martyrdom of King Charles the First.

111  The Twenty-ninth Day of May, being the day kept in Memory *of the Return* of King Charles the Second.[22]

A Table of the Moveable Feasts
calculated for Fourty years.    (1661 - 1700)[23]
[stands unaltered]

A Table to Find Easter for Ever.
[stands unaltered]

When ye have found the Sunday Letter in the uppermost Line, guide your Eye downward from the same, till ye come right over against the Prime *or Golden number:*[24] and there is shewed both what month, and what day of the Month Easter falleth that Year. But note, that the name of the Month is set at the left Hand, or else just with the Figure, and followeth not, as in other Table, by descent, but collateral.

## THE ORDER FOR MORNING AND EVENING PRAYER
Daily to be said and used throughout the year.

The Morning and Evening Prayer shall be used in the accustomed Place of the Church, Chappel, or Chancel; Except it shall be otherwise determined by the Ordinary of the Place. And the Chancels shall remain as they have done in times past.

*mem: a* Canon *to specify ye vestments.*[1]

*Whereas ye Surplice is appointed to be used by all Ministers in performing Divine Offices, it is hereby declared, That it is continued onely as being an Antient & Decent Habit. But yet if any Minister shall come & declare to his Bishop, that he cannot satisfye his Conscience in ye Use of ye Surplice in Divine Service, In that case ye Bishop shall dispense with his not using it, and if he shall see cause for it, He shall appoint a Curate to officiate in a Surplice.*

*Me: This Rubric was suggested, but not agreed to; but left to further Consideration.*

# THE ORDER FOR MORNING PRAYER
Daily throughout the year.[2]

At the beginning of Morning Prayer, the Minister shall read with a loud voice some one, or more of these Sentences of the Scriptures, that follow. And then he shall say that which is written after the said Sentences.

When the wicked man turneth away. . . .

Dearly beloved brethren, the Scripture moveth us in sundry places to acknowledge and confess our manifold sins and wickedness. . . .

A general Confession to be said of the whole Congregation after the Minister, all kneeling.

Almighty and most merciful Father, We have erred and strayed from thy ways like lost sheep. We have followed too much the devices, and desires of our own hearts. We have offended against thy holy laws. We have left undone those things which we ought to have done; and we have done those things which we ought not to have done; And there is no health in us.[3] But thou, O Lord, have mercy upon us, miserable offenders. Spare thou them, O God, which[4] confess their faults. Restore thou them that are penitent; According to thy promises declared unto mankind in Christ *Jesus*[5] our Lord. And grant, O most merciful Father, for his sake; That we may hereafter live a godly, righteous and sober life, To the glory of thy holy Name. Amen.

The *Absolution to*[7] be pronounced by the[6] Priest alone, standing; the People still kneeling.

Almighty God, the Father of our Lord Jesus Christ, who desireth not the death of a sinner, but rather that he may turn from his wickedness, and live; and hath given power and commandment to his Ministers, to declare and pronounce to his people, being penitent, the absolution, and remission of their sins: He pardoneth and absolveth all them that truly repent, and unfeignedly believe his holy gospel. Wherefore let us beseech him to grant[8] us true repentance, and his Holy Spirit, that those things may please him which we do at this present, and that the rest of our life hereafter may be pure and holy, so that at the last we may come to his eternal joy, through Jesus Christ our Lord.

The People shall answer here, and at the end of all other prayers, Amen.

Then the Minister shall kneel, and say the Lords Prayer with an audible voice; the People also kneeling, and repeating it with him, both here, and wheresoever else it is used in Divine Service.

Our Father. . . . For thine is the Kingdom, and the Power, And the Glory, For ever and ever. Amen. [9]

Then likewise he shall say.

O Lord, open thou our lips.

Answer.   And our mouth shall shew forth thy praise.

*Minister.*   *Enlighten our minds O Lord.* [10]

*Answer.*   *That we may understand the great Things of thy Law.*

*Minister.*   O God, make speed to save us.

Answer.   O Lord, make haste to help us.

Here all standing up, the *Minister* [11] shall say

Glory be to the Father, and to the Son: and to the Holy Ghost;

Answer.   As it was in the beginning, is now, and ever shall be: world without end. Amen.

Priest.   Praise ye the Lord.

Answer.   The Lords Name be praised.

Then shall be said or sung this Psalm following; Except on Easter Day, upon which another Anthem is appointed: and on the Nineteenth day of every Month it is not to be read here, but in the ordinary course of the Psalms.

Venite Exultemus Domino.

Psalm 95

O come, let us sing unto the Lord. . . . [12]

Then shall follow the Psalms in order as they are appointed. And at the end of every Psalm throughout the Year, and likewise at the end of *ye 148 Psalm, ye 100 Psalm, Benedictus, The 8 Psalm, The 134 Ps,* shall be repeated, [13]

Glory be to the Father, and to the Son: and to the Holy Ghost; Answer. As it was in the beginning, is now, and ever shall be: world without end. Amen.

Then shall be read distinctly with an audible voice the First Lesson, taken out of the Old Testament, as is appointed in the Kalendar; (except there be proper Lessons assigned for that day:) He that readeth, so standing, and turning himself, as he may best be heard of all such as are present. And after that, shall be said or sung in English, the hymn called Te Deum Laudamus, daily throughout the Year.

Note, that before every Lesson the Minister shall say, Here beginneth such a Chapter, or Verse of such a Chapter of such a Book: And after every Lesson, Here endeth the First, or the Second Lesson.

# Te Deum Laudamus.

We praise thee, O God: we acknowledge thee to be the Lord.

All the earth doth worship thee: the Father everlasting.

To thee all Angels cry aloud: the Heavens, and all the powers therein.

To thee Cherubin, and Seraphin: continually do cry,

Holy, Holy, Holy: Lord God of *Hosts*,[14]

Heaven, and Earth are full of the Majesty: of thy Glory.

The glorious company of the Apostles: praise thee

The goodly fellowship of the Prophets: praise thee

The noble Army of Martyrs: praise thee

The holy Church throughout all the world: doth acknowledge thee;

The Father: of an infinite Majesty;

*Thy True & Thy only begotten Son;*[15]

Also the Holy Ghost: the Comforter.

Thou art the King of Glory: O Christ. . . .

## *or Psalm. 148.*[16]

*O Praise the Lord of Heaven: Praise him in ye Heights.*

*Praise him All ye Angells of His; praise Him all his Hosts.*

*Praise him sun & moon: praise him, all ye starrs & Light.*

*Praise him all ye Heavens: & ye waters yt are above the Heavens.*

*Let them praise ye name of the Ld: for he spake the word & they were made, he comanded, and they were created.*

*He hath made them fast for evr & ever: he hath given them a Law wch shall not be broken.*

*Praise ye Lord upon Earth: ye Dragos & all deeps:*

*Fire & hail, snow & vapour: wind & storme fulfilling his word.*

*Mountains & all hills; fruitfull Trees & all Cedars;*

*Beasts & all Cattle: worms & feathered fowls;*

*Kings of ye Earth & all People: Princes & all Judges of ye world;*

*Young men & Maidens: old Me & Children;*

*Praise ye name of ye Lord: for his name only is excellent, & his praise above Heaven & Earth.*

*He shall exalt ye horn of his People: All his Saints shall prays him even ye Children of Israell, even ye People yt serveth him.*

*Glory be to ye Father &c*

*As it was &c. Amen*

Then shall be read in like manner the Second Lesson, taken out of the New Testament. And after that *This Psalm Jubilate Deo. Psal 100.*[17]

*O be joyfull in ye Lord*, all ye lands: . . . .

Or the following Hymn, except when yt shall happen to be read, in ye chapter for ye day, or for ye gospell on S John Baptists day.

## Benedictus

### S Luk 1.86[18]

Blessed be the Lord God of Israel: . . . . To perform the oath which he sware to our forefather Abraham: that he would *graunt us*. . . . .[19]

Then shall be[20] *said the Creed comonly called the Apostles Creed* by the Minister, and the People standing. Except only such days as the Creed *comonly called St Athanasiuss Creed*, is appointed to be read.

I believe in God the Father Almighty. . . .

And after that, these Prayers following, all devoutly kneeling, the Minister first pronouncing with a loud voice,

<blockquote>The Lord be with you.</blockquote>

Answer.   And with thy Spirit.

Minister.   Let us pray

<blockquote>[21]Lord, have mercy upon us.

Christ, have mercy upon us.

Lord, have mercy upon us.</blockquote>

Then the Minister, Clerks, and People shall say the Lords Prayer *when there is neither Litany nor Communion.*

Our Father. . . .

Then the *Minister shall* say

<blockquote>O Lord shew thy mercy upon us.</blockquote>

Answer.       And grant us thy salvation.

Priest.        O Lord save the King and Queen.

Answer.       And mercifully hear us when we call upon thee.

Priest.        Endue thy ministers with righteousness.

Answer.       And make thy chosen people joyful.

Priest.        O Lord, save thy people.

Answer.       And bless thine inheritance.

*Minister*.     Give peace[22] in our time, O Lord.

Answer.       [23]*That we may serve Thee without Fear All ye daies of our Lives.*

*Minister*.     O God make clean our hearts within us.

Answer.       And take not thy holy Spirit from us.[24]

Then shall follow *these*[25] collects; The first of the Day, which shall be the same that is appointed at the Communion; The second for Peace; The third for Grace to live well. And the two last Collects shall never alter, but daily be said at Morning Prayer throughout all the Year, as followeth; all kneeling.

*The Collect for ye day is not* (to) *be used in ye morning service when there is either Litany, or Comunion-service with It.*

### The second Collect for Peace.

O God, who art the author of peace and lover of concord, in knowledge of whom standeth our eternal life, whose service is perfect freedom: [26]. . . .

### The third Collect for Grace.

O Lord and heavenly Father, Almighty and everlasting God, who hast safely brought us *to this*[27] day. . . .

In Quires and Places where they Sing, here followeth the Anthem.

Then *these*[28] *Prayers* following are to be read here, except when the Litany is read; and then onely the two last are to be read as they are there placed.

### A Prayer for the King and Queens Majesties.

O Lord our heavenly Father, high and mighty, King of kings, Lord of lords, the only Ruler of princes, who dost from thy throne behold all the dwellers upon earth; Most heartily we beseech thee with thy favour to behold *our Sovereign*[29] Lord and Lady, King William and Queen Mary and so replenish them with the grace of thy Holy Spirit, that they may always incline to thy will, and walk in thy way: Endue them plenteously with heavenly gifts. *Direct all their cousels to thy Honour and glory: Bless all their righteous undertakings;* grant them in health and wealth long to *live, and that* after this life, they may attain everlasting joy and felicity, through Jesus Christ our Lord. Amen.

### A Prayer for the Royal Family.

Almighty God, the fountain of all goodness, we humbly beseech thee to bless[30] Catherine the Queene Dowager, *The* Princess Anne of Denmark, and all the Royal family: Endue them with thy Holy Spirit; enrich them with thy heavenly grace; prosper them with all happiness; and bring them to thine everlasting Kingdom, through Jesus Christ our Lord. Amen.

### A Prayer for the Clergy and people.

Almighty and everlasting God, the *Giver of all Spiritual Gifts*[31]; Send down upon our Bishops *Pastors* and Curates, and all Congregations committed to their charge, the healthful Spirit of thy grace; and that they may truly please thee, pour upon them the continual dew of thy blessing. Grant this, O Lord, for the honour of our Advocate and Mediator, Jesus Christ. Amen.[32]

A Prayer comonly calld St Chrysostom's.[33]

Almighty God, who has given us grace at this time with one accord to make our common supplications unto thee. . . .

2 Cor xiij 14

The grace of our Lord Jesus Christ, and the love of God, and the fellowship of the Holy Ghost be with us all evermore. Amen.

**Here endeth the Order of Morning Prayer throughout the Year.**

## THE ORDER FOR EVENING PRAYER[1]

Daily throughout the year.

**At the beginning of Evening Prayer, the Minister shall read with a loud voice. . . .**

When the wicked man turneth away from his wickedness. . . .

Dearly beloved brethren, the Scripture moveth us. . . .

A General confession to be said of the whole congregation. . . .

Almighty and most merciful Father, we have erred and strayed. . . .

**The *Absolution to* be pronounced by the *Minister* alone, standing; the People still kneeling.**

Almighty God, the Father of our Lord Jesus Christ. . . .

**The People shall answer here. . . .**

**Then the Minister shall kneel, and say. . . .**

Our Father. . . .

**Then likewise he shall say.**

O Lord, open thou our lips.

| | |
|---|---|
| Answer. | And our mouth shall shew forth thy praise. |
| *Minister.* | *Enlighten our minds O Lord.* |
| *Answer.* | *That we may understand the great Things of Thy Law.* |
| *Minister.* | O God, make speed to save us. |
| Answer. | O Lord, make haste to help us. |

**Here all standing up, the *Minister* shall say,**

Glory be to the Father, and to the Son: and to the Holy Ghost.

| | |
|---|---|
| Answer. | As it was in the beginning, is now, and ever shall be: world without end. Amen. |
| Priest. | Praise ye the Lord. |
| Answer. | The Lords Name be praised. |

Then shall be said or sung the Psalms in order as they are appointed. Then a Lesson of the Old Testament, as is appointed: And after that, *the 8 Psalm or* Magnificat (or the song of the blessed Virgin Mary) in English.[2]

*Psalm 8*                *& 98 X*

Magnificat. S. Luke 1.46

My soul doth magnifie the Lord. . . .

*X;* except it to be on the Nineteenth Day of the Month, when it is read in the ordinary course of the Psalms.

Cantate Domino. Psalm 98

O sing unto the Lord a new song. . . .

Then a Lesson of the New Testament, as is appointed: and after that *Ps 134.*

Or else this Psalm; Except it be on the Twelfth day of the Month.

Deus misereatur. Psalm 67

God be merciful unto us, and bless us. . . .

Then shall be *said*[3] the Creed *comonly calld ye Apostles Creed* by the Minister and people standing.

I believe in God. . . .

And after that, these Prayers following, all devoutly kneeling the Minister first pronouncing with a loud voice,

The Lord be with you.

Answer.      And with thy Spirit.

Minister.    Let us pray.
                Lord, have mercy upon us.
                Christ, have mercy upon us.
                Lord, have mercy upon us.

Then the Minister, Clerk, and People shall say the Lords Prayer with a loud voice.

Our Father . . . . but deliver us from evil. *For thine is ye Kingdom, ye Power & the glory for ever & ever.* Amen.

Then the *Minister* standing up,[4] shall say,

O Lord shew thy mercy upon us.

Answer.      And grant us thy salvation.

*Minister.*   O Lord save the King and Queen.

Answer.      And mercifully hear us when we call upon thee.

*Minister.*   Endue thy ministers with righteousness.

Answer.      And make thy chosen people[5] joyful.

| | |
|---|---|
| Priest. | O Lord, save thy people. |
| Answer. | *That we may serve Thee without Fear all ye days of our Lives.* |
| Priest. | O God make clean our hearts within us. |
| Answer. | And take not thy holy Spirit from us. |

Then shall follow three Collects;[6] The first of the Day; The second for Peace; The third for Aid against all Perils, as hereafter followeth: which two last Collects shall be daily said at Evening-Prayer without alteration.

The second Collect at Evening Prayer.
O God, from whom all holy desires. . . .

The third Collect for Aid against all Perils.[7]
[8]*Almighty God who hast hitherto preserv'd us in safety this day, by thy* great mercy defend us from all perils and dangers of this night, for the love of thy onely Son, our Saviour Jesus Christ. Amen.

*or*                    B. Patr

————*night. Pardon whatsoever we have done amiss, & settle our holy purposes to do better for ye time to come: That, laying our selves dow to sleep with these godly Resolutions in our hearts, They may awaken with us in ye morning, & we may daily grow more watchfull in all or waies, for ye love of thy only Son or Saviour Jesus Christ. Amen.*

In quires and places where thy sing, here followeth the Anthem.

[9]A Prayer for the King and Queens Majesties . . . .
A Prayer for the Royal Family . . . .
A Prayer for the Clergy and people . . . .
A Prayer *comonly calld St Chrysostom's* . . . .
2 Cor xiij 14

Here endeth the Order of Evening Prayer
throughout the Year.

## THE CREED *COMONLY CALLD YE CREED OF* ST ATHANASIUS.

Upon these Feasts; *Christmas-day, Easter-day, Ascension-day, Whitsun-day, Trinity Sunday and upo All Saints* shall be *said at* Morning Prayer *by ye Minister & People standing,* instead of *ye creed comonly called* the Apostles Creed, this Confession of our Christian Faith, commonly called the creed of Saint Athanasius, *The Articles of which ought to be receiv'd & beleiv'd as being agreable to ye Holy Scriptures. And ye Condemning clauses are to be undrstood as relating only to those who obstinately deny ye substance of the Xn Fayth.*

Quicunque vult.

Whosoever will be saved: before all things it is necessary that he hold the Catholic Faith.

Which Faith . . . . [unaltered]

## THE LITANY[1]

*Me: o y/fa: Creator c 11-Eh*[2]

Here followeth the Litany, or General Supplication, to be *said* after Morning Prayer upon Sundays, Wednesdays and Fridays, and at other times, when it shall be commanded by the Ordinary.

*The Litany nevr to be sung.*

*Qu. if an Alias. or shorter Litanie to be us'd upon Occasion?*

O God the Father *Creator* of heaven *& Earth*: [3] have mercy upon us miserable sinners.

O God the Father *Creator of* heaven *& Earth*: have mercy upon us miserable sinners.

O God the Son, Redeemer of the world: have mercy upon us miserable sinners.

O God the Son, Redeemer of the world: have mercy upon us miserable sinners.

O God the Holy Ghost, *our Sanctifyer & Comforter*: [4] have mercy upon us miserable sinners.

O God, the Holy Ghost, *our Sanctifyer & Comforter*: have mercy upon us miserable sinners.

O Holy, blessed and glorious Trinity, three persons and one God: have mercy upon us miserable sinners.

O Holy, blessed and glorious Trinity, three persons and one God: have mercy upon us miserable sinners.

Remember not Lord our offences, nor the offences of our forefathers, neither take thou vengeance of our sins: spare us good Lord, spare thy people whom thou hast redeemed with thy most precious bloud, and be not angry with us for ever.

Spare us, good Lord.

*Good Ld, pserve & delivr us from* all evil and mischief, from sin, from *all the deceipts (& temptatios q) of the world, the flesh and* the devil;[5] from thy wrath, and from everlasting damnation.

Good Lord, deliver us.

*From all Infidelitie & Error, from all Impietie & profaneness, fro all Superstition & Idolatry.*[6]

*Good Ld. deliver us.*

*From* pride, vain-glory, and hypocracie; from envy, hatred and *Revenge, from all rash Censure, contention & uncharitableness.*

Good Lord, deliver us.

*From drunkenness & Gluttony; from sloth & misspending of our Time; From Fornication, Adultery & all uncleanness.*

*Good Ld delivr us.*

*From lying and Slaundering, from vain Swearing, Cursing & perjury, from Covetousness Opression & all Injustice.*

*Good Ld delivr us.*

From Lightning and tempest; from plague, pestilence and famine; from battel, and murder, and from *dying suddainly & unprepared.*[7]

Good Lord, deliver us.

From all sedition, privy conspiracy, and rebellion; from all false doctrine, heresie and schism; from hardness of heart, and contempt of thy Word and Commandment.

Good Lord, deliver us.

By[8] the mystery of thy holy Incarnation; by thy holy Nativity and Circumcision; by thy Baptism, Fasting and Temptation.

Good Lord, deliver us.

By thine Agony, and Bloudy Sweat; by thy[8] *Passion on the Cross;* by thy precious Death, and Burial; by thy glorious Resurrection and Ascension: *by thy sending of* the Holy Ghost, *and by thy continuall Intercession at the Right hand of God.*

Good Lord, deliver us.

In all time of our tribulation;[9] in all time of our wealth; in the hour of death, and in the day of judgment.

Good Lord, deliver us.

We sinners do beseech thee to hear us, O Lord God, and that it may please thee to rule and govern thy holy church universal in the right way, *& this in particular of wch we are members,*

We beseech thee to hear us, good Lord.

That it may please thee to *Guide*[10] and strengthen in the true worshipping of thee, in righteousness and holiness of life, thy servants William and Mary *our King* and Queen.

We beseech thee to hear us, good Lord.

That it may please thee to rule their hearts in thy faith, fear, and love, and that they may evermore have affiance in thee, and ever seek thy honour and glory;

We beseech thee to hear us, good Lord.

That it may please thee to be their defender and keeper, *giving Them a prosperous & happy reign over us.*[11]

We beseech thee to hear us, good Lord.

That it may please thee to bless and preserve, Catherine the Queen Dowager, *The* Princess Anne of Denmark, and all the Royal Family.[12] *That it may please Thee to direct & psp ye H. Court of Parliament in all their Consultations, to ye Advancement of thy glory, ye good of thy Church, ye Safety honr & welfare of their Majesties & their Kingdoms.*

*We beseech thee to hear us Good Ld.*

That it may please thee to illuminate[13] all Bishops, Priests, and Deacons, with true knowledge and understanding of thy Word, and that both by their preaching and living they may set it forth, and shew it accordingly;

We beseech thee to hear us, good Lord.

That it may please thee to endue the Lords of the Council, and all the Nobility, with grace, wisdom, and understanding;

We beseech thee to hear us, good Lord.

That it may please thee to bless and keep the Magistrates, giving them grace to execute justice, and to maintain truth; *That it may please Thee to take their majesties forces by Sea and Land into thy most gracious protection, & to make them victorious over all our Enemies.*

We beseech thee to hear us, good Lord.

That it may please thee to bless and keep all thy people;

We beseech thee to hear us, good Lord.

That it may please thee to give to all Nations unity, peace, and concord;

We beseech thee to hear us, good Lord.

B.P. That it may please thee to give us an heart to love[14] *thee above all things, to dread to offend thee & dil:*(igently) to live after thy commandments; *That it may please Thee to incline & enable us to pray all way wth fervt affection, in evry thing to give thaks, to depend upo Thee, & chearfully to resign orselves to thy holy will & pleasure.*

We beseech thee to hear us, good Lord.

That it may please thee to give to all thy people increase of grace, to hear meekly thy Word, and to receive it with pure affection, and to bring forth[15] the fruits of the Spirit.

We beseech thee to hear us, good Lord.

*That it may please Thee to endue us wth ye Graces of humility & meekness, of contentedness & patiense, of True Justice, of Temperance & purity, of peaceableness & charitie.*[16]

*We beseech Thee to hear us, Good Ld.*

That it may please thee to bring into the way of truth all such as have erred and are deceived;

We beseech thee to hear us, good Lord.

That it may please thee to strengthen such as do stand, and to comfort, and help the weak-hearted, and to raise up them that fall, and finally to beat down Satan under our feet;

We beseech thee to hear us, good Lord.

That it may please thee to succour, help, and comfort all that are in danger, necessity, and tribulation;

We beseech thee to hear us, good Lord.

That it may please thee to preserve[17] *such as* travel by land or by water, all women labouring of child, all *young children, all sick & dying persons.*

We beseech thee to hear us, good Lord.

*That it may please Thee to show thy pity upon all Prisoners & captives, upon all that are persecuted for Truth and righteousness sake; upon all that are in Affliction; (especially those for whome our prayers are desired).*[18]

*We beseech Thee to hear us, Good Lord.*

That it may please thee to defend, and provide for the fatherless children and widows, and all that are desolate and oppressed;

We beseech thee to hear us, good Lord . . . .

O Lamb of God: that takest away the sins of the world;
Have mercy upon us.

O Christ, hear us.[19]

O Christ, hear us.

Lord, have mercy upon us.

Lord, have mercy upon us.

Christ, have mercy upon us.

Christ, have mercy upon us.

Lord, have mercy upon us.

Lord, have mercy upon us.

Then shall the *Minister*, and the people with him, say the Lords prayer.[20]

Our Father, which art in heaven; Hallowed be thy Name. Thy Kingdom come. Thy will be done in Earth, As it is in Heaven. Give us this day our daily bread. And forgive us our trespasses, As we forgive them that trespass against us. And lead us not into temptation; But deliver us from evil. *for &c. Amen.*[21]

Priest.        O Lord, deal not with us after our sins.

Answer.      Neither reward us after our iniquities.[22]

[23]O God merciful Father, that despiseth not the sighing . . . .

O Lord, arise, help us, and deliver us for thy Names Sake.

O God we have heard with our ears, and our fathers have declared unto us the noble works that thou didst in their days, and in the old time before them.

O Lord, arise, help us, and deliver us for thine honour.

*From* our enemies defend us, O Christ.

Graciously look upon our afflictions.

Pitifully behold the sorrows of our hearts.

Mercifully forgive the sins of thy people.

Favourably with mercy hear our prayers.

O Son of David, have mercy upon us.

Both now and ever vouchsafe to hear us, O Christ.

Graciously hear us, O Christ; graciously hear us, O Lord Christ.

**Priest.**       O Lord, let thy mercy be shewed upon us,

**Answer.**    As we do put our trust in thee.

[24]We humbly beseech thee, O Father, mercifully look upon our infirmities; and for the glory of thy Name turn from us all those evils that we most *justly*[25] have deserved; and grant that in all our troubles we may put our whole trust and confidence in thy mercy, and evermore serve thee in holiness and pureness of living, to thy honour and glory, through our only Mediator and Advocate, Jesus Christ our Lord. Amen.

*Then ye minister continuing in his Place shall use ys Collect,*[26]

*Almighty God to whome all hearts &c Amen.*

*Then shall the minister rehearse distinctly the Tenn Commandments, & ye People, still kneeling, shall after evry comandment ask Gods mercy for their Transgression thereof for the time past, & Grace to keep ye same for ye time to come; as followeth*

### Minister.

*God spake these words & said, I am the Lord thy God which hath brought Thee out of ye Land of Aegypt out of ye house of Bondage. Thou shalt have no other Gods before me.*

### People.

*Ld have mercy upo us, & incline our hearts to keep this Law.*

### Minister.

*Thou shalt not make unto Thee any graven Image or any likeness of any Thing that is in Heaven above, or yt is in ye earth beneath,*

71

*or yt is in ye water undr ye Earth: thou shalt not bow down thy self to Them nor serve Them, for I the Lord thy God am a jealous God, visiting ye iniquities of ye Father upo ye children unto ye 3d & 4th Genration of Them yt hate me, & shewing mercy unto thousands of them yt love me & keep my Comandments.*

### People.

*Ld have mercy &c*

*Thou shalt not take ye name of thy Lord God in vain: for the Ld will not hold him guiltless that taketh his name in vain.*

### People.

*Ld have mercy &c*

*Remember ye Sabbath day\* to keep it holy: 6 daies shalt thou labour & do all thy work; but ye 7th day is the Sabbath of ye Ld thy God: In it Thou shalt not do any work, Thou, nor thy sonn, nor Thy daughter, thy manservant nor thy maidservant, nor thy Cattle, nor thy strangr yt is wthin thy Gates. for in 6 daies ye Ld made heaven & Earth, ye sea & all yt in Them is; & rested ye 7th day; wherefore the Lord blessed ye Sabbath day & hallowed It.*

*\*Which is now the Lords day.*

### People.

*Ld have mercy &c*

Or sometimes the 8 Beatitudes, especially on Comunion daies. See the comunio Service....

Then shall follow the Collect for ye Day.

Then ye Epistle & Gospell.

Then (If there be No Comunion) the Nicene Creed.[27]

Then the Genral Thanksgiving &c

The Prayer commonly call'd S Chrysostom's.[28]
                    2 Cor. 13.14

Then the Minister shall declare unto ye people what Holydaies or Fasting-daies, are, in ye week following to be observ'd; and then also, if occasion be, shall notice be given of the Comunion, & ye Banns of Matrimony published & Briefs, Citations, & Excomunications read; & nothing shall be proclaimed or published in the Church during ye Time of divine service but by ye Minister, nor by him any Thing but what is prscribed in ye Rules of this book or enjoyned by ye King or by ye Ordinary of ye Place, not being contrary to ye Laws of this Realm.

> This rubric was occasioned by K James's enjoining his declaratio (wch was ag: law) to be read in Churches.

*The Singing Psalm.*

*Q of what translation.*

*QQ whether the Minister may not here be directed to use in ye Pulpit before Sermon the Prayer for the whole state of Christs Church &c accomodated to yt purpose; or some such other Prayer?*

Note that when there is no comunion at all, this shall be read in ye same place with ye rest of ye service.

# PRAYERS
## PRAYERS AND THANKSGIVINGS UPON SEVERAL OCCASIONS,

To be used before the two final Prayers of the Litany, or of Morning and Evening Prayer.

*Prayers.*[1]

*A Pparatory Prayr for ye receiving of ye Comunion, to be read on ye Lords day or some week day or days before.*

*O God who hast ordained holy mysteries for a Comemoration*[2] *of our Saviours wondrfull Love in laying dow his life for us, & for ye comunication of ye benefits of his death & passion to Us; we beseech Thee to dispose all Those, who intend to receive the holy Sacrament to come to thy Table wth such sincere repentance of all their sins, & unfeigned Resolutions of bettr obedience; wth such an humble fayth & ardent Love unto Thee & unto All men, that they may comfortably hope for thy Gracious pardon, & for ye powr of thy holy Spirit, to carry them, by patient continuance in well doing, unto aetrnall life, through Jesus Christ or Ld. Amen.*

### A prayr to be said in any time of Calamitie.[3]

*Almighty God & most mercifull Father: we miserable sinners do here humbly acknowledge before Thee, that we are unworthy of ye least of all thy mercies: We confess, O Ld, in ye bittrness of or souls yt we have grievously sined against Thee: that all orders of men amongst us have transgressed thy righteous Laws: that we have hitherto rendered both thy mercies and thy Judgments ineffectuall to or amendment. It is of thy mere mercy, O Ld, that we are not consum'd; for wch or souls do magnify & bless Thy name. O God who hast hitherto spar'd us to ye End yt thy goodness might lead us to repentance: let It be thy good pleasure to give unto us All yt godly sorrow wch worketh repentance to salvation not to be repented of; That thou maist turn from thy heavy displeasure against us, & maist rejoyce over us to do us good, through ye merits & mediation of Jesus Christ our Ld & only Saviour. Amen.*

*Q of Prayers for ye Army & Navy.*

### For Rain.

O God heavenly Father, who by thy Son Jesus Christ . . . .

*A Generall Collect for fair weather*

O Almighty Lord God, who for the sin of man didst once drown all the world, except eight persons, and afterward of thy great mercy didst promise never to destroy it so again; We humbly beseech thee, that although we for our iniquities have worthily deserved a plague of rain and waters,[4] yet upon our true repentance thou wilt send us such weather, as that we may receive the fruits of the earth in due season, and learn both by thy punishment to amend our lives, and for thy clemency to give thee praise and glory, through Jesus Christ our Lord. Amen.

### In time of Dearth and Famine.

O God heavenly Father, whose gift it is . . . .

### Or this,

O God merciful Father, who in the time of Elisha . . . .

### In the time of War and Tumults.

Almighty God, King of all kings, and Governour of all things, whose power no creature is able to resist, to whom it belongeth justly to punish sinners and to be merciful to them that truly repent; Save and deliver us, we humbly beseech thee, from the hands of our Enemies; abate their pride, asswage their malice, and *disappoint* their devices,[5] that we, being armed with thy defence, may be preserved evermore from all perils, to glorifie thee, who art the only giver of all victory, through the merits of thy onely Son, Jesus Christ our Lord. Amen.

### In the time of any common Plague or sickness.

O Almighty God, who in thy wrath didst send a plague upon thine own people in the wilderness for their obstinate rebellion against Moses and Aaron, and also in the time of King David didst slay with the plague of pestilence threescore and ten thousand, and yet remembring thy mercy didst save the rest; Have pity upon us miserable sinners, who now are visited with great sickness and mortality;[6] that like as thou didst accept of atonement, and didst command the destroying Angel to cease from punishing; so it may now please thee to withdraw from us, *who humbly acknowledge our sinns, and truly repent us of them,* this plague of grievous sickness; *yt being deliver'd we may glorify thy name* through Jesus Christ our Lord. Amen.

*Rubric.*

*(This rubric . . . .)*

**Whereas ye Apostles did use Prayr & fasting before They ordained, & yt it has bin ye practice of ye church to enjoyn Fasts in ye 4 weeks of ye year comonly called Ember weeks**

*before ye Lordsdays appointed for Ordination to implore ye blessing*[7] *of God upon them yt are to ordain, & upo Those yt are to be ordained; It is therefore earnestly recomended to All persons to spend somme part of those days in Prayr to God for his blessing on ye Church, & on all yt are to be sent out to officiate in It. & It is most solemnly charged on All yt are concerned in Ordinations, chiefly on ye Persons yt are to be ordained, to spend those days in fervent Prayer & Fasting, for ye due prparing of ymselves to be initiated into holy Orders.*

*This rubric is to be read imediatelie after ye Apostles Creed on ye Lords day next before any of ye Ember weeks.*[8]

*put ys at ye beginning.*[9]

In the Ember Weeks to be said every day, for those that are to be admitted to holy Orders.

Almighty God our heavenly Father, who hast purchased to thyself an universal Church . . . .

Or this,

Almighty God, the giver of all good gifts . . . .

A Prayer for the High Court of Parliament,[10]

to be read during their *sitting, wn ye Litany is not appointed to be said.*

Most gracious God, we humbly beseech thee, as for this Kingdom in general, so especially for the High Court of Parliament, under *our soveraign Ld* King *William* and Queen *Mary*[11] at this time assembled: . . . .

A Collect or Prayer for all Conditions of Men, to be used at such times when the Litany[12] is not appointed to be said.

O God, the creator and preserver of all mankind . . . .

A Prayer that may be said after any of the former.

*To be left out. This did not come in here by any Authoritie of Convocation or Parlt.* [13]

## THANKSGIVINGS

### A General Thanksgiving.[1]

Almighty God, Father of all mercies, we thine unworthy servants do give thee most humble and hearty thanks . . . .

### For Rain.

O God our heavenly Father, who by thy gracious providence dost cause . . . .

For fair Weather.

*A new collect was here design'd but not pfected.*

O Lord God, who hast justly humbled us by thy late plague[2] of immoderate rain and waters . . . .

For Plenty.

O Most merciful Father, who of thy gracious goodness hast heard the devout Prayers of thy Church, and turned our dearth and scarcity into cheapness and plenty; We give thee humble thanks for this thy special bounty, beseeching thee to continue thy loving-kindness unto us, that our land may yield us her fruits of increase,[3] *& yt we may use Them* to thy glory and our comfort, through Jesus Christ our Lord. Amen.

For Peace and Deliverance from our Enemies.

O Almighty God, who art a strong tower of defence . . . .

For restoring Publick Peace at Home.

O Eternal God, our heavenly Father, who alone makest men to be of one mind in a house . . . .

For deliverance from the Plague, or other common Sickness.

O Lord God, who hast wounded us for our sins . . . .

Or this.

We humbly acknowledge before thee, O most merciful Father, that all the punishments which are threatened in thy law . . . .

THE COLLECTS, EPISTLES AND GOSPELS

to be used through the year.

Note, that the Collect appointed for every Sunday, or for any Holy-day that hath a Vigil or Eve, *Q*[1] shall be said at the Evening Service next before.

The First Sunday in Advent.

The Collect.

Almighty God, give us grace that we may cast away the works of darkness . . . .

This collect is to be repeated every day with the other Collects in Advent, until Christmas-Eve.

Epistle; Rom. 13.8-14<br>Gospel; S. Matt. 21.1-13

The Second Sunday in Advent.

The Collect.

Blessed Lord, who hast caused all holy Scriptures to be written for our learning . . . .

Epistle; Rom. 15.4-13<br>Gospel; S. Luke 21.25-33

76

### The Third Sunday in Advent.
#### The Collect.

O Lord *Jesus*[2] Christ, who at thy first coming didst send thy messenger to prepare thy way before thee . . . .

Epistle; 1 Cor. 4.1-5
Gospel; S. Matt. 11.2-10

### The Fourth Sunday in Advent.[3]
#### The Collect.

*O Lord, who hast given us Cause of perpetual Joy by ye Coming of thy Son, our Saviour among us, raise up thy Power (we pray thee) & possess us with a mighty sense of thy wonderfull Love. that whereas thro ye Cares of this Life we are sore let and hindered in runing ye Race yt is set before us, we may be carefull for nothing, but thankfully commending ourselves in everything to thy bountifull Grace & Mercy, the Peace of thee our God, wch passeth all Understanding, may keep our hearts and Minds, thro' ye Satisfaction of thy Son or Lord, To whom with thee & ye Holy Ghost be Honour & Glory, world without End. Amen.*

Epistle; Phil. 4.4-7
Gospel; S. John 1.19-28

### The Nativity of our Lord, or the Birth-day of Christ, commonly called CHRISTMAS DAY.[4]
#### The Collect.

*Allmighty God, who hast given us thy onely begotten Son, ye brightness of thy Glory, & ye Express Image of thy Person, to take our Nature upon Him, & to be born of a pure Virgin. Grant that we being regenerate & made thy Children by Adoption & Grace, may dayly be renewed by thy Holy Spirit; till Christ be perfectly formed in us, & we be made Partakers of a Divine Nature, thro' ye same our Lord Jesus Christ, who liveth & reigneth with thee and ye same Spirit; ever one God World without End. Amen.*

Epistle; Heb. 1.1-12
Gospel; S. John 1.1-14

### Saint Stephens Day.[5]
#### The Collect.

Grant, O Lord, that in all our sufferings here upon earth . . . .

Then shall follow the Collect of the Nativity, which shall be said continually unto New-Years Eve.

Epistle; Acts 7.55-60
Gospel; S. Matt. 23.34-39

### Saint John the Evangelists Day.[6]
#### The Collect.

*Merciful God, who art Light, & in whom is no darkness at all, enlighten or Minds, we most humbly beseech thee, wth such a full Understanding of the Doctrine taught by thy Blessed Apostle & Evangelist John, that we walking in ye Truth in all Purity & Holiness of Life, may have Fellowship wth thee & thy Son Jesus Christ; by whose Blood being cleansed from all or Sins, we may at length attain to Everlasting Life, thro' ye same or Lord Jesus Christ, Amen.*

Epistle; 1 John 1.1-10
Gospel; S. John 21.19-25

### The Innocents Day.[7]
#### The Collect.

*O most Blessed God, who haveing sent thy Son in or Nature, didst preserve him in his Infancy from ye Malice of Herod, by whom many other children were slain; Grant yt in all dangers & Adversities we may put or whole Trust & confidence in thee, & do thou by thy good Providence preserve us from ye Rage of unreasonable & wicked men, or strengthen us by patient Sufferings to glorify thy holy Name thro' Jesus Xt our Lord. Amen.*

Epistle; Rev. 14.1-5
Gospel; S. Matt. 2.13-18

### The Sunday after Christmas Day.[8]
#### The Collect.

Almighty God, who hast given us thy onely-begotten Son to take our nature upon him, & to be born of a pure virgin; Grant that we being regenerate, and made thy children by adoption and grace, may daily be renewed by thy holy Spirit, *which we beseech thee to send forth more & more into our hearts as a Testimony of thy fatherly love unto us, and to fill us with Fervent Love towards thee, thro' Jesus Christ our Ld. Amen.*

Epistle; Gal. 4.1-7
Gospel; S. Matt. 1.18-25

### The Circumcision of Christ.[9]
#### The Collect.

Almighty God, who madest thy blessed Son to be circumcised, and obedient to the law for man; Grant us the true circumcision of the Spirit, that our hearts and all our members, being mortified from all worldly and carnal lusts, we may in all things obey thy *Holy* will, & *thereby obtain ye Remission of our sins, & ye righteousness wch is by ye Fayth of Jesus Christ or Lord. Amen.*

Epistle; Rom. 4.8-14
Gospel; S. Luke 2.15-21

The same Collect, Epistle, and Gospel shall serve for every day after, unto the Epiphany.

## The Epiphany.[10]
### The Collect.

*O God who by ye leading of a Starr didst manifest thy onely begotten Son to ye Gentiles, & guide them to ye place where he lay; Mercifully grant that we to whom thou hast revealed him more clearly by ye Light of thy glorious Gospel, may make such progress in Faith & Holyness, and be so entirely led & govern'd by thy Spirit, that we may be brought after this Life into that blessed place where he now is, and there have ye Fruition of thy glorious Presence for ever & ever, thro' Jesus Christ or Lord. Amen.*

Epistle; Eph. 3.1-12
Gospel; S. Matt. 2.1-12

## The First Sunday after the Epiphany.[11]
### The Collect.

*O God, whose infinite Mercies in our Blessed Saviour incourage us to call upon thee; we beseech thee gratiously to hear us, & grant that we may both perceive & know what is thy good, & acceptable, & perfect Will revealed to us: and also have Grace & Power so faithfully to fulfill ye same, yt we may present ourselves a Liveing Sacrifice, holy, & acceptable, unto thee, thro' Jesus Christ our Lord. Amen.*

Epistle; Rom. 12.1-5
Gospel; S. Luke 2.41-52

## The Second Sunday after the Epiphany.[12]
### The Collect.

Almighty and everlasting God, who dost govern all things in heaven and earth; Mercifully hear the supplications of thy people, & *so rule & guide us yt we may do or Duties faithfully in ye severall places & Relations: constantly abhoring yt wch is evill & cleaving to yt wch is good; being fervent in Spirit, serving ye Lord, rejoyceing in hope, patient in Tribulation, & continuing so instant in Prayer, yt we may enjoy thy Peace all ye days of or Life, thro' Jesus Xt our Lord. Amen.*

Epistle; Rom. 12.6-16
Gospel; S. John 2.1-11

## The Third Sunday after the Epiphany.[13]

### The Collect.

Almighty and everlasting God, mercifully look upon our infirmities, *& endue us wth the spirit of meekness & patience; yt no Evill we suffer from others, may move us to doe Evill unto them, but we may overcome ym by doing ym good, providing things honest in ye sight of all men, & if it be possible as much as lieth in us, live peaceably with All men, thro Jesus Xt or Ld. Amen.*

Epistle; Rom. 12.16-21
Gospel; S. Matt. 8.1-13

## The Fourth Sunday after the Epiphany.[14]

### The Collect.

O God, who knowest us to be set in the midst of so many *temptatios &* dangers, that by reason of the frailty of our nature *in many ways we offend All,* Grant to us such strength and protection, as may support us in all dangers, and carry us through all temptations, *that being faithfull unto thee, obedient to or governours, rendering to every one their Due, & doing yt wch is good, we may be graciously accepted of thee, thro' Jesus Xt or Ld. Amen.*

Epistle; Rom. 13.1-7
Gospel; S. Matt. 8.23-34

## The Fifth Sunday after the Epiphany.[15]

### The Collect.

O Lord, we beseech thee to keep thy Church, and household continually in thy true religion, *and to stirr up every Member of ye same to adorn their Holy Profession, by putting on Bowels of Mercy, kindness, humbleness of Mind, Meekness, Long-suffering: that resting onely upon ye hope of thy Heavenly Grace, & doing all in ye Name of or blessed Savr we may evermore be defended by thy Mighty Power, giving thanks unto thee thro' Jesus Xt or Lord. Amen.*

Epistle; Col. 3.12-17
Gospel; S. Matt. 13.24-30

## The Sixth Sunday after the Epiphany.[16]

### The Collect.

O God, whose blessed Son was manifested, that he might destroy the works of the devil . . . .

Epistle; 1 John 3.1-8
Gospel; S. Matt. 24.23-31

## The Sunday called Septuagesima,[17]
## or the Third Sunday before Lent.

### The Collect.

O Lord, we beseech thee favourably to hear the prayers of thy people, *that we who by thy Grace are call'd to ye Course of A Christian life may be temperate in all things; and so run ye Race, yt is set before us as to obtain yt Incorruptible Crown, wch thou hast promised to ym yt Love thee, thro' Jesus Xt or Saviour who liveth & reigneth with thee & ye Holy Ghost ever one God world without End. Amen.*

Epistle; 1 Cor. 9.24-27
Gospel; S. Matt. 20.1-16

## The Sunday called Sexagesima[18]
## or the Second Sunday before Lent.

### The Collect.

O Lord God, who seest that we put not our trust in any thing that we do; Mercifully grant, that by thy power we may be defended against all *adversitys or so mightily aided by thy Grace, yt we may not faint under them; but having heard thy holy Word wth honest & good Hearts, we may keep it, & bring forth Fruit with Patience, thro' Jesus Xt or Lord. Amen.*

Epistle; 2 Cor. 11.19-31
Gospel; S Luke 8.4-15

## The Sunday called Quinquagesima[19]
## or the next Sunday before Lent.

### The Collect.

O Lord, who hast taught us, that all our doings without charity are nothing worth; Send thy Holy Ghost, and pour into our hearts that most excellent gift of charity, *wch is humble, meek, kind long-suffering & patient, ye very bond of peace & of all vertues. Grant this for thine onely Son Jesus Xts sake. Amen.*

Epistle; 1 Cor. 13.1-13
Gospel; S. Luke 18.31-43

The First Day of Lent commonly called Ashwednesday.[20]

### The Collect.

Almighty and everlasting God, who hatest nothing that thou hast made, and dost forgive the sins of all them that are penitent; Create and make in us new and contrite hearts, that we *truly* lamenting our sins *with unfeigned sorrow & abhorence* and acknowledging our wretchedness, *wth sincere Resolution of amendment of Life, may* obtain of thee, the God of all mercy, perfect remission and forgiveness; through Jesus Christ our Lord. Amen.

This Collect is to be read every day in Lent, after the Collect appointed for the Day.

For the Epistle; Joel 2.12-17
Gospel; S. Matt 6.16-21

### *See the Comination.*[21]
#### *A Sermon or Homily then to be used.*

*Whereas the observation of ye Fast of Lent is an antient & usefull Custom, designed for ye bringing of all Christians to a serious Examination of their Lives past; to repent of their Sinns & fitt Themselves for ye worthy receiving the Comunion at Easter; It is most earnestly recomended to All Persons, but more particularly to all Churchmen, to observe that time religiously, not placing Fasting or devotion in any distinction of Meats, but spending larger portions of their time in prayr, meditation & true abstinence, & in works of Charity, forbearing Feasting & entertainments.*

This is to be read the Lords day before Ashwednesday.

### The First Sunday in Lent.[22]
#### The Collect.

*O Lord, who for or sake didst fast fourty days and forty nights & vanquish all ye Temptations of ye Devill by wch our first Parents were overcome, Grant yt we may not receive (The) grace of God in vain, but use such Abstinence, yt our Flesh being subdued to ye Spirit, no desire of pleasure, Glory, or Worldly Advantage, may tempt us from our Duty; but we may ever obey thy godly Motions, in Righteousness & true Holiness, to thy Honour & Glory, who livest & reignest with ye Father & ye Holy Ghost One God world without end. Amen.*

Epistle; 2 Cor. 6.1-10
Gospel; S. Matt. 4.1-11

## The Second Sunday in Lent.[23]
### The Collect.

Almighty God, who seest that we have no power of our selves to help our selves; Keep us both outwardly in our bodies, and inwardly in our souls, that we may be defended from all adversities which may happen to the body, and from all evil thoughts which may assault and hurt the soul, *and as we have received how we ought to walk and please thee, so we may abound more & more, thro' or Lord & Saviour Jesus Xt. Amen.*

Epistle; 1 Thess. 4.1-8
Gospel; S. Matt. 15.21-28

## The Third Sunday in Lent.[24]
### The Collect.

We beseech thee, Almighty God, look upon the hearty desires of thy humble servants, *and as thou hast enlightened us wth ye Knowledge of thy Truth, so enable us to walk as children of ye Light, and to have no Fellowship with ye Unfruitfull Works of Darkness; that bringing forth ye Fruits of ye Spirit in all Goodness, Righteousness, & Truth, we may be ever under thy Divine Protection, thro' Jesus Xt or Ld. Amen.*

Episle; Eph. 5.1-14
Gospel; S. Luke 11.14-28

## The Fourth Sunday in Lent.[25]
### The Collect.

*Allmighty God who hast made a Covenant of unspeakable Grace & Mercy wth us in Christ Jesus, & conveyed unto us therein an heavenly Inheritance upon sincere Obedience to his Commands, wch is or reasonable Service; Grant that we may Evermore rejoyce in thee, & walk worthy of our holy calling, thro' or Ld & Savr Jesus Xt.*

Epistle; Gal. 4.21-31
Gospel; S. John 6.1-14

## The Fifth Sunday in Lent.[26]
### The Collect.

*O Allmighty God, who hast sent thy Son Christ to be an High-Priest of good things to come, & by his own Blood to enter in once into ye Holy Place, having obtained an Eternall Redemption for us; Mercifully look upon thy People; that by ye same Blood of or Saviour who thro' ye Eternal Spirit offer'd himself wthout Spott unto thee, our Consciences may be purged from dead works to serve thee ye Living God, that we may receive ye Promise of Eternal Inheritance, thro' Jesus Xt our Lord. Amen.*

Epistle; Heb. 9.11-15
Gospel; S. John 8.46-59

# The Sunday Next before Easter.[27]

## The Collect.

Almighty and everlasting God, who of thy tender love towards mankind, hast sent thy Sour, our Saviour Jesus Christ, to take upon him our flesh, *and that in ye Form of a Servant; & to suffer Death, even ye Death of ye Cross, for our Redemption, & that we should follow ye Example of his great Humility, Patience & Obedience; Mercifully grant, yt this Mind may be in us, wch was in Xt Jesus, that we may both follow the Example of his humble Obedience, & patient Suffering, and also be made partakers of his glorious Resurrection, to live with thee for ever. Grant this for ye Sake of thy Son, or Savr Jesus Xt. Amen.*

Epistle; Phil. 2.5-11

Gospel; S. Matt. 27.1-54


Munday before Easter.
For the Epistle; Isa. 63.1-19
Gospel; S. Mark 14.1-72

Tuesday before Easter.
For the Epistle; Isa. 50.5-11
Gospel; S. Mark 15.1-39

Wednesday before Easter.
Epistle; Heb. 9.16-28
Gospel; S. Luke 22.1-71

Thursday before Easter
Epistle; 1 Cor. 11.17-34
Gospel; S. Luke 23. 1-49

Good Friday.


## *A Sermon or Homily then to be used.*

### *1 Collect*[28]

*Allmighty God, ye Father of Mercies, we beseech thee graciously to hear ye Prayers of thy Church, for wch or Ld Jesus Xt was content to be betrayed, & given up into ye hands of wicked Men, & to suffer Death upon ye Cross; & according to that New Covenant, wch he sealed there wth his precious blood, put thy Laws into all or hearts, & write ym in or Minds; & then remember or Sins & Iniquities no more; for ye sake of him, who, when he had offered One Sacrifice for Sin, for ever sat down, on thy Right Hand, & now liveth & reigneth wth thee & ye Holy Ghost, ever one God World without End. Amen.*

## 2 Coll.[(29)]

Almighty and everlasting God, by whose Spirit the whole body of the Church is governed and sanctified; Receive our supplications and prayers which we offer before thee for all estates of men in thy holy Church, *that every Member of ye same drawing near unto thee with a true Heart, & in full Assurance of Faith, haveing their Souls & Bodies purified from all Uncleanness, may hold fast ye Profession of Faith without wavering; & in their Vocation and Ministry truely & Godly serve thee, thro' our Lord and Saviour Jesus Xt. Amen.*

## 3 Coll.[(30)]

O Merciful God who hast made all men, and hatest nothing that thou hast made, nor wouldest the death of a sinner, *but by ye Death of thy dear Son for ye Sins of ye world hast shewn thou hadst rather he should be converted & live, have Mercy upon all Jews, Turks, Infidels, & Hereticks: Make known thy Blessed Gospel unto ym, take from ym all Ignorance, Hardness of heart, & contempt of thy Word; Work such a lively Faith in them that they may be brought home to thy Flock, and there be made One Fold under One Shepherd, Jesus Xt or Lord. Amen.*

Epistle; Heb. 10.1-25
Gospel; S. John 19.1-37

## Easter Even[(31)]

### The Collect

*Blessed Lord, whose onely Son or Saviour Jesus Xt hath once suffered for our Sins, the Just for ye unjust, that he might bring us to thee our God; we beseech thee, that as we are baptized into his Death, so by continuall* mortifying our corrupt affections, we may be buried with him; and *at last through* the grave, and gate of death, *pass* to our joyful resurrection; for his merits, who died, and was buried, and *rose again, thy* Son Jesus Christ our Lord. Amen.

Epistle; 1 Pet. 3.17-22
Gospel; S. Matt 27.57-66

## Easter Day[(32)]

At Morning Prayer, instead of the Psalm: O Come let us &c these Anthems shall be sung or said.

*Min.*   Christ our passover is sacrificed for us: therefore let us keep the feast.

*People.*   Not with the old leaven, nor with the leaven of malice and wickedness: but with the unleavened bread of sincerity and truth. 1 Cor. 5.7, 8

*Minister.*  Christ being raised from the dead, dieth no more: death hath no more dominion over him.

*People.*  For in that he died, he died unto sin once: but in that he liveth he liveth unto God.

*Minister.*  Likewise reckon ye also your selves to be dead indeed unto sin:

*People.*  But alive unto God, through Jesus Christ our Lord.  Rom. 6.9, 10, 11

*Minister.*  Christ is risen from the dead: and become the first-fruits of them that slept.

*People.*  For since by man came death: by man came also the resurrection of the dead.

*Minister.*  For as in Adam all die: even so in Christ shall all be made alive.  1 Cor. 15.20, 21, 22

*People.  Who is he yt condemneth? It is Christ yt died.*

*Min.  Yea rather yt is risen Again.*

*Peo.  Who is even at ye right hand of God; who maketh Intercession for us.*

*Min.*  Glory be to the Father, and to the Son: and to the Holy Ghost.

*People.*  As it was in the beginning, is now, and ever shall be: world without end. Amen.

## The Collect

*Allmighty God, who by ye Resurrection of thy onely begotten Son Jesus Xt, hast overcome Death, & opend to us ye Gate of Everlasting Life, We humbly beseech thee yt we may die to sin & live to righteousness & stedfastly set our Hearts upon those things wch are above, yt when Christ, who is our Life, shall appear, we may also appear with him in Glory, where he now liveth & reigneth wth thee & ye holy Ghost, ever one God, world without End. Amen.*

Epistle; Col. 3.1-7
Gospel; S. John 20.1-10

## Munday in Easter Week[33]

*This collect the same wth that upon Easter day.*
For the Epistle; Acts 10.34-43
Gospel; S. Luke 24.13-35

## Tuesday in Easter Week

*The collect ye same wth that for Easter day*
For the Epistle; Acts 13.26-41
Gospel; S. Luke 24.36-48

## The First Sunday after Easter[34]

### The Collect

Almighty Father, who hast given thine onely Son to die for our sins, and to rise again for our justification: *increas & strengthen our Fayth in thee & in thy Sonn whome Thou hast sent, that so, believing in Him, we may overcome the world, and attain unto eternal life through Jesus Christ our Lord. Amen.*

Epistle; 1 S. John 5.4-12
Gospel; S. John 20.19-23

## The Second Sunday after Easter.[35]

### The Collect

Almighty God, who hast given thine onely Son to be unto us both a sacrifice for sin, and also an *example* of godly life; Give us grace, that we may always most thankfully receive that his inestimable benefit, and also daily *endevour to* follow the blessed steps of his most holy life, *that dying unto sin & living unto Righteousness we may at last obtain eternal Life through ye same Jes. Ch. or Ld. Amen.*

Epistle; 1 Pet. 2.19-25
Gospel; S. John 10.11-16

## The Third Sunday after Easter.[36]

### The Collect

Almighty God who shewest to them that be in errour the light of thy truth, to the intent that they may return into the way of righteousness; Grant unto all them *who* are admitted into the fellowship of Christs religion, *yt as strangers & Pilgrims they may abstain from fleshly lusts & follow all such things as are agreable to their holy Profession, thro* our Lord Jesus Christ. Amen.

Epistle; 1 Pet. 2.11-17
Gospel; S. John 16.16-22

## The Fourth Sunday after Easter.[37]

### The Collect.

O Almighty God, who alone canst order the unruly wills and affections of sinful men: Grant unto *us* thy people that *we* may love the thing which thou commandest, and desire that which thou dost promise; that so among the sundry and manifold changes of the world, our hearts may surely there be fixed, where true joys are to be found, through Jesus Christ our Lord. Amen.

Epistle; Jas. 1.17-21
Gospel; S. John 16.5-15

## The Fifth Sunday after Easter.[38]
### being *Rogation Sunday*.[39]

*Allmighty God who hast blessed ye Earth yt it should be fruitfull & bring forth every Thing yt is necessary for ye life of man, & hast comanded us to work wth quietness & Eat our own bread; bless us in all our Labours & graunt us such seasonable weather yt we may gather in ye fruits of ye Earth & ever rejoyce in thy Goodness to ye prays of thy holy name, through Jesus Christ or Lord. Amen.*

*For ye Epistle.*

### Rogation Sunday.

#### For The Epistle. Deut 28. from 1 to 9

*It shall come to pass, If thou shalt hearken diligently unto ye Voice of ye Lord thy God, to observe & to do all his Commandments wch I comand Thee this day, ye Ld thy God will sett Thee on high above all nations of ye Earth; & all these blessings shall come on Thee, & ovrtake Thee; If thou shalt hearken unto ye voice of ye Ld thy God. Blessed shalt Thou be, in ye City, & blessed shalt thou be in ye Field, blessed shall be ye fruit of thy body, & ye fruit of ye ground, & ye fruit of thy Cattell, ye increas of thy Kine, & ye flocks of thy sheep. Blessed shall be thy basket & thy store. Blessed shalt thou be when Thou comest in, & Blessed shalt thou be when thou goest out. The Ld shall cause thine enemies yt rise up against Thee to be smitten before thy Face. They shall come out against Thee one way & flee before Thee 7 ways. The Ld shall command ye blessing upon ye in thy storehouses, & in all yt Thou settest thine hands unto, & He shall bless thee in ye land wch ye Ld thy God giveth Thee. The Lord shall establish Thee a holy people to himself, as He hath sworn unto thee, if Thou shalt keep ye Comandments of ye Ld thy God and walk in his ways.*

### The Gospell.  S Matt 6.25 to ye End.

*—— I say unto you, take no thought for yr life, wt ye shall eat, or wt ye shall drink, nor yet for yr body, what you shall put on. Is not ye life more yn meat & ye body more than rainment? behold ye fowls of ye air, for they sow not, neither do they reap, nor gather into barns; yet yr heavenly Father feedeth Them. are ye not much bettr yn They? wch of you by taking thought can add One Cubit unto his stature? & why take ye thought for raiment? considr ye Lillies of ye Field, how they grow; They toil not, neither do they spinn, & yet I say unto you, yt even Solomo in all his glory was not arrayed like One of These. Wherefore if God so cloath ye grass of ye Field wch to day is & to morrow is cast into ye Oven, shall he not much more cloath you, o ye of little Fayth? Therefore take no*

thought saying, wt shall we eat or wt shall we drink, or wherewthall shall we be cloathed? for after all these things do ye Gentiles seek. for your heavenly Father knoweth yt ye have need of all these Things. But seek ye first ye Kingdom of God & his righteousness & all these Things shall be added unto you. Take therefore no thought for ye morrow, for ye morrow shall take thought for ye Things of It Self: sufficient unto ye day is ye Evill thereof.

## The Ascension Day[(40)]

### *A Sermon or Homily then to be used*

### The Collect

*O God ye King of Glory who hast exalted thy Sonn Jesus Christ wth great triumph into the Kingdom of Heaven; graunt we beseech thee yt we may also in heart & mind thither ascend & wth him continually dwell who livest & reignest wth Thee & ye H. Gh. one God world without End, Amen.*

For the Epistle; Acts 1.1-11

Gospel; S. Mark 16.14-20

## The Sunday after Ascension Day[(41)]

### The Collect

O God the King of Glory who hast exalted thine onely Son Jesus Christ with great triumph unto thy Kingdom in Heaven, & *yet didst not leave thy Apostles Comfortless. Vouchsafe, we beseech Thee, to give us thy holy Spirit to guide & comfort us, yt, being sober and watching unto Prayer, & above all things having fervent Charity among orselves we may be exalted into ye same place whither or Saviour Ch: is gone before who liveth &c   Amen*

Epistle; 1 Pet. 4.7-11

Gospel; S. John 15.26-16.4

## Whitsunday[(42)]

### The Collect

*O etrnall God, who, according to thy faithfull pmise didst send ye Holy Ghost on ye day of Pentecost, graunt us by ye same Spirit to have a right Judgment in all Things, & showing our love to Thee by keeping thy Comandments, may evrmore rejoyce in Him, through the merits of Christ J. or Savr: who liveth &c Amen.*

For the Epistle; Acts 2.1-11

Gospel; S. John 14.15-31

## Munday in Whitsun-Week.[43]

### The Collect

*This Collect to be ye same wth that on Whitsunday.*

For the Epistle; Acts 10.34-48
Gospel; S. John 3.16-21


## Tuesday in Whitsun-week

### The Collect

*This Collect ye same wth that on Whitsunday*

For the Epistle; Acts 8.14-17
Gospel; S. John 10.1-10


## Trinity Sunday.[44]

### The Collect

*Holy, Holy, Holy, Ld God Almighty. Thou art worthy to receive glory & Honour & Power; for thou hast created all things, & for thy pleasure they are & were created. Blessed be thy divine majestie who hast given us thy servants Grace by ye Confession of a true Fayth to acknowledge ye glory of ye eternall Trinity, & to worship One God Father Son & holy Ghost. We beseech Thee yt thou wouldst keep us stedfast in this Fayth, & in holiness of Life, & give us Grace to walk worthy of Thee who livest & reignest evr One God world wthout End. Amen.*

For the Epistle; Rev. 4.1-11
Gospel; S. John 3.1-15


## The First Sunday after Trinity.[45]

### The Collect.

O God, the strength of all them that put their trust in thee; Mercifully accept our prayers: and because through the weakness of our mortal nature we can do no good thing without thee grant us the help of thy grace, *that stedfastly believing in thy Son Jes: Xt, and loveing one another as he hath given us commandment, may please thee both in Will and Deed, thro Jesus Xt or Ld. Amen.*

Epistle; 1 John 4.7-21
Gospel; S. Luke 16.19-31

## The Second Sunday after Trinity.[(46)]
### The Collect.

*O Lord who never failest to help & govern ym who continue stedfast in thy fear & Love, keep us, we beseech thee under ye Protection of thy good Providence and give us grace to fear & love thee above all things; and to have Bowels of Compassion tow'rds all our Brethren, that so we may have Confidence tow'rds thee & whatsoever we ask we may receive of thee thro' Jesus Xt. or Ld. Amen*

Epistle; 1 John 3.13-24
Gospel; S. Luke 14.16-24

## The Third Sunday after Trinity.[(47)]
### The Collect.

*O God of all Grace, who hast called us unto thy Eternall Glory by Christ Jesus, we beseech thee mercifully to hear the Prayers, wch with hearty Desires we make unto thee; and grant that we, being clothed with Humility, & casting all our care on thee, may be sober, & vigilant, & continuing stedfast in the Faith may resist all ye Temptations of ye Devill, & at length obtain ye Crown of life, through Jesus Ch. or Ld. Amen.*

Epistle; 1 Pet. 5.5-11
Gospel; S. Luke 15.1-10

## The Fourth Sunday after Trinity.[(48)]
### The Collect.

*O God who hast taught us yt ye sufferings of ye prsent time are not worthy to be compared with ye glory yt shall be revealed in us,* Increas and multiply upon us thy mercy, that thou being our ruler and guide, we may so pass through things temporal, that we finally lose not the things eternal: grant this, O Heavenly Father, for Jesus Christs sake our Lord. Amen.

Epistle; Rom. 8.18-23
Gospel; S. Luke 6.36-42

## The Fifth Sunday after Trinity.[(49)]
### The Collect.

*O Lord whose Eyes are over ye Righteous & thine Eares open to their prayers, we most humbly beseech thee, to make us all of one Mind, having Compassion One of another, loveing as Brethren, being pitifull & Courteous, eschewing all evill in Word & Deed, & doing Good, seeking Peace wth all men, yt so we may attain yt peace wch passeth all undrstanding, through J. Ch. or Ld. Amen.*

Epistle; 1 S Pet. 3.8-15
Gospel; S. Luke 5.1-11

## The Sixth Sunday after Trinity.[(50)]
### The Collect.

O God, who hast prepared for them that love thee, such good things as pass mans understanding; *Graunt yt we loving Thee above all things & walking before thee in Newness of Life, may obtain thy Promises thro Jes. Chr. or. Ld. Amen.*

Epistle; Rom. 6.3-11
Gospel; S. Matt. 5.20-26

## The Seventh Sunday after Trinity.[(51)]
### The Collect.

Lord of all power and might, who art the author and giver of all good things; Graft in our hearts the love of thy Name, increase in us true religion, *that we being made free from Sin, and become the Servants of thee our God, may have our fruit unto Holiness & ye end everlasting Life, thro' Jesus Christ our Lord. Amen.*

Epistle; Rom. 6.19-23
Gospel; S. Mark 8.1-9

## The Eighth Sunday after Trinity.[(52)]
### The Collect.

O God, whose never-failing providence ordereth all things both in heaven and earth; we humbly beseech thee to put away from us all hurtful things, and to give us those things which be profitable for us, through Jesus Christ our Lord.

*This to be put among ye Collects at ye End of ye Comm: service.*

*Most gracious God, who hast given us ye Spirit of Adoption whereby we call Thee or Father, Graunt yt we, mortifying ye deeds of ye body, & being led by thy holy Spirit, may live as becomes thy children, & joynt heirs wth Christ, & finally be glorifyd together wth him who liveth &c Amen.*

Epistle; Rom. 8.12-17
Gospel; S. Matt. 7.15-21

## The Ninth Sunday after Trinity.[(53)]
### The Collect.

*O God who hast in thy holy Word set before us thy righteous Judgments upon thine antient People the Jews for or Admonition, & Example, preserve us by thy Grace from all those Sins, by which they provoked thy Wrath against them, and never suffer us to be tempted above what we are able, but make a Way for us to escape ye Temptation or enable us to bear it thro Jes: Xt. or Ld. Amen.*

Epistle; 1 Cor. 10.1-13
Gospel; S. Luke 16.1-9

## The Tenth Sunday after Trinity.[(54)]
### The Collect.

*O God who was pleased to bestow great diversity of Spiritual Gifts for ye first planting of thy Church; we beseech Thee still to pour out such a measure of thy holy Spirit upon evry member of ye same as may be for ye pfit & edification of ye whole body united together in Love by one & ye same Spirit, through Jesus &c Amen.*

Epistle; 1 Cor. 12.1-11
Gospel. S. Luke 19.41-47

## The Eleventh Sunday after Trinity.[(55)]
### The Collect.

*O God who has brought life & Imortality to Light by yr Gospell, & hast begotten us again to a lively hope by ye Resurrection of Jesus Christ fro the dead, make us stedfast & immoveable in ye Fayth, allways abounding in ye work of ye Lord, who died for or Sins & rose again & now liveth & reigneth with Thee &c.*

Epistle; 1 Cor. 15.1-11
Gospel; S. Luke 18.9-14

## The Twelfth Sunday after Trinity.[(56)]
### The Collect.

*O most mercifull Father who by ye glorious Ministration of ye Spirit hast given us a cleare Revelation of thy will in ye Gospell of thy Sonn, we beseech Thee to enlighten or minds, that we may rightly undrstand It & duly value It, & frame or Lives according to It, to thy honr & glory, through Jesus Christ our Ld. Amen.*

Epistle; (2 Cor. 3.4-9)
Gospel; S. Mark 7.31-37

## The Thirteenth Sunday after Trinity.[(57)]
### The Collect.

*O Aetrnall God who hast called all Nations to be One by Faith in Christ Jesus, grant that we who are baptized into him may* so faithfully serve thee in this life, that we fail not finally to attain thy heavenly promises, through the merits of Jesus Christ our Lord. Amen.

*The Epistle. Gal 3 from 22 to the End.*

———— *The Scripture hath concluded All under Sin, that the Promise by Fayth of Jesus Christ might be given to Them that beleive. But before Fayth came, we were kept undr ye Law, shut up unto ye Fayth wch should afterwards be revealed. Wherefore ye Law was our Schoolmr to bring us unto Christ, yt we might be justify'd by Fayth. but after that Fayth is come, we are no longr udr a Schoolmaster. For ye are All ye children of God by Fayth in Christ Jesus. for as many of you as have bin baptized into Christ, have put on Christ. There is neither Jew nor Greek, there is neither bond nor free, there is neither male nor female: for ye are all One in Christ Jesus. And if ye be Christs, then are ye Abrahas Seed, & heirs according to ye pmise.*

## Gospel; S. Luke 10.23-37

## The Fourteenth Sunday after Trinity.[58]
### The Collect.

*Almighty & Evrlasting God we beseech thee enable us more & more to mortify ye flesh with ye Affectios & Lusts, & to bring forth ye fruit of ye Spirit in Love, joy, peace, longsuffering, Gentleness, Goodness, Fayth, meekness temperance; that we loving what Thou dost Comand, may obtain that wch Thou dost pmise through Jesus Christ our Lord. Amen.*

### Epistle; Gal. 5.16-24
### Gospel; S. Luke 17.11-19

## The Fifteenth Sunday after Trinity.[59]
### The Collect.

*Almighty God, who having made thy Sonn Jes. Christ perfect through sufferings, hast called us to be his Disciples & followers, indue us, we beseech Thee, wth ye same Spirit wch was in Him; yt we being crucify'd to ye World, may patiently bear ye Cross, &, being renewd in or Natures, in righteousness & true holiness, and walking according to this Rule, Peace & mercy may be upon Us, through Jesus Christ or Lord. Amen.*

### Epistle; Gal. 6.11-18
### Gospel; S. Matt. 6.24-34

## The Sixteenth Sunday after Trinity.[(60)]
### The Collect.

*O God ye Father of our Ld. Jes. Christ, of whome ye whole Family of Heaven & Earth is named, grant, we beseech Thee, according to ye Riches of thy Glory yt we may be strengthened wth might by thy Spirit in the inner man; yt Christ may dwell in our hearts by fayth, & we, being routed & grounded in Love, may be able to comprehend thy Love in Christ, wch passeth knowledge, & be filled wth all divine Graces & virtues, through Jesus Christ our Lord. Amen.*

Epistle; Eph. 3.13-21
Gospel; S. Luke 7.11-17


## The Seventeenth Sunday after Trinity.[(61)]
### The Collect.

*O God ye Father of All, who art above All, through All, & in All, grant we pray thee yt thy Grace may allwaies prevent & follow us, yt we may walk worthy of ye Vocation wherewith we are call'd, wth all lowliness & meekness, wth Longsuffering, forebearing one Another in Love, endevouring to keep ye unity of ye Spirit in ye bond of Peace. That, being continually given to all good works, we may finally attain to evrlasting joy & felicitie, through our Ld. & Saviour Jesus Christ. Amen.*

Epistle; Eph. 4.1-6
Gospel; S. Luke 14.1-11


## The Eighteenth Sunday after Trinity.[(62)]
### The Collect.

*O Lord who hast enriched us wth ye knowledge of thy holy Gospell; graunt us grace, we beseech Thee, so to wait for ye coming of our Lord Jesus Christ, to judge ye world in righteousness, yt we may wthstand ye Temptations of ye world ye flesh & ye devill, & wth such pure hearts & minds follow Thee the only God, yt we may be confirmed unto ye End, & be blameless in ye day of our Ld. Jesus Christ. Amen.*

Epistle; 1 Cor. 1.4-8
Gospel; S. Matt. 22.34-46

### The Nineteenth Sunday after Trinity.[(63)]
### The Collect.

O God, forasmuch as without thee we are not able to please thee; Mercifully grant that thy holy Spirit may in all things direct, and rule our hearts, *and renew us in ye Spirit of our mind: that putting away all bitterness & wrath, Anger & malice. & every othr evill Affection, & being kind One to Another, tendrhearted, forgiving One another, even as Thou, O God, for Christs sake hast forgiven us; we may comfortably look wth an assured hope for ye day of Redemption from all Evills, unto etrnall life, through Jesus Christ our Ld. Amen.*

Epistle; Eph. 4.17-32
Gospel; S. Matt. 9.1-8

### The Twentieth Sunday after Trinity.[(64)]
### The Collect.

*O Almighty & most mercifull God, who hast given us to undrstand thy holy will, we beseech Thee to grant us thy Grace to walk circumspectly, not as fools but as wise, redeeming ye time, in all sobrietie & heavenly mindedness: yt being filled wth ye Spirit we may rejoyce in Thee, & giv thanks allwaies for all things in ye name of our Lord Jesus Christ. Amen.*

Epistle; Eph. 5.15-21
Gospel; S. Matt. 22.1-14

### The One and Twentieth Sunday after Trinity.[(65)]
### The Collect.

*O mercifull God who, according to thy divine Power, hast given us all Things pertaining to Life & Godliness; make us strong in ye Lord, & in ye power of his Might: That putting on ye whole armour of God, we may be able to resist all ye temptations of ye devill, praying to Thee Allways wth fervent Prayer & watching thereunto wth all perseverance, through Jesus Christ our Lord. Amen.*

Epistle; Eph. 6.10-20
Gospel; S. John 4.46-54

### The Two and Twentieth Sunday after Trinity.[66]
### The Collect.

*O Mercifull God, perfect, we beseech Thee, ye good work wch Thou hast begun in Us; that or Love may abound yet more & more in knowledge & in all Judgment: that, approving things wch are Excellent, we may be sincere & wthout offense, till ye day of Christ; being filled with ye fruits of righteousness wch are to ye prays & glory of Thee or God, through Jesus Christ our Ld. Amen.*

Epistle; Phil. 1.3-11
Gospel; S. Matt. 18.21-35

### The Three and Twentieth Sunday after Trinity.[67]
### The Collect.

*O God who hast set before ys many & great Exaples of a holy & heavenly Life, assist us by thy Grace, to be Followers of Them as They were of Christ; yt we may not mind earthly things, but having our Conversation in Heaven, may look for ye Saviour our Lord Jesus Christ, to change our vile bodies & fashion Them like unto his glorious body, in wch he liveth & reigneth wth Thee & ye holy Sp. evr One God world wthout End. Amen.*

Epistle; Phil. 3.17-21
Gospel; S. Matt. 22.15-22

### The Four and Twentieth Sunday after Trinity.[68]
### The Collect.

*O God ye Father of our Ld. Jesus Christ, give us Grace, we beseech Thee, to walk worthy of Thee unto all pleasing; that being fruitfull in evry work & increasing in ye knowledge of Thee or God, & thereby made meet to be partakers of ye inheritance of ye Saints in Light, we may allwaies give thanks unto Thee in thy holy Church, through Jesus Christ our Ld. Amen.*

Epistle; Col. 1.3-12
Gospel; S. Matt. 9.18-26

The Twenty Fifth Sunday after Trinity.[69]
The Collect.

*O eternal God who art faithfull & True &, according to thy*
*gracious pmises, hast raised up a glorious deliverer to us who is the*
*Lord Our Righteousness; we beseech Thee to stir up ye Wills of thy*
*faithfull People, that, bringing forth plenteously the fruit of good*
*works, they may be a people prepared for ye Ld: And, we pray Thee,*
*hasten his kingdom when he shall reign & psp & execute Judgmnt*
*& Justice in all ye Earth. Grant this for thy infinite Mercies sake in*
*Jesus Christ, to whome wth thee, O Father & ye holy Ghost be*
*eternall prais. Amen.*

For the Epistle; Jer. 23.5-8
Gospel; S. John 6.5-14


Saint Andrews Day
Saint Thomas the Apostle                    unaltered
Conversion of Saint Paul


The Presentation of Christ in the Temple,[70]
commonly called, The Purification of Saint Mary the Virgin.

The Collect.

Almighty and everliving God, we humbly beseech thy Majesty that
as thy onely begotten Son *was presented* in the temple in substance
of our flesh; so we may be presented unto thee with pure and clean
hearts, by the same thy Son Jesus Christ our Lord. Amen.

For the Epistle; Mal. 3.1-5
Gospel; S. Luke 2.22-40

Saint Matthiass Day                         unaltered
The Annunciation of the blessed Virgin Mary


Saint Marks Day.
The Collect.

O Almighty God, who hast instructed thy holy Church with the
heavenly Doctrine of *thy Evangelist Mark*; Give us grace, that being
not like children carried away with every blast of vain doctrine, we
may be established in the truth of thy holy Gospel, through Jesus
Christ our Lord. Amen.

Epistle; Eph. 4.7-16
Gospel; S. John 15.1-11

Saint Philip and Saint Jamess Day.
The Collect.

O Almighty God, whom truly to know is everlasting life; Grant us perfectly to know thy son Jesus Christ to be the way, the truth, and the life; that following the steps of thy holy Apostles *Philip and James* we may stedfastly walk in the way that leadeth to eternal life, through the same thy Son Jesus Christ our Lord. Amen.

Epistle; Jas. 1.1-12
Gospel; S. John 14.1-14

Saint Barnabas the Apostle                                unaltered
Saint John Baptists Day

Saint Peters Day.
The Collect.

O Almighty God, who by thy Son Jesus Christ didst give to thy *Apostle Peter* many excellent gifts, and commanded him earnestly to feed thy flock; Make, we beseech thee, all Bishops and Pastors diligently to preach thy holy Word, and the people obediently to follow the same, that they may receive the crown of everlasting glory, through Jesus Christ our Lord. Amen.

For the Epistle; Acts 12.1-11
Gospel; S. Matt. 16.13-19

Saint James the Apostle.[71]
The Collect.

Grant, O merciful God, that as thine holy *Apostle James*, leaving his father and all that he had, without delay was obedient unto the calling of thy Son Jesus Christ, and followed him; so we forsaking all worldly and carnal affections may be evermore ready to follow thy holy commandments *as he did, & wth him to lay down our lives for ye testimonie of thy Truth, through Jesus Christ our Lord. Amen.*

For the Epistle; Acts 11.27-12.3
Gospel; S. Matt. 20.20-28

## Saint Bartholemew the Apostle.[72]
### The Collect.

O Almighty and everlasting God, who didst give *to Bartholemew & the other Apostles,* grace truly to believe and to preach thy Word *& power to confirm It with many Signs & wonders, grant* we beseech thee unto thy Church, to love that word which *they* believed, and both to preach and receive the same, through Jesus Christ our Lord. Amen.

For the Epistle; Acts 5.12-16
Gospel; S. Luke 22.24-30

Saint Matthew the Apostle                                  unaltered
Saint Michael and All Angels

### Saint Luke the Evangelist.[73]
### The Collect.

*Almighty God who didst inspire Luke ye Evangelist to write in order ye Gospell of or Lord Jesus Christ; grant yt we, being instructed in ye certainty thereof, may most surely believe It, & conform ourselves to ye holy precepts & Examples of or blessed Ld. & Saviour who liveth &c. Amen.*

Epistle; 2 Tim. 4.5-15
Gospel; S. Luke. 10.1-7

Saint Simon and Saint Jude, Apostles                      unaltered
All Saints Day

## THE ORDER FOR THE MINISTRATION OF THE HOLY COMMUNION

*When there is no Comunion, there is not to be any Comunion-service.* [1]

So many as intend to be partakers of the Holy Communion shall signifie their Names to the Curate *sometime* the *week* [2] before.

*The Minister that Consecrates ought allwaies to be a Archbp, Bishop or Presbyter. Q.* [3]

And if any of those be an open and notorious evil liver, or have done wrong to his neighbours by word or deed, so that the congregation be thereby offended; the Curate, having knowledge thereof, shall call him and advertise him, that in any wise he presume not to come to the Lords Table, until he have openly declared himself to have truly repented, and amended his former naughty life, that the congregation may thereby be satisfied,[4] which before were offended; . . . .

The same order shall the Curate use . . . .

The Table at the Communion-time having a fair white linen Cloth upon it, shall stand in the body of the Church, or in the Chancel, where Morning and Evening Prayer are appointed to be said. *And ye minister shall at ye Northside of ye Table say the Lords Prayer with ye collect following, All Kneeling.* [5]

*Q. of another Collect &c & Then Let yr Light &c & of those for ye K.*

Our Father, which art in heaven; Hallowed be thy Name. Thy Kingdom come. Thy will be done in earth, As it is in heaven. Give us this day our daily bread. And forgive us our trespasses, As we forgive them that trespass against us. And lead us not into temptation; But deliver us from evil. *For thine &c Amen.* [6]

Collect.

Almighty God, unto whom all hearts be open, all desires known, and from whom no secrets are hid; Cleanse the thoughts of our hearts by the *operation* [7] of thy holy Spirit, that we may perfectly love thee, and worthily magnifie thy holy Name, through Christ our Lord. Amen. [8]

*to be put at ye End of ye Litany:* [9]

*Or the 8 Beatitudes, the People still kneeling &, after every Beautitude, praying as is hereafter directed.*

*Italic.*

*Minister.*
*Our Lord Christ spake these Words and sayd*
*Blessed are ye poor in spirit, for ther's is ye Kingdom of Heaven.*

*People.*
*Lord have mercy upon us, & make us Partakers of ys blessing.*

*Minister.*
*Blessed are They yt mourn, for They shall be comforted.*

*People.*
*Ld have mercy upon us, & make us partakers of ys blessing.*

*Minister.*

*Blessed are the meek for They shall inherit ye Earth.*

*People.*

*Ld have mercy upon us, & make us partakrs of ys blessing.*

*Minister.*

*Blessed are They who*[10] *hugr & thirs after righteousness: for They shall be filled.*

*People.*

*Ld have mercy upon us, & make us partakrs of ys blessing.*

*Minister.*

*Blessed are the merciful, for they shall obtain mercy.*

*People.*

*Ld have mercy upon us, & make us partakrs of vs blessing.*

*Minister.*

*Blessed are ye pure in heart: for They shall see God.*

*People.*

*Ld have mercy upon us, & make us partakrs of ys blessing.*

*Minister.*

*Blessed are ye Peacemakers: for they shall be called ye childre of God.*

*People.*

*Ld have mercy upon us, & make us partakers of ys blessing.*

*Minister.*

*Blessed are They wch are persecuted for Righteousness sake: for theirs is ye Kingdom of Heaven.*

*People.*

*Ld have mercy upon us & indue us wth all these Graces, & make us partakers of ye blessedness pmis'd to Them we humbly beseech thee.*

*Then . .*[11]

*Our Lord Jesus Christ spake these words, & said,*[12]

*Blessed are the poor in spirit: for theirs is the kingdom of heaven.*

*Lord have mercy upon us & endue us with an humble & contented Spirit.*

*Blessed are they that mourn: for they shall be comforted.*

*Lord have mercy upon us, and give us that godly favour wch worketh repentance, never to be repented of.*

*Lord have mercy upon us, & give us grace to shew all meekness*

*Blessed are the meek: for they shall inherit the Earth.*

*Lord have mercy upon us, & give us grace to shew all meekness & gentleness towards all men.*

*Blessed are thy wch do hunger & thirst after righteousness: for they shall be filled.*

*Lord have mercy upon us, & fill us with all the fruits of righteousness wch are by Christ Jesus, to thy praise & glory.*

*· Blessed are the mercifull: for they shall obtain mercy.*

*Lord have mercy upon us, and make us mercifull as thou our heavenly Father art mercifull.*

*Blessed are the pure in heart: for they shall see God.*

*Lord have mercy upon us, & clense us from all filthiness of flesh & spirit, & inable*[13] *us to perfect holyness in the fear of thee our God.*

*Blessed are the peacemakers: for they shall be called the Children of God.*

*Lord have mercy upon us, and incline us to eschew evill & do good, to seek peace & ensue it.*

*Blessed are they wch are persecuted for righteousness sake: for theirs is the kingdom of heaven.*

*Lord have mercy upon us, when we are called to suffer for thy name, and strengthen us*[14] *according to thy glorious power, unto all patience & long-suffering, with joyfullness.*[15]

**This to be used after or instead (of) the X comandmts upon the great Festivals.**

Then shall follow one of these two Collects for the King[16] and Queen, the Priest standing as before, and saying

Let us pray[17]

Almighty God, whose kingdom is everlasting, and power infinite; have mercy upon the whole church, and so rule the hearts of *thy servants*[18] King William and Queen Mary, that they (knowing whose Ministers they are) may above all things seek thy honour and glory; and that we and all their subjects (duly considering whose authority they have) may faithfully serve, honour, and humbly obey them, in thee, and for thee, according to thy blessed Word and Ordinance, through Jesus Christ our Lord, who with thee and the Holy Ghost, liveth and reigneth ever one God, world without end. Amen.

Or,

Almighty and everlasting God, we are taught by thy holy word, that the hearts of kings are in thy rule and governance, and that thou dost dispose and turn them as it seemeth best to thy godly wisdom; We humbly beseech thee so to dispose and govern the hearts of *thy servants*[18] King William and Queen Mary, that in all their thoughts, words and works, they may ever seek thy honour and glory, and study to preserve thy people committed to their charge, in wealth, peace, and godliness. Grant this, O merciful Father, for thy dear Sons sake Jesus Christ our Lord. Amen.

X

Then[19] shall be said the Collect of the Day. And immediately after the Collect, the Priest shall read the Epistle saying, The Epistle (or the portion of Scripture appointed for the Epistle) is written in the — — — Chapter of — — — beginning at the — — — verse. And the Epistle ended, he shall say, Here endeth the Epistle. Then shall he read the Gospel (the People all standing up) saying, The Holy Gospel is written in the — — — Chapter of — — — beginning at the — — — verse. And the Gospel ended, shall be sung or said the Creed following, the people still standing, as before.

I Believe in One God, . . . .

And I believe in the Holy Ghost, the Lord and giver of life, Who proceedeth from the Father and the Son[20]

*It is humbly submitted to ye Convocation whether a Note ought not here to be added wth relation to ye Greek Church, in order to our maintaining Catholic Comunion.*

Who with the Father and the Son together is worshipped and glorified, who spake by the prophets. And I believe one Catholick and Apostolick Church, I acknowledge one Baptism for the remission of sins, And I look for the Resurrection of the dead, And the life of the world to come. Amen.

*See at ye End of ye Litany.* [21]

Then the *Minister* shall declare unto the People what Holydays, or Fasting-days are in the Week following to be observed. And then also (if occasion be) shall notice be given of the Communion; and Briefs, Citations, and Excommunications read. And nothing shall be proclaimed or published in the church, during the time of Divine Service, but by the Minister: Nor by him any thing, but what is prescribed in the Rules of this Book, or enjoyned by the King, or the Ordinary of the place; *& is agreable to the Laws of the Land.*

Then shall follow the Sermon, or one of the Homilies already set forth, or hereafter to be set forth by Authority.

*Q. Concerning Another Book of Homilies to be added to ye formr; & of correcting some obsolete phrases in yt former book.*

Then shall *the Minister begin the* Offertory,[22] saying one or more of these Sentences following, as he thinketh most convenient in his discretion.

Let your light so shine before men. . . .

Lay not up for your selves treasure. . . .

Whatsoever ye would that men should do. . . .

Not every one that saith unto me, Lord, Lord. . . .

Zaccheus stood forth, and said unto the Lord. . . .

He that soweth little, shall reap little. . . .

While we have time, let us do good. . . .

Godliness is great riches. . . .

Charge them who are rich in this world. . . .

God is not unrighteous. . . .

To do good, and to distribute, forget not. . . .

Whoso hath this worlds good. . . .

He that hath pity upon the poor. . . .

Blessed be the man that provideth for the sick and needy: the Lord shall deliver him in the time of trouble. Ps. 41.1 [23]

*These sentences are to be read only in those Churches where ye Custom is that ye minister has any share of ye offerings.*

*Who goeth a warfare at any time of his own cost? who planteth a vineyard, and eateth not of ye Fruit thereof? or who feedeth a flock, & eateth not of the milk of ye flock?* 1 Cor. 9.7

*If we have sown unto you Spiritual Things, is it a great mattr if we reap ye worldly things?* 1 Cor. 9.11

*Do ye not know that they who minister about holy Things live of the Sacrifice? & they who wait at ye Altar are partakers with ye Altar? Even so hath ye Lord also ordained, that They who preach ye Gospell should live of ye Gospell.* 1 Cor. 9.13, 14

*Let him that is taught in ye word minister unto him yt teacheth in all good Things. Be not deceived, God is not mocked: for whatsoever a man soweth that shall he reap.* Gal. 6.6, 7

Whilst these sentences are in reading, the Deacons, Churchwardens or other fit Persons appointed for that purpose, shall receive the Alms of the Poor, and other Devotions of the People, in a decent Basin, to be provided by the Parish for that purpose; and reverently bring it to the *Minister,* who shall humbly present and place it upon the holy Table.[24]

*And the Minister shall* place upon the Table so much Bread and Wine, as he shall think sufficient. After which done, the *Minister* shall say,

Let us pray for the whole state of Christs Church militant here in earth.[25]

Almighty and Everliving God, who by thy holy Apostle hast taught us to make prayers and supplications, and to give thanks for all men; We humbly beseech thee most mercifully (to accept our alms and oblations, and) to receive these our prayers, which we offer unto thy divine

If there be no alms or oblations, then shall the words (of accepting our alms and oblations) be left out unsaid.

Majesty, beseeching thee to inspire continually the universal Church with the spirit of truth, unity, and concord: and grant that all they that do confess thy holy Name, may agree in the truth of thy holy Word, and live in unity and godly love. We beseech thee also to save and defend all Christian Kings, Princes and Governors; and especially thy servants William and Mary, our King and Queen, that under them we may be godly and quietly governed: and grant unto their whole council, and to all that are put in Authority under them, that they may truly and *impartially* minister justice, to the punishment of wickedness and vice, and to the maintenance of thy true Religion and vertue. Give grace, O heavenly Father, to all Bishops, *Pastors* and Curates, that they may both by their life and doctrine set forth thy true and lively Word, and rightly and duly administer thy holy Sacraments: And to all thy people give thy heavenly grace; and especially to this Congregation here present, that[26] *they may allwaies with* meek heart and due reverence *hear* and receive thy holy Word; truly serving thee in holiness and righteousness all the days of their life And we most humbly beseech thee of thy goodness, O Lord, to comfort and succour all them, who in this transitory life are in trouble, sorrow, need, sickness, or any other adversity. And we also bless thy holy Name, for all thy servants departed this life in thy faith and fear; beseeching thee to give us grace so to follow their good examples, that with them we may be partakers of thy heavenly kingdom. Grant this, O Father, for Jesus Christs sake our onely Mediatour and Advocate. Amen.

*See Collects at ye End of ye Comunion Service.*

*A preparatory Prayer for ye Comunion to be read on ye Lds day, or o some week day, or daies before, at ye discretio of ye Minister.*

*O God who has ordained holy Mysteries for a comemoratio*[27] *of or Saviour's wonderfull love in laying dow his life for us; & for ye comunicatio of ye benefits of his death & passion to Us; we beseech yee to dispose all Those who intend to be made partakers of them, to come to thy holy Table with such sincere repentance of all their sinns, & ufeigned Resolutios of better Obedience; wth such an humble Fayth & ardent love uto Thee & unto All men: That*

106

*They may cofortably hope for thy gracious Pardon, & for ye powr of thy holy Spirit, to carry them, by patience in well doing, unto aetrnal life, through Jesus Christ our Lord. Amen.*

When the minister giveth warning for the celebration of the holy Communion (which he shall always do upon the Sunday, or some holy-day immediately preceding) after the Sermon or Homily ended, he shall read this exhortation following.

*A shorter Form of warning to be made, seeing in many Parishes the Returns of monethly Comunions are comonly known!*[(28)] *ys referred to ye Dea of Pet. D. Patrick.*

Dearly beloved, on — — — — day next, I purpose, through Gods assistance, to administer to all such as shall be religiously and devoutly disposed, the most comfortable Sacrament of the Body and Blood of Christ . . . .

The ways and means thereto is . . . . Repent you of your sins, or else come not to that holy Table, *least by profaning that holy Sacrament you draw down ye heavy, displeasure of God upon you.*

And because it is requisite, that no man should come to the holy Communion, but with *trust* in Gods mercy, and with a *good* conscience; Therefore if there be any of you, who by this means cannot quiet his own conscience herein, but requireth further comfort or counsel: let him come to me, *or to some other Minister of Gods word & open his Greif,*[(29)] *that he may receive such spiritual Advice & Comfort as may tend to ye quieting of his Conscience,*[(30)] *& his better prparation for ye holy Comunion.*

Or in case he shall see the people negligent to come to the Holy Communion, instead of the former, he shall use this exhortation.

Dearly beloved brethren, on — — — — — I intend by Gods grace to celebrate the Lords Supper: unto which, in Gods behalf, I bid you all that are here present; and beseech you for the Lord Jesus Christs sake, that ye will not refuse to come thereto, being so lovingly called and bidden by God himself . . . .

At the time of the celebration of the Communion, the Communicants being conveniently placed for the receiving of the holy Sacrament, the Priest shall say this Exhortation.

Dearly beloved in the Lord, ye that mind to come to the holy Communion of the body and bloud of our Saviour Christ, must consider how Saint Paul exhorteth all persons diligently to try and examine them selves, before they presume to eat of that Bread, and drink of that Cup. For as the benefit is great, if with a true penitent heart and lively faith we receive that holy *Sacrament, so* is the danger great, if we receive the same *unworthily. Judge therefore*[31] your selves, brethren, that ye be not judged of the Lord; repent you truly for your sins past; have a lively and stedfast faith in Christ our Saviour; amend your lives, and be in perfect charity with all men; so shall ye be meet partakers of those holy mysteries.[32] . . .

Then shall the *Minister* say to them that come to receive the holy Communion.

Ye that do truly and earnestly repent you of your sins, and are in love and charity with your neighbours, and intend to lead a new life, following the commandments of God, and walking from henceforth in his holy ways; Draw near with faith, and take his holy Sacrament to your comfort; and make your humble confession to Almighty God, meekly kneeling upon your knees.[33]

Then shall this general Confession be made, in the name of all those that are minded to receive the holy Communion, by one of the Ministers, both he and all the people kneeling upon their knees, and saying,

Almighty God, Father of our Lord Jesus Christ, Maker of all things, Judge of all men . . . .

Then shall the *Minister*[34] (or the Bishop being present) stand up, and turning himself to the People, pronounce this Absolution.

Almighty God our heavenly Father, who of his great mercy hath promised forgiveness of sins . . . .

Then shall the *Minister*[35] say,

Hear what comfortable words our Saviour Christ saith unto all that truly turn to him . . . .

After which the Priest[36] shall proceed, saying,

Lift up your hearts.

Answer. We lift them up unto the Lord.

Priest. Let us give thanks unto our Lord God.

Answer. It is meet and right so to do.

Then shall the Priest turn to the Lords Table, and say,

It is very meet, right and our bounden duty that we should at all times, and in all places give thanks unto thee O Lord, (Holy Father) Almighty, Everlasting God.

These words (Holy Father) must be omitted on Trinity Sunday.

Here shall follow the proper Preface, according to the time, if there be any specially appointed: or else immediately shall follow,

Therefore with Angels and Archangels, and with all the company[37] of heaven, we laud and magnifie thy glorious Name, evermore praising thee, and saying, Holy, holy, holy, Lord God of hosts, Heaven and earth are full of thy glory. Glory be to thee, O Lord most High. Amen.

## Proper Prefaces.

### Upon Christmas-day, and seven days after.[38]

Because thou didst give Jesus Christ thine onely Son to be born at this time[39] for us . . . . Therefore with Angels &c.

### *Upon Good-friday:*

*Who hast not spared thine own Son, but deliver'd him up for Us All, that by making himself a Sacrifice for our sins, he might redeem us from all iniquity & purify to himself a peculiar people zealous of good works. Therefore with Angells &c.*

### Upon Easter-day, and seven days after.

But chiefly are we bound to praise thee for the glorious Resurrection of thy Son Jesus Christ our Lord . . . . Therefore &c.

### Upon Ascension-day, and seven days after.

Through thy most dearly beloved Son Jesus Christ our Lord, who after his most glorious Resurrection . . . . Therefore &c.

### Upon Whitsunday, and six days after.

Through Jesus Christ our Lord; according to whose most true promise, the Holy Ghost came down as at this time from heaven . . . . Therefore with Angels &c.

### Upon the Feast of Trinity onely.[40]

Who are one God, one Lord; not one onely person . . . . Therefore with Angels &c.

After each of which Prefaces, shall immediately be sung or said,

Therefore with Angels and Archangels, and with all the company[41] of heaven, we laud and magnifie thy glorious Name, evermore praising thee, and saying; Holy, holy, holy, Lord God of hosts, Heaven and earth are full of thy glory. Glory be to thee, O Lord most high. Amen.

Then shall the [42], kneeling down at the Lords Table, say in the name of all them that shall receive the Communion, this prayer following.

We do not presume to come to this thy Table, O merciful Lord, trusting in our own righteousness, but in thy manifold and great mercies. We are not worthy so much as to gather up the crumbs under thy Table. But thou art the same Lord, whose property is always to have mercy; Grant us therefore, gracious Lord, so to eat the flesh of thy dear Son Jesus Christ, and to drink his bloud, that our *soules & Bodies may be wash'd & cleansed by the Sacrifice of his most precious Body & bloud,*[43] and that we may evermore dwell in him, and he in us. Amen.

When the *Minister,*[44] standing before the Table, hath so ordered the Bread and Wine, that he may with the more readiness and decency break the Bread before the People, and take the Cup into his Hands, he shall say the Prayer of Consecration, as followeth.

Almighty God, our heavenly Father, who of thy tender mercy didst give thine onely Son Jesus Christ to suffer death upon the Cross for our redemption, who made there (by his one oblation of himself once offered) a full, perfect and sufficient sacrifice, oblation, and satisfaction for the sins of the whole world, and didst institute, and in his holy Gospel command us to continue a perpetual memory of that his precious death, until his coming again; Hear us, O merciful Father, we most humbly beseech thee, and grant that we receiving these thy creatures of bread and wine, according to thy Son our Saviour Jesus Christs holy institution, in remembrance of his death and passion, may be partakers of his most precious body and bloud: Who in the same night that he was betrayed (a) took bread, and when he had given thanks (b) he brake it, and gave it to his disciples, saying, Take, eat, (c) this is my body which is given for you, do this in remembrance of me. Likewise after Supper, (d) he took the cup, and when he had given thanks, he gave it to them saying, Drink ye all of this, for this (e) is my bloud of the New Testament, which is shed for you and for many for the remission of sins: Do this, as oft as ye shall drink it, in remembrance of me. Amen.

(a) here the Priest is to take the Paten into his hands:

(b) and here to break the bread:

[45](c) and here to lay his hand upon all the bread:

(d) here he is to take the cup into his hand:

(e) And here to lay his hand upon every vessel (be it Chalice or Flagon) in which there is any wine to be consecrated:

Then shall the Minister first receive the Communion in both kinds himself, and then proceed to deliver the same to the Bishops,                ,[46] and Deacons, in like manner (if any be present) and after that to the people also in order, into their Hands, all *kneeling humbly.*[47] And when he delivereth the Bread to any one, he shall say,

The Body[48] of our Lord Jesus Christ, which is given for thee, preserve thy body and soul unto everlasting life. *Amen*. Take and eat this in remembrance that Christ died for thee, and feed on him in thy heart by faith with thanksgiving.

And the Minister that delivereth the Cup to any one, shall say,

The bloud of our Lord Jesus Christ, which was shed for thee, preserve thy body and soul unto everlasting life. *Amen*. Drink this in remembrance that Christs bloud was shed for thee, and be thankful.

If the consecrated Bread or Wine be all spent before all have communicated; *the Minister shall use this form.*

*O Mercifull Father! hear the Prayers of thy Church that have now bin made unto Thee in ye name of thy Sonn or Lord Jesus Christ, who, ye same night yt he was betrayed, took bread (or ye Cup) &c*[49]

When all have communicated, the Minister shall return to the Lords Table, and reverently place upon it what remaineth of the consecrated Elements, covering the same with a fair Linen Cloth.

Then shall the Priest say the Lords Prayer, the People repeating after him every Petition.[50]

Our Father . . . .

Then shall be said as followeth.

O Lord and heavenly Father, we thy humble servants entirely desire thy Fatherly goodness, mercifully to accept this our sacrifice of praise and thanksgiving; most humbly beseeching thee to grant, that by the merits and death of thy Son Jesus Christ, and through faith in his bloud, we and all thy whole Church may obtain remission of our sins, and all other benefits of his passion. And here we offer and present unto thee, O Lord, our selves, our souls and bodies, to be a reasonable, holy, and lively sacrifice unto thee; humbly beseeching thee, that all we who are partakers of this holy Communion, may be *filled*[51] with thy grace and heavenly benediction. And although we be unworthy through our manifold sins, to offer unto thee any sacrifice; yet we beseech thee to accept this our bounden duty and service; not weighing our merits, but pardoning our offences, through Jesus Christ our Lord; by whom, and with whom, in the unity of the Holy Ghost, all honour and glory be unto thee, O Father Almighty, world without end. Amen.

### Or this

Almighty and everliving God, we most heartily thank thee, for that thou dost vouchsafe to feed us, who have duly received these holy Mysteries, with the spiritual food of the most precious body and bloud of thy Son our Saviour Jesus Christ; and dost *further* assure us thereby of thy favour and goodness towards us; and that *we are incorporate*[52] in the mystical body of thy Son, which is the blessed company of all faithful people; and are also heirs through hope of thy everlasting kingdom, by the merits of the most precious death and passion of thy dear Son. And we most humbly beseech thee, O Heavenly Father, so to assist us with thy grace, that we may continue in that holy fellowship, and do all such good works as thou hast prepared for us to walk in, through Jesus Christ our Lord, to whom with thee, and the Holy Ghost, be all honour and glory world without end. Amen.

Then shall be said or sung;

Glory be to God on high, and in earth peace, good will towards men. We praise thee, we bless thee, we worship thee, we glorifie thee, we give thanks to thee for thy great glory, O Lord God, heavenly King, God the Father Almighty.

O Lord, the onely begotten Son Jesus Christ; O Lord God, Lamb of God, Son of the Father, that takest away the sins of the world, have mercy upon us. Thou that takest away the sins of the world, have mercy upon us. Thou that takest away the sins of the world, receive our prayer. Thou that sittest at the right hand of God the Father, have mercy upon us.

For thou onely art *ye holy One of God,* thou onely art the Lord, *thou only art ye eternall son of God;*[53] thou onely, O Christ, with the Holy Ghost, art most high in the glory of God the Father. Amen.

Then the *Minister* (or Bishop, if he be present) shall let them depart with this Blessing.

The peace of God which passeth all understanding, keep your hearts and minds in the knowledge and love of God, and of his Son Jesus Christ our Lord: And the blessing of God Almighty, the Father, the Son, and the Holy Ghost, be amongst you, and remain with you always. Amen.

Collects to be said *when there*[54] is no Communion, every such day one or more; and the same may be said also as often as occasion shall serve, after the Collects either of Morning or Evening Prayer, Communion, or Litany, by the discretion of the Minister.

Assist us mercifully, O Lord, in these our supplications and prayers, and dispose the way of thy servants towards the attainment of everlasting salvation; that among the *changes of this* mortal life, they may ever be defended by thy most gracious and ready help, through Jesus Christ our Lord. Amen.

O Almighty Lord, and everlasting God, vouchsafe . . . .

Grant, we beseech thee, Almighty God, that the words . . .

Prevent us, O Lord, in all our doings . . . .

Almighty God the fountain of all wisdom . . . .

Almighty God, who hast promised to hear the petitions . . . .

*O God whose neverfayling Providence ordereth all things both in Heaven & Earth: we humbly beseech Thee to put away from us all hurtfull Things, & to give us those Things wch be pfitable for us, through Jesus Christ our Lord. Amen.*

*To be added here to this collect (viz for ye 8th Sunday aftr Trinity) these following the 5th. 12. 16. 17. 21. 22. 23. And the Prayer for Repentance Compos'd by A.B.S. &c in K. Jamess time, & a praeparatorie Collect for ye Comunio.*[55]

### 5

*Graut O Ld we beseech Thee, yt ye Cours of ys world may be so peaceably order'd by thy Governance, that thy Church may joyfully serve Thee in all godly quietness, through Jes: Ch. or Ld Amen.*

### 8 as above
### 12

*Alm: & Evr God, who art allwaies more ready to hear than we to pray, & art wont to give more than eithr we desire or deserve, Pour down upo us ye abudance of thy mercy, forgiving us those things whereof or Conscience is afraid, & giving us those good Things wch we are not worthy to ask but through ye mer: & med: of J.Ch. thy So or Ld. Amen.*

### 16

*O Ld we beseech thee, let thy cotinuall Grace*[56] *cleans & defend thy church; & because it canot continue in safety wthout thy succor,*[57] *prserve it evrmore by thy help & goodness thro J. Ch. or Ld. Amen.*

### 17

*Lord we pray thee yt thy Grace may allwaies prvent & follow us, & make us continually to be given to all good works, thro J. Ch. or Ld. Amen.*

### 21

*Graut, we beseech thee, mercifull Ld, to thy faithfull people pardon & Peace, that They may be cleansed from all their sinns, & serve Thee with a quiet mind, through J. Ch. or Ld. Amen.*

*22*

*Ld, we beseech Thee, to keep thy household ye church in continual Godliness, that through thy ptection, It may be free fro all Advrsities, & devoutly given to serve Thee in good works, to the glory of thy name, through Jesus Christ our Ld. Amen.*

*23*

*O God, or Refuge & Strength, who art ye Author of all Godliness, be ready, we beseech Thee, to hear ye devout prayrs of thy church; & grant yt those things wch we ask faythfully we may obtain effectually, through Jesus Christ our Lord. Amen.*

*Collect for Repentance*

*See warning for ye Comun:*

(58)Upon the *Lords days* and other Holidays (if there be no Communion) shall be said all that is appointed at the Communion, until the end of the general Prayer (For the good estate of the Catholick Church of Christ) together with one or moe of these Collects last before rehearsed, concluding with the Blessing.

*There* shall be no Celebration of the Lords Supper, except there be a convenient number to communicate with *the Minister, Three, at ye least.*

*In* Cathedral and Collegiate Churches and Colledges, where there are many Priests and Deacons, they shall all Receive the Communion with the *Minister every Lords day except*(59) they have a reasonable cause to the contrary. *And in evry Great Town or Parish there shall be a Comunion once a Moneth: And in every Parish at least four times in ye year, yt is on Christmass-day, Easter-day, Whitsunday, & some Lords day soon after Harvest at ye Ministers discretion. And All Ministers shall exhort their People to comunicate frequently. And evry Parishioner shall comunicate at least three Times in ye year of wch Easter to be one.*

And to take away all occasion of dissension, and superstition, which any Person hath or might have concerning the Bread and Wine, it shall suffice that the Bread be such as is usual to be eaten; but the best and purest wheat Bread that conveniently may be gotten.

And if any of the Bread and Wine remain unconsecrated, the Curate shall have it to his own use: but if any remain of that which was Consecrated, it shall not be carried out of the Church, but the *Minister*, and such other of the Communicants as he shall then call unto him, shall immediately after the Blessing, reverently eat and drink the same.(61)

The Bread and Wine for the Communion shall be provided by the Curate and the Church-wardens, at the Charges of the Parish.

And note, *yt yearly* at Easter every parishioner shall reckon with the Parson, Vicar, or Curate, or his or their Deputy, or Deputies, and pay to them or him all Ecclesiastical Duties, accustomably due, then and at that time to be paid.

After the Divine Service ended,[62] *or at some other Convenient Time,* the Money given at the Offertory shall be disposed of to such pious and charitable uses, as the Minister and Church-wardens shall think fit. Wherein if thy disagree, it shall be disposed of as the Ordinary shall appoint.

Whereas it is ordained in this Office for the Administration of the Lords Supper, that the Communicants should receive the same Kneeling; (which Order is well meant, for a signification of our humble and grateful acknowledgement of the benefits of Christ therein given to all worthy Receivers, and for the avoiding of such profanation, and disorder in the holy Communion, as might otherwise ensue) Yet, lest the same Kneeling should by any persons, either out of ignorance and infirmity, or out of malice and obstinacy, be misconstrued and depraved; It is here declared, That thereby no Adoration is intended, or ought to be done, either unto the Sacramental Bread and Wine there bodily received, or unto any Corporal Presence of Christs Natural Flesh and Bloud. For the Sacramental Bread and Wine remain still in their very Natural Substances, and therefore may not be adored; (for that were Idolatry, to be abhorred of all faithful Christians) and the Natural Body and Bloud of our Saviour Christ are in Heaven, and not here; it being against the truth of Christs Natural Body, to be at one time in more places than one.

*But, to take off all prtence of Scruple, If any, not being satisfyd herewith shall, some day in ye week before They intend to receive the holy Comunion, come to ye minister of their Parish, & declare that they are verily psuaded in Conscience that They canot receive it kneeling wthout sinn, Then ye minister shall endevour to give Them satisfaction*[63] *in this matter, after wch if they still persist, then ye minister shall give Them ye Sacramentall bread & wine in some Convenient Place or Pew wthout obliging Them to Kneel.*[64]

## THE MINISTRATION OF PUBLICK BAPTISM OF INFANTS
### To be used in the Church.

*Q. conc: a Cure by a Canon of Ministers Christning Children in other ministers Parishes without their leave, & when there is no urgent Occasion?*

The People are to be admonished, that it is most convenient that Baptism should not be administered but upon *Lords days*, and other Holy-days, when the most number of People come together . . . .

And Note, That there shall be for every male-child to be Baptized, two Godfathers and one Godmother: and for every female, one Godfather and two Godmothers.

*None are to be Sureties but such as either have receiv'd the Comunion, or are ready to do It.*

*Whereas it is appointed by ys office that all Children shall be presented by Godfathers & Godmothers,*[1] *to be Baptizd, wch is still continued according to ye antient custom of ye Church, yt so, besides ye obligation yt lies on ye Parents to breed up their children in ye Xn Religion, there may be likewise other Sureties to see yt ye Parents do their duty, & to look to ye Xn educatio of ye psons baptizd, in case of ye default or death of ye Parents: yet there being some difficulties in observing ys good & useful constitution, It is hereby pvided yt, if any pson comes to ye Minister & tells him he canot coveniently pcure Godfathers & Godmothers for his child, & yt he desires his child may be baptizd upo ye Engagement of ye Parent or Parents only, in yt Case, ye minister, after discours wth him, if he persists, shall be oblig'd to baptize such child or children upo ye Suretyship of ye Parent or Parents, or some other near Relation or Friends.*

When there are children to be Baptized, the Parents *(q)* shall give knowledge thereof over night, or in the morning before the beginning of Morning Prayer, to the Curate. And then the *Sureties* and the People, with the children must be ready at the Font, either immediately after the last Lesson at Morning Prayer, or else immediately after the last Lesson at Evening[2] Prayer *(if it may be)*, as the *Minister* by his discretion shall appoint. And the *Minister* coming to the Font[3] (which is then to be filled with pure water) and standing there, shall say, *if the case be in ye least doubtfull,*[4]

Hath this Child been already Baptized, or no?

If they answer, No: then shall the *Minister* proceed as followeth.[5]

Dearly beloved, forasmuch as all men are conceived . . . .

Then shall the *Minister* say,

116

Let us pray.

Almighty and everlasting God, who of thy great mercy didst save Noah and his family in the Ark from perishing by water, and also didst safely lead the children of Israel thy people through the Red Sea, figuring thereby thy holy baptism; and *after ye* Baptism[6] of thy well-beloved Son Jesus Christ in the river Jordan, didst *appoint water to be used in this Sacrament for*[7] the mystical washing away of sin; We beseech thee for thine infinite mercies, that thou wilt mercifully look upon this child; wash him and sanctifie him with the Holy Ghost, that he being delivered from thy wrath, may be received into the Ark of Christs Church; *& perservering in Fayth, hope & charity, may so pass through this present Evill world, that finally He may come to Evrlasting life, through Jes. Ch. or Ld. Amen.*[8]

Almighty and immortal God, the aid of all that need, the helper of all that flee to thee for succour, the life of them that believe, and the resurrection of the dead; We call upon thee for this infant, that he coming to thy holy Baptism, *may be regenerated & receive remission of sin.*[9] Receive him, O Lord, as thou hast promised by thy well-beloved Son, saying, Ask, and ye shall have; seek, and ye shall find; knock and it shall be opened unto you: So give now unto us that ask; let us that seek find; open the gate unto us that knock; that this infant may enjoy the everlasting benediction of thy heavenly washing, and may come to the eternal Kingdom which thou hast promised, by Christ our Lord. Amen.

**Then shall the People stand up, and the *Minister* shall say,**

Hear the words of the Gospel, written by Saint Mark in the Tenth Chapter, at the Thirteenth verse.

They brought young children to Christ . . . .

**After the Gospel is read, the Minister shall make this brief Exhortation upon the words of the Gospel.**

Beloved, ye hear in this Gospel the words of our Saviour Christ, that he commanded the children to be brought to him; how he blamed those that would have kept them from him; how he exhorteth all men to follow their innocency. Ye perceive how by his outward gesture and deed[10] he declared his good will toward them; for he embraced them in his arms, he laid his hands upon them, and blessed them. Doubt ye not therefore, but *stedfastly* believe, that *according to his gracious Covenant*, he will likewise favourably receive this present infant, that he will embrace him in the arms of his mercy, that he will give unto him the blessing of eternal life, and make him a partaker of his everlasting Kingdom.[11] Wherefore we being thus perswaded of the good will of our heavenly Father towards this infant, declared by his Son Jesus Christ, and nothing doubting but that he favourably alloweth this charitable work of ours, in bringing this Infant to his holy Baptism, let us faithfully and devoutly give thanks unto him, and say,

117

Almighty and everlasting God, heavenly Father . . . .

*Then shall ye Minister speaking to ye Congregation, ask,*[12] *Who are ye Sureties for this child?*

*Then may ye Parent or Parents prsent ye Sureties, if there be any other besides Themselves.*

Dearly beloved, ye have brought this Child here to be Baptized, ye have prayed that our Lord Jesus Christ would vouchsafe to receive him, to release him *of sin*,[13] to sanctifie him with the Holy Ghost, to give him the Kingdom of heaven, and everlasting life. Ye have heard also that our Lord Jesus Christ hath promised in his Gospel to grant all these things that ye have prayed for: which promise he, for his part, will most surely keep and perform. Wherefore after this promise made by Christ, this Infant must also faithfully for his part, promise by you that are his Sureties (until he come of age to take it upon himself) that he will renounce the devil and all his works, and constantly believe Gods holy Word, and obediently keep his commandments.

## I demand therefore,

Dost thou in the Name of this child, renounce the devil and all his works, *the pomps and vanities of ye wicked world*, with all covetous desires of the same, and *all ye sinfull Lusts*[14] of the flesh so that thou wilt not follow nor be led by them?

Answer; I renounce them all.

## Minister.

Dost thou believe in God . . . .

Answer;     All this I stedfastly believe.

Minister;   Wilt thou be baptized in this Fayth?

Answer;     That is my desire.

Minister;   Wilt thou then obediently keep Gods holy will and commandments, and walk in the same all the days of thy life?

Answer;     I will, *God being my helper*.[15]

*Then shall the Minister say,*

O merciful God, grant that the old Adam[16] in this child may be so buried . . . .

118

Almighty everliving God, whose most dearly beloved Son Jesus Christ, for the forgiveness of our sins, did shed out of his most precious side both water and bloud, and gave commandment to his disciples, that they should go teach all Nations, and baptize them in the Name of the Father, and of the Son, and of the Holy Ghost;[17] Regard we beseech thee, the supplications of thy Congregation; sanctifie this Water to the mystical washing away of sin: and grant that this child, now to be baptized therein, may receive the fulness of thy grace, and ever remain in the number of thy faithful and elect children, through Jesus Christ our Lord. Amen.

Then the *Minister* shall take the child into his hands, and shall say to the *Sureties,*

Name this child.

And then naming it after them, *he shall pour or sprinkle water upon It; or (if They shall certify Him that ye Child may well endure It) he shall dip It in ye Water discreetly & warily saying,*[18]

N. I Baptize thee In the Name of the Father, and of the Son, and of the Holy Ghost. Amen.

Then shall the priest say,

We receive this child into the Congregation of Christs flock, and
* do sign him with the sign of the cross,[19] *to mind him hereafter not to* be ashamed to confess the Faith of Christ crucified, *but* manfully to fight under his banner against sin, the world, and the devil; and to continue Christs faithful souldier and servant unto his lives end. Amen.

*Here the Priest shall make a cross<br>upon the child's forehead.

Then shall the Priest say,

Seeing now, dearly beloved brethren, that this child *is regenerated*[20] and grafted into the body of Christs Church, let us give thanks unto Almighty God for these benefits, and with one accord make our prayers unto him, that this child may lead the rest of his life according to this beginning.

Then shall be said, all kneeling,

Our Father . . . .

Then shall the *Minister* say,

We yeild thee hearty thanks, most merciful Father, that it hath pleased thee to regenerate this Infant with *water and* thy holy Spirit,[21] to receive him for thine own child by adoption, and to incorporate him into thy holy Church . . . .

119

Then all standing up, *the Minister* shall say to the *Sureties* this Exhortation following;

Forasmuch as this child hath promised by you his Sureties . . . .[22]

*Then ye Minister shall say to ye Parents, if there, or to some of their near Relations. You have heard now what is yr duty, do you pmise conscientiously to perform It?*

Then shall he add, and say

Ye are to take care that this child be brought to the Bishop to be confirmed by him, so soon as he can say the Creed, the Lords Prayer, and the Ten Commandments in the Vulgar tongue,[23] and be further instructed in the Church-Catechism *& be otherwise duly praepared according to ye Charge in ye Exhortation to be made before Confirmation.*

| | |
|---|---|
| *This rubric is either to be omitted, or to be pved by pticular places of Scripture to be sett in ye Margent.* | It is certain by Gods Word, that children which are Baptized, dying before they commit actual sin, are undoubtedly saved.[24] |

*Whereas ye sign of ye Cross is, by this Office, appointed to be used in Baptism according to ye Antient & laudable Custom of ye Church, It is not thereby intended to add any new Rite to ye Sacrament as a part of it, or as necessary to it; or that ye Using that Sign is of any Vertue or Efficacy of itself; but onely to remember all Christians of ye Death & Cross of Christ, wch is their Hope & their Glory, & to put ym in Mind of their obligation[25] to bear the Cross in such manner as God shall think fitt to lay it upon them, & to become conformable to Christ in his Sufferings.*

| | |
|---|---|
| *This was proposed but not agreed to, but left to further considratio.* | *Yet if there are any who, not satisfied with this Declaration, shall come some day before they offer their Children to be baptised, & declare to their Minister yt they are perswaded in their Conscience, that they cannot without Sin offer their Child to be baptiz'd according to the Form here prescrib'd, by admitting to ye Sign of the Cross, then it shall not be used.[26]* |

*If any Minister at his Institution shall declare to his Bp. yt He canot satisfy his Conscience in Baptizing any wth ye Sign of ye Cross; then ye Bp shall dispense with Him in yt pticular, & shall name a Curate who shall baptize ye children of Those in that Parish who desire it may be done with ye Sign of ye Cross according to ys Office.*

# THE MINISTRATION OF PRIVATE BAPTISM OF
## CHILDREN IN *CASES OF NECESSITIE*.[1]

The *Ministers* of every Parish shall often admonish the People, that they defer not the Baptism of their children longer than the first or second Sunday next after their Birth, or other Holy-day falling between, unless upon a great and reasonable cause, to be approved by the *Minister.*

And also they shall warn them . . . .

First let the Minister of the parish (or in his absence, any other lawful Minister that can be procured) with them that are present, call upon God, and say the Lords Prayer, and so many of the Collects appointed to be said before in the Form of Publick Baptism, as the time and present exigence will suffer. And then, *the Minister shall ask the Parents or Parent or ye Person that prsents ye Child,*

*Min. Dost thou &c (as in public baptism) if ye Exigence will suffr It. And ye Sign of ye Cross to be used where ye Parents or those yt prsent ye Child are satisfy'd.*[2]

*Otherwise he shall pceed thus.*

*Min. Dost thou, in the name of this Child, believe ye Articles of the Christian fayth?*

*Answer.*     *All these I stedfastly believe.*

*Min.*         *Dost thou renounce ye world the flesh & ye Devill?*

*Ans.*         *I renounce Them All.*

*Min.*         *Wilt thou keep ye Comandments of Christ and psevere in Them?*

*Answer.*     *I will, God being my helper.*

The child being named by some one that is present, the Minister shall pour water upon it, saying these words;

N. I Baptize thee in the Name of the Father, and of the Son, and of the Holy Ghost. Amen.

Then all kneeling down, the Minister shall give thanks unto God, and say,

We yield thee hearty thanks, most merciful Father, that it hath pleased thee to regenerate this infant *by water & ye holy Ghost;*[3] to receive him for thine own child by adoption, and to incorporate him into thy holy Church. And we humbly beseech thee to grant, that as he is now made partaker of the Death of thy Son, so he may be also of his Resurrection: and that finally with the residue of thy Saints, he may inherit thine everlasting Kingdom, through the same thy Son Jesus Christ our Lord. Amen.

(4) And let them not doubt. . . .

I certifie you . . . .

But if the child were baptized . . . .

And if the Minister shall find by the answers . . . .
I Certifie you, that in this case all is well done, and according to due order, concerning the baptizing of this child; who being born in original sin, and in the wrath of God,(5) is now by the laver of Regeneration . . . .

They brought young children to Christ . . . .

(6) After the Gospel is read, the Minister shall make this brief exhortation upon the words of the Gospel.

Beloved, ye hear in this Gospel the words of our Saviour Christ, that he commanded the children to be brought unto him; how he blamed those that would have kept them from him; how he exhorted all men to follow their innocency. Ye perceive how by his outward gesture and deed he embraced them in his arms, he laid his hands upon them, and blessed them. Doubt ye not therefore, but *stedfastly believe that according to his gracious Covenant* he hath likewise favourably received this present Infant . . . .

Our Father . . . .

Almighty and everlasting God, heavenly Father, we give thee humble thanks . . . .

(7) Then shall the *Minister* demand the Name of the Child, which being by the *Sureties* pronounced, the Minister shall say,

Dost thou in the name of this child, renounce the devil and all his works, the *pomps and* (8) *world,* with all covetous desires of the same, and *all ye sinfull Lusts of the flesh,* so that thou wilt not follow nor be led by them?

Answer.  I renounce them all.

### Minister.

Dost thou believe in God . . . .

Answer.  All this I stedfastly believe.

Minister.  (9) Wilt thou then obediently keep Gods holy will and commandments, and walk in the same all the days of thy life?

Answer.  I will, *God being my helper.*

122

**Then shall the Priest say,**

We receive this child into the Congregation of Christs flock, and do * sign him with the sign of the cross, in token that hereafter he shall not be ashamed to confess the Faith of Christ crucified, and manfully to fight under his banner, against sin, the world, and the devil; and to continue Christs faithful souldier and servant unto his lives end. Amen.

**\* The Priest shall make a cross upon the childs forehead.**
**Then shall the Priest say,**

*Added Latelie Q*
*by ye Printer*
*in K James's time*[11]

[10] Seeing now, dearly beloved brethren, that this child is *(by Baptism)*

*regenerated*, and grafted into the body of Christs Church, let us give thanks unto Almighty God for these benefits, and with one accord make our prayers unto him, that he may lead the rest of his life according to this beginning.

**Then shall the Priest say,**

We yield thee hearty thanks most merciful Father, that it hath pleased thee to regenerate this Infant. . . .

**Then all standing up, the Minister shall make this Exhortation to the *Sureties.***

Forasmuch as this child hath promised by you his Sureties . . . .

**But if they which bring the Infant to the Church do make uncertain answers to the Priests questions, as that it cannot appear that the child was Baptized with Water, In the Name of the Father, and of the Son, and of the Holy Ghost (which are essential parts of Baptism) then let the *Minister* Baptize it in the Form before appointed for Publick Baptism of Infants; saving that at the *pouring of water on the child or sprinkling or dipping of It in the Font,* he shall use this Form of Words,**

**If thou art not already Baptized, N. I Baptize thee, In the Name of the Father, and of the Son, and of the Holy Ghost. Amen.**

## THE MINISTRATION OF BAPTISM TO SUCH AS ARE OF RIPER YEARS AND ARE ABLE TO ANSWER FOR THEMSELVES.

**When any such persons, as are of riper years, are to be baptized, timely notice shall be given to the Bishop, or whom he shall appoint for that purpose, a Week before**[1] **at the least, *if it can be convenientlie done,* by the Parents, or some other discreet persons: . . . .**

And if they shall be found fit, then the *chosen witnesses*[2] (the people being assembled upon the *Lords day* or Holy-day appointed) shall be ready to present them at the Font *(unless ye Bp shall direct othrwise)* immediately after the Second Lesson, either at Morning or Evening Prayer,[3] *or at some other convenient Time,* as the *Minister* in his discretion shall think fit.

And standing there the *Minister* shall ask . . . .
Dearly Beloved . . . .[4]
Then shall the Priest say[5] . . . .
Almighty and everlasting God[6] . . . .
Almighty and immortal God . . . .
Then shall the people stand up . . . .
Hear the words of the Gospel . . . .
There was a man . . . .
After which . . . .
Beloved, ye hear in this Gospel . . . .
Almighty and everlasting God . . . .

Then the *Minister* shall speak to the persons to be baptised on this wise:

Well-beloved, who are come hither . . . .

Then shall the *minister* demand of each of the Persons to be Baptized, severally, these Questions following.

### Question.

Dost thou renounce the devil and all his works, the *pomps and vanities of this wicked world,* with all covetous desires of the same, and *all the sinfull Lusts* of the flesh, so that thou wilt not follow nor be led by them?

Answer. I renounce them all.
Dost thou believe . . . .
Answer. All this I stedfastly believe.
Wilt thou be baptized . . . .
Wilt thou then obediently . . . .
O Merciful God, grant that the old Adam . . . .
Almighty, everliving God . . . .
Then shall the Priest take . . . .
N I Baptize thee . . . .
Then shall the Priest . . . .
We receive this person . . . .
Then shall the *minister say,*
Seeing now, dearly beloved . . . .
Then shall be said . . . .
Our Father . . . .

We yield thee humbly thanks, O heavenly Father . . . reigneth
with thee, in the unity of the same holy Spirit, *ever one God
world without End. Amen.*

**Then all standing up, the *Minister* shall use this Exhorta-
tion following; speaking to the *Sureties* first.**[7]
Forasmuch as these persons . . . .[8]

# A CATECHISM, THAT IS TO SAY, AN INSTRUCTION TO BE LEARNED OF EVERY PERSON, BEFORE HE BE BROUGHT TO BE CONFIRMED BY THE BISHOP

*This to be retaind, & also A larger One to be considerd of, &
that made by D. Williams to be pposd in Convocation, in order to a
Review & Acceptance of It.*[1]

## Question.

What is your Name?

## Answer.

N. or M.

## Question.

Who gave you this Name?

## Answer.

My *Sureties* in my Baptism,[2] wherein I was made a Member of
Christ, the child of God, and an *heir* of the kingdom of heaven.

## Question.
What did your *Sureties* then for you?

## Answer.

They did promise and vow three things in my Name.[3] First, that
I should renounce the devil and all his works, the pomps and
*vanitys*[4] of this wicked world *with all covetous desires of ye same,*
and all the sinful lusts of the flesh: Secondly, that I should believe
all the Articles of the Christian Faith. And thirdly, that I should keep
Gods holy will and Commandments, and walk in the same all the
days of my life.

## Question.

Dost thou not think that thou art bound to believe, and to do, as
they have promised for thee?

## Answer.

Yes verily; and by Gods help so I will. And I heartily thank our
heavenly Father, that he hath called me to this state of salvation,
through Jesus Christ our Saviour. And I pray unto God to give me
his grace, that I may continue in the same unto my lives end.

**Catechist.**

Rehearse the Articles of thy belief.

**Answer.**

I Believe in God . . . .

**Question.**

What dost thou chiefly learn in these Articles of thy belief?

**Answer.**

First, I learn to believe in God the Father, who hath made me, and all the world.

Secondly, in God the Son, who hath redeemed me, and all mankind.

Thirdly, in God the Holy Ghost, who sanctifieth me, and all the elect people of God.

**Question.**

*What do you learn further in this Creed?*

**Answer.**

*I learn that Christ hath had,*[5] *still hath & ever will have a Church somewhere on Earth.*

**Question.**

*Wt are you there taught concerning this Church?*

**Answer.**

*I am taught yt it is Catholic or Universal, as it receivs into it all Nations upon ye Profession of ye Christian Fayth in baptism.*

**Question.**

*What priviledges belong to Christians by their being receivd*[6] *into this Catholic Church?*

**Answer.**

[7]*Four. First ye Comunion of Saints or fellowship of all true Christians in Fayth, wp & charity. Secondly, ye Forgiveness of Sins obtained by ye Sacrifice of Christs death, & given to us, upon Fayth in him, & repetance fro dead works. Thirdly, the Rising again of or bodys at ye last day to a State of Glory. Fourthly, Everlasting life wth our Saviour in ye Kingdom of Heaven.*

**Question.**

You said that your Godfathers and Godmothers did promise for you, that you should keep Gods Commandments.[8] Tell me how many there be?

**Answer.**

Ten.[9]

**Question.**

Which are they?

### Answer.

The same which God spake in the twentieth Chapter of Exodus, saying,

*To be put as in Exodus.*[10]

### Question.

What dost thou chiefly learn by these Commandments?

### Answer.

I learn two things: my duty towards God, and my duty towards my Neighbour.

### Question.

What is thy duty towards God?

### Answer.

My duty towards God is to believe in him, to fear him, and to love him with all my heart, with all my mind, with all my soul, and with all my strength; to worship him, to give him thanks, to put my whole trust in him, to call upon him, to honour his holy Name and his Word; and to serve him truly all the days of my life, *especially on Lords days.*[11]

### Question.

*Now to apply (or referr q) this to the 4 first comandments. Tell me first wt you learn by ye first of Them?*[12]

### Answer.

*I learn yt it is my duty towards God to believe in him, to fear him, &c strength.*

### Question.

*Wt learn you by ye Second Comandmt?*[13]

### Answer.

*To worship him, & him only, to give him thaks &c upo him.*

### Question.

*Wt learn you by ye 3d Comandment?*

### Answer.

*To Honour his holy name & his word.*

### Question.

*Wt learn you by ye fourth Comandment?*

### Answer.

*To serve him truly all ye days of my life, especially on Lords days.*

### Question.

What is thy duty towards thy Neighbour?

### Answer.

My duty towards my Neighbour, is to love him as my self . . . .

*Q.*

*Now to apply (or referr) this to ye 6 last Comandments; Tell me wt you learn by ye 5t?*[14]

*A.*

*To love honr &c betters.*

*Q.*

*Wt learn you by the 6t Comandmt?*

*A.*

*To hurt no body by word or deed.*

*Q.*

*Wt &c by ye 7th?*

*A.*

*To keep my body in temp. sob. & chastity.*

*Q.*

*Wt &c by ye 8th?*

*A.*

*To be true & just &c stealing.*

*Q.*

*Wt &c by ye 9th?*

*A.*

*To keep my tongue fro evill speaking, lying & slandering.*

*Q.*

*Wt &c by ye tenth?*

*A.*

*Not to covet &c call me.*

### Catechist.
My good child, know this . . . .

### Answer.
Our Father . . . .

### Question.
What desirest thou of God in this Prayer?

### Answer.
I desire my Lord God our heavenly Father . . . . and that it will please him to save and defend us in all dangers ghostly and bodily;[15] and that . . . .

*Q.*

*Now to apply this to ye several Petitions. Tell me wt you desire of God in ye 1st Petition.*[16]

128

**A.**

*I desire my Lord God &c that we may worship him.* [17]

**Q.**

*Wt desire you in ye 2d & 3d Petitions.* [18]

**A.**

*That we may serve him & obey him as we ought to do.*

**Q.**

*Wt desire you in ye 4th.*

**A.**

*That he would send us all things needfull both for or Souls & Bodies.*

**Q.**

*Wt desire you in ye 5t.*

**A.**

*That he will be mercifull unto us & forgive us or sinns, & yt we may have grace to forgive or Enemies.*

**Q.**

*Wt des you in ye 6t.*

**A.**

*That &c evrlasting death.*

**Q.**

*What is ye conclusion?*

**A.**

*This I trust he will do &c Amen. or So be It.*

### Question.
How many Sacraments hath Christ ordained in his Church?

### Answer.
Two *onely; that* is to say, Baptism, and the Supper of the Lord. [19]

### Question.
*Are These necessary.*

### Answer.
*Yes. They are generally necessary to Salvation.*

### Question.
What meanest thou by this word Sacrament?

### Answer.
I mean an outward and visible sign of an inward and spiritual grace, given unto us, ordained by Christ himself, as a means whereby we receive the same, and a pledge to assure us thereof.

**Question.**

How many parts are there in a Sacrament?

**Answer.**

Two: the outward visible sign, and the inward spiritual grace.

**Question.**

What is the outward visible *sign in*[20] Baptism?

**Answer.**

Water: wherein the person is baptized, In the Name of the Father, and of the Son, and of the Holy Ghost.

**Question.**

What is the inward and spiritual grace?

**Answer.**

A death unto sin, and a new birth unto righteousness: for being by nature born in sin, and the children of wrath,[21] we are hereby made the children of grace.

**Question.**

*What are persons to be baptized to be engag'd unto?*

**Answer.**

Repentance,[22] whereby they forsake sin; and faith, whereby they stedfastly believe the promises of God, made to them[23] in that Sacrament.

**Question.**

Why then are Infants baptized, when by reason of their tender age they cannot perform *These conditions of Fayth & Repentance?*

**Answer.**

Because they promise *both these*[24] by their Sureties; which promise, when they come of age, them selves are bound to perform.

**Question.**

Why was the Sacrament of the Lords Supper ordained?

**Answer.**

For the continual remembrance of the sacrifice of the death of Christ, and of the benefits which we receive thereby, *& to renew our Engagement to all ye Duties we ow to Him yt dy'd for us.*

**Question.**

*What are ye outward & visible signs in the Lords Supper?*[25]

**Answer.**

Bread and Wine, which the Lord hath commanded to be received.[26]

**Question.**

*What are the things signified by ye Bread & wine?*[27]

### Answer.

The Body and Bloud of Christ, which *were offered for us upon ye Cross once for All.*[28]

### Question.

*What is ye inward & spiritual Grace?*

### Answer.

*The Benefits of ye Sacrifice of Christs body & blood wch are verily & indeed taken & receiv'd by ye Faythfull in ye Lords Supper.*

### Question.

*What are these Benefits there receiv'd by ye faithfull?*

### Answer.

*Remission of Sinns & all blessings wch follow upon It; & particularly the strengthening & refreshing* of our souls by the body and bloud of Christ, as our bodies are by the bread and wine.

### Question.

What is required of them who come to the Lords Supper?

### Answer.

To examine themselves *1* whether they repent them truly of their former sins, stedfastly purposing to lead a new life; *2 whether they have a true and lively faith* in God's mercy through Christ, *3 whether they are devoutly dispos'd to make a Thakfull* remembrance of his death, *4 whether they are* in charity with all men.

The Curate of every Parish shall diligently upon Sundays and Holy-days, *either before Evening Prayer, or* after the Second Lesson at Evening Prayer, openly in the Church Instruct and Examine so many Children of his Parish sent unto him, as he shall think convenient, in some part of this Catechism.

And all Fathers, Mothers, Masters and Dames shall *take care to instruct their children & servants & Apprentices in ye Church Catechism, And cause Them to come to ye Church at ye time appointed, & obediently to hear & be ordered by ye Curate untill such time as they be fitt for Confirmation & ye holy Comunion.*

So soon as Children are come to a competent age, *& are well instructed in ye short Catechism, & resolved to renew in their own Persons their baptismall vow, they shall be presented by their minister to ye Bp to be confirmed.*[29]

And whensoever the Bishop shall give knowledge for Children to be brought unto him for their Confirmation, the Curate of every Parish shall either bring, or send in Writing, with his Hand subscribed thereunto, the Names of all such Persons within the Parish, as he shall think fit to be presented to the Bishop to be confirmed. And if the Bishop approve of them, he shall Confirm them in the manner following.

*An Exhortation to be read the Lords day before a Confirmation.* [1]

*Dearly Beloved, I am appointed by ye Bp. to give you notice that he will be ready to Confirm such as shall be found duly prepared for it on — — — — ye*           *Day of*

It is a weighty Business that he comes about; And I signify this to you before hand to ye End yt such of you as have not yet been confirmed may have time to consider ye Vows & Promises that were made in your Name when you were Baptiz'd, & ye Obligation yt lyes on you both to observe ym all ye Days of your Lives & to renew ym in your own Persons at your Confirmation.

You ought, first of all, to read over ye Offices of Baptism, & to consider, both ye Blessings that belong to yt holy Ordinance & the Engagements which you lay under by it. You are in ye next place to consider what Sins you have committed since you have grown up to be capable of discerning between Good & Evill, and how ye Sins are aggravated by this, that they have bin so many Breaches of ye Conditions of your Baptism, & of ye Solemn Promises & Vows yt were then made to God in your Name. Of all wch I exhort & require you seriously to bethink yourselves & to repent of all your known Sins, & to amend your Lives & live like Christians.

This you must do if ever you hope to be ye better for having been admitted into that Holy Profession.

I am to mind [2] you further, that, now you are come to an Age of Discretion, You ought according to ye Charge yt was given at your Baptism, to be confirmed by ye Bishop. and in order to this you are to come to me, and to give me such an Account of your Knowledge of ye Christian Religion, according to ye Scriptures, & ye doctrine of ye Church of England, as it is set forth in ye Catechism; and your Stedfast Purpose of leading your Lives according to ye Christian Religion, that I may with a good Conscience, present you to ye Bp to be Confirmed by him.

Consider what a dreadfull thing it is to make Promises to Allmighty God, & never to think of ym afterwards, or so much as intend to keep them. Think how great a Sin it must be to lye to God, & to take his holy Name in Vain, wch he declares, whosoever does, He will not hold them Guiltless.

It is not enough for you to be able to repeat the Catechism, unless you well understand ye meaning of it, & truely believe it, & unless you give up yourselves to God with all your hearts, being fully resolved to conform yourselves in all things to his Holy Gospel: For all such as are so disposed, they may assure themselves that coming to Confirmation, & solemnly renewing their Baptismall Vow; they shall be graciously received by God, and inwardly Strengthened by

132

*his Holy Spirit to perform these holy Resolutions. Of ourselves we are not able to do it, we cannot so much as think a good Thought without his Help & Assistance; But we are assured by the promise of or Blessed Saviour, that our heavenly Father will give his Holy Spirit to Them that ask Him.*

*Come then & ask yt ye may receive, but come duly prepared according to ye Rules yt I have given you. Come wth a full Resolution not to rest with ye renewing of your Vows, but to carry them on to full Perfection, by your worthy receiving of ye Holy Comunion, assoon as may be afterwards, & so from time to time as you have Opportunity.*

*Remember you are not to look upon this as onely the Receiving of ye Bishops Blessing, but as ye Engageing of yourselves solemnly to persevere in your holy Faith, upon wch according to ye Practice of ye Apostles, & the constant Custom of ye Church of God, you are to be blessed & confirmed by him. And upon ye performing on your part you may most certainly believe yt you are sealed by ye holy Spirit of God unto ye Day of your Redemption.*

Q

*Such as have been once confirmed, should not come to be Confirm'd again, unless they have fallen under a Sentence of Excomunication, or into ye sin of Separating from ye Body of Christ: Otherwise such as come to be confirm'd over & over again; do but discover their own Ignorance of ye Nature & Design of Confirmation.*

[3]*Beware therefore as well of ye Guilt of neglecting this Benefit, when God offers it to you by his good Providence; as of carelessness in coming to it without a due Measure both of Knowledge & Faith & of Repentance & new Obedience.*

*You are to dedicate yourselves to be ye Temples of ye Living God, that He may dwell in you by his Holy Spirit. He will receive you & become your God, if you are a Willing & Obedient People. I will be your God & you shall be my Sons & Daughters saith ye Lord God Allmighty.*

[4]*Having therefore these Promises, Dearly Beloved, let us cleanse ourselves from all Filthiness both of Flesh & Spirit, perfecting Holiness in ye Fear of God. And ye good God, who by his preventing Grace has put into your Minds good Desires, enable you by his continual Help to bring ye same to good Effect; through Jesus Christ our Lord, who liveth & reigneth with ye Father & ye Holy Spirit ever one God world without End. Amen.*

133

## THE ORDER OF CONFIRMATION
## OR LAYING ON OF HANDS UPON THOSE THAT ARE
## BAPTIZED AND COME TO YEARS OF DISCRETION.

Upon the day appointed, all that are to be then Confirmed, being placed, and standing in order before the Bishop; he (or some other Minister appointed by him) shall read this Preface following.

*You have bin lately inform'd for what end you ought to come hither. And I hope that you are come prepared according to ye Exhortation then made to you; That is, with a serious Desire & Resolution openly to ratify & Confirm before the Church, with your own Mouth & Consent, what your Sureties promised in your Names, when you were baptized; and also to promise that, by ye Grace of God, you will evermore endeavour yourselves faithfully to observe such things, as You, by your own Confession, have assented unto.*[1]

Then shall the Bishop say,

Do ye here in the presence of God and of this Congregation, renew the solemn promise and vow[2] that was made in your name at your Baptism;[3] ratifying and confirming the same in your own persons, and acknowledging your selves bound to believe and to do all those things which your Godfathers and Godmothers then undertook for you.

And every one shall audibly answer,
I do.

*Q. do you renounce &c. as in baptism.*

| | |
|---|---|
| The Bishop. | Our help is in the Name of the Lord; |
| Answer. | Who hath made heaven and earth. |
| Bishop. | Blessed be the Name of the Lord, |
| Answer. | Henceforth world without end. |
| Bishop. | Lord, hear our prayers, |
| Answer. | And let our cry come unto thee. |

### Bishop

Almighty and everliving God, who has vouchsafed to regenerate these thy servants by water and the Holy Ghost[4] *for ye forgiveness of sinn. Renew & strengthen Them, we beseech Thee O Lord, more and more, by ye Holy Ghost ye Comforter, & daily increase thy Graces in Them. fill Them wth ye knowledge of thy will in all wisdom & spiritual undrstanding: & enable them to walk worthy of their holy Calling wth all lowliness & meekness. That they may be blameless and harmless ye sons of God wthout rebuke, shining as Lights in ye world, to ye prays & glory of thy name through Jesus Christ or Lord. Amen.*

Then all of them in order kneeling before the Bishop, he shall lay his Hand upon the Head of every one severally, saying,

Defend, O Lord, this thy child (or this thy servant) with thy heavenly grace, that he may continue thine for ever: and daily increase in thy holy Spirit more and more, until he come unto thy everlasting Kingdom. Amen.

Then shall the Bishop say,

The Lord be with you.

Answer. And with thy Spirit.

And (all kneeling down) the Bishop shall add,

Let us pray.

Our Father, which art in heaven; Hallowed be thy Name. Thy Kingdom come. Thy will be done in earth, As it is in heaven. Give us this day our daily bread. And forgive us our trespasses, As we forgive them that trespass against us. And lead us not into temptation; But deliver us from evil. *For thine &c Amen.*

### And this Collect.

Almighty and everlasting God, who makest us both to will and to do those things that be good and acceptable unto thy divine Majesty; We make our humble supplications unto thee for these thy servants upon *whom we*[5] have now laid our *hands. Let* thy Fatherly hand, we beseech thee, ever be over them; let thy holy Spirit ever be with them; and so lead them in the knowledge and obedience of thy Word, that in the end they may obtain everlasting life, through our Lord Jesus Christ, who with thee and the Holy Ghost liveth and reigneth, ever one God, world without end. Amen.

O Almighty Lord, and everlasting God, vouchsafe we beseech thee, to direct . . . .

*Accept good Lord of ye dedication wch these thy Servants have made of Themselves unto thee by ye Renewall of their baptismall Vow & Covenant. And as They have now given up Themselves unto Thee & consented to be governed in all Things by thy will: so do Thou vouchsafe to receive Them into thy speciall favour & Grace, to fulfill in Them all ye good pleasure of Thy Goodness & ye work of Fayth wth power. Possess their minds perpetually wth a serious & lively remembrance of what they have now pmisd. Confirm & settle ye godly resolutions They have now made. Sanctify Them throughout that They may become ye Temples of ye Holy Ghost, & in ye End be presented faultless before ye prsence of thy glory with exceeding Joy, through Jesus Christ or Ld. Amen.*

135

*Then shall follow this exhortatio to ye confirmed who are required to stay and hear It.*

(6)*Dearly Beloved you have now dedicated yrselvs in yr own psons to ye fear & service of God, & have pfessed yr Fayth in or Ld Jesus Christ. I do therefore require & charge you, as you will aswr It in ye great day of ye Lord, yt you observe Religiously ye vows wch ye have now made, & walk worthy of yr holy Calling. That so yr Conversation may be in all things such as becomes ye Gospell of Christ. Mortify all yr unruly Appetites & inordinate Affections. Abstain from Adultery, Fornication, Uncleanness & Covetousness wch is Idolatry, for wch Things sake ye wrath of God cometh upo ye children of disobedience: put away likewise all Anger, wrath, malice, evill speaking, Lying, Swearing & filthy comunication out of yr mouths; & put on as ye Elect of God, Holy & Beloved, bowells of mercies, kindness, humbleness of mind, meekness, & Long-suffering. Be ye Followers of Christ. Take his yoke & learn of Him, who was meek & lowly in heart, & be ye holy as He who has called you was holy, in all manner of Conversation. Be ye obedient to yr Parents & masters, diligent in yr Callings, allways building up yrselves in ye Love of God, looking for ye mercy of or Ld Jesus Christ unto eternall life. He who establisheth us wth you in Ch. Jesus, & hath anointed us, is God who hath also sealed us, & given us ye earnest of his Spirit in our hearts. And if you continue faithfull to ye death, He will give you ye crown of Life. But if any man draws back, his soul shall have no Pleasure in Him, since he hath grieved ye holy Spirit of Grace. for, if after you have escaped ye Pollutions of the Pollutions of ye world through ye knowledge of or Ld & Saviour Jesus Christ, you are again entangled therein & overcome; yr latter End will be wors than yr beginning. Watch ye therefore & pray yt you entr not into Temptation, for ye Spirit indeed is willing, but ye flesh is weak. And seing ye are compassed about wth such a cloud of witnesses, lay aside evry weight, & run wth patience ye race yt is set before you. Be you stedfast, unmoveable, allways abounding in ye work of ye Lord, forasmuch as yr Labour is not in vain in ye Lord. And I pray God to sanctify you wholly, yt yr whole spirit & soul & body may be prserved blameless unto ye coming of our Ld Jesus Christ.*

*Then ye Bishop* shall bless them, saying thus,

The blessing of God Almighty, The Father, the Son, and the Holy Ghost, be upon you, and remain with you for ever. Amen.

And there shall none be admitted to *Confirmation, but such as shall be judged fitt to receive the Comunion upon ye next Occasion.*

# THE FORM OF SOLEMNIZATION OF MATRIMONY.

*The considration about restraining Licences to be referred to ye Canon.*

*see at ye End of ye Litany* First the Banns of all that are to be Married together, must be published in the Church three several Sundays (or Holy-days) in the time of Divine Service; the *Minister* saying after the accustomed manner,

I publish the Banns of Marriage . . . .

At the day and time appointed for Solemnization of Matrimony, the Persons to be Married shall come into the body of the Church with their Friends and Neighbours: And there standing together, the Man on the right Hand, and the Woman on the left, the *Minister* shall say,

Dearly Beloved, we are gathered together here in the sight of God . . . . like brute beasts that have no understanding;[1] but reverently, discreetly, advisedly, soberly and in the fear of God, duly considering the causes for which Matrimony was ordained.

First, it was ordained for the *Blessing* of Children,[2] to be brought up in the fear and nurture of the Lord, and to the praise of his holy Name.

Secondly, it was ordained for a remedy against sin, and to avoid fornication, that such persons as have not the gift of continency, might Marry, and keep themselves undefiled members of Christs Body.

Thirdly, it was ordained for the mutual society, help and comfort, that the one ought to have of the other both in prosperity and adversity: Into which holy Estate these two persons present come now to be joyned. Therefore if any man can shew any just cause why they may not lawfully be joyned together, let him now speak, or else hereafter for ever hold his peace.

And also speaking unto the Persons that shall be Married, he shall say,

I Require and charge you both, (as ye will answer at the dreadful day of judgement, when the secrets of all hearts shall be disclosed) that if either of you know any impediment why ye may not lawfully be joyned together in Matrimony, ye do now confess it. For be ye well assured, that so many as are *married*[3] together otherwise then Gods Word doth allow, are not joyned together by God, neither is their Matrimony lawful.

At which day of Marriage . . . .[4]

If no impediment be alledged, then shall the Curate say unto the man,

N wilt thou have this Woman to thy wedded Wife . . . .

The Man shall answer; I will.

Then shall the Priest say unto the Woman,

N wilt thou have this Man to thy wedded Husband . . . .

The Woman shall answer; I will.

Then shall the Minister say,

Who giveth this Woman to be Married to this Man?

Then shall they give their Troth to each other in this manner.

The Minister receiving the Woman at her Fathers or Friends Hands, shall cause the Man with his right Hand to take the Woman by her right Hand, and to say after him as followeth.

I N take thee N to my wedded Wife . . . .

Then shall they loose their Hands, and the Woman with her right Hand taking the Man by his right Hand, shall likewise say after the Minister;

I N take thee N to my wedded Husband . . . .

Then shall they again loose their Hands, and the Man shall give unto the Woman a Ring *(wch is here used only as a civil Ceremonie, & pledge)* laying the same upon the Book, with the accustomed Duty to the Priest and Clerk. And the Priest taking the Ring, shall deliver it unto the Man, to put it upon the fourth Finger of the Womans left Hand. And the Man holding the Ring there, and taught by the Priest, shall say,[5]

*With this Ring I thee wed, with my worldly Goods I Thee endow: & by this our marriage we become One according to Gods holy Institution. And this I declare in ye prsence of Almighty God, Fathr Sonn & Holy Ghost. Amen.*[6]

Then the Man leaving the Ring upon the fourth Finger of the Womans left Hand, they shall both kneel down, and the Minister shall say,

Let us pray.

O Eternal God, Creator and Preserver of all mankind, giver of all spiritual grace, the author of everlasting life; Send thy blessing upon these thy servants, this Man and this Woman,[7] whom we bless in thy Name; that as Isaac and Rebecca lived faithfully together, so these Persons may surely perform and keep the Vow and Covenant betwixt them *made, and* may ever remain in perfect love and peace together, and live according to thy laws, through Jesus Christ our Lord. Amen.

Then shall the *minister* joyn their right Hands together, and say,

Those whom God hath joyned together, let no man put asunder.

Then shall the Minister speak unto the People.

Forasmuch as N and N have consented together in holy Wedlock, and have witnessed the same before God and this Company, and thereto have given and pledged their Troth either to other, and have declared the same by giving and receiving of a Ring, and by joyning of Hands; I pronounce that they be Man and Wife together, In the Name of the Father, and of the Son, and of the Holy Ghost. Amen.

And the Minister shall add this Blessing.

God the Father, God the Son, and God the Holy Ghost, bless, preserve and keep you; the Lord mercifully with his favour look upon you, and so fill you with all spiritual benediction and grace, that ye may so live together in this life, that in the world to come ye may have life everlasting. Amen.

Then the Minister or Clerks *being eithr in ye body of ye Church, or at the Comunion Table* shall say or sing this Psalm following.[8]

Beati Omnes, Psalm 128

*Q. New Transl.*[9]

Or this Psalm.

Deus misereatur, Psalm 67.

God be merciful unto us and bless us . . . .

The Psalm ended, and the Man and the Woman *kneeling, the minister* shall say,

|  | Lord, have mercy upon us. |
|---|---|
| Answer. | Christ, have mercy upon us. |
| Minister. | Lord, have mercy upon us. |

Our Father . . . .

| Minister. | O Lord, save thy servant, and thy handmaid;[10] |
|---|---|
| Answer. | Who put their trust in thee. |
| Minister. | O Lord, send them help from thy holy place. |
| Answer. | And evermore defend them. |

| Minister. | *Unite Them to One Another in sincere Love.* |
|---|---|
| Answer. | *That they may rejoyce in each other All the days of their Lives.* |
| Minister. | O Lord, hear our prayer. |
| Answer. | And let our cry come unto thee. |

### Minister.

O God of Abraham, God of Isaac, God of Jacob,[11] bless these thy servants, *& plant thy fear in their hearts,* that whatsoever in thy holy Word they shall profitably learn . . . .

**This Prayer next following shall be omitted, where the Woman is past Child-bearing.**

O Merciful Lord and heavenly Father, by whose gracious gift mankind is increased; We beseech thee *to bless these Thy Servants with Children, if Thou, in thy wisdom seest It to be convenient for Them, & graunt them to live*[12] together so long in godly love and honesty, that they may see their Children Christianly and vertuously brought up, to thy praise and honour, through Jesus Christ our Lord. Amen.

O God, who by thy mighty power hast made all things of nothing . . . . and also that this Woman may be *loving, faithful*[13] and obedient to her Husband, and in all quietness and sobriety, and peace be a follower of holy and godly Matrons. O Lord, bless them both, and grant them to inherit thy everlasting Kingdom, through Jesus Christ our Lord. Amen.

### Then shall the *Minister turning towards Them* say,

Almighty God, who at the beginning did create our first parents, Adam and Eve, and did sanctifie and joyn them together in Marriage; Pour upon you the riches of his grace, sanctifie and bless you, that ye may please him both in body and soul and live together in holy love unto your lives end. Amen.

**After which, if there be no Sermon declaring the Duties of Man and Wife, the Minister shall read as followeth.**

*Ye that are here present,* hear what the holy Scripture doth say as touching the Duty of Husbands towards their Wives, and Wives towards their Husbands.[14]

Saint Paul in his Epistle to the Ephesians . . . .

Hitherto ye have heard the duty of the husband to the wife. *Now hear the dutie* toward your husbands, even as it is plainly set forth in holy Scripture.[15]

140

Saint Paul in the aforenamed Epistle to the Ephesians teacheth you thus . . . .

Saint Peter also doth instruct you very well . . . . Whose adorning let it not be that outward adorning of plaiting the hair, and of wearing gold, or of putting on apparel; but let it be the hidden man[16] of the heart, in that which is not corruptible, even the ornament of a meek and quiet spirit, which is in the sight of God of great price.[17] For after this manner in the old time the holy women also who trusted in God, adorned them selves, being in subjection unto their own husbands; even as Sarah obeyed Abraham, calling him Lord; whose daughters ye are as long as ye do well, and are not afraid with any amazement.

*Let us pray.*

*O Almighty Lord and everlasting God, vouchsafe we beseech Thee to direct sanctify & govern both our hearts & bodies in the ways of thy Laws, & in ye works of thy Comandments, that through thy most mighty ptection both here & ever we may be prserved in body & soul, through our Ld & Saviour Jesus Christ. Amen.*

*The Peace of God &c*

*If the new married Persons signify beforehand to ye Minister that they desire the holy Sacrament, there shall be a Comunion. If they do not, they shall be exhorted to receive It as soon as they have an Opportunitie.*[18]

## THE ORDER FOR THE VISITATION OF THE SICK.[1]

When any Person is sick, *early* notice shall be given thereof to the Minister of the Parish; *When ye Persons are come together the Minister shall say,*

Peace be to this House, and to all that dwell in it.[2]

*Then kneeling dow he shall pray as follows.*

Remember[3] not, Lord, our iniquities, nor the iniquities of our forefathers. Spare us, good Lord, spare thy people, whom thou hast redeemed with thy most precious bloud, and be not angry with us for ever.

Answer.     Spare us, good Lord.

Then the Minister shall say,

Let us pray.
Lord, have mercy upon us.
Christ, have mercy upon us.
Lord, have mercy upon us.

Our Father, which art in heaven; Hallowed be thy Name. Thy Kingdom come. Thy will be done in Earth, As it is in heaven. Give us this day our daily bread. And forgive us our trespasses, As we forgive them that trespass against us. And lead us not into temptation; But deliver us from evil, *for thine &c Ame.*

| | |
|---|---|
| Minister. | O Lord, save thy servant;[4] |
| Answer. | Which putteth his trust in thee. |
| Minister. | Send him help from thy holy place, |
| Answer. | And evermore mightily defend him. |
| Minister. | Let the enemy have no advantage over him; |
| Answer. | Nor the wicked approach to hurt him. |
| Minister. | Be unto him, O Lord, a strong tower, |
| Answer. | From the face of his enemy. |
| Minister. | O Lord, hear our prayers. |
| Answer. | And let our cry come unto thee. |

### Minister.

O Lord, look down from heaven . . . .

Hear us, Almighty and most merciful God and Saviour; extend thy accustomed goodness to this thy servant, who is grieved with sickness.[5] Sanctifie, we beseech thee, this thy Fatherly correction to him; that the sense of his weakness[6] may add strength to his faith and *increas the* seriousness[8] to his repentance. *If it be thy good pleasure,[7] restore Him to his formr Health, & bless ye means usd in ordr to his recovery. & graunt that He may lead ye residue of his life* in thy fear, and to thy glory: *And give* him grace so to take thy visitation, that after this painful life ended he may dwell with thee in life everlasting, through Jesus Christ our Lord. Amen.

**Then shall the Minister exhort the sick Person after this form, or other like.**

Dearly beloved, know this, that Almighty God is the Lord of life and death, and of all things to them pertaining, as youth, strength, health, age, weakness and sickness.[9] Wherefore whatsoever your sickness is, know you certainly, that it is Gods visitation. And for what cause soever this sickness is sent unto you, whether it be[10] to try your patience for the example of others, and that your faith may be found in the day of the Lord, laudable, glorious, and honourable, to the increase of glory and endless felicity; or else it be sent unto you to correct and amend in you whatsoever doth offend the eyes of[11] your heavenly Father; know you certainly, that if you truly repent you of your sins, and bear your sickness patiently, trusting in Gods mercy for his dear Son Jesus Christs sake, and render unto him humble thanks for his Fatherly visitation, submitting your self wholly unto his will, it shall turn to your profit, and help you forward in the right way that leadeth unto everlasting life.

If the Person visited be very sick, then the *Minister*[12] may end his Exhortation in this place, or else proceed.

Take therefore in good part the chastisement of the Lord: For (as Saint Paul[13] saith in the twelfth Chapter to the Hebrews) whom the Lord Loveth he chasteneth, and scourgeth every son whom he receiveth . . . . And there should be no great comfort to Christian persons, than to be made like unto Christ, by suffering patiently adversities, troubles, and sicknesses.[14] For he himself went not up to joy, but first he suffered pain; he entred not into his glory before he was crucified. So truly our way to eternal joy, is to suffer here with Christ;[15] and our door to enter into eternal life, *is to* die with Christ; that we may rise again from death, and dwell with him in everlasting life . . . .

Here the Minister shall rehearse the Articles of the Faith, saying thus,

Dost thou believe in God . . . .

The sick Person shall answer.

All this I stedfastly believe.


### Minister.

*Do you truly & sincerely repent of all yr sinns & begg of God forgiveness of Them through Jesus Christ?*

*Do you, in this yr sickness, submit yrself to the holy Will of God, to be dispos'd of for life or death, as to him*[16] *shall seem Good?*

*Do you solemnly pmise & vow, that if it shall please God to rays you up again, you will spend ye rest of yr life in his fear, & live according to yr holy pfession?*

*Do you forgive all the world, even yr greatest Enemies, as you now desire forgiveness of God?*

*Are you truly sorry for all ye wrongs you may have done any pson whether in their good name or Goods, or in any othr kind?*

*Are you willing to make reparation & restitution according to yr Abilitie, in case you have not already done It?*

*Have you to ye best of yr knowledge, so made your will & settled yr Estate, yt no pson may be defrauded by It? or if you have not already done It, do you pmise to do It, if you have time?*

*Is yr Conscience troubled wth any weighty matter in wch you desire my Advice & Assistance?*

But men should often be put in remembrance to take order for the settling of their temporal Estates, whilst they are in health.

These words before rehearsed, may be said before the Minister begin his Prayer, as he shall see cause.

The Minister should not omit earnestly to move such sick Persons as are of ability, to be liberal to the poor.

Here shall the sick Person be moved to make a special confession of his sins, if he feel his conscience troubled with any weighty matter.[17]

Then shall the *Minister* say the Collect following.[18]

Let us pray.[19]

O Most merciful God, who according to the multitude of thy mercies, dost so put away the sins of those who truly repent, that thou remembrest them no more; Open thine eye of mercy upon this thy servant, who most earnestly desireth pardon and forgiveness. Renew in him (most loving Father) whatsoever hath been decayed by the fraud and malice of the devil, or by his own carnal will and frailness; preserve and continue this sick member in the unity of the Church; consider his contrition, accept his tears, asswage his pain *(or mitigate his sickness)* as shall seem to thee most expedient for him. And forasmuch as he putteth *his trust* onely in thy mercy, impute not unto him his former sins; but strengthen him with thy blessed Spirit; and when thou art pleased to take him hence, take him unto thy favour, through the merits of thy most dearly beloved Son Jesus Christ our Lord. Amen.

*Then the Priest shall Absolve Him (if he humbly & heartily desireth It) in this Form.*

*Our Ld Jes: Ch: who hast left power to his Church to absolve all Sinnrs who truly repent, & believe in Him, of his great mercy forgive Thee thine Offences; & upon thy true fayth & repentance by his Authoritie comitted to me, I pnouce (q) thee absolved from all thy Sinns, in ye name of ye Father, & of ye Sonn, & of ye h. Gh. Amen.*

Q. about a Rubric or Canon for ye Abs. of ye Excom: wn[20] in Extremis.

*Then shall ye Minister say ys Hymn.*[21]

*Unto Thee do I lift up mine Eys O thou yt dwellest in ye Heavens.*

*My help cometh fro thee, O Ld, who hast made Heaven & Earth.*

*O Ld. rebuke me not in thine Anger, neither Chasten me in thy displeasure.*

*Have mercy upo me for I am weak; O save me for thy mercies sake.*

*Look upon my Affliction & my pain: & forgive me all my sin.*

*If thou, Lord, wilt be extreme to mark what is done amiss: O Ld who may abide it.*

*But there is forgiveness wth Thee, that thou mayst be feared.*

*O Comfort ye Soul of thy servant, for unto thee, O Ld, do I lift up my soul.*

*For thou, Ld, art good & gracious, & of great mercy unto all Them yt call upon Thee.*

*Whome have I in heave but Thee? & There is none upo Earth yt I desire besides Thee.*

*My heart & my flesh faileth: But God is ye strength of my heart: & my portion for ever.*

*It is good for me to draw near to God, & to put my trust in ye Ld God, that I may declare all thy works.*

*Glory be to ye Father &c*

adding this,

O Saviour of the world, who by *thy precious bloud shed on ye Cross*[22] hast redeemed us, save us and help us, we humbly beseech thee O Lord.

Then shall the Minister say,

The Almighty Lord who is a most strong tower . . .

And after that shall say,

Unto Gods gracious mercy and protection . . . .

A Prayer for a sick Child.

O Almighty God and merciful Father, to whom alone belong the issues of life and death . . . .

A Prayer for a sick Person, when there appeareth<br>small hope of Recovery.

O Father of mercies, and God of all comfort, our onely help in time of need . . . .

A Commendatory Prayer for a sick Person at<br>the point of departure.

O Almighty God, with whom do live the spirits of just men made perfect . . . .

*A Prayer to be said with ye Family if ye Min: be prsent when the pson is departed, or be desired to come soon after.*

*This form was not composed.*

*Q. of more Prayrs to be added to ys Office?*[23]

A Prayer for Persons troubled in Mind or in Conscience.

O Blessed Lord, the Father of mercies, and the God of all comforts . . . .

# THE COMMUNION OF THE SICK [1]

*The whole office for ye sick may be usd if the Persons concerned can bear It, & desire It. otherwise ye minister is to pceed as is here appointed.*

Forasmuch as all mortal Men be subject to many sudden Perils, Diseases and Sicknesses, and ever uncertain what time they shall depart out of this life; . . . . then he must give timely notice to the Curate, signifying also how many there are to Communicate with him (which shall be *Two or more if they may conveniently be had)* [2] and having a convenient place in the sick Mans House, with all things necessary so prepared, that the Curate may reverently Minister, he shall there Celebrate the holy Communion, beginning with the Collect, Epistle and Gospel here following.

## The Collect.

Almighty everliving God, maker of mankind, who dost correct those whom thou dost love, and chastise every one whom thou dost receive; We beseech thee to have mercy upon this thy servant visited with thine hand, and to grant that he may take his sickness patiently, and recover his bodily health (if it be thy gracious will) and whensoever [3] his soul shall depart from the body, it may be without spot presented unto thee, through Jesus Christ our Lord. Amen.

## The Epistle. Heb. 12.5 [4]
## The Gospel. S. John 5.24

After which, the Priest [5] shall proceed according to the form before prescribed for the holy Communion, beginning with these words (Ye that do truly &c)

At the time of the distribution of the holy Sacrament, the Priest [6] shall first receive the Communion himself, and after minister unto them that are appointed to Communicate with the Sick; and last of all to the sick Person, *unless ye Minister perceive Him ready to expire.* [7]

But if a man, either by reason of extremity of sickness, or for want of warning in due time to the Curate, or for lack of company to receive with him, or by any other just impediment, do not receive the Sacrament of Christs Body and Bloud, the Curate shall instruct him, That if he do truly repent of his sins, and stedfastly believe that Jesus Christ hath suffered death upon the Cross for him, and shed his Bloud for his Redemption, earnestly remembring the benefits he hath thereby, and giving him hearty thanks therefore, he doth eat and drink the Body and Bloud of our Saviour Christ profitably to his souls health, although he do not receive the Sacrament with his mouth. [8]

When the sick person is visited, and received the holy Communion all at one time, the Priest, for more expedition, shall cut off the form of the Visitation at the Psalm (In thee, O Lord, have I put my trust) and go straight to the Communion.

In the time of the Plague, Sweat,[9] or such other like contagious Times of Sickness or Diseases, when none of the Parish or Neighbours can be gotten to Communicate with the Sick in their Houses, for fear of the Infection, upon special request of the Diseased, the Minister *alone may*[10] Communicate with him.

## THE ORDER FOR THE BURIAL OF THE DEAD.[1]

Here is to be noted, That the Office ensuing is not to be used for any that die unbaptized, or excommunicate, *or have bin found to lay violent hands upon Themselves unless such of Them as were capable had receiv'd Absolution according to ye former Office in ye Visit. of ye Sick.*

The Priest and Clerks meeting the Corps at the entrance of the Church-yard, and going before it, either into the Church, or towards the Grave, shall say or sing,

I am the resurrection and the life . . . .

And after they are come into the Church,[2] shall be read one or both of these Psalms following.

Dixi, Custodiam    Ps. 39[3]

Domine, refugium    Ps. 90

Then shall follow the Lesson taken out of the fifteenth Chapter of the former Epistle of Saint Paul to the Corinthians.

1 Cor. 15.20 - 58[4]

*Or this in colder or later seasons taken out of ye 1 Thess 4, from vers 13 to ye End.*

*I would not have you to be ignorant, Brethren, concerning Them wch are asleep, yt ye sorrow not even as Others who have no Hope. for if we believe yt Jesus dyed & rose again, even so ym also wch sleep in Jesus will God bring with him. For this we say unto you by ye word of ye Lord, yt we, wch are alive, & remain unto ye coming of ye Lord, shall not prevent ym, wch are asleep. For ye Lord himself shall descend from Heaven wth a Shout, wth ye Voice of ye Archangel, & wth ye Trump of God, & ye dead in Christ shall rise first; Then we, wch are alive, & remain, shall be caught up together wth ym in ye Clouds to meet ye Lord in ye Air, & so shall we ever be wth ye Lord. Wherefore Comfort one another wth these words.*

When they come to the Grave, while the Corps is made ready to be laid into the Earth, the *Minister*[5] shall say, or the Priest and Clerks shall sing,

Man that is born of a woman . . . . Thou knowest, Lord, the secrets of our hearts; shut not thy merciful ears to our prayer; but spare us, Lord most holy, O God most mighty, O holy and merciful Saviour, thou most *Righteous* Judge eternal, suffer us not at our last hour, *Thro' any Temptations* to fall from thee.

Then while the Earth shall be cast upon the Body by some standing by, the Priest shall say,

Forasmuch as it hath pleased Almighty God *to take out of this world ye soul of our Brother (or Sister) here departed,* we therefore commit his body to the ground; earth to earth, ashes to ashes, dust to dust, *in a firm belief* of the resurrection *of ye dead at ye last day in wch They who die in ye Lord shall rise again to eternal Life, through* our Lord Jesus Christ, who shall change our vile body, that it may be like unto his glorious body, according to the mighty working, whereby he is able to subdue all things to himself.[6]

Then shall be said or sung,[7]

I heard a voice from heaven, saying unto me, Write; From henceforth blessed are the dead which die in the Lord: even so saith the Spirit; for they rest from their labours. Rev 14.13

Then the *Minister*[8] shall say,

Lord, have mercy upon us.

Christ, have mercy upon us.

Lord, have mercy upon us.

Our Father, which art in heaven; Hallowed be thy Name. Thy Kingdom come. Thy will be done in earth, As it is in heaven. Give us this day our daily bread. And forgive us our trespasses, As we forgive them that trespass against us. And lead us not into temptation; But deliver us from evil. *for thine &c.*

### *Minister*[8]

*Almighty God with whome do live ye spirits of Them* that depart hence in the Lord, and with whom the souls of the faithful, after they are delivered from the burden of the flesh, are in joy and felicity: we give thee hearty thanks for that it hath *pleased Thee to instruct*

*us in this heavenly knowledge, beseeching Thee so to affect our hearts therewth, yt seeing we believe such a happy estate hereafter, we may live here in all holy Conversation & Godliness, looking for & hastening unto ye coming of ye day of God:*[(10)] *That being then found of Thee in Peace wthout Spott & blameless, we may have or pfect Consumation &* bliss, both in body and soul, in *thy everlasting* glory, through Jesus Christ our Lord. Amen.

## The Collect.

O Merciful God, the Father of our Lord Jesus Christ, who is the resurrection and the life; in whom whosoever believeth shall live, though he die; and whosoever liveth and believeth in him, shall not die eternally; who also hath taught us (by his holy Apostle Saint Paul) not to be sorry as men without hope, for them that sleep in him; We meekly beseech thee, O Father, to raise us from the death of sin unto the life of righteousness; that when we shall depart this life, we may rest in *him;*[(12)] *and* that at the general resurrection in the last day we may be found acceptable in thy sight, and receive that blessing which thy well-beloved Son shall then pronounce to all that love and fear thee, saying, Come, ye blessed children of my Father, receive the Kingdom prepared for you from the beginning of the world. Grant this, we beseech thee, O merciful Father, through Jesus Christ our Mediatour and Redeemer. Amen.

The Grace of our Lord Jesus Christ, and the love of God, and the fellowship of the Holy Ghost, be with us all evermore. Amen.

## THE THANKSGIVING AFTER CHILD-BIRTH COMMONLY CALLED THE CHURCHING OF WOMEN.

The Woman at the usual time after her Delivery, shall come into the Church decently apparelled,[(1)] and there shall kneel down in some convenient place, as hath been accustomed, or as the Ordinary shall direct: and then the *Minister*[(2)] shall say unto her,

Forasmuch as it hath pleased Almighty God of his goodness to give you safe deliverance, and hath preserved you in the great danger of Child-birth, you shall therefore give hearty thanks unto God, and say,

(Then shall the *Minister*[(3)] say this *Psalm or Hymn*)
*Blessed be ye Lord who hath not turnd away my Prayer, nor his mercy from me.*

*I was in pain & I called on ye name of ye Lord, O Ld, I beseech thee, delivr my soul.*

*Gracious is ye Ld & righteous: yea or God is mercifull.*

*I love ye Lord, because he hath heard my Voice & my supplication;*

*Because he hath inclined his Ear unto me: Therefore will I call upo him as long as I live.*

*I will pay my vows unto ye Lord, & walk before him wth an upright heart.*

*Shew me thy waies O Lord: Teach me thy paths.*

*Lead me in thy Truth, & learn me; for Thou art ye God of my salvation.*

*Give me understanding & I shall keep thy Law; yea I shall observe it wth my whole heart.*

*Make me to go in ye path of thy Comandments, for therein is my delight.*[4]

*Glory &c*

## Or this Psalm.

Nisi Dominus, Psalm 127

Except the Lord build the house . . . .

Then the *Minister*[5] shall say,

*Lord,* have mercy upon us.

Christ, have mercy upon us.

Lord, have mercy upon us.

Our Father . . . .

**Minister.**  O Lord *save thy* servant;[6]

**Answer.**  *Who now returns her Thanks to Thee.*[7]

**Minister.**  Be thou *her help & her defence.*

**Answer.**  *That she may serve Thee in holiness & right: all the days of her life.*[8]

**Minister.**  Lord, hear our prayer.

**Answer.**  And let our cry come unto thee.

## Minister.[9]

O Almighty God, we give thee humble thanks for that thou hast vouchsafed to deliver *this thy* servant from the great pain and peril of Child-birth, *make her ever mindfull of thy great mercy to Her, & of her vows unto Thee, & graunt,* we beseech thee most merciful Father, that she through thy help may both faithfully live, and walk according to thy will in this life present, and also may be partaker of everlasting glory in the life to come, through Jesus Christ our Lord. Amen.

The Woman that cometh to give her Thanks, must offer the accustomed Offerings; and if there be a Communion, it is convenient that she receive the holy Communion.

*Then ye Blessing is to be usd if this Office be usd before or after Service.*

*A Collect wch may be said imediatelie aftr ye woman is deliverd.*

[No text given]

## THE PROPER OFFICE FOR ASHWEDNESDAY

*See Ashwednesday.*[1]

*The latter part of ye Office for Ashwednesday.*

*After morning Prayer, ye Litany ended according to ye accustom'd manner the Minister shall in ye Reading Pew or Pulpit say.*[2]

*Brethren this time of Lent upon wch we are now entred was by ye Antient Church observed very religiously, & set apart All men to examine them selves, for true fasting, & for ye due preparation of all persons for ye worthy receiving of ye Comunion at Easter; & was of good Use till Superstition corrupted it, When all ye Fasting of this Season came to be placed in a distinction of Meats, upon wch an undue Value was set; And instead of Mens humbling themselves before God, & mourning for their Sins, & turning to God with all their Hearts, & bringing forth Fruits worthy of Repentance, Auricular Confession, together wth outward Penances, were ye things mainly insisted on. But in order to ye rectifying these abuses, & returning to ye Antient Practice, you must know yt Fasting is of no value, but as it is joyn'd wth Prayer, & ye Afflicting of our Souls before God. Nor does it consist in ye distinction of Meats but in such a restraint of bodily Appetites as disposes the Mind more for Prayer. Nor are Fasting, Prayer, or our sorrowing for Sinn, of any Value in ye Sight of God, but as they tend to work in us true Repentance, wch is a reall Change both of our Heart & Life, by wch we become assured of Gods love & Favour to us; since by this onely we can certainly know that God has forgiven our Sins, if we ourselves do truely forsake them. But in order to your Understanding aright ye Necessity of Fasting & Prayer, I shall set before you good & Evill, Life & Death, Blessing & Cursing, in ye Words of God himself, who cannot lye, & in whom there is no Variableness nor Shadow of turning. I shall read to you both some of ye Blessings of ye Gospell, as also some of the heavy Denunciations of Gods Wrath, yt are set down in ye New Testament, that in these you may see both ye Blessedness to wch our Saviour calls us, as also ye Dreadfull Judgments of God against impenitent Sinners; & yt by these you may be warned to flee from ye Wrath wch is to come & to lay hold on Eternal Life.*

### Min. [3]
*Blessed are ye poor in spirit: for theirs is ye Kingdo of Heaven.*

### People.
*Ld have mercy upon us, & make us partakrs of ys blessing.*

### Min.
*Blessed are they yt mourn: for They shall be comforted.*

### People.
*Ld have mercy &c.*

### Min.
*Blessed are ye meek: for they shall Inherit ye Earth.*

### People.
*Ld have mercy upo us & make us partakrs &c.*

### Min.
*Blessed are They wch do hunger & thirst aftr Righteousness: for They shall be filled.*

### Peo.
*Ld have &c.*

### Min.
*Blessed are ye mercifull: for They shall obtain mercy.*

### Peo.
*Ld have mercy &c.*

### Min.
*Blessed are ye pure in heart: for They shall see God.*

### Peo.
*Ld have mercy &c.*

### Minister.
*Blessed are ye Peacemakers: for They shall be called ye Children of God.*

### People.
*Lord have mercy upon us & indue us wth all these Graces, & make us partakers of ye blessedness pmised to Them, we hubly beseech Thee.*

### Minister.
*You have already heard ye blessings pmised to ye obedient, now hear ye Judgmts of God denounced against Sinners.*

*Know ye not yt ye unrighteous shall not inherit ye Kingdom of God? be not deceived neither fornicators, nor Idolaters, nor Adulterers, nor effeminate, nor abusers of themselves wth mankind, nor Thieves, nor Covetous, nor drukards, nor Revilers, nor Extortioners, shall inherit ye Kingdom of God?*     1 Cor. 6.9 to 10

**People.**

*O Ld prserve us fro these Sinns, & fro thy wrath wch they justly deserve.*

**Min.**

*The works of ye Flesh are manifest wch are these, Adultery, fornication, uncleanness, Lasciviousness, Idolatry, witchcraft, hatred, variance, emulations, wrath, strife, seditios, Heresies, Envyings, murthers, drukenness, revellings & such like: of ye wch I tell you before as I have also told you in time past that they wch do such things, shall not inherit ye Kingdom of God.        Gal. 5.19 to 22*

**People.**

*O Ld prserve us fro these Sinns, & fro thy wrath wch they justly deserve.*

**Min.**

*—This you know that no whoremonger, nor unclean pson, nor Covetous man who is an Idolater, hath any Inheritance in the Kingdom of Christ & of God. Let no man deceive you with vain words, for because of these Things cometh ye wrath of God upo ye children of disobedience.        Ephes. 5.5, 7*

**People.**

*Fro these & all other Sinns, & fro thy wrath wch they justly deserve, save & deliver us we humbly beseech thee O Ld.*[4]

**Minister.**

Now seeing that *all They are blessed who truly obey God according to his holy word;*[5] *let his Goodness lead us to repentance, & to such a godly righteous & sober life, yt we may not fall short of ye blessedness wch he hath pmised to all that love him. And seeing that All they are accursed* (as the prophet David beareth witness) who do err and go astray from the commandments of God, let us (remembring the dreadful *judgments* hanging over *the heads of the wicked,* and always ready to fall upon *them*) return unto our Lord God with all contrition and meekness of heart; bewailing and lamenting our sinful life, acknowledging and confessing our offences, and seeking to bring forth worthy fruits of *Repentance.* For now is the ax put unto the root of the trees . . . .

Then shall they all kneel upon their knees, and the Priest and Clerks kneeling (in the place where they are accustomed to say the Litany) shall say this Psalm.

Miserere mei, Deus. Psalm 51

Lord, have mercy upon us.

Christ, have mercy upon us.

Lord, have mercy upon us.

Our Father . . . .

| Minister. | O Lord, *hear* thy servants; |
|---|---|
| Answer. | *Who have now made their Supplicatios to yee.* |
| Minister. | *Ld cause thy face to shine upo us.* |
| Answer. | *Yt we may evrmore rejoyce in yee.* |
| *Minister.* | *Put thy Laws in our Hearts.* |
| *Answer.* | *And remembr or Sins & Iniquities no more.* |
| Minister. | Help us, O God our Saviour. |
| Answer. | And for the glory of thy Name deliver us; be merciful to us sinners, for thy Names sake. |
| Minister. | O Lord, hear our prayer. |
| **Answer.** | And let our cry come unto thee. |

### Minister.[6]

O Lord, we beseech thee mercifully hear our prayers, and spare all those who confess their sins unto thee, that they whose consciences *accuse Them of sin,* by thy merciful pardon may be absolved, through Christ our Lord. Amen.

O Most mighty God and merciful Father, who hast compassion upon all men . . . . but so turn thine anger from us, who *humbly* acknowledge our vileness, and truly repent us of our faults *and so help us* in this world *by thy Grace* that we may ever live with thee in the world to come, through Jesus Christ our Lord. Amen.

**Then shall the People say this that followeth, after the Minister.**

Turn thou us, O good Lord, and so shall we be turned . . . .

**Then the Minister alone shall say.**

The Lord bless us, and keep us; the Lord lift up the light of his countenance upon us, and give us peace, now and for evermore. Amen.

# THE PSALTER OR PSALMS OF DAVID,


## AFTER THE TRANSLATION OF THE GREAT BIBLE,
## POINTED AS THEY ARE TO BE SUNG OR SAID
## IN CHURCHES


London Printed by the Assigns (&c)


1683 Cum Privilegio


*This Translation was to be revis'd. D. Kidder had
done it. But 'twas not examined for want of time.*


[No alterations in Psalter]


## FORMS OF PRAYER TO BE USED AT SEA


[No alterations]

# THE FORM AND MANNER OF MAKING, ORDAINING, AND CONSECRATING OF BISHOPS, *PRESBYTERS (comonly call'd* PRIESTS*)* AND DEACONS, ACCORDING TO THE ORDER OF THE CHURCH OF ENGLAND.

## The Preface[1]

It is evident *from* holy Scripture and antient Authors, that from the Apostles *times* there have been these Orders of Ministers in Christ's Church; Bishops, Priests, and Deacons . . . .

And none shall be Admitted a Deacon . . . .

And the Bishop knowing either by himself . . . .

*The Persons who desire to be ordaind, shall send their Testimonials to the Bishop from the Place of their present Residence at least a moneth before: And come[2] Themselves to be examined at least a week before.*

*After ye Receipt of ye Testimonials the Bishop shall give order that public notice be given of their desiring holy orders, in the Church, Chappell, or College where they reside, the Lords-day before the Ordination-day.*

---

*Whereas we have bin often impos'd upon by men pretending to Orders in the Church of Rome, it is therefore humbly propos'd whether since we[3] can have no certainty concerning the Instruments of Orders wch They show, They may be admitted to serve as deacons or Presbyters of this church without being ordain'd according to the following Offices?* [4]

*The Commissioners proceded no further for want of time; The Convocation being mett.* [5]

## THE FORM AND MANNER OF MAKING OF DEACONS. [6]

(Rubric before the Litany)

Then the Bishop . . . shall, with the Clergy and people present, *say* the Litany, with the Prayers, as followeth.

(first interrogation)

Do you think that you are truly called, according to the will of our take upon you this office and ministration *having a sincere & fervent desire to* serve God, for the promoting of his glory, and the edifying of his people?

(second interrogation)

Do you trust that you are inwardly moved by the Holy Ghost to Lord Jesus Christ, and the due order of this *Church of England,* to the *Order & ministry of Deacon?*[7]

156

# THE FORM AND MANNER OF

## ORDERING OF PRIESTS *IE PRESBYTERS.*

Seeing The Reformed Churches abroad are in that imperfect State that They canot receive ordination from Bishops;[8] It is humbly propos'd, whether They may not be receiv'd by an Imposition[9] of A[10] Bishops hands, in these or such like words.

Take Thou Authoritie to preach the Word of God & to minister ye Holy Sacraments in this Church as (Q where) thou shalt be lawfully appointed thereunto.

---

Whereas it has bin ye Constant practice of ye Antient Church to allow of no Ordinations of Priests (i.e.) Presbyters, or Deacons[11] wthout a Bishop, & that it has bin likewise ye constant Practice of this Church ever since ye Reformation, to allow none that were not ordained by Bps. where They could be had; yet in regard that several in this Kingdo have, of late years, bin ordained only by Presbyters, The Church being desirous to do all yt can be done for Peace, & in order to ye healing of our divisions, has thought fitt to receive such as have bin ordained by Presbyters only to be ordained according to this Office with ye Addition of These words in these following Places.

Archd:   Reverend Father &c order of Priesthood, If they have not bin already Ordain'd.

Bp:     Good People &c Priesthood &c If They have not bin already ordaind.

Q Bp.   Receive ye H. Gh. for ye office & work of a Priest in ye Ch. of God now comitted unto Thee by ye imposition of our hands, if Thou hast not bin already ordain'd.

By which as she retains her opinion and Practice wch make a Bp necessary to the giving of Orders when He can be had; so she do's likewise leave all such Persons as have bin ordain'd by Presbyters only, the freedom of their own Thoughts concerning their former Ordinations. It being, wth all, expressly pvided that this shall never be a Precedent for ye time to come, & yt It shall only be graunted to such as have bin ordained before the          Day of

*Letters of Orders are to be given them in so much of the Form*[12] *as was used in Ireland upon the Return of K. Ch. ye 2d to his Kingdomes, by D Bramhall Archbp. of Ardmagh.*

—————— *Non annihilantes priores ordinis (si quos habuit) nec validitatem nec invaliditatem eorundem determinantes, multo minus omnes ordines sacros Ecclesiarum Forinsecarum condemnantes, quos proprio Judici relinquimus; sed salummodo supplentes quicquid prius defuit per canones Ecclesiae Anglicanae requisitum, et providentes paci Ecclesiae ut Schismatis tollatur occasio, et conscientijs Fidelium satisfiat, nec ullo modo dubitent de ejus Ordinatione, aut actus suos presbyteriales tanquam invalidos aversentur: In cujus rei Testimonium.*[13]

When the day appointed by the Bishop is come, after Morning Prayer is ended, there shall be a Sermon or Exhortation, declaring the Duty and Office of such as come to be admitted Priests; . . .[14]

[The service continues as in the BCP except;
Both versions of Veni Creator deleted, and written beside them is]

*New Hymns to be compos'd*[15]

[That done . . . .
Let us Pray.
Almighty God and heavenly Father . . .]

When this prayer is done the Bishop with the Priests present shall lay their hands severally upon the head of every one that receiveth the order of Priesthood; the receivers humbly kneeling upon their knees, and the Bishop saying[16]

*Whereas It was ye constant Practice of ye Church to ordain by Prayer, wch practice continu'd for many Ages & yt ye pnouncing these words (Receive ye Holy Ghost) in ye Imperative Mood, was brought into ye Office of Ordination in ye darkest Times of Popery; It is humbly submitted to ye Convocation, whether it be not more suitable unto ye general Rule the Ch. of E. has gone upon of conforming her self to ye primitive Church to put these words in some such form as this.*

" *Pour down, O Father of Lights, ye holy Ghost on this thy Servant, for ye Office & work of a Priest in ye church of God, now comitted unto Him by ye Imposition of our hands that whose sinns he do's forgive they may be forgiven, & whose sinns he doth retain, they may be retained, & yt he may be a faithfull dispenser of Gods Word and Sacraments, to ye aedification of his Church, & ye glory of his holy name through Jesus Christ, to whom with ye Father & ye Holy Ghost be all Honour & glory world wthout End. Amen.*

*S. Aug. 1.15 de Trin. Cap. 27. Quomodo ergo De⁹ no est Qui dat Spm Sanctu? imo quant⁹ De⁹ est Qui dat deu? neq3 enim Aliquis Discipuloru ei⁹ dedit Spm Sm. Orabat quippe ut veniret in Eos quib⁹ man⁹ imponebat, no Ipsi enim dabant. Quem morem in suis prpositis etia nunc servat ecclesia.*

**Then the Bishop shall deliver to every one of them kneeling, the Bible into his Hand, saying,**

*In the name of ye Fathr, & of ye Sonn & of ye holy Ghost,*
Take thou authority to preach the Word of God, and to Minister the holy Sacraments in the Congregation, where thou shalt be lawfully appointed thereunto.[17]

**When this is done . . . .**

The Communion . . . .

Most merciful Father, we . . . . . Grant also that we may have
Q grace to hear and receive what they shall deliver out of thy most holy word . . . .

### FORM OF ORDAINING OR CONSECRATING OF AN ARCHBISHOP OR BISHOP, WHICH IS ALWAYS TO BE PERFORMED UPON SOME SUNDAY OR HOLY-DAY[18]

[Hymns Veni Creator Spiritus deleted; note written]

*New Hymns to be compos'd*

[and by doxology of metrical version] *Q.*

### A FORM OF PRAYER WITH THANKSGIVING TO BE USED UPON THE FIFTH DAY OF NOVEMBER. A FORM OF PRAYER TO BE USED UPON THE THIRTIETH DAY OF JANUARY, A FORM OF PRAYER TO BE USED YEARLY UPON THE NINE AND TWENTIETH DAY OF MAY.

(In that for 30 January ' being the Day of the Martyrdom of the Blessed King Charles the first . . . .')

### The First Collect.

O Most mighty God, terrible in thy judgments . . . .
But, O Gracious God, when thou makest inquisition for bloud, lay not the guilt of this innocent bloud,
*This may be* (the shedding whereof nothing but the bloud of thy
*sd of every* Son can expiate) . . . .
*Sin, & is,*
*therefore ye*
*less pp.*

# APPENDIX 1

## THE DIARY OF JOHN WILLIAMS

### SECKER MS. 24/6[1]

To be put into the publick MS Library at Lambeth.[2]

A Diary Of the proceedings of the Commissioners appointed by K. William & Q. Mary to revise the Common prayer, 1689.

Taken by Dr. Williams now Bishop of Chichester, one of the Commrs. every night, after He went home from the several Meetings.

There was an appointment made by direction from the Lord Bishop of London, for their meeting at the Jerusalem Chamber at 9 o Clock, Octor. 3. 1689

Sess 1. ⎱ The first thing done was the opening of the Comissn.
Oct 3. ⎰ Dr Sharp Dean of Norwich being desired to read it.

The tenor of it was in these Words[3] " We do authorise, empower & require you — — — — Archbp of York &c and any Nine or more of You whereof 3 to be Bishops, to meet from time to time, as often as shall be needfull and to prepare such alterations and Amendments of the Liturgy & Canons, and such proposals for the Reformation of Ecclesiastical Abuses and to consider of such other matters as in Your Judgment[4] may most conduce to the ends above mentioned; so that the things so by you considered and prepared may be in readiness to be offered to the Convocation at their next Meeting, and when approved by them may be presented to Us & Our 2 houses of Parliament, and that if it shall be judged fitt they may be established in due form of Law ——— Sept 17. 1689 ".

The Names of the Persons appointed to be Commissioners.

Ten Bps. viz. Dr. Lamplugh Arch Bp. of York 1, Dr. Compton Bp. of London 2, Dr. Smith Bp. of Carlisle 3, Dr. Mews[5] Bp. of Winchester 4, Dr. Floyd Bp. of St Asaph 5, Dr. Sprat Bp. of Rochester 6, Dr. Burnet Bp. of Salisbury 7, Dr. Trelawny Bp. of Exon 8, Dr. Humphreys Bp. of Bangor 9, Dr. Stratford Bp. of Chester 10.

Six Deans, Tillotson of Canterbury 1, Stillingfleet of St. Pauls 2, Patrick of Peterb 3: Meggot of Winton 4, Sharp of Norwich 5, Aldridge of Xt. Church 6.

Four Professors & Drs. of Universities } Oxford { Hall } Jane } Cambridge { Beaumont } Montague }

4 Arch Deacons —— Goodman, Beveridge, Alston, Battley[6]

6 of the London Clergy —— viz, Tenison, Grove, Scott, Fowler, Kidder, Williams.

Of those there met at that time 17 viz. 5 Bps. whereof 2 Elect, 5 Deans and 7 others.

Bps. of London, Rochester, St. Asaph —— Elect of Worcest. Stilling. and Chichr. Patr. Deans of Canterb. Norwich, Winchest. Xt. Church, Gloucester. others, Beveridge, Tenison, Grove, Scott, Alston, Kidder & Williams.

N.B.[7] 1. Before the 2d Sess. Dr Stillingfleet was Bp. of Worcester and Dr. Patrick Bp. of Chichester.

2. In Sess. 9 Dr. Tillotson appears as Dean of Pauls, and Dr. Sharp as Dean of Canterbury.

3. Of the aforesaid Comssrs. never sat York, Carlisle, Exeter, Beaumont, Montague, Battley —— Bp. of Rochester came only twice and not after Sess. 2. Octob. 16. Drs. Jane, Aldridge, Meggott came not after Sess. 3. Oct. 18.

After the reading of the Comission the first point proposed to be debated[8] was the reading the Apochrypha in the Church.

For it there were 3 things offered,

1. That leaving it out wou'd give great offence to the People —— thus Dr. B.

2. That if not the whole allowed to be read yet some parts of the most useful should be retained —— By Dr. Jane[9].

3. It was desired that We should not proceed in these matters till We had a greater Number, and without[10] more time to Consider —— Dn. of Winton.

To the two former it was answered, That besides the Objections against particular parts of it, the Whole was of no Authority, That it gave too great a Countenance to the Pretentions of the Church of Rome, and shewed too great a Respect to the Books themselves —— To the last it was said—That the Time was short and the matter would not admit long delays. 2 That what was done here was no determination and that the whole was to be left to the Convocation —— It was carry'd against the Apochrypha.

The next point in Debate was the Version of the Psalms in the Common Prayer. It was debated whether keep the Old Translation, or have yt altered, or wholly take in the new.[11]

161

Here Mr. Kidder was desired to give some account of what He (at the desire of some of the Bps.) had observed. He shewed that the first half was faulty, the latter much better, (and from thence he collected[12] that the Translator by that Time he had gone through the first half grew weary of his Work, and rather chose to Translate it a new, then patch it up as before) and that it differed from the LXX as well as from the Hebrew.

Mr. K and Mr. W. then withdrew (about 12 a Clock) going out of Town.

It seems They gave several Their parts, and Adjourned till Monday, Oct. 14.

On Monday Oct. 14[13] only 7 or 8 met viz. . . . and adjourned till Wednesday following at 10 in the Morning.

Sess 2. ⎫ On Wednesday Oct. 16. at 10 o'Clock[14], met 18 of
Oct 16. ⎬ the Comissrs. Viz.

> 6 Bishops, London, Winton, Rochester, St. Asaph, Worcester, Chichesr.

> 6 Deans, Cantery, Norwich, Winchestr. Xt Church, Glocr. Peterbro.

> 6 others, Beveridge, Tenison, Grove, Scot, Alston, Williams.

In the first place the Bp. of Rochester[15] spoke to this purpose, That He questioned the Authority of this Comissn; and whether it was not pmunire to meet according to it, That a burnt Child dreads the Fire, and that he shou'd not think himself safe unless He had it under the hands of the 12 Judges, having in his former Case had Judges on his Side, That if it was legal, yet however He questioned whether this was not dissolved, and that there needed a new Commission, and that[16] 1. Because the quality of some of the Persons therein concerned[17] was altered; Such as He a few days ago had the Honour to lay his hands upon; and 2. because there were but 7 at the last meeting that[18] Adjourned the Court; and that the Comiss: made 9 at least of the Quorum. He urged further that He could not See how We could enter upon such matters having given Assent and Consent to Them;[19] That it was to accuse the Church, and Condemn it as if it needed; That this was to prevent the Convocation, and that it could not be taken well by them to be called together to Confirm that which They had no hand in: That this wou'd provoke the Parliament.

This ended, the Dn. of Glocr. Dr. Jane stood up and said, that what the Bp. of Rochester said, had convinced him and He was of the same mind.

To this was reply'd especially by Dr. Patrick Bp. of Chichestr, 1. That sure[20] there was no comparison between the late Ecclcal Comission and this: For here was nothing to be determin'd, and They were only called together to advise and give their Opinion; not to determine concerning right and wrong[21] (The Bp. of Rochestr. said He would not compare Them). 2. Nor betwixt the Judges then that[22] were corrupted and gave Verdict against Law, and these that acted according to Law; and that They had consulted some of them (as well as the King had) and They said it was lawfull; for there was no Law to hinder the King from calling any Persons together for Their Advice, and this the Words of the Commission shewed was no more. 3. The Bishop of London said, that it was approved by the Lords House, and besides if this Comission shou'd end[23] without effect, the Work wou'd be taken out of Our hands[24] and done without the Clergy. 4. That this was not to prevent the Convocation but to shorten their Work, and that was usual in Parliament, and great[25] Assemblies. 5. That all signify'd nothing unless the Convocation approv'd it.

Several other things were said by the Bps., but being at some distance at first, I heard them not so well.

After some Debate, the B. of St. Asaph moved, that those that[26] were not satisfyed about the Comission might withdraw and not be Spies upon the rest. Upon which Dr. Jane rose up to be gone, but was prevailed with to stay. And a motion was made to debate matters before them as Friends or a private Comittee, but this others were against, because then They did not know how far the acting[27] without a Comission might come within the Statute of Premunire.

However They sat down, and continued out that Assembly and it was desired that all things that happened at that Time might be kept Secret. Before which the Dn. of Peterborough was desired to read his Observations on the Psalms (as He had digested them) which He did, and that matter was again discoursed.

At last it was moved that They wou'd take Their Parts (but this the Deans of Xt. Church and Glocr. and Winchestr. did not shew a concurrence in) and bring them again the next meeting.

So They Adjourned to Friday Oct. 18 at 1 of the Clock.[28]

Oct. 16[29] The Bps. of London and Worcesr, Dr Alston and Williams, din'd at Dr. Patricks the Bp. of Chichr. whither after dinner came Dr. Tenison and Dr. Grove and They together went over most of the Questions upon the Service.

Oct. 17. 10 in the Morning, there met at Dr. Beveriges the Dean of Peterburrow[30] Dr. Grove Dr. Scott & Williams who went over the Calendar about the Lessons for Holydays and then came the Bp. of St. Asaph, and They went over part of those of the Week Days.

Sess 3. ⎱  Friday Oct. 18 at 1 in the Afternoon the Committee
Oct 18. ⎰  sat. Present 19 ————

Bps. of London, Winton, St. Asaph, Salisbury, Worcestr. Chichr.——

Deans—— Cantry. Winton, Norwich, Xt. Ch: Glocr. Peterb:

Doctors, Beveridge, Tenison, Grove, Scott, Alston, Wms & afterds. Dr. Hall.

Then were read over the Queries upon the whole Service by Dr. Tenison.

The First thing taken into debate was the Ceremonies; but they had not gone far, before the Deans of Xt. Ch: and Glocr. went out; who came no more. [31]

They considered the Case of Godfathers, and it was propos'd that Parents (comprehending therein Grandfathers &c) might upon occasion be admitted.

As for the posture of the Sacrament [32], it was first moved that it might be kneeling or standing at Liberty, but at last it was agreed for those that scrupled kneeling, that it shou'd be in some posture of Reverence, and in some Convenient Pew or Place in the Church so that none but those that kneeled, shou'd come up to the Rails or Table [33], And that the Persons scrupling shou'd some Week Day before come to the Minister; and declare that they cou'd not kneel with a good Conscience. This was agreed to, and drawn up. Only the B. of Winchester moved that the Names of such Persons might be written down, but that was not approved, and after all He dissented from the whole.

They proceeded to the Cross. Dr Bev: said, They might as well object against [34] holding the Child in Arms, and that there was no end if We wou'd take away all Scruples. It was argued this [35] was a distinct thing from the other Ceremonies, For there must be some Time, Place, Posture, Habit; but this depended wholly upon human Institution, And after a full debate [36] it was agreed, 1. That the Persons indulged were to declare in their Conscience They thought it Sinfull to have it used. 2. That the Children should be Baptized last, that were to be baptized without the Cross. This was drawn up and Assented to.

Then the Court rose up and adjourned till Monday Oct. 21 at 3 a clock.

164

} Oct. 21 at 3 a Clock.[37] Present 15.

Bishops, London, St. Asaph, Salisb: Worcestr, Chichester.

Deans, Canterbury, Norwich, Peterburrow.

Doctors, Beverige, Hall, Tenison, Grove, Scot, Alston, Williams.

Went over what was done about the Cross, (because the Bp. of London went then away before the rest) and agreed to leave out that of the Childrens being Baptised last —— It was desired that some expedient shou'd be thought of for the ease of Ministers in the Use of the Cross.

They then proceeded to the Case of Godfathers. It was pleaded by Dr. Beverige, 1. That it was very Antient, 2. That We shou'd have a Care of going off from the practise of the Universal Church, and that no instance cou'd be given in Antiquity where this was not used.

To which it was[38] answered, That it was a very usefull and laudable practice and shou'd be encouraged, but withal it was too often made a matter of Interest. 2. That it was — — — — — — as is publisht by Balurius[39] — — — — — 3. That it was hard to find an instance of a Child Baptised before St. Cyprians Time.

At last it was agreed that a Rubrick should be drawn up, that if the Parent should say He cou'd not conveniently procure Godfathers, He himself shou'd be admitted to be a Sponsor.[40]

Then it was proceeded to the Surplice, which held a long debate. All agreed, it was a matter of the least consequence; and it was debated whether to lay it wholly aside, but in Cathedrals, or to leave it as it is, or indifft. To lay it wholly aside would be to give offence and make a Schism, or encourage the Schism that was now setting a foot.[41] To leave it as it is wou'd not be to answer the end of the meeting, and to make what was the least necessary, the most. To leave it indifferent wou'd be the Occasion of continual Divisions.

The Bp. of London went here away, & adjourned till Wednesdy. 3 a Clock.

Here We continued a Sub-Commee. At last it was agreed, that a Rubrick shou'd be drawn up, to signify that We us'd it only as decent and Antient, and that if any Minister thought it unlawfull he might go to the Bp., who shou'd (as He thought fit) Appoint One to Officiate in the Service for Him. It was desired, We shou'd meet ye next Day[42] at 10 a Clock as a Sub-Commee and Sit all Day.

Oct 22. A Sub-Commee. Tuesday Oct 22 Met as a Sub-Commee about 10.[43] Present.

Bps. St. Asaph, Salisb. Worcr. Chichesr.

Deans, Canterb: Norwich, Peterburrow.

Doctors, Hall, Beverige, Tenison, Grove, Scot, Williams.

Enter'd upon the Kalendar about Sts. Days, and determined only such to be inserted, that were allowed by Our Church, according to the First Book of Edw. 6. —— Went over the Service Book in Order; Resolved to omit the Benedictus &c.—— Agreed to leave out the Collect, *We are ty'd with the Chain &c* as not being in the Original Book — — — — — Quere that[44]; for in some of the Books, it is not left out, but put into another place: — — — said, in that of Ely[45] —— Continu'd till about 5 a Clock.

Sess 5. ⎫ On Wednesday Oct. 23[46] the Commee Sat about 3 a
Oct 23. ⎭ Clock. Present 14.

Bps. London, Asaph, Salisb: Worcestr. Chichester.

Deans. Canterbury, Norwich.

Drs. Hall, Beverige, Tenison, Grove, Scot, Alston, Williams.

Went over what was done by the Sub-Commee —— The cheif debate was about the Athanasian Creed —— It was moved, either to leave it with an alias, or to leave out the Damnatory Clauses, or to leave it as it is with a Rubrick. For it was alledg'd 1. That it was Antient. 2 Received[47] by Our Church ever since the Reformation. 3 Offence to leave it out; but granted that if it was to do now, it were better to omit it.

It was reply'd by the Bp. of Salisb: 1 That the Church of England received the 4 first General Councils that the Ephesine Council condemns any new Creeds. 2. That this Creed was not very antient, and the Filioque especially. 3. That it condemned the Greek Church whom yet We defend. —— It was propos'd by the Bp. of Worcest. to have a Rubrick, that it shou'd be interpreted by Article — — — — of Our Church, and that the condemning Sentences were only as to the Substance of the Articles; which was drawn up and approv'd of.

We sat till 6. and adjourned till 10 next day.

Sess 6. ⎫ Thursday Oct. 24 — met about 10[48] Present 13
Oct 24. ⎭ Bps. London, Asaph, Salisb: Worcest. Chichester.

Deans, Norwich, Peterburrow.

Doctors, Hall, Beverige, Tenison, Scot, Alston, Williams.

Went upon the Offices of Baptism, and the Lords Supper.

About Dipping ———— said it was the Custom[49] to dip in England ———— Bp. of St. Asaph said, it was so still in some parts of Wales; putting in the head, and letting it run over the Body.[50] ———— Orderd that both be inserted.

About the Lords Supper; Debated the Prayer of Consecration; that it was not the words, but the setting it apart by Prayer, that was the Consecration.

Ordered that when they Consecrate afresh they begin with the Prayer ———— In the Trisagion, alter'd it to Thou O Holy One ———— ———— Thou O Son of God with the Holy Ghost.

Here Dr. Tenison reproving Dr. Bev: he took so ill, that he was leaving; but Dr. T. ask'd his Pardon.[51]

Adjourned till Friday, 1 a Clock.

Sess 7. ⎱ Friday, Oct. 25. one a Clock, the Comissrs. Sat. Prt.
Oct 25. ⎰ 15.[52] Bps. London, Asaph, Salisb: Worcest. Chichester.

Deans, Norwich, Peterburrow.

Drs. Goodman, Hall, Beverige, Tenison, Scot, Fowler, Alston, Williams.

Went over the Office of Baptism ———— Disputed the point of Regeneration ———— Beverige went away early ———— Enter'd upon the Catechism ———— went away ———— Bp. of London &c. Adjourned till Monday 3 a Clock,[53] So We became a Sub-Commee, viz. Bps. Salisb: Asaph, Worcest. Chichr. Drs. Tenison, Hall, Williams, ———— went over the rest of the Catechism.

Sess 8. ⎱ On Monday Oct. 28. 3 a Clock[54] ———— Present
Oct 28. ⎰ 12. Bps. London, Asaph, Salisb: Chester, Worcest. Chichester.
Drs. Hall, Tenison, Grove, Fowler, Scot, Williams.

There was a long Debate about Baptismal Regeneration, and the Phrase in the office *Regenerated by Thy Holy Spirit*. It was desired by Dr. T.[55] that either the latter part of it, *by thy Holy Spirit* might be left out,[56] or explain'd, Forasmuch as the Phrase (as now used) implies an actual Change. It was answered, that the Phrase has been antiently apply'd to Baptism, and if there were not more in Baptism than the outward washing it would give away the Cause to the Anabaptists. But it was again reply'd, Not so, because it was a Federal Regeneration; and what gave a Title to the Privileges of

167

that Covenant, (of which the Assistance of the H. Spirit was One) according as They were capable of Them. It was Argued further, that this was a Phrase disputed by the Non-Conformists, and by all those that[57] were against falling from Grace ───── It was said further, Baptism did unite us to the Spirit.

They proceeded to the Office of Confirmation, In the first place was read an Exhortation to be used sometime before Confirmation (as there is before the Sacrament) The first thing debated in that was that Hebr. 6 was applyed to it, and so apply'd as if Confirmation was of the Foundation. The B. of S. said it was of the Foundation respecting Government. ───── B. of A. said that it appeard to be so, because immediately follows the baptismoi,[58] by which the Baptism of Christ was distinguish'd from that of St. John. But B.W.[59] that He thought it was ─────

It was agreed to be left out in the Exhortation. The Collect was mended by putting in New Testament Phrases into the place of the old. And it was agreed to, that there should be a Charge or Exhortation drawn up, to be used by the Bishop in the Close.

Adjourned till Wednesday 3 a Clock.

Sess 9.  } On Wednesday, Oct. 30. 3 a Clock.[60] Present 15.
Oct 30.  } Bishops, London, Chester, Salisb: Worcestr. Chichestr.

Deans, Pauls, and Canterbury (Dr. Sharp)[61]

Drs. Goodman, Tenison, Beveridge, Grove, Fowler, Scot, Alston, Williams.

Then was read what was done the last meeting about Confirmation and the phrase *Regenerated* in the Prayer was objected against. Dr. Goodman, S. and T. said it was fitt[62] to be expunged especially in the Thanksgiving, or moderated because of the Dissenters & because . . . . It was answer'd, That this was the Doctrine of all Reformed Churches, and that this could not be without altering the Office of Baptism the Catechism &c. and it was put to the Vote, whether it was not to be done, or left to the Convocation. Carry'd for the latter. Then they read the Charge to be used at the Conclusion of that Office, and after some Amendments proceeded to the Office of *Matrimony*. Agreed to make a Rubrick about the Ring; and to leave out *with my Body* &c. and put in other words for it.

The Bp. of London went away about 5. The Court Adjourned till Thursday 3 a Clock.

Sess 10. }
Oct 31. }  Thursday Oct. 31. 3 a Clock.[63] Present 9.

Bishops, London, Salisb: Chester, Worcestr. Chichestr. Bangor.[64]

Dn. of Pauls (Dr. Tillotson)[65]

Drs. Scot, Alston,
Considered the Office of Visitation of the Sick.[66]

Adjourned til Friday Novr. 1.2 a Clock.


Sess 11. }
Nov 1. }  Met Novr. 1. Friday about 2 a Clock.[67] Present 12.

Bishops, London, Salisb. Chester, Bangor. Chichr.

Dean of Canterbury. (Dr. Sharp)

Drs. Tenison, Fowler, Beveridge, Grove, Scot, Williams

Review'd the Commination —— Considered[68] the Alterations to be made in it.

Then Dr. F. moved, that the business of the Athanasian Creed might be reheard, and he desired it might be left at Liberty with a *may be read* since[69] he had convers'd with several Conformists and Nonconformists. The Conformists were Men of Eminence that were of that mind and some of them had[70] not read it for many Years. The Nonconformists were desirous of it and were of the mind that no Creed should be used, but what was conceived in Scripture Expressions. However, it was thought more advisable to leave it as it was and let the Convocation consider it. Both B. of Salisb: and Dean of Cant. undertaking to promote it in both Houses of Convocation.

Then they proceeded to the Business of *Ordination* which the B. of S. reduced to 3 Cases. 1. That of the Church of Rome. 2. Of the foreign Churches. 3. Of the Dissenters[71] at home. As to the Church of Rome it was urged we had very great Reason now to question the validity of their Orders, because they Ordained without imposition of Hands (. . . . till after Ordination) and without the Form of Words *whosesoever Sins* &c.[72] and then it was requisite that there should be an Intention, which cou'd never[73] be proved. Bur here it was reply'd, We ought to be Cautious, because it has always been own'd by our Church. And we also received Orders from them. And therefore the Bp. of L. said that We[74] did not question the validy of their Orders, but the Sufficiency

169

of the Evidence. And this was confirm'd, not only by the Cheats put upon us, but also because we had no Communion with that Church. Dr. Bev. reply'd, So it wou'd be with the Reformed. It was answer'd Not; Because there We have Communion, and they were willing to give us Satisfaction, but that the Church of Rome wou'd not do.[75] And this was no more than what the Antient Church did, which wou'd not admit without Literae formatae. It was agreed to propose it, whether therefore[76] they shou'd not be Reordain'd with a Conditional Ordination, *If thou art not already Ordained*. 2. As for that of Foreign[77] Churches, it was urg'd by B. Sy. that the Church of England had allowed it, as in Du Moulin Prb. of Canterb: Dr. Bev. reply'd that might be, for that it was not necessary where there was no Cure of Souls. Nay, the Dean of Canterb: said, that he had heard Laymen had been P'bendaries (if not Camden) many.[78] But the Bp. laid before them the Case of the Scotch Bishops who were Consecrated Bps. without being Reordain'd Priests; and that K. James 1st. stifly insisted upon it,[79] and was psent at the Consecration in Westmr. Abby. That Bp. Andrews opposed it but yielded; and that He somewhere says of such Ordination[80] .... 2. It was said, it was never made necessary til 1661. 3. That it was allowed in a Case of necessity, by those that were most violent, and that in positive Institutions necessity rul'd, And at last it was propos'd to draw up a Rubrick to signify that it was sufficient ᵗho' imperfect Ordination; and that they shou'd be received by imposition of the hands of the Bp. only to Officiate in the Church of England. o———*
3. As for Dissenters, the Bp. of Salisb. said, that it was a kind of necessity in our prt. circumstances; and that the Antient Church did give us some directions, when notwithstanding the Canons of the Church against admitting two Bps. to one Altar, yet they were willing to Receive ye Donatists into the same City, and that the Survivour shou'd be the Bp. tho' the Donatists had been very vexatious. But to this Dr. Bev: reply'd They had Episcopal Ordination. But it was[81] answer'd, that there could be no more two Bps. than a Presbyter be Ordained without a Bishop, and if the Necessity of affairs was a Reason for the One, it was a Reason for the other; and that the Stopping of the prt. Schism made it a necessity. It was then queried[82] how it should be done; and it was agreed, that it shou'd be only for this turn, those that were in Orders, but not to proceed further. The further debate was adjourned til Monday 3 a Clock. o——— It was sometimes queried, What good wou'd this do as to the Dissenters. It was answered by Dr. Still:[83] We sat there to make such Alterations as were fitt, which wou'd be fit to make were there no Dissenters, and which wou'd be for the improvement of the Service.

It was said, I think by Dr. F. that some of the Nonconformists desired to be heard. It was reply'd by Dr. Still: that was not to be allowed, because doubtless they had no more to say by word of mouth than they had in their Writings. And that They might do them Justice there were several of their Books laid before the Commee, that They might consult if there be occasion.

On Monday Nov. 3. at 3 a Clock. Present 16.

Bps. London, Asaph, Sarum, Bangor, Chichester.

Deans, Canterbury, Pauls.

Drs. Goodman, Hall, Beveridge, Tenison, Grove, Fowler, Scot, Alston, Willms.

Reassumed the debate of Reordinations; and a Rubrick read[84] about it, signifying the Reasons of this proceeding. But Dr. Bev: said, if the Ordination should be put[85] hypothetically viz. *If thou art not Ordained*, it lookt like Equivocation on the part of the Ordainer and Ordained: Of the Ordainer, because it is likely he believ'd him not ordained before; Of the Ordained, because he Questioned not his former Ordination. To this the B. of S. answer'd, that there was no reason for this because here was a Declaration annexed, that each should reserve his opinion.

Then Dr. K.[86] made another proposal. . . .

Then Dr. Scot read Bp. Bramhals method that he took in Ordaing. such.

Then Dr. Grove propos'd, that the Ordination might be lookt upon as imperfect only, not invalid. Not invalid, because then all acts done by them, must be so accounted and that They would never allow; but as Imperfect and then the Bp. without Presbyters shou'd lay his hands on them, as it was in the Form before of Foreign Churches. But to this the Dean of St. Pauls reply'd that in this point we were to respect 2 things. 1. The Preservation of the Churches principle about the necessity of Episcopal Ordination when it might be had; and the Case of[87] the Dissenters; and that it was much like the marrying of the Man and the Woman refusing, but after a Term of Years She consenting to go on, the Woman was then married alone, without beginning again with the Man.

The Dn. of Cant. ask'd why it might not be allowed as well as that the Church of Rome formerly allow'd ours (as in Q. Marys Letter to Gardiner) Quod illis deerat, Supplebit Episcopus; which they conceived was the Potestas Sacrificandi, Mason 1.5.c.14 P. 671. 672 and so it might be here (v Mason P. 172) where we were to say, If thou art not already Ordained &c. To this it was reply'd that then the question only was as to the matter of fact (as in Baptism) allowing their right, if prov'd; but here it was a matter of right. After this it was proposed and carryed (Dr. Bev. & Scot dissenting) to be hypothetically expressed, and after an examination of the Phrase it was also agreed, that the like Phrase should be inserted at the Archdeacons Presentation[88] in Ordination.

Before the Bp. of London went away adjourned till Wednesday 3 a Clock.

Sess 13.⎱ On Wednesday Nov. 6. 3 a Clock[89] ——— Present 13.
Nov 6.   ⎰

Bishops, London, Asaph, Sarum, Chester, Chichester.

Deans ——— Pauls and Canterbury.

Drs. Hall, Tenison, Grove, Scot, Alston, Williams.

Begun with the Office of Ordination, and particularly with the Care that ought to be taken in conferring Orders; that at least a Month before they should send in their Testimonials and at least a Week before make their appearance. It was proposed that among the things the Candidates were to be try'd in, one shou'd be the composing some short discourse upon the place, in writing upon some point or Article. Upon which the B. of S. told the Board, what was wont to be in his Time in Scotland, first[90] that He shou'd compose some practical Discourse, then Doctrinal, then mixt; shou'd be examin'd in the Originals, and then in Sacred Chronology. So that it took up a Months Space.

It was proposed also, that the Names of the Persons to be Ordain'd shou'd be expos'd some Days before and Notice given to the parish He was to be Instituted to. Bp. of London said, He thought,[91] this belong'd to the Canons; but it was reply'd, that the Canons were but little consulted, and the Rubrick more in use.

Then they proceeded to the Phrase, *Receive the Holy Ghost.* Bp. of Sarum said, this was not above 400 Years standing, and that it was brought in in those Ages when the Design[92] was to exalt the Priesthood; That the Forms originally were by way of Prayer, *Exaudi Nos &c.* And so it was in the Apostolical Constitutions, in Dionys. Areopi. and the Council of Carthage,[93] and that it begun to be alter'd in Hildebrands time. Bp. of S. Asaph reply'd, he thought the Form to be very fitt, because tho' spoke upon extraordinary, yet the Ordinary was convey'd with the extraordinary and so[94] insisted upon the conveying of the Spirit by Baptism and the Lords Supper, *Drink into one Spirit. (Accipe Sp. Sanctum* i.e. istiusmodi Sanctam et Spiritualem potestatem, Seu Spiritus Sti gratiam, qualis ad hoc requiritur, ut quis ex Presbytero fiat Ep'us. Mason. 1.4. c. 1. p. 10. *Receive the Holy Ghost*, i.e. the Grace of the Holy Ghost, to exercise and discharge the Office of Priesthood: Bramhal, Consecran. of Prot. Bps. defended p. 486 ——— Gratiam quae peccata remitteret Hieron.

172

Chrys. Amb. ―――― Remittere i.e. declarare, praedicare, ib: p 633 &c. v. plura). And to *receive* was so to Receive as to bestow it upon others in the Sacraments. To this Dr. Scot agreed. B. of S. reply'd, that this was not contending for any thing else, but leaving out the Word *receive* and that these Texts did not prove it. Bp. of Chichr. said, that Sense was hard. The Professor[95] and others said, they thought no more was intended by it, than *Receive* ye Commission to preach the Word and Administer the Sacraments, in the due Use of which the Holy Ghost in convey'd. This was left to further consideration.

Went upon the Collects for Sunday and adjourned till Friday 1 a Clock.

Sess 14. ⎱
Nov 8. ⎰ Met Friday Novr. 8: 1 a Clock[96] ―――― Present 13.

Bishops, Lond. Asaph, Salisb. Chester. Chichesr.

Deans, Pauls and Canterbury.

Doctors, Tenison, Grove, Fowler, Scot, Alston, Williams.

In the first place went over the first 10 Collects[97] after Trinity.

Then reassumed the debate about the Form of Ordination. Bp. of Sarum read it by way of Prayer. Here Dr. Scot interposed, and said that He thought the Form used by our Saviour, tho' in an extraordinary Case, yet did contain the Ordinary; as, that *as my Father hath sent me So &c* and that it seemed more Solemn to keep it, as it has been used in the Church since the Reformation; and if this be not retained,[98] there is no Form of Ordination Authoritatively. To this it was reply'd, That the Form aforesaid, used by our Saviour did not seem to be the Form necessary to be used;[99] and if it was necessary to be used in that manner Authoritatively, then there had been no Ordination when that had not been used. 2. It was evident that the Church never used it in that Form for 1300 Years together; as Appears by 16 Rituals[100] produc'd by Morinus de Ordinatione and what was in the Council of Carthage, &c nor is now used in any Church but Our's. 3. That it was not us'd in Ordination in the Church of Rome (where it is by way of Prayer, *Exaudi Nos* &c but after it, when the Bp. alone impos'd his hands. Dr. W. said; that Bp. Bramhal and Mr. Mason did instance in this as the primitive Practice (The Beleif and practice of the Primitive Church who knew no other matter than Imposition of hands, nor Form, than *Receive the Holy Ghost* &c Bramhal, Protest. Ordinat. defended, p. 994) So *Mason*,[101] who tho' He saith in one place, In Baptismo est certa verborum Formula, quam Christus ipse per modum praecepti Sanxit in Ordine non item. 1.2. c. 14. p. 665[102] yet soon after adds p. 666.

that in the Church of Rome is used, *quicquid ad Presbyteratus essentiam est necessarium confertur autem per eadem verba quibus hodie utitur Ecclesia Anglicana, imo quibus usus est ipse Christus.*

To this the Bp. of Sarum reply'd, it was their mistake, and if Mr. Mason had liv'd since Morinus publish'd his Book, He would have made good work with it. Here the Dean of Cant. shewed a quotation out of St. Austin de Trinitate 1.15. c. 27 proving Christ to be God because he gave the H. Ghost; but the Church only prays for it. *Quomodo ergo Deus non est, qui dat Spiritum Sanctum; imo quis Deus est qui dat Deum? neque enim aliquis discipulorum ejus dedit Spiritum Sanctu orabant quippe ut veniat in Eos quibus manus imponebant, non ipsi Eum dabant,*[103] *quem morem in suis propositis etiam nunc servat Ecclesia.* Bp. of St. Asaph shew'd how the Apostles did therefore pray, that the H. Ghost might be confer'd by the Imposition of their hands Acts 8.15.17 and he said, that Simon then receiv'd the H. Ghost himself. Dr. Scot offred further, that We ought to consider the prudence of such an Alteration. It was answer'd that the Commissrs. made some Alteration in 1661 And the Church of Rome great and many. And besides this was[104] to bring the Case to its true State.

The Bp of London went away about 5. Adjourned the Court till 3 on Monday ————— But they sat and went over many other Collects.

Sess 15. ⎱ Monday, Nov. 11 met about 3 a Clock[105] —————
Nov 11. ⎰ Present 10.

Bishops, Lond. Asaph. Sarum. Bangor. Chester, Chichesr. Dean, of Pauls.

Doctors, Tenison, Fowler, Williams.

Proceeded on the Collects and for the most part kept to it as a Rule (where it cou'd be observ'd) to take the matter of ye Collect out of the Epistle and Gospel; especially considering that this was done in the 5 new Collects composed in 1661 ————— Order'd, That the Collects that are good but not suitable to the Epistle and Gospel be retained but put into the Number of the voluntary Prayers.

Went thro' the rest of the Collects after Trinity; and after the Bp. of London, &c[106] went away, they continued on, and went through some of the Saints-days, as far as Phil. & Jac. Adjourned til Wednesday 3 a Clock.

There was a debate about shortning the Service. Bp. of Sarum moved that on Sundays, the Epistle and Gospel shou'd go for the Lessons; but it was answer'd, that that wou'd be offensive, and besides it would not be so proper and beneficial to the People, as to read the Scriptures in Course. It was Answer'd this[107] might be in the

Afternoon. It was proposed by others, that rather they would abridge it, by ending the Litany at the Lords Prayer (the latter part seeming now but a botch, and cheifly respecting times of Persecution) and after that read the Commandments and so conclude.

Sess 16. ⎫
Nov 13. ⎭ Wednesday Nov. 13 : [108] Present 15.

Bishops, Lond. S. Asaph. Sarum, Bangor, Chester, Chichester.

Deans, Pauls, Canterbury, (stayd not)[109] Peterburrow.

Doctors, Tenison, Beveridge, Grove, Scot, Alston, Williams.

Went over the rest of the Collects for the Holy Days — — — — Adjourned til Friday 9 in the Morning.

Sess 17. ⎫
Nov 15. ⎭ Friday Nov. 15, met about 10 ——— Present 14.

Bishops, London. S. Asaph. Sarum. Bangor. Chester.

Deans, Pauls, Canterbury, Peterburrow.

Doctors, Tenison, Grove, Scot, Fowler, Alston, Williams.

Went over the Whole again; made some few Alterations[110] and Amendments; the most considerable was in the Athanasian Creed; where after it was suggested, that they were the Articles, and not the Terms in which those Articles were expressed, that were assented to; it was concluded, that the word *obstinately* should be inserted, and the reference to Article — — — — omitted. Added a new Service for Rogation-Sunday ——— Proceeded as far as the Sunday after Trinity —— Then rose about 5 and adjourned till Monday 9 a Clock.

Nov 18.    Monday Nov: 18 about 10 in ye Morning Present 8.

Bishops, Lond. Asaph, Sarum.

Dean of Peterburrow.

Doctors, Tenison, Grove, Alston, Williams.

Not being a *Quorum,* we only read over what was done before, beginning at                    Sunday after Trinity and proceeded to the Office of Baptism.[111] It was proposed by W. that a Rubrick shou'd be drawn up respecting those Ministers that shou'd Scruple the use of the Cross; that being the most material point in question among[112] the Non-conformists, and which they all agreed in their dissent from.

It was moved by Dr. G. that however, this should extend to those that were to come in, not to those that[113] were already in the Church. It was agreed, that it should be much after the way taken in the Rubrick about kneeling. The Bp. of Sarum drew it up ———— There were some few Alterations, as particularly that dipping shou'd be continu'd in Baptism ———— Parted till 3. Afternoon.[114]

Sess 18. ⎱
Nov 18. ⎰ Afternoon — Present 9.

p.m. Bishops, London, Asaph, Sarum, Bangor, Chester.

Doctors, Tenison, Grove, Alston, Williams.

There being a Quorum, the Bp. of Sarum proposed the Rubrick for their Consent; which was agreed to.

Then there was a debate about the extent of the Comissn Whether We were to Sit after the Convocation began? And that We shew'd[115] from the Commission that We were to offer to it.

Then how far the Power of the Convocation did extend? The Bp. of Sarum said, that since the Act of Submission in H.8s. time, they cou'd not enter upon any matter but what was proposed by the King; and the King now did propose by the Commission: So that they cou'd begin nothing, tho' by the Commission thy might debate and reject[116] as they pleased after the proposal.

Proceeded to review the rest of the Offices, and finished.

There was remaining, the Form of Subscription (which the B. of Sarum proposed before there was a Quorum, but it was forgot) and Excommunication was spoke of, but it was too late.

Rose up sine Die.

And thus this Assembly concluded, after above 6 Weeks continuance, and 18 Sessions;[117] besides about 6 Sub-Comittees there and elsewhere.

The Alterations and Improvements are in the interleav'd Common Prayer Book, deposited with Dr. Tenison.

The Convocation began Nov. 6.

Commissioners that never sat 6. viz. York, Carlisle, Exeter, Beaumont, Montague, Battley.[118]

Bishop of Rochester was only twice, and came not after Sess: 2. Oct: 16 ———— Nor Dr. Jane, Aldridge, Meggott, after Sess: 3. Oct: 18.[119]

Memorand.

Nov. 5. 1708. This transcript Collated with Bp. Williams's original Papers, by

Edmund Gibson
John Garnett.

This Copy is transcribed, & on collating it I think exactly, from one in 4⁰, containing 20 pages, & belonging to Mr Sturges Prebendary of Winchester, but lent me in 1761 by Dr Lowth Prebendary of Durham, with Leave from Mr Sturges, that I might have a Copy of it taken.[120]

## APPENDIX 2

An Account of the proceedings of the Commissioners of 1689, by Dr Nicholls

(Apparatus ad Defens. Eccles. Angl. p. 95)

This account is understood to have been obtained by Dr Nicholls from the papers of Bishop Williams (of Chichester) who was one of the Commissioners. Kennet, Comp. Hist. Vol. iii. p. 591. Quoted in Cardwell, *Conferences* p. 432-3

Imperato operi viri reverendi se protinus accingunt, et in Liturgia denuo limanda labores auspicantur. Primum in examen vocatur Calendarium, ex quo lectionibus Apocryphis exturbatis, Canonicae Scripturae capita suffecta sunt, cum majore populi fructu perlegenda. Symbolum quod vulgo Sancti Athanasii dicitur, quia a multis improbatur propter atrocem de singulis, secus quam hic docetur credentibus, sententiam ministri arbitrio permittitur, ut pro apostolico mutetur. Collectae in totum anni cyclum de novo elaborantur, ad epistolae et evangelii doctrinam congruentius factae; et cum tanta verborum elegantia atque splendore, tantaque Christianae mentis vi atque ardore compositae sunt, ut nihil possit animos audientium magis afficere et accendere, et eorum mentes ad Deum evehere. Eas primum contexuit, summus hujus rei artifex, Simon Patricius; ulteriorem vim sanguinem spiritumque adhibebat Gilbertus Burnetius; eas denique cum magno judicio, singulis verbis diligenter expensis, examinante Edvardo Stillingfleto; ultimam limam addente ac verbis enodibus et dulcis facilisque eloquentiae fluentis iterum perpoliente Joanne Tillotsonio. Novam Psalmorum versionem ornabant originibus Richardo Ciddero, viro in linguis orientalibus versatissimo. Singulas dictiones et vocabula, quae sparsim per Liturgiam improbarant illius hostes, exquisita indagine collegit Thomas Tenisonius; in eorum loca suffectis verbis perspicuis et distinctis, nec a morosiori aliquo cavillandis. Alia quaedam proposita sunt, sed quae integre ad synodum referenda judicabantur. Primum ut crux baptismalis seu infantium frontibus signetur, seu prorsus omittatur, penes parentes sit eligere. Deinde si nonconformista minister ad Ecclesiam revertatur, novis mysteriis vulgari ritu non iterum initiandus, sed ordinatione quadam conditionali potius insigniendus, uti nobis in usu est baptismum infantibus, de quorum baptizatione non admodum compertum est, inferre; benedictione episcopi addita, ut mos erat apud antiquos, clericos ab haereticis ordinatos recipiendi (Dionys. Alex. ap. Euseb. Hist. Eccl. 1. 7. c.2. Concil. Nic. 1. Can. 8. Just. sive Author Resp. ad orthodox. resp. 18. Theod. Hist. Eccl. 1.i. c.8.) In sacris ordinibus tali modo conferendis exemplo praeiverat vir de ecclesia optime meritus Dominus Bramallus, Hiberniae Primas, cum Scotos Presbyteros in Ecclesiam reciperet.

Haec eorum summa erat quae in hoc congressu viri doctissimi moliebantur.

# ABBREVIATIONS IN NOTES

| | |
|---|---|
| 1549 | *The First Prayer Book of King Edward VI* (Everyman Edn. No. 448. London, 1964). |
| 1552 | *The Second Prayer Book of King Edward VI* (Everyman Edn). |
| 1559 | *The Prayer Book of Queen Elizabeth* The Antient and Modern Libr. of Theol. Lit. (London, 1890). |
| D.B. | *The Durham Book* ed. G. J. Cuming. (Oxford, 1961). |
| S.L. | *The Making of the Scottish Prayer Book of 1637,* Gordon Donaldson. (Edinburgh, 1954). |
| 1662 | *The Book of Common Prayer.* |
| Exceptions | *The Exceptions of 1661 against the Prayer Book,* quoted in Cardwell, *Conferences.* |
| Let. Min. | *A Letter from A Minister in the Country* Burnet (1689). |
| Let. Friend | *A Letter to a Friend relating to the present Convocation at Westminster,* H. Prideaux (1690). |
| V. Cleri | *Vox Cleri, Or the Sense of the Clergy,* Thomas Long (1690). |
| V. Populi | *Vox Populi, Or the Sense of the Sober Lay-men* (1690). |
| JRC | *The Judgment of the Foreign Reformed Churches* (1690). |
| New Survey | *A New Survey of the Book of Common Prayer* (1690). |
| Vindication | *A Vindication of two letters concerning alterations* (1690). |
| The Way | *The Way to Peace amongst All Protestants* (1688). |
| Terms | *An Explanation of the Terms, Order and Usefulness of the Liturgy 1717* (1st Edn. 1690/91). |
| Let. Till. | *Letter to Tillotson from U.M.,* quoted in *Conferences* p. 452f. |
| Brief Discourse | *A Brief Discourse concerning the lawfulness of worshipping God . . .* by Bp. Williams, (2nd Edn. 1694). |
| Wickham Legg | *English Church Life from the Restoration to the Tractarian Movement* by W. L. (London, 1914). |

# NOTES TO THE INTRODUCTION

1. E. Cardwell, *A History of Conferences* (1841), p. 282.

2. The members of the Commission included, amongst others, Bishops: Cosin, Sheldon, Sanderson, Walton, Sparrow, Pearson and Gunning. Presbyterians: Reynolds, Tuckney, Lightfoot, Baxter, Bates, and Jacombe.

3. For a full discussion see Dr Cuming 'The Grand Debate' (*Church Quarterly Review*, January 1962).

4. Anthony Sparrow, *A Rationale upon the Book of Common Prayer of the Church of England* (1657), preface.

5. The following account is a collation from N. Sykes, *From Sheldon to Secker* (Cambridge, 1959); ed. G. Nuttall and O. Chadwick, *From Uniformity to Unity* (1962); A. H. Wood, *Church Unity with Uniformity* (1963); E. Cardwell, *A History of Conferences*.

6. Pepys Diary 21 Dec 1667, (Dent edn., 1924) p. 208.

7. Article on 'The Protestant Reconciliation in the Exclusion Crisis' (*Journal of Ecclesiastical History*, 1964).

8. Thomas Long, *Vox Cleri or the Sense of the Clergy* (1690) p. 3-5.

9. G. Burnet, *History of his own time* (1815), Vol. II. p. 345; William Claget, *The Present State of the Controversy between the Church of England and the Church of Rome* (1687); William Wake, *Continuation of the Present state of the controversy* (1686). *A Catalogue of all discourses published against popery during the reign of James II* (anon) 1689.

10. As for example the Ecclesiastical Commission's treatment of Sharp and Compton. Baxter also suffered at their hands, Jeffreys suggesting that the old man should be whipped through the streets.

11. E. Cardwell, *Conferences* p. 399.

12. William Sancroft (1617-93) At the restoration he was chaplain to Charles II and acted as scribe for Cosin at the Savoy Conference. In 1678 he succeeded Sheldon as Archbishop of Canterbury.

13. George D'Oyly, *Life of William Sancroft* Vol. I, p. 312.

14. Ibid., p. 251-2.

15. *The Autobiography of Symon Patrick* (Oxford, 1839) p. 131.

16. Thomas Tenison (1636-1715) Educated Corpus Christi, Cambridge where he was admitted Scholar in 1653. Graduated in the same year and after a time of studying 'physick' received his M.A. in 1660, when his ordination which had been kept secret was made public. He became a Fellow (1659) and later a Reader at Corpus Christi (1665) In 1680 became D.D. and was presented to the rectory of St. Martin-in-the-Fields. From 1686-92 he was also Minister of St. James' Piccadilly. In 1683 and the following years he was involved in talks on reunion with the dissenters, and continued these activities intermittently until 1690. In 1691 he became Bishop of Lincoln, and on the death of Tillotson in 1694, Archbishop of Canterbury. (DNB, 1908 edn.)

17. The following events are collated from *The Autobiography of Symon Patrick* (Oxford, 1839), p. 131-3; and from Clarendon's Diary, *Correspondence of Henry Hyde* 2 vols. ed. S. W. Singer (1828) p. 171-2.

18. D'Oyly, *Life of William Sancroft* Vol. I, p. 262-4.

19. John Tillotson (1630-94) Educated at Clare Hall, Cambridge, graduating in 1650. In 1660 took his D.D., and became chaplain to Charles II, and Prebend of Canterbury, in 1672 becoming Dean. He became Archbishop of Canterbury in 1690 on the deprivation of Sancroft.

Edward Stillingfleet (1635-99) Educated at St. John's, Cambridge, graduating in 1653, when he received a fellowship. In 1664 he was appointed to the Rolls Chapel, and the following year to the rectory of St. Andrew's, Holborn. In 1668 became D.D. 1677 was made Archdeacon of London, and in 1678 Dean of St. Paul's and in 1689 he became Bishop of Worcester.

Symon Patrick (1626-1707) Educated at Queen's College, Cambridge, graduating in 1647. Received Presbyterian Orders, but was converted to Episcopacy being privately ordained by Dr Joseph Hall, Bishop of Norwich in 1654. In 1662 he was presented to the rectory of St. Paul's Covent Garden where he remained until 1672 when he became a Prebend of Westminster. Dean of Peterborough in 1679, and in 1689 became Bishop of Chichester, translated to Ely in 1691.

Robert Grove (1634-96) Educated at St. John's, Cambridge, graduating in 1657. For several years lived at College as a tutor, becoming D.D. in 1681. In 1670 after several minor preferments, became Rector of St. Andrew Undershaft, and in 1679 Canon of St. Paul's. In 1690 he became Archdeacon of Middlesex, and in 1691 was consecrated Bishop of Chichester.

William Lloyd (1627-1717) Educated at Oriel, Oxford, graduating in 1639, becoming D.D. in 1667. After minor preferments, became Prebend of Ripon in 1660; 1667 Prebend of Salisbury; 1672 Archdeacon of Merioneth; 1672 Dean of Bangor holding many appointments in plurality. In 1680 he became Bishop of St. Asaph, being translated to Lichfield and Coventry in 1692 and Worcester in 1700. (DNB 1908 edn.).

20. A. T. Hart, *William Lloyd* (1952), ch. 3 *passim.*

21. *Clarendon Diary* vol. II p. 240.

22. A. T. Hart, *William Lloyd* p. 103ff.

23. Ibid., p. 128, 133.

24. *Clarendon Diary,* p. 266, 269, 304.

25. D'Oyly, *Life of William Sancroft* vol. I p. 156.

26. Sir John Reresby, *Memoirs,* p. 302.

27. Ellis Correspondence (1829) vol. II p. 63.

28. G. Every, *The High Church Party* (1956), p. 22-3.

29. D'Oyly *Life of William Sancroft* Vol. I p. 324-5.

30. Ibid., p. 324-5.

31. Title page has no date. The moveable feasts are those of 1681-1720. State prayers except in the Communion Servive which refer to Charles, all refer to James. The Constitutions and Canons bound in with them are dated Oxford 1683.

32. A useful study on the whole of this subject may be found in George Every, *The High Church Party,* ch. 2 and 3.

33. *Autobiography of Symon Patrick* p. 137-8.

34. E. Cardwell, *Conferences,* p. 403-4.

35. Humphrey Prideaux *A Letter to a Friend* (1690), p. 2.

36. Clarendon vol. II p. 240.

37. *Autobiography of Symon Patrick* p. 140.
38. *High Church Party* p. 32.
39. Birch, *Life of Tillotson* p. 368.
40. For his relationship to Tillotson see Birch p. 229; and for his relationship with Tenison see E. Carpenter, *Thomas Tenison* (London, 1948) p. 42-9.
41. A. T. Hart, *William Lloyd* p. 133.
42. For relationship of Lloyd and Burnet see Hart *William Lloyd* p. 115.
43. Scott is seen working with the pressure group on 11 January cf. Letter of Bishop Turner of Ely to Sancroft. Hyde Correspondence vol. II p. 507, and Carpenter on Tenison p. 92.
44. E. Carpenter *The Protestant Bishop* (1956), p. 109ff, and 162ff.
45. Sprat had been on the Ecclesiastical Commission of James II and was fearful of reprisals after the revolution. He became strictly high Church overnight. (cf. Letter to Sancroft, Hyde Correspondence vol. II p. 510).
46. P. 1.
47. P. 4-5.
48. P. 12, 16, 20, 23-4.
49. *Vox Cleri, or the Sense of the Clergy* (1689), p. 1.
50. Full titles given in the Bibliography.
51. Humphrey Prideaux *Letter to a Friend* p. 2, 3-4.
52. Ibid., p. 5-7. *Answer to Vox Cleri* p. 22, 30.
53. Ibid., p. 19. *Answer to Vox Cleri* p. 13-14. Tenison's *Discourse* p. 24. *A Letter to a Member of Parliament in favour of the Bill for a Protestant Union* p. 5.
54. *The Way to peace among all Protestants* p. 2, 3. *Vox Populi* p. 8-9.
55. *Vox Cleri,* p. 45.
56. Ibid., p. 44, 6. *Just Censure to the Answer* p. 25.
57. *Judgment of Reformed Churches,* preface. *Remarks from the Country* p. 15.
58. *Vox Cleri,* p. 7, 10, 17, 45. *Remarks from the Country* p. 6-7. *Judgment of Reformed Churches* p. 7.
59. *Letter to a Minister* p. 17, 27. *Letter to a Friend* p. 20. *Answer to Vox Cleri* p. 26, 28-30. *The Remarks from the Country* p. 14, hold that the issue is simply a legal one.
60. *Letter to a Friend* p. 21, *Answer to Vox Cleri* p. 9.
61. *Letter to a Friend* p. 21-3.
62. *Answer to Vox Cleri* p. 6-7, 30. *Vindication of two letters* p. 4-7.
63. *Vox Cleri* p. 2, 10, 54. *Just Censure* p. 17. *Vox Laici* p. 11.
64. *Vox Cleri* p. 46. *Judgment of reformed Churches* p. 10-11 *Remarks from the Country* p. 8-11.
65. *Vox Cleri* p. 3, 6, 45, 2, 20, 34, 41, 47. *Judgment of reformed Churches* p. 58-9.
66. *Remarks from the Country* p. 8-11. Cf. also *To the Rev. and Merry Answerer.* p. 9.
67. *Letter to a Minister* p. 18ff. *Letter to a Friend* p. 7-8.
68. *Letter to a Friend* p. 12-13.

69. *Letter to a Minister* p. 4. *Letter to a Friend* 14-15, 16-17. *Answer to Vox Regis et Regni* p. 2.

70. *Letter to a Minister* p. 23, *Letter to a Friend* p. 13, *Answer to Vox Cleri* p. 16-18.

71. *Vox Cleri* p. 6, 11, 28. *Just Censure* p. 4. *Judgment of Reformed Churches* p. 56. *Vox Laici* p. 13, 16, 22.

72. *Vox Cleri*, 16, 23-4, 53 *Remarks from the Country* p. 1-2, 5-6, 12. *Vox Laici* p. 8.

73. *Remarks from the Country* p. 16-17.

74. *Letter to a Friend* p. 18. *Vox Cleri* p. 51. *Answer to Vox Cleri* p. 2. etc.

75. T. Birch, *The Life of Tillotson* p. 190. Burnet's comment on the failure of the revision was ' that the providence of God was displayed in the proceedings which led to a refusal to make alterations in the Liturgy '. cf. Carpenter on *Thomas Tenison* p. 108-9.


# NOTES ON THE PAGES
# BEFORE THE TITLE PAGES

*1.* E. L. are the initials of Edmund Gibson, Bishop London (1669-1748) into whose hands the MSS passed. See the Introduction page 46.

*2.* This comprises three pieces of paper stuck into the inner binding of the Book. The first is the section labelled ' Directions ', the second the list of MSS endorsed by Thomas Herring, Archbishop of Canterbury (1693-1757), and the third, ' From the Dean of the Arches '. On the page opposite, there is a fair copy of these pieces of paper, endorsed by Henry Hall.

*3.* This is added to a blank page before the start of the printed text. (f. iii) It was not in the Preces Privatae of 1564, but was added in the 1573 Edition under the title ' Admonitio ad Lectorem ' being placed immediately before the Catechism. The full text of the Preces may be found in *Private Prayers of the Reign of Queen Elizabeth* by W. K. Clay, for the Parker Society, Cambridge, 1851. This note is to be found on p. 428. Cf also Notes on the Calendar for Saints Days (JRC note 16).

1688: At the Beginning of 1688, at a similar juncture on blank interleaves, the following is written out by Tenison.
' D. Comber analyseth ys Book logically: he shows a method wch others see not in it. ye order may be mended, but to mend it nicelie, is to spoil it.

No Psalm to be set by the Clerk but the appointment of the minister: Some lessons more proper to be used in the place of them taken from Leviticus &c: The Chronicles will supply us wth some & the 3 first Chap. of Revelation.

I. J. Price.
N. J. Ibrice.
Church matters & persons.

1. how they fell (ii degenerated) from primitive simplicitie.
2. by what means they are again to be reduced to it.
   1. men are to gett over ye Comon hindrance of all Reformation. viz, ye thought of innovation, & that those who have bin otherwise accustom'd will be disturb'd at ye Alteration.

We see it otherwise in ye late Alter. in ye Com: Prayr wch were nigh 600 & no body minded ye chage so as to be shock'd at it.

Where ye Alteration is made on the Priests part, there will be no averseness in ye people: there Difficultie will arise fro new Responses cheifly, wch they will not be presently ready at; nor care they to be put out of their road, & to take pains tho in a bettr way. The Greatest diff: as to them is in ye Transl. of ye Psalms, wch may, with very little Alteration, be made bettr than those in ye middle of ye book.

In ye constitution of a Religious Societie, there should be

1. nothing Unaccountable
2  nothing merely defensible
3  nothing urg'd as a Term of Comunion wch is not some way more usefull than ye Omission of it would be. indeed nothing like a particular Church Covenant.
4. nothing phantasticall. Mr Calvin, wn he sd of some of or Rites that they were ' tolerabiles ineptiae ' spake very injudiciously. for no sort of impertinence in Religion is tolerable.
5. Nothing of Superfluous formalitie.
6. Multitude of Repititions should be avoided. & if distinct services (as is or prsent case) be performed at ye same time, in every one of them ye same forms (as ye Lds Prayer, & ye Collect for ye day in ye first & 2d serve) might perhaps be omitted.

By reason of the varietie of Tempers & capacities of men in a Nationall= Church, The public service appointed for them should be so formed as not to be too strait for them in indifferent matter, that they may be easie in ye Comunion of such a church, & have no temptation to Seperation: & because ye People, who are ye greater number, are unlearned; nothing should be introduc'd wch is not easily accountable, tho a learned ma might justify it with his less obvious reasons. as wping towds ye East &c.'

Some Notes on this insertion.

' D. Comber '. Thomas Comber: *Short Discourses upon the whole Common Prayer* London 1684 (2nd Edn. 1688).

' No Psalm . . .' This was inserted by another hand.

' I J. Price '. These two names are difficult to decipher, and it is with hesitation that these two renderings are included. The first surname is ' Price ', but there is no record of anyone of that name who could have taken part in these talks, either Dissenter or Churchman.

' In ye constitution '. Compare this whole section with;

Exceptions: ' First, that all the prayers, and other materials of the Liturgy may consist of nothing " doubtful or questioned " amongst pious, learned, and orthodox persons, inasmuch as the professed end of composing them is for the declaring of the unity and consent of all who join in the publick worship; it being too evident that the limiting of church-communion to things of " doubtful disputation " hath been in all ages the ground of schism and separation, according to the saying of a learned person.
' To load our publick forms with the private fancies upon which we differ, is the most soveraign way to perpetuate schism to the world's end. Prayer, confession, thanksgiving, reading of the Scriptures, and administration of the Sacraments in the plainest, and simplest Liturgy, though nothing either of private opinion, or of church-pomp, of garments, or prescribed gestures, of imagery, of musick, of matter concerning the dead, of many superfluities

which creep into the Church under the name of " order " and " decency " did interpose itself. To charge Churches and Liturgies with things un-necessary, was the first beginning of all superstition, and when scruple of conscience began to be made or pretended, then schism began to break in. If the special guides and fathers of the Church would be a little sparing of incumbering churches with superfluities, or not over-rigid, either in reviving obsolete customs, or imposing new, there would be far less cause of schism, or superstition; and all the inconvenience were likely to ensure, would be but this, they should in so doing yield a little to the imbecillity of inferiors; a thing which St. Paul would never have refused to do. Mean while wheresoever false or suspected opinions are made a piece of Church-Liturgy, he that separates is not the schismatick; for it is alike unlawful to make profession of known, or suspected falshood, as to put in practice unlawful or suspected.' (Quoted from John Hales, *Tract of Schism* p. 215).

It will be noted that Tenison's version is more Anglicanised, for while he included many of the principles ennunciated here, he omits the sections which would completely alter the ethos of Anglican worship; ritual, vestments, church music and prayer for the dead.

' Tolerabiles ineptiae '. The 1552 Prayer Book enraged many of those who had been forced into exile at the accession of Queen Mary. Knox and Whittingham who had fled to Frankfort therefore wrote to Calvin in Geneva, denouncing it as ' a huge volume of ceremonies ' and asking for ' his judgment therein.' To this Calvin replied, ' In Anglicana Liturgia, qualem describitis, multas video fuisse tolerabiles ineptias.' (*A Brieff discours off the troubles begonne at Frankfort in Germany A.D. 1554 Abowte the Booke of Common Prayer and Ceremonies MDLXXV.* (Reprinted London 1846) *Calvin Opp Epist et Responsa* p. 98. Cf. Proctor and Frere p. 129ff).

' Repitition '. See notes on the Gloria Patri; note 8 p. 186f.


## NOTES ON THE SECTIONS BEFORE
## MORNING PRAYER

*1.* 1688. (Title Page reads)
The Title as here
in this book

The Book of Common Prayer and
Administrations of the
Sacraments
and other Rites and Ceremonies
of the
Church of England
With ye Psalter or Psalms of
David.
Oxford Printed.
for M. Pitt, at the Angel in
St. Paul's Churchyard. (n.d.)

*2.* For the difference between Priest and Presbyter in popular estimation, cf. *The Anglican Ordinal* by Dr Paul Bradshaw, *passim*. The popular view may be summarized in Thomas Cartwright's own words; ' For so much as the common and usual speech of England is to note by the word " Priest " not a minister of the Gospel but a sacrificer, which the minister of the Gospel is not, therefore we ought not to call the ministers of the Gospel ' Priests '. And that this is the English speech, it appeareth by all the English translations, which translate always " hiereis " which were sacrificers " Priests "; and do not on the other side for any that ever I read translate " presbuteros " " a Priest ". Seeing therefore a Priest with us and in our tongue doth signify both by the papists' judgment in respect of their abominable mass, and also by the judgment of the protestants in respect of the beasts which were offered in the law, a sacrificing office, which the minister of the Gospel neither doth nor can excuse; it is manifest that it cannot be without great offence so used.' (T. C. lib. i, p. 198). The view of the Commissioners, would seem to be that of Richard Hooker: 'I rather term the one sort Presbyters than Priests, because in a matter of so small moment I would not willingly offend their ears to whom the name of Priesthood is odious though without cause. . . .' (*Ecclesiastical Polity*, v. LXXVIII (2) Everyman Edn. 1964, vol. 2 p. 429).

3. Deleted from the bottom of the title: Printed by the Assigns of John Bill Deceas'd: And by Henry Hills and Thomas Newcomb, Printers to the Kings Most Excellent Majesty, 1683.

. 4. Note, that the Commination Office has its title changed to the 'Latter part of the Office for Ashwednesday'. However, to save confusion, throughout the notes it is referred to as the Commination Service.

5. The Preface is not deleted, but this note is added. There does not seem to be any surviving draft of this, if one was composed. The alteration was necessary, as the general tenor of the 1662 preface, controverted the aims of the commission; particularly perhaps, 'Our general aim therefore in this undertaking was, not to gratify this or that party in any their unreasonable demands; but to do that, which to our best understandings we conceived might most tend to the preservation of Peace and Unity in the Church: . . . .'

6. Prev. Reading i. Cure of our souls.

7. 1688: (a) The Psalter shall . . . .

8. Prev. Reading i. And at the end of all the Psalms. ii. And at the end of the last at morning & Evening Service shall be repeated.
1688: (c) and at the end . . . .

Exceptions: (Concerning the Rubric in Morning Prayer for the Psalms) 'By this rubrick, and other places in the Common Prayer books, the Gloria Patri is appointed to be said six times ordinarily in every morning and evening service, frequently eight times in a morning, sometimes ten, which we think carries with it at least an appearance of that vain repitition which Christ forbids: for the avoiding of which appearance of evil, we desire it may be used but once in the morning, and once in the evening.'

New Survey: 'Such yielding as this would make no such Alteration but that our present Common-Prayer Books would serve; which they might do, if several Repetitions were left out . . . as of the Gloria Patri after every Psalm (yielded to be left out by those who met at the Bishop of Lincoln's House in King Charles I time) . . . .' (p. 33).

V. Populi: 'The Gloria Patri is sometimes said, for Instance on the first day of the Month, five times at the end of the Psalms read for the Morning-Service; again, at the end of the Lords Prayer after the absolution; again, at the end of the 95th Psal. O Come Let us Sing &c. again, at the end of the Benedicite; again, at the end of Benedictus; and again in the Litany; that is ten times in the ordinary Morning Service. (The Frequent Repetition of this, is one of those things which A. B. Usher, Bp. Williams, Prideaux, and Brownrig, Dr Ward, Featly, and Hacket took notice of, and would have consider'd, whether it were not fit to be amended . . . .) . . . . This hath a semblance of those vain Repititions forbidden by our Saviour; and when we reproach the Fanaticks for their Tautologies in Prayer, they immediately flap us in the mouth with this; and we profess sincerely we are not able to reply upon them.' (p. 2-3).

Let. Till: ' Since the age seems so averse to frequent repetitions in Divine worship, whether the Lords Prayer, Gloria Patri &c may not be more seldom used? ' (I).

Terms: ' Q. Why is Glory be to the Father, and to the Son, and to the Holy Ghost, so often used? And why at the end of every Psalm, and why standing?

A. Because it is of antient Use, by which we avouch our Doctrine and Faith of the Trinity against all Opposers.

2. That we may reduce that to practice, which is the Scope of every Psalm; and that is to give Glory to God . . . .' (p. 6).

Sparrow; (*Rationale* p. 32) ' This hymn of Glory is fit to conclude the Psalms, so especially this Christian hymn . . . . by which . . . we do as it were, fit this part of the Old Testament for the service of God under the Gospel, and make them evangelical offices.'

The Tanner MS (vol. cclxxxii) quoted in Conferences (p. 429) as ' An account of the proceedings . . . . communicated to Dr Calamy by a friend ' represents the findings of the Commission that ' the Gloria Patri shall not be repeated at the end of every Psalm, but of all, appointed for morning and evening prayer.' This is inaccurate. Originally the words above (i) ' all the Psalms ' was substituted but this was replaced by the more definite ' at the end of the last . . . . (ii). This however was also deleted, and the final phraseology is much more ambiguous. That this means that the Gloria should be repeated after each Psalm, is substantiated by the fact that the rubric after the Venite is unaltered in this respect.

Throughout the eighteenth century, one of the great objections to the Book of Common Prayer, was its frequent use of Repetitions; a situation which was brought about by reading Morning Prayer, Litany and Ante-Communion almost as if they were one service, rather than distinct acts of worship. Invariably those defending it, point to the fact that the services are intended to be separate entities, but this seems to have sounded merely as a ' valiant try ', in relation to practice. The main objections were centred in the frequent repetition of the Lords Prayer, Gloria Patri, Kyrie Eleison, and par excellence, the Litany. Each complaint is given under its respective head in the notes that follow. At this point, however, it may be worthwhile quoting Bishop William's Reply to Increase Mather's ' *A brief discourse concerning the unlawfulness of the Common Prayer worship* (1689), particularly as he was one of the Commissioners.

' For tho he cannot find " Incense " and " Holy Water ", & his " et caetera " among us, yet he saith, " What vain Repititions does the Common-Prayer-Book abound with? In one Service the worshippers must repeat the words, Good Lord deliver us, Eight times over. And, we beseech thee to hear us, Twenty times over. The Gloria Patri is to be repeated Ten times in the same Morning or Evening Service. That the Heathens were wont to worship their Idols just after the same manner, is clear from Matth. 7. &c ' . . . .

We yet do maintain, That there are such Repititions in Divine Worship, as are not vain, that are neither Heathenish or popish. Such do we read of in the Old Testament, as Ps 57. 1, 75. 1, 4, 5. 94. 1 103. 1, 2, 22, 107. 5, 15, 21, 31, 136 throughout. And thus our Saviour repeated the same words thrice in his Agony in the Garden, Matt. 26. 44, and twice on the Cross. Matt. 27. 46. And consequently all Repititions are no more condemned by our Saviour in Matt. 6. 7 than all long Prayers are, Matt. 23. 14. . . .

We are to consider wherein the Vanity of Repititions consists, so as to be after the manner of the Heathens. This admits great variety, and just bounds cannot be set; so that it's not to be exactly said, Here the vain Repititions begin. But they are such;

1. When they that use them, think that they shall be ' heard for their much speaking' as our Saviour saith, the Heathens did: . . . .

2. When it is nothing but Tautology, viz, a Repitition of the same words without new Matter; or of the same matter, but in different words. . . . . But when there are distinct Petitions, as when we say, ' We beseech thee to hear us good Lord', its as lawful to close after that manner, as it is to say, ' Amen', which we find to follow every particular Petition, and was distinctly repeated for twelve times together after that manner, Deut. 27. 15.

3. Vain Repititions, are when the words are thought sufficient, tho the Heart be not in them; but this is common to any. . . .

*(A Brief Discourse concerning the Lawfulness of Worshipping God.* 1st Edn. 1689-90), 2nd Edn corrected 1694. p. 5-7).

9. The Gloria Patri and the Psalms were said alternately by the Priest and people, the choir turning to face the East for the former. Similarly when they were sung, they were sung alternately, in metric versions. On the whole these versions, which were often printed at the end of Prayer Books, were appalling, and their contemporaries had no hesitation in saying so.

10. 1688 : Note also (d) . . . .

11. Note that the Roman numerals of the Prayer Book have been changed for arabic ones, and the format of the Tables slightly simplified, for the convenience of the Reader. No changes have, however, been made in what was written by the Commissioners, and where they used Roman numerals, these have been printed as such.

12. Exceptions: XI ' and that instead of the word " Sunday ", the word " Lord's-day ", may be every where used.'

13. Prev. Reading i. Ash. Wed. M. Isai 58 E. Jonah 23.

14. MSS 933 in Lambeth Palace Library, is an exact copy of these lessons, including the alterations.

15. All the alterations in the ' Lessons Proper for Holy Days ' are ones which replace Apocryphal Lessons with Canonical Scripture, except that for St Luke's Day, where, in the Evening Service, Job 1 is changed to Ecclesiates 12 to complete the reading of that book.

The Reading of the Apocrypha.

Williams Diary : (3 Oct.) " After the reading of the Comission the first point proposed to be debated was the reading the Apochrypha in the Church. For it there were 3 things offered,

1. That leaving it out wou'd give great offence to the People—thus Dr. B.

2. That if not the whole allowed to be read yet some parts of the most usefull should be retained—By Dr. Jane.

3. It was desired We should not proceed in these matters till We had a greater Number, and without more time to Consider—Dn. of Winton. To the two former it was answered, That besides the Objections against particular parts of it, the Whole was of no Authority, That it gave too great a Countenance to the Pretensions of the Church of Rome, and shewed too great a Respect to the Books themselves—To the last it was said—That the Time was short and the matter would not admit long delays. 2 That what was done here was no determination and that the whole was to be left to the Convocation—It was carry'd against the Apochrypha."

(The Calendar itself was altered in Sub-committee, cf. Williams Diary, 17 Oct.).

Exceptions IX : " That inasmuch as the Holy Scriptures are able to make us wise unto salvation, to furnish us throughly unto all good works, and

188

contain in them all things necessary, either in doctrine to be believed, or in duty to be practised; whereas divers chapters of the apocryphal books appointed to be read, are charged to be in both respects of dubious and uncertain credit: it is therefore desired, that nothing be read in the church for lessons, but the Holy Scriptures of the Old and New Testament."

Let. Min.: "The Kalendar. And herein the first thing that is to be considered is the Apocrypha, the Books of which being only of Humane Composure, have not only been all along objected against by Dissenters, but also wished by many amongst our selves might be exchanged for Lessons out of the Canonical Scripture, as by the Bishops, and other Episcopal Divines, assembled to consider of these matters in 1641. It's acknowledged that some of these Books contain matter of excellent use, and have been anciently read in the Christian Church. But the first of these is no Reason for those Books which contain things neither profitable not true: nor can it be of any force, when there are Chapters of Canonical Scripture, that may with great profit be read, and are omitted for their sake." (p. 5).

Let. Friend: "Must the Story of Tobit and his Dog and that of Bell and the Dragon always supplant Canonical Scripture in our Churches, and we be forced to read such ridiculous things to our people instead of the Word of God? " (p. 15).

V. Cleri (re Arguments in Let. Min): " he would have the Apocryphal Lessons exchanged, for as many taken out of the Canon of Scripture, as by the Bishops and other Divines Assembled to consider of that matter, 1641: He doth not say was agreed; for I find in an Answer to a Petition presented to the King's Majesty, by above a Thousand Ministers, as it was there said, that there was no such concession made; for pag 14. the Answer to the Objection says, ' That they are grosly ignorant if they know it not, or wilfully malicious and turbulent, if knowing it to be lawful, they yet oppugne the Reading of the Apocryphal Writings in the Church; Non ad confirmationem fidei sed ad reformationem morum: . . . . . . . (The dissenters are only against reading the Apocrypha as Lessons, not against their reading in church in general) . . . . . . That they are not of equal Authority with the Scriptures; which is known of their own People, who therefore will not have them Bound with Bibles; besides no part of the Apocrypha is read on Sundays, but on the Week-days, when there are too few to hear them, and those few better instructed than to think them Canonical." (p. 25-6).

Let. Till. " Whether the lessons out of the Apocrypha may not be omitted? " (VI).

Vindication: " Apocryphal Lessons, which ought in reason and prudence to be changed for Canonical Scriptures; because these containing some things unseemly, some improbable, and others evidently false, do scandalize not only them without the Church, but many of those who are frequenters of our daily prayers. . . . Some nonconformists give this as a great Reason of their Dissent, that they cannot be satisfied, but that the Assent and Consent required by the Act of Uniformity, doth reach not only the Use but the Truth of these Books." (p. 22-3).

JRC: (Having discussed the matter fully, particularly in relation to the foreign churches which use the Apocrypha (p 15ff) he concluded) " First, that no Papist ever made use of this as an argument that our Church own'd these Books as Canonical, so that there can be no real ground for this objection. Secondly, That there neither is, now ever was any one Christian Church in the whole World that had set Lessons appointed for every day in the year, as we have, but some of them were taken out of the Apocrypha. Thirdly, that no one Foreign Church whatsoever did ever declare themselves offended with the Church of England in this matter, but as I have shewed, generally approved. Fourthly, That these very persons who complain of our reading the Apocryphal Chapters for Lessons, make no complaint of having Hymns printed in their Bibles before and after David's

Psalms in meeter, and being frequently used in Church instead of them. . . .'
(p. 20).

Other Authorities mentioning the subject are Vox Populi p. 1, Brief Discourse concerning the unlawfulness p. 170-1 Brief Discourse concerning the lawfulness p. 19f. A real distinction was often drawn between Canonical Scripture and the Apocrypha in practice; e.g. Sir Matthew Hale begs his Family to kneel at prayers, but to stand for the Epistle and Gospel—from which mark of respect they should abstain if any of the Apocrypha was read. (Wickham Legg p. 183).

*16.* All the Black letter saints have been deleted, except St Blasius (3 Feb.) which seems to have been left in by mistake, due to its position at the top of the page. The Fasts have also been deleted except that of the 20 September; again, probably a mistake.

Williams Diary: (22 Oct.) 'Enter'd upon the Kalendar about Sts. Days, and determined only such to be inserted, that were allowed by Our Church, according to the First Book of Edw. 6. . . .'

1688: By January is the letter, '(a)'; on a small piece of the interleaf which remains, is decipherable 'Hilary &c'. It may well be that the query was whether to delete, black letter saints, or not.

Exceptions VI: "That the religious observation of saints-days appointed to be kept as holy-days, and the vigils thereof without any foundation (as we conceive) in Scripture, may be omitted. That if any be retained, they may be called festivals, and not holy-days, not made equal with the Lord's-day, nor have any peculiar service appointed for them, nor the people be upon such days forced wholly to abstain from work, and that the names of all others now inserted in the Calender which are not in the first and second books of Edward the Sixth, may be left out."
JRC: "I may very well pass by also the objecting of the Saints and Bishops Names continued in our Kalender, which as it's generally used in the Lutheran Churches, so is evidently done for a Civil, and not any Religious use, as hath been long since declared in the Preface to Preces Privatae published by authority, A.D. 1573. The words are, 'Not that we repute them all for Saints or holy men, but that they may be as notes of some certain things, and fixed seasons, the knowledge of which is very beneficial;' of which sort are 'Hilary, Valentine, David, St George, Martin, Swithin, Lammas, Giles, Holyrood, Evispine, All-Souls, Leonard, Cicilia, O Sapientia &c'.

And so far as I can see, the only way to continue peace and union amongst our selves, and with other Protestant Churches, is to continue the Kalender as it is." (p. 25-6). cf. this Last quotation with The Insertion in the Commissioners text (p. 48).

Prev. Reading. In the Margin by the Annunciation, the following was added, and subsequently deleted: 'Ash Wednesday M. Isa 52 E. Jonah 23.'

This was added to the Lessons for Lords-days, where it was also deleted. Possibly the Commissioners were unsure as to which category would be best for it.

*17.* There are no deletions or alterations in the table of Lessons, but the replacement of the Apocryphal Lessons in the Lords-day Table, and the omission of this rubric, would suggest that the intention was to alter them in a similar manner.

*18.* 1688: Beside 'Easter day (on which the rest depend)' there is the note; 'qu', and an illegible comment.

There were a number of problems in finding Easter from the tables and suggestions made in the Prayer Book, which could be very innacurate. It is not however regarded as a major point of Controversy in the pamphlets, and is really only dealt with in JRC p. 22-5.

19. 1688: ' all Lords days in ye year Comonly calld Sundays.'
20. Prev. Reading i. A Sermon or Homily to be used.
21. Table of Vigils &c omitted by the Commissioners. 1688: by Title '(c)' and read: ' Abstinence ye observation of wch is recomended.'
22. 1688: (in 111) the words ' being the day of the birth and return of King Charles the Second ' are boxed in.
23. 1688: The table runs from 1681-1720, and in the margin has been added, " made up to 40 ".
24. 1688: read ' against the Golden number; and. . . .'

## NOTES ON MORNING PRAYER

1. 1688: By the rubric " And here is to be noted " add: " A ".

1552: " And here is to be noted that the minister at the tyme of the comunion, & at al other times in his ministracion, shall use nether Albe, Vestmet, nor Cope: but beyng Archebishop, or Bishop, he shal haue and weare a rochet: & beeyng a priest or Deacon, he shall have and weare a surples only."

1662: " And here is to be noted, That such Ornaments of the Church, and of the Ministers thereof, at all times of their Ministration, shall be retained, and be in use as were in this Church of England by the authoritie of Parliament, in the second year of the reign of King Edward VI."

Cosin's interpretation of this, was as follows: " Provided alwayes, & be it enacted, that Such Ornaments of the Church (whereunto the adorning & decent furniture of the Comunion-Table relate) & of the Ministers thereof (as the Albe or Surplice, the Vestment or Cope, with the Rochet & Pastorall Staffe before mentioned). . . . (D. B., p. 56-7)

Exceptions: " Forasmuch as this rubrick seemeth to bring back the cope, albe &c and other vestments forbidden by the Common Prayer Book, 5 and 6 Edw. VI. and so our reasons alledged against ceremonies under our eighteenth general exception, we desire it may be wholly left out." XVIII: " Because this Liturgy containeth the imposition of divers ceremonies which from the first reformation have by sundry learned and pious men been judged unwarrantable, as 1. That publick worship may not be celebrated by any minister that dare not wear a surpless . . . . these ceremonies have for above an hundred years been the fountain of manifold evils in this church and nation, occasioning sad divisions between ministers and ministers, as also between ministers and people, exposing many orthodox, pious, and peaceable ministers, to the displeasure of their rulers, casting them on the edge of the penal statutes, to the loss not only of their livings and liberties, but also of their opportunities for the service of Christ and his Church. . . ."

Bishops Reply: 13 cer 3: " This in brief may here suffice for the surplice; that reason and experience teaches that decent ornaments and habits preserve reverence, and are held therefore necessary to the solemnity of royal acts, and acts of justice, and why not as well to the solemnity of religious worship. And in particular no habit more suitable than white linen, which resembles purity and beauty, wherein angels have appeared, (Rev. xv) fit for those, whom Scripture calls angels: and this habit was ancient."

Williams Diary: (21 Oct) " Then it was proceeded to the Surplice, which held a long debate. All agreed, it was a matter of the least consequence; and it was debated whether to lay it wholly aside, but in Cathedrals, or to leave it as it is, or indifft. To lay it wholly aside would be to give offence and make a Schism, or encourage the Schism that was now setting a foot. To leave it as it is wou'd not be to answer the end of the meeting, and to make what was the least necessary, the most. To leave it indifferent wou'd be the Occasion of continual Divisions. . . . . . at last it was agreed, that a Rubrick shou'd be drawn up, to signify that We us'd it only as decent and Antient, and that if any Minister thought it unlawfull he might go to the Bp. who shou'd (as He thought fit) Appoint One to Officiate in the Service for Him."

(Note that here Williams takes it that the rubric was agreed by the Commissioners, but this is at variance with the actual text which adds, " This Rubrick was suggested, but not agreed to; but left to further Consideration.")

Let. Min.: " And therefore to accommodate in this matter, some have thought it most convenient to leave the case wholly indifferent, to wear or not wear a Surplice, or to use or not use the Cross, to kneel, stand, or sit in the Lords Supper; but I am afraid instead of uniting, this would more divide us, and set Clergy against Clergy, and People against People, and sometimes People against Clergy. And therefore in my poor opinion, the best expedient is first of all to have some Rubricks drawn up to set forth for what reason the Church doth use and retain them, . . . . And then to find out some way for a mitigation. As for instance if the Minister to be admitted, yet scruples the use of the Surplice of Cross, upon application to the Bishop, another may be appointed to do that Service; and if one of the Laity scruples the use of the Cross, the Minister may be permitted in that case to Baptize without it: Or if Kneeling at the Sacrament, that the person so scrupling may have it delivered unto him in another posture, provided it be not at the Table, but in some convenient Pew or Place appointed by the Minister." (p. 8-9)

(This account is remarkable in its similarity of content and wording to both Williams Diary, and the results of the Revision itself. See notes on its Authorship, p. 32f.)

The Lett Friend (p. 10-1) is also prepared to give up the surplice for the sake of a comprehension, and Let. Till, VIII likewise, provided that some explanation is given of why it is being altered, so that there will be no reflection upon the Ancient practice or that of the Church of England. Vox Cleri of course defends it curtly (p. 49). In favour of those who wished to abandon it, there is evidence that many of the Clergy only wore the Surplice when a sacrament was administered, and did not do so on other occasions (Bonasus Vapulans 1672 p. 41); similarly in practice we find examples of people receiving the Communion in a sitting posture in some London Churches. (Baxter's *Plea for Peace* p. 160 &c; quoted Lathbury p. 390) References to the neglect of the Surplice abound, one of which reads; " Some read not all the Common Prayer they are enjoined; some use not the surplice; some omit the cross in Baptism; some dare not put away any from the sacrament merely because they are not satisfied to receive it kneeling." (*Rector of Sutton committed with Dean of St Paul's.* 1680 p. 27.) A study of a slightly later period than this may be found in Wickham Legg p. 374ff. The Note in 1689 " mem: a Canon to specify ye vestments " was necessary because many clergymen did not know what vestments were allowed, and what were not. Cosin, in his Particulars of 1660, points out " But what those Ornamts of the Church & of the Ministers were, is not here specified, & they are so unknowne to many, yt by most they are neglected. Wherefore it were Requisite that those Ornamts used in the 2d yeere of K. Edward, should be here particularly named & sett forth, that there might be no difference about ym." (D. B. p. 57) Cosin's own interpretation has been quoted above. There was much confusion about what was allowable in the Second year of Edward VI. Many commentators show a knowledge of the rubric at the end of the book, allowing the use of Surplice and Hood, to the Parochial and Cathedral Clergy, and the " Rochette, a Surples or albe, and a cope or vestment " to a Bishop (Certayne notes for the more playne explication. . . . . Everyman p 288) They seem however to have neglected, or not been aware of the rubric before the Communion, " the Priest that shal execute the holy ministery, shall put upon hym the vesture appoincted for that ministracion, that is to saye: a white Albe plain, with a vestement or Cope. And where there by many Priestes, or Decons, there so many shalbe ready to helpe the Priest, in lykewise the vestures appointed for their ministery, that is to saye, Albes with tunacles." This Rubric allows the Celebrant, even if he is not a Bishop, to wear a Cope. The interpretations current at this time are delineated in Wickham Legg p. 351-74, Suffice it to say, that in general (where they were not neglected) only the Surplice, Hood and sometimes Cope were worn. Edmund Hickeringill, a fierce opponent of Anglican worship, attacks the Clergyman for " his Cope, his Hood his Surplice, his Cringing Worship, his Altar with Candles on it (most Nonsensically unlighted too) his Bagpipes or Organs, and in some place Viols and Violins, singing Men and singing Boys &c are all so very like Popery, (and all but the Vestments illegal). . . ." (*The Ceremony Monger—His Character*. 1689 p. 18) Had Hickeringill been able to attack more, he would have done.

2. Details of the Observance of the Duty of the daily service by the Clergy, the people's attendance, and the hours when and where it was conducted, may be found in Wickham Legg p. 77-110.

3. 1688: The words ' no health ' are boxed in.

4. 1688: Altered to ' who confess '.

5. Black fails to record the alteration of the word ' Jesu ' to ' Jesus '. This alteration is also made in 1688.

   Exceptions: " The Confession is very deffective, not clearly expressing original sin, nor sufficiently enumerating actual sins, with their aggravations, but consisting only of generals; whereas confession being the exercise of repentance, ought to be more particular." (XVII. 2).

   Reply of Bishops: (2 Exc. 2) " This which they call a defect, others think they have reason to account the perfection of the Liturgy, the offices of which being intended for common and general services, would cease to be such by descending to particulars, as in confession of sin; while it is general, all persons may and must join in, since in many things we offend all. But if there be a particular enumeration of sins, it cannot be so general a confession, because it may happen that some or other may by God's grace have been preserved from some of those sins enumerated, and therefore should by confessing themselves guilty, tell God a lie: which needs a new confession."

6. Prev. Readings. i. minister. ii. ' stet ' written above the word ' priest '. Note that in Evensong the word is altered to ' minister '.

7. 1688: ' or Remission of Sins ' is underlined. This phrase was added in 1662; 1552 read " The absolucion to be pronounced by the minister alone." Perhaps it is underlined, at least in sympathy (because the argument after 1662 no longer applies) with Cosin's Particulars 1660. 21: ' The words . . . . " Or Remission of Sins " were added at ye instance of the Ministers in the Conference at Hampton Court; but it is no legall Addition, for ye Act of Parliament forbiddeth it.'

8. 1688: ' Grant us true repentance and his Holy Spirit ' underlined; and an x placed by the word ' grant '.

9. Exceptions: " We desire that these words, ' For thine is the kingdom, the power and the glory, for ever and ever. Amen ', may be always added unto the Lord's Prayer; and that this prayer may not be enjoyned to be so often used in morning and evening service."

   1662 added the Doxology in conformity with this objection in the first Lords Prayer of the Offices, but not in the second.

   1689 adds the doxology to the second Lord's Prayer at Evensong, and although there is no similar note in Morning Prayer, it may be presumed that it was intended to add it there also.

Bishops Reply: "Lord's Pr. often used. It is used but twice in the morning and twice in the evening service; and twice cannot be called often, much less so often. For the Litany, Communion, Baptism, &c., they are offices distinct from morning and evening prayer, and it is not fit that any of them should want the Lord's Prayer."

V. Populi: "The Lords Prayer is said once at the end of the Absolution; again, after the Apostles Creed; again, in the Litany; and again, in the beginning of the Communion-Service; and again, in the second part of the Communion-Service; and again, in the pulpit before the Sermon; so that 'tis repeated five times every Sunday Morning constantly, and six if there be a Communion." (p. 2).

Terms: "Q. Why is the Lord's Prayer so frequently used in our Liturgy? A. 1. Because it is the pattern of Prayer. 2. Because it is the most absolute and perfect Form, and gives perfection to all the rest. 3. In Imitation of your Saviour, who often repeated the same Words." (p. 6). For notes on Repitition cf. note 8 p. 186f.

10. This phrase is added in several places throughout the revision (e.g. the Collects for St John Evangelist and Trinity 12). Its history is a complicated one; it seems to have stemmed from the Collect for Advent 3 in the Sarum Missal: "Aurem tuam quesumus domine precibus nostris accomoda. et mentis nostre tenebras gracia tue uisitacionis illustra." The phrase "et mentis nostre tenebras illustra" was translated in 1549 as "lighten the darkness of our hearte". D. B. has rewritten the third Collect for Evening Prayer in the light of this collect from 1549. The 1689 Commissioners took it a step further, and retranslated the original substituting the word "mind" for "heart", and linking it in a number of cases with Ps 119. 18, "Open thou mine eyes: that I may see the wondrous things of thy law". (for connection cf 2 Cor 4. 6, 2 Cor 3. 14 and Eph 1. 18 etc). It is interesting to note that these developments have been united in the American Liturgy of 1786, when the beginning of the third Collect at Evening Prayer was altered to read, "Enlighten our Minds O Lord. . . . ."

11. Exceptions XI: ' That as the word " minister " and not priest, or curate, is used in the Absolution, and in divers other places; it may throughout the whole book be so used instead of those two words; . . .'
This alteration is made throughout the Revision, although each single case is not specified by the Commissioners.

12. 1688: There is a line drawn in the margin from, ' Today if ye will hear his voice ' to ' enter into my rest ', and the comment added ' omitt Ru '.

13. Cf. note 8 p. 186f. Prev. Reading i. the 8 Psalm, Magnificat, The 134 Ps.

It was the custom to follow the Psalms with an Organ Voluntary; a custom praised in the *Spectator*: ' Methinks there is something very laudable in the Custom of a Voluntary before the first Lesson '. (No 630. 8 Dec 1714).

14. Wren's Advices counselled the alteration of the word ' Sabaoth ' to " Hosts " (D. B. p. 69). This alteration was also made independently by four other Liturgies in the eighteenth Century, the most well-known being those of Samuel Clarke and William Whiston.
1688: word " Sabaoth " altered to " Hosts ".

15. 1688: read: " Thy true & onely begotten Son " (with an illegible comment).
Prev. Reading i. Thine honourable, true, and thy only begotten Son.

16. 1688: (By the Benedicite) " omit ". The words " O Ananias, Azarius, and Misael " in the Benedicite are underlined.

Psalm 148.

The text of this Psalm is interesting in that while it is based on the Prayer Book version of the Psalter, there are certain alterations made in conformity with the Biblical (AV) version: (1) The words " Height " and " Host " (V. 1 and 2) have been put in the plural. (2) The word " vapour " is put in the singular. (3) The phrase " Young men and maidens, old men and children " has been made into a separate verse as in the AV

The Alteration of the Benedicite to Psalm 148 follows the recommendation of the Exceptions: ' We desire that some Psalm or Scripture hymn may be appointed instead of that Apocryphal '.

*17.* Prev. Reading i. or ye hymn calld Benedictus except.

*18.* The Benedictus of course begins at Lk. 1.68. The reading Lk. 1.86 is a misprint in the Prayer Book the Commissioners used.

Williams Diary: (22 Oct) ". . . resolved to omit the Benedictus &c. . . ." (This is another example of Williams Diary conflicting with the evidence of the Text itself.)

*19.* The Jubilate is deleted, and by it is written, ' This C Ps to be put before Benedictus.'

*20.* 1688: ' Then shall be sung or said the Apostles Creed by the Minister, and the People standing; Except onely such Days as the Creed of St Athanasius is appointed to be read.'

Within this alteration, the words " sung or " are underlined, and put in parentheses. The words " St Athanasius " were then deleted, and the word " Nicene " added before " Creed " thus reading: ' . . . Days as the Nicene Creed of is appointed to be read." Lastly, the whole section from ' Except onely . . . .' to the end of the rubric was deleted.

1688: Adds also in the margin; ' a rubric for ys on Holidays."

Vindication: ' The Rubric is that after the second Hymn in the Morning-Service, and runs thus, Then shall be sung or said the Apostles Creed—excepting only such days as the Creed of St Athanasius is appointed. Where I shall prove that it is not a meer notion, but a mighty concern to Alter it thus, viz, The Creed commonly called the Apostles: and so the other. . . . Now this Rubrick gives a mighty advantage to the Socinians, who plead, that as our Church ascribes this Creed to the Apostles, so it suits not but the Unitarian Doctrin, as asserting the Divinity of the Father only; and many of our own Writers affirm, that it contains all the Credenda necessary to Salvation, as the Decalogue doth the Agenda: Whence it follows, either, 1. That the Doctrin of Christs Divinity was not known in the Apostles time: Or 2. That the Apostles have given us an imperfect Rule of Faith: Or 3. That the Belief of this Doctrin is not necessary to Salvation. Whence we must either deny this Creed to be theirs, and thereby set up our private light in opposition to the Church, and thence fall under that last which we have laid upon Dissenters; or grant, that this Apostolical Rule is wanting in some things necessary to Salvation; or else yield, that this Doctrin (if true) is yet of no moment. All which adsurdities will be avoided only by intituling it, The Creed, Commonly called the Apostles'. (p. 25, 28).

V. Populi: " We think it very odd, that Te Deum, Benedicite, The Psalms in prose, and the three Creeds, should be appointed to be SUNG or said. The Lessons in the Old Common Prayer-Book were order'd to be Sung in a plain Tune. That is reform'd, and they are now appointed to be read distinctly with an audible voice. And is there not the same reason for the other two? Were this canting way laid aside, we might then have the Psalms in the New Translation; for 'tis for the sake of their being pointed to be SUNG or said, that though in some places it be corrupt, and in others several Verses that are not in the Original, but the Septuagint only, the old one is still retained." (p. 4).

21. 1688: The words " Lord, Christ, Lord " in the lesser Litany are deleted, and in the left hand margin is added: Heavenly Father

Sonn of God

Holy Spirit

and in the right hand margin: Bl. Creator

Bl. Redeemr

Bl. Sanctifyer.

The whole of the Lesser Litany was then deleted, together with the salutation and its response.

V. Populi: " Not to speak of the Kyrie Eleesons, nor of all the Congregations, even Women too, saying after the Minister with a loud voice, nor of their alternate reading the Verses of the Psalms, for which later, we don't find any Rubrick; all which seem to make such a confused Babling, that we can hardly reconcile it to the Apostles Discourse in the first Epistle to Corinth. and 14th Chapter; and make a man think he were in Dover-Court, rather than a Christian Assembly. . . . . . . This hath such a semblance of those vain Repititions forbidden by our Saviour. . . . (p. 2-3).

Terms: ' Q. Why is, Lord have Mercy upon us, thrice repeated? And why before the Lord's Prayer? A. 1. To notify the Trinity we pray to, is it thrice repeated. 2. Before the Lord's Prayer, because it is expedient we implore God's Mercy before we use that Prayer.' (p. 11).

22. 1688: The word " Peace " is underlined.

23. 1688: The word "Fighteth " is underlined, and " can defend us q " written above it. The whole answer was then deleted, and referred to the interleaf by ' (a) '.

The new Response in 1689, seems to be a precis of Lk. 1. 74-5 from the Benedictus; the connection probably being that of ' give peace in our time ' and ' being delivered out of the hands of our enemies ', which have much the same content.

24. 1688: ' And take not the aid of thy holy Spirit from us.'

25. Altered because the rubric below, allows the omission of the Collect for the Day when the Litany or Communion follows, to avoid Repetition; in this case only two would be said, and not three.

26. 1688:' In knowledge of whom standeth our eternal life, whose service is perfect freedom ' is underlined and put in parentheses.

27. 1688: ' the beginning of ' put in parentheses, probably because as Morning Prayer might be said at any time before noon, it was frequently inapplicable.

28. 1688: The word " Five " put in parentheses, with the note: " omit five & let all prayers to be read be printed loyot her in order as they are to be read."

29. 1688: In the phrase, " behold our most gracious soveraign Lord King James " the words " most gracious " are underlined, and put in parentheses, and the letter (c) refers to the interleaf. The phrase " Strengthen him that he may vanquish and overcome all his enemies " is underlined and put in parentheses, and the letter (c) added. In the margin is also added " thine and their " presumably to replace the word ' his '.

This last phrase had many overtones for the Churchman of the period, for while King James imprisoned the Bishops in the Tower whom they supported, they found themselves praying that he would overcome them. This is brought out in some of the pamphlets:

Let. Friend: "Must we always be forced in our addresses to God Almighty with a flattery not to be warrented, to call every King that reigns over us most Religious, though the whole tenor of his life may be quite the contrary; and pray that he may be kept and strengthened in the true worshipping of God, though openly professing so false a worship as that of Popery?" (p. 15).

Let. Till: V. "Whether the prayers for the King and Queen may not be put in such general words as will be applicable to all circumstances? we being, as it is well known, not long since crampt by a form, not without some seeming advantage to our enemies, and scandal to some of our friends?"

30. 1688: "bless our gracious Queen Mary; Catherine the Queen Dowager; their Royal Highnesses Mary Princess of Orange, and the Princess Anne of Denmark and all the Royal Family" is all put in parentheses. Inside, the words "gracious" and "their Royal Highnesses" are deleted. There is also a line down the margin, referring to this section.

Note: 1689 also omits "Their Royal Highnesses" before the "Princess Anne".

31. 1688: "who alone workest great marvels" is underlined; and there is a line beside the whole prayer, with the word "Quaer:" written in. The word "healthful" is underlined and put in parentheses. The alternative is illegible.

Let. Min: "Who alone workest great marvels" is regarded as obscure. (p. 24).

V. Cleri: "Who dares deny, saith Dr Comber, that the assistance granted to the Ministers for the conversion of sinners are as marvellous, as was the Creation of Light out of Darkness or the Resurrection from the Dead." (p. 38).

32. 1688: adds "Gener: Prayrs & Thanks to be printed here.

33. 1688: "A Prayer Commonly Called St Chrysostom's".

## NOTES ON EVENING PRAYER

1. Let. Till: I: "Whether, too, a greater variety of prayers may not be allowed, two or three different forms being set down upon every occasion, that he who officiates may sometimes take one and sometimes another? And whether even the whole evening service may not be made to differ from that of the morning?

2. Let. Till: "IV: Whether some psalms, proper to express our ordinary wants, and to be thankful in for general blessings, or else anthems to the same effect, made up of select expressions of Scripture, would not do well in the room of the Magnificat, Nunc dimittis, and even the Benedictus?

New Survey: "Whether the Hymns and Offices of Praise after the Lessons, (especially in the Evening Service) are not become less edifying in their present use, where those Spiritual Songs are barely Read, (as in Parish Churches) and not Sung; 'there being one way of Singing', or an Harmonious Reading of them useful and edifying, though another way not so much to Edification, because but few understand it in the way of an Anthem. There are some things of particular respect to the Virgin

Mary, and good Old Symeon, not so suitable to the Congregation. Whither the Wisdom of our Governours may not see reason to forbear those Anthems wholly in Parish Churches, or to leave the use of them indifferent, or to limit them ' pro hic & nunc ', according as times of Joy and Victory require our Praise, or other times of Humiliation to forbear them." (p. 6-7).

Magnificat.

Dr Cuming says that ". . . Magnificat and Nunc Dimittis give way to Psalms 8 and 134 " (History p. 175), and many have agreed with this interpretation in the past. The evidence of the text itself however is very complicated, and holds of a much more complex interpretation. It has therefore been printed, as near as is possible to the original. The material evidence connected with it, is as follows :

(1) In the rubric before the first lesson at Morning Prayer, the Magnificat was originally included as a hymn after which the Gloria should be said. This was subsequently deleted in pencil, which means as part of a final revision.

(2) The phrase " The 8 Psalm & " has been added to the Rubric before the word " Magnificat "; this was later altered to " The 8 Psalm or ".

(3) " Psalm 8 " is also added between the rubric and the Magnificat, on one side of the page; at the other side, at a similar elevation was written " or 98 X ", which is altered to " & 98 X "

(4) The Magnificat remains unaltered.

(5) The first four words of the rubric before Ps. 98 are deleted, and the Mark X added, referring to the note above.

This leaves the fate of the Magnificat a little in doubt. It is quite evident, that in some way, it was intended that Ps. 8 and Ps. 98 should be used at this point. Two alternatives seem possible, both of which however include the Magnificat. It is unlikely that if it was intended to omit the Magnificat, no mention should be made in Evensong of it, and the only reference be a deletion of the word in Morning Prayer (1 above).

(a) The alternative Hymns are: Psalm 8 or the Magnificat and Ps. 98.

Thus two hymns are sung, one perhaps seen in the light of an Office hymn. If this is correct, the text relates as follows:

(i) It was intended that Psalm 8 and the Magnificat should both be said.

(ii) The question then arose, " What to do with Psalm 98 "?

(iii) It was decided that it should be retained as an alternative and the phrase " or 98 " was added, with the mark X, showing that it should be added to the beginning of the Rubric below. There was thus a threefold alternative; Psalm 8 or the Magnificat, or Ps 98. (The " Psalm 8 and " having in the meantime been altered to " Psalm 8 or ")

(iv) It was then decided that a threefold alternative was too much, and so the " or 98 " was altered to " & 98 ".

(v) The alternatives, are thus Ps 8 or the Magnificat, and Ps 98.

(b) The other alternative reading is: Ps 8 and Ps 98 or Magnificat.

The arguments are much the same as above, with one material difference; the phrase " & 98 " is not to be added to the rubric below, but the rubric is referred to that place by the letter X. In favour of this one might add, that it would not have been difficult to add " & 98 " to the rubric, but would have been difficult to transfer the whole rubric and Psalm to this place before the Magnificat. The case rests as follows:

(i) It was originally intended that Ps. 8 and the Magnificat should both be said.

(ii) The problem of Ps. 98 was solved by making it an alternative to them; Ps. 8 and Magnificat or Ps. 98.

(iii) This was altered to Ps. 8 or the Magnificat or Ps. 98.

(iv) The threefold alternative was felt to be too much, and so the scheme was altered. Ps. 8 was made an alternative to Magnificat, and the phrase added beneath the rubric, with an alteration of " or 98 " to " & 98 ".

(v) This left the case: Ps. 8 or the Magnificat
                    Ps. 8 and Ps. 98,

(vi) It was intended therefore that the rubric should be added after the phrase " & 98 X " in the Printed Prayer Book as an alternative to Ps. 8, and the Magnificat was an alternative to them. There was a choice of either saying two Psalms or the Magnificat.

Either of the alternatives is allowable on the textual evidence and neither does violence to it. The second may well be felt to be preferable.

3. 1688: The word " sung " is underlined, and a small x placed above it. Cf. notes on Morning Prayer No. 20.

4. In Morning Prayer the phrase " standing up " is omitted.

5. 1688: The word " chosen people " is underlined.
Wren's Advices; " In the last line of that Page, the word (People) should be left out, thus, Answer. And make Thy Chosen joyfull." (D.B. p. 75).

6. 1688: The words " three Collects " are put in parentheses.

7. The text is printed as it stands, because it is uncertain whether it is intended that Bishop Patrick's version should begin with the revised opening of the Prayer or not. There are no insertion marks, and it might have been intended as an alternative prayer or simply an alternative ending.

8. 1688: ' Lighten ' is underlined, and the phrase " from all perils and dangers of this night " is underlined, and put in unclosed parentheses. An illegible comment is added.

Wren's Advices: " That this Prayer also is to be sayd in the afternoons in Summer, is but very improper, unless it shall be thought fit to say it, thus, Lighten the Darknes, we beseech thee, O Lord, that the night will bring upon us, and by Thy great Mercy defend us from all Dangers of the same, for the Love of thy onely Sonne our Saviour Jesus Xt. Amen.

9. New Survey: ' Whether it were not desirable to have a Prayer for particular Graces in the Evening Service, (the Petitioning part being less perfect then) and at such times when the Letany is not used. We have such a Prayer in the ' Whole Duty of Man ', called a Prayer for Grace, comprehensive of particular Graces. And then no doubt the use of it would be more acceptable in Families than it is now, when it runs out so much in Intercessions, and so little in Petitions.' (p. 6).

## NOTES ON THE ATHANASIAN CREED

Prev. Readings i. (a note) the daies to be reduced to ye 1st book of K. Edwd.
              i. Condemning clauses . . . . only to ye substance of the Xn Fayth, according to ye 18th Article of this Church.

1688: (a fair copy) '. . . . S. Matthew, S. Simon and S. Jude, S. Andrew and upon Trinity Sunday, instead of ye Apostles Creed, and may be The Nicene Creed or this following said at Morning Prayer, the Creed commonly called the Creed of S. Athanasius. . . .'

The text is laid out as follows:

| The Nicene Creed | S. Andrew and upon Trinity Sunday,/Instead |
| or this following* | of ye Apostles Creed (a) shall be* (sung or) |

(a) May — said at Morning Prayer, instead of the Apostles Creed (this Confession of our Christian faith) (the Creed commonly &c) commonly called the Creed of S Athanasius. Rubric for Nicene.

The additions on the left are in the margin; ' Instead of ye Apostles Creed ' is an insertion into the text. The words ' S. Andrew . . . . shall . . . sung or . . . commonly called ' are all underlined, and the word ' May ' in the margin likewise The phrase " Instead of the Apostles Creed " (not the insertion) is deleted, as is " this Confession of our Christian faith '.

It is quite impossible to discover a sequence in these alterations.

1549. " In these feastes of Christmas, Thepiphanie, Easter, Thascencion, Penticost, and upon Trinitie Sonday, shall be song or sayed immediately after Benedictus this confession of our christian fayth."

1552: " In the feastes of Christmas, the Epiphanie, saincte Mathie, Easter, Thassencion, Pentecost, Sainct Iohn Baptist, Sainct Iames, Sainct Bartholemew, Sainct Mathewe, Sainct Symon and Iude, Sainct Andrewe, and Trinitie Sundaye; shalbe song, or sayd immediately after Benedictus this confession of our Christen fayth."

1662: " Upon these Feasts: Christmas day, the Epiphany, Saint Matthias, Easter day, Ascension day, Whitsunday, Saint John Baptist, Saint James, Saint Bartholemew, Saint Matthew, Saint Simon and Saint Jude, Saint Andrew, and upon Trinity Sunday, shall be sung, or said at morning Prayer, instead of the Apostles Creed, this Confession of our christian Faith, commonly called the Creed of Saint Athanasius, by the Minister and people standing."

Williams Diary: (23 Oct) " The cheif debate was about the Athanasian Creed—It was moved, either to leave it with an alias, or to leave out the Damnatory Clauses, or to leave it as it is with a Rubrick. For it was alledg'd 1. That it was Antient. 2. Received by Our Church ever since the Reformation. 3 Offence to leave it out; but granted that if it was to do now, it were better to omit it. It was reply'd by the Bp. of Salisb: 1. That the Church of England received the 4 first General Councils that the Ephesine Council condemns any new Creeds. 2. That this Creed was not very antient, and the Filioque especially. 3. That it condemned the Greek Church whom yet We defend. — It was propos'd by the Bp. of Worcest. to have a Rubrick, that it shou'd be interpreted by Article—of Our Church, and that the condemning Sentences were only as to the Substance of the Articles; which was drawn up and approv'd of . . . . (1 Nov) Dr. F. moved, that the business of the Athanasian Creed might be reheard, and he desired it might be left at Liberty with a ' may be read ' since he had convers'd with several Conformists and Nonconformists. The Conformists were Men of Eminence that were of that mind and some of them had not read it for many Years. The Nonconformists were desirous of it and were of the mind that no Creed should be used, but what was conceived in Scripture Expressions. However, it was thought more adviseable to leave it as it was and let the Convocation consider it. Both the B. of Salisb: and Dean of Cant. undertaking to promote it in both Houses of Convocation. . . . (15 Nov) . . . made some few Alterations and Amendments; the most considerable was in the Athanasian Creed; where after it was suggested, that they were the Articles, and not the Terms in which those Articles were expressed, that were assented to; it was concluded, that the word ' obstinately ' should be inserted, and the reference to Article — omitted."

Let. Min: (Cf. with Williams above; especially Burnet's statements) " He (the young ordinand) proceeds further, and comes to the Creeds, and because that of Athanasius is the larger, and so may be presumed should be the plainer, he begins to examine the Articles of it, and though he is abundantly satisfied in the Doctrine of the Sacred Trinity, and the Deity of the Son and Holy Ghost, yet he finds a great Dispute betwixt the Greek and Latin Church about the ' procession of the Holy Ghost from the Son '. Now the first Question is, whether of these two Churches is in the right? And secondly, whether this be a Fundamental article of the Faith ' which except a man believe faithfully, he cannot be saved '? And the third Question is, whether he may declare the Greek Church in a state of Damnation for what is questionable, whether it be a Fundamental Article or not? And that it is questionable he finds, for this is not made necessary by Athanasius himself, nor was originally either in the Nicene (truely so called) or the Athanasian Creed. Nor lastly, is it so thought by our Church, which receiving the four first General Councils, consequently agrees with the third, that of Ephesus, which made a peremptory Decree ' against all Additions to be made here-after to the Creed ': From whence it follows that nothing else was then accounted necessary to be believed, but what was contained in the Nicene. . . . And therefore it's convenient that the Forms of Subscription and Declaration be explained. And it would be worth your while perhaps to consider also, whether it will not be requisite to have a Rubrick drawn up, and inserted before the Athanasian Creed, signifying, That ' this Creed may be read ', or with an Alias, ' This or the Nicene; ' or that the Condemning Sentences be left out, or if continued, it may be express'd, that they are to be applied only to those that obstinately deny the Fundamental Articles of the Christian Faith, contained in that Creed. The want of which doth give occasion of scruple to many of our own People, that will not say ' Amen ' to it, as well as to the Dissenters, and trouble several of the Order that subscribe it." (p. 14-5).

Let. Friend: " And must we always be necessitated to pronounce all damn'd that do not believe every tittle in Athanasius's Creed, which so few do under-stand. . . .' (p. 15).

V. Cleri: " (Let. Min.) he restrains the Damnatory Sentences to one Article of the Creed, which is to be referred to the whole, for so says the Preface, ' This is the Catholick Faith &c '. Moreover I think it not necessary to Salvation, that every Man should believe that Article of the Procession of the Holy Ghost from the Father to the Son, seeing there are several Articles in the Creed called the Apostles, as we receive it now, which in the most Primitive Times, were not extant in that Creed; . . . . And so the Damnatory Sentences not appearing to be the Addition of Athanasius, nor respecting any Article, but what is fundamental and necessary to Salvation. . . ." (p. 32-3).

Other Authorities: Against its inclusion or with qualifications mentioned above: V. Populi p. 4; Let. Till. VII. In Favour of the Creed as it is: JRC p. 32ff.

## NOTES ON THE LITANY

1. Exceptions IV: ' That in regard the Litany (though otherwise containing in it many holy petitions) is so framed, that the petitions for a great part are uttered only by the people, which we think not to be so consonant to Scripture, which makes the minister the mouth of the people to God in prayer, the particulars thereof may be composed into one solemn prayer to be offered by the minister unto God for the people.'

V. Populi: " Good Lord deliver us, is repeated eight times in the Litany; and We beseech thee to hear us good Lord, no less than two and twenty times in the same . . . This hath a resemblance of those ' vain Repititions ' forbidden by our Saviour." (p. 2-3).

Terms: " Q. Why do we pray by way of Respond? A. In Conformity to the primitive Practice; and the Reasons are, 1. To stir up Devotion. 2. To strengthen affection. 3. To oblige the Worshippers to greater Attention and Intention." (p. 6).

Cf. Notes on Repetition note 8 p. 186f.

2. This is an abbreviation of " Memorand: O God ye Father, Creator of Heaven and Earth."

3. Prev. Reading i. q heavenly father.
   1688: O God our heavenly Father.

   Note: In the Congregational response, the Commissioners supplied the word ' of ' due to an omission in the printed book.

4. 1688: The phrase ' proceeding from the Father and the Son ' is underlined and put in parentheses, being replaced by ' our Sanctifyer and Comforter '. (Cf. Notes on Athanasian Creed). The Clauses to the Holy Ghost and the Trinity were then both deleted.

5. 1688: ' from sin ' and ' from the crafts and assaults of the devil ' are deleted. In the margin is the note: ' fm all ye deceits of ye fl. Q '.

6. 1688: At this point there are a large number of additions written into the margin, all of which are crossed out. A Fair copy of these reads:

   From all blindness of mind; from pride, vain-glory, and by hypocricie; from envy, hatred, and revenge, from all rash censure contention and all uncharitableness.

   From all Infidelitie, ignorance & errr; from all impietie & profaneness from all Superstition & Idolatry. Good Lord &c.

   From Fornication (Q Adultery) & all uncleanness, & from rioting, drunkenness & gluttony; fro sloth & mispending of our time, and from all other heinous sins.

   forn & adult. & all uncl.

   The phrase " From all blindness of mind " is subsequently deleted.

   Exceptions: ' In regard that the wages of sin is death; we desire that this clause may be thus altered: " From fornication, and all other heinous, or grievous sins ".'

7. Exceptions: " Because this expression of " sudden death " hath been so often excepted against, we desire, if it be thought fit, it may be thus read: " From battel and murther and from dying suddenly, and unprepared."

8. 1688: In each case, the word " by " is put in parentheses, and altered through a marginal note to " through ". The words " thy Cross and Passion " are underlined, and " the coming of thy Holy Ghost " put in parentheses.

9. 1688: In ' our tribulation ' the word " our " is boxed in; the words " our wealth " are boxed in also, but separately.

10. 1688: The word " keep " is replaced by the word " guide ". Then this petition, and the two following are deleted.

11. 1688: Petition deleted. Inside the deletion " his enemies " is altered to " thine and their enemies ".

12. 1688: read " preserve the King, the Queen, and all the Royal Family."

In 1689 there is a note in the margin, " Italic " beside the Petition for the High Court of Parliament. A similar note is placed beside the new petition for the Land and Sea Forces. Black suggests that this petition forms a new Versicle with its Response. It is more probable however that the petition, like that of the Forces Petition, is designed to be added to the existing versicle;

the rubric " Italic " implying that it should only be said when applicable, in this case, during the parliamentary session, and in the case of the Forces, in time of war. The only other place where " Italic " is put in the margin is " especially those for whome our prayers are desired ", where this is obviously the case. Furthermore the textual position of the addition makes this interpretation certain: '. . . Family; That it . . .'.

13. 1688: The word " illuminate " is boxed in, and the word " stet " written above it.

14. 1688: " to love thee above all things, and to fear to offend, and diligently . . . ".

Black again gives this new petition as a separate versicle. However the two new petitions above both begin with the word " That ", so that this is no argument for a separation here. There is no response added to this new petition, and no mark of insertion which would be necessary if it were a separate versicle. (B.P. are the initials of Bishop Patrick.)

15. 1688: ' forth all the fruits of the . . . '.

16. Prev. Reading i. Patiense, of justice, & Temperance, of purity, peace-ableness. . . .

17. 1688: The word " all " is put in parentheses, and " all sick persons, and young children; and to shew they pity upon all prisoners and captives " is underlined.

   Exceptions: " We desire that the term ' all ' may be advised upon, as seeming liable to just exceptions; and that it may be considered, whether to may not better be put indefinitely, ' those that travel ' &c. rather than universally."

18. In the margin is the word " Ital " referring to this section in Parentheses. Let. Till.: " Whether a prayer for preservation be not wanting in our Common Prayer Book, as it now is, wherein particular persons (on their giving notice) may be commended to the Divine protection, a thing frequently desired in some places, especially port-towns? Also another for the sick or afflicted, to be used when the Litany is read; there being none appointed at those times?

19. 1688: Delete " O Christ hear us " and the whole section down to the end of the Lords Prayer.

   Prev. Reading i. From this point to the Gloria Patri, which follows " O Lord arise . . . thine honour ", there is a line drawn down the side of the page, as if it were to be omitted.

   ii. The word " stet " is written three times beside the line. The Gloria is not however included in the restoration of the text.

20. Prev. Reading i. Q. Whether, when there ever is a comunion, the Lds prayer, is not to be omitted?

Black reads " When there is a comunion " in this previous Reading, but it is evident that another word is included, " ever " has been suggested here as a possible, but not certain, rendering of that word.

21. 1688: There are a large number of deletions at the conclusion of the Litany. What remains is:

O Lamb of God: that takest away the sins of the world.

Have mercy upon us.

O Lord, deal not with us after our sins.

Neither reward us after our iniquities.

We humbly beseech thee, O Father, mercifully. . . .

A Prayer Commonly called S. Chrysostom's

The Grace

In the last deletions there are marks indicating a previous attempt to revise the text of the prayers. These are noted in their respective places.

*22.* 1688: "Let us pray" before "O God merciful Father" deleted.

*23.* 1688: The prayer is deleted. Inside the deletion the word "craft" is underlined and put in parentheses, and the phrase "the providence of thy goodness" is boxed in.

*24.* 1688: The salutation before "We humbly beseech thee": a note in the margin, "omitt it".

*25.* 1688: "Righteously" altered to "justly".

*26.* Prev. Reading i. Then if there is no communion the minister shall read continuing in his place.

*27.* Prev. Reading i. the Nicence Creed. I believe in One God &c.

*28.* Prev. Reading i. A Prayer of S. Chrysostom's.

1688: 'A prayer commonly called S. Chrysostom's.

For Notes on the Sequence and what is intended in these rubrics by the Commissioners, see the Communion Service (note p. 234f.)

## NOTES ON THE PRAYERS

*1.* Positioning of the "Pparatory Prayr" and prayer "to be said in any time of Calamitie."

The interleaf bears these two prayers and a rubric. Before this rubric is the mark XX, which by a corresponding mark places it before the Ember Collect. There is however no indication as to the positioning of the two prayers in question. They have been placed in this position, firstly because it is evident that they are not intended to precede the rubric; secondly, because the general heading "Prayers" would seem to imply this position, and would be the natural place to put a prayer which would be in such common use as the one to be said before Communion.

Authorship.

At the conclusion of the Holy Communion Service are the following notes: "To be added here to this collect. . . . And the Prayer for Repentance Compos'd by A.B.S. &c in K. Jamess time, & a praeparatorie Collect for ye comunio:" After the insertion of the Collects: 'Collect for Repentance' and 'See warning for ye Comun:'

These rubrics or notes, obviously refer to the prayers in Question. George Every identifies the Prayer "Compos'd by A.B.S. &c" as being the "Pparatory Prayr" (High Church Party, p. 47-8) but this is most unlikely. Both notes above differentiate between the prayer composed by A.B.S. &c and the preparatory prayer. The Preparatory prayer also occurs written out with slight differences before the Exhortations in the Communion Service, as a "Warning" for the Communion, entitled "A preparatory Prayer for ye Comunion to be read on ye Lds day, or o some week day, or daies before, at ye discretio of ye Minister." It would therefore seem that the second note above corresponds to the first note, as one might expect. The Collect for Repentance was to be printed out there, and this was to be followed by the Preparatory prayer, which was written on an interleaf as a warning for the Communion. Such an interpretation is substantiated by the fact that the Prayer "to be said in any time of Calamitie" originally had the title "For Repentance", and deserves such a title more than the preparatory prayer. It was perhaps altered to fit in with the titles of the Prayers and Thanksgivings, and indeed would have seemed a most suitable prayer for any time of crisis. "A.B.S. &c" is an abbreviation of the name "ArchBishop Sancroft". It has been considered that the Prayer was a composition of Sancroft himself; but this interpretation takes no note of the "&c" which follows it. In view of the fact that it was composed in the reign of James II, it was probably a compilation of those who sat to revise the Prayer Book in 1688, over which Sancroft presided. A Photograph of these two prayers is included in *A History of the Anglican Liturgy* by G. J. Cuming, facing p. 176.

2. Black reads "mysteries for a Comunication". The word should read "Comemoration".

   Prev Reading i. to be made partakers of them, to come to thy holy Table. (This reading is retained in the "Warning for Communion.)

3. Composed during the revision of 1688.
   Prev. Reading of the Title i. For Repentance.

4. 1688: The phrase "a plague of rain and waters" is underlined, and the word "plague" deleted.

5. 1688: The phrase "confound their devices" is underlined.

6. In the text there is an insertion mark after the word "mortality", but there is no addition phraseology given.

   Prev. Reading i. humbly acknowledge our vileness, and repent of our faults. ii. (word 'vileness' altered to) wickedness.

7. Prev. Reading i. Ordination for imploring ye blessing.

8. Prev. Readings i. Q. about reading this in ye Church before Each of ye 4 weeks, the (Sunday) Lords day before each of the Ember weeks. (The word 'Sunday' is deleted, and replaced by Lords day).    ii. This rubric is to be read in ye Church at ye end of morning prayer before the.

9. As the marks XX mentioned above, refer the rubric to this place, the comment "put ys at ye beginning" must refer only to the rubric "This rubric is to be read . . . ."

10. Prev. Reading i. When ye Litany is read, this to be omitted.

11. Prev. Reading i. soveraign Ld & Lady. (Black includes this as part of the text, but the words "& Lady" are deleted.)

    1688: The words "under our most religious and gracious King" are underlined.

    For notes on the omission of certain titles of the King and Queen, see State Prayers after Morning Prayer (p. 196f.).

12. 1688: "when the Litany" is underlined.

13. Williams Diary: (22 Oct.) "Agreed to leave out the Collect, We are ty'd with the Chain &c. as not being in the Original Book—Quere that; for in some of the Books, it is not left out, but put into another place: —said, in that of Ely."

    The Prayer was to be found in many Primers before 1549, but was not included in that revision. In the Grafton edition of 1559 it was placed at the end of the Litany, and in 1662 it was placed here.

## NOTES ON THE THANKSGIVINGS

1. New Survey: "And as to the General Thanksgiving, perhaps it were to be desired, that to the Redemption by Jesus Christ, and the Means of Grace, were added, and for the Spirit of Grace sanctifying an Holy

Catholick Church, and the Resurrection of the Body unto Eternal life. Some have thought our Thanksgiving too general, in that there is no mention made in it of Sanctification . . ." (p. 7).

2. 1688: The words " plague of "are placed in parentheses. The new collect for Rogation day, may well have been designed either as, or in conjunction with, the new collect which was " not pfected ". (Cf. Collects note 39).

3. 1688: An insertion mark is placed after the word " increase ". Perhaps to include a phrase similar to the one inserted by the Commissioners.

## A GENERAL NOTE ON THE REVISION OF THE COLLECTS

Exceptions: " The collects are generally short, many of them consisting but of one, or at most two sentences of petition; and these generally ushered in with a repeated mention of the name and attributes of God, and presently concluding with the name and merits of Christ; whence are caused many unnecessary intercisions and abruptions, which when many petitions are to be offered at the same time, are neither agreeable to scriptural examples, nor suited to the gravity and seriousness of that holy duty. 2. The prefaces of many collects have not any clear and special respect to the following petitions; and particuarly petitions are put together, which have not any due order, nor evident connection one with another, nor suitableness with the occasions upon which they are used, but seem to have fallen in rather casually, than from an orderly contrivance. It is desired, that instead of those various collects, there may be one methodical and intire form of prayer composed out of many of them."

Williams Diary: (11 Nov.) ' Proceeded on the Collects and for the most part kept to it as a Rule (where it cou'd be observ'd) to take the matter of the Collect out of the Epistle and Gospel; especially considering that this was done in the 5 new Collects composed in 1661—Order'd, That the Collects that are good but not suitable to the Epistle and Gospel be retained but put into the Number of the voluntary Prayers."

Williams Diary: (6 Nov.) "Went upon the Collects for Sundays and adjourn'd . . . (8 Nov.) In the first place went over the first 10 Collects after Trinity. . . . The Bp of London went away about 5. Adjourned the Court till 3 on Monday—But they sat and went over many other Collects . . . (11 Nov) Proceeded on the Collects. . . . Went thro' the rest of the Collects after Trinity; and after the Bp. of London &c, went away, they continued on, and went through some of the Saints-days, as far as Phil. & Jac. . . . (13 Nov) Went over the rest of the Collects for the Holy Days. . . . (15 Nov) Added a new Service for Rogation-Sunday—Proceeded as far as the Sunday after Trinity—. . . . (18 Nov.) Not being a Quorum, we only read over what was done before, beginning at          Sunday after Trinity and proceeded to the Office of Baptism. . . ."

Let. Min: " In the Collects, which, though good, may be made, as I conceive, more useful for exciting the Devotion of the People, if (where it may conveniently be done) they be so formed, as to have a respect to the Epistle and Gospel then read. This I perceive was a design the Commissioners of the Savoy had in their eye; such were the third Sunday in Advent, and the sixth Sunday after Epiphany. It was great pity they had not time (as I suppose) to have gone through with the whole; for we may easily apprehend by what was then done, the difference, and advantage that might have been gained by it." (p. 25).

V. Populi: " Most of the Collects have but one Petition in them. Were several of our short Prayers well digested into one, we humbly conceive it would be like the uniting of the little Sparkles of Heaven into a constellation that renders them the more conspicuous. . . ." (p. 3).

JRC: "And if some late Collects are intended as a Specimen, by which the old are to be mended, I believe few will rejoice in the change." (p. 40).

Let. Till: "Since short collects do not very well suit the humour of the people, whether several of those in our Liturgy may be contrived into one? as, for instance, those of petition together, intercession together, &c." (II).

Terms: "Q. What is the Collect for the Day? A. A Prayer summing up the chief things contained in the Epistle and Gospel for the Day, and a pious Application of them." (p. 15).

The method of compiling the new Collects took a long time. It was first begun by the revisers of the Prayer Book in 1688. Archbishop Wake, in his Speech at the Sacheverell Trial which refers to the setting up of the 1688 Revision, says: "The time was towards the end of the late unhappy reign, when we were in the height of our labours defending the Church of England against the assaults of Popery . . . The Scheme was laid out, and the several parts of it were committed, not only with the approbation, but by the direction of that great prelate, to such of our divines as were thought the most proper to be intrusted with it. His Grace took one part to himself; another was committed to a then pious and reverend Dean, afterwards a bishop, of our church." (A Note identifies this "Dean" with Symon Patrick.) In Dr. Nicholl's *Apparatus ad Defens.* (p. 95) quoted in Conferences p. 432 ff, the following is said about the compilation of the collects: "Collectae in totum anni cyclum de novo elaborantur, ad epistolae et evangelii doctrinam congruentius factae; et cum tanta verborum elegantia atque splendore, tantaque Christianae mentis vi atque ardore compositae sunt, ut nihil possit animos audientium magis afficere et accendere, et eorum mentes ad Deum evehere. Eas primum contexuit, summus hujus rei artifex, Simon Patricius; ulteriorem vim sanguinem spiritumque adhibebat Gilbertus Burnetius; eas denique cum magno judicio, singulis verbis diligenter expensis, examinante Edvardo Stillinfleto; ultimam limam addente ac verbis enodibus et dulcis facilisque eloquentiar fluentis iterum perpoliente Joanne Tillotsonio."

From these authorities, it is obvious that Patrick began the revision of the Collects on Sancroft's order in 1688. The part played by Stillingfleet, Burnet and Tillotson is harder to determine. One possibility is that although they were not mentioned by Wake as being part of Sancroft's 1688 Committee, they were in fact involved. Only two other members were mentioned by Wake, both of whom were still alive and in the House, namely Sharp and Moore of Ely, and their names were only mentioned "to bear witness to the truth of my relation "; the "such of our divines as were thought the most worthy to be intrusted with " the Revision, cannot have been limited to three alone, and so it must be presumed that there were others on the committee.

The New Collects themselves are written into the 1689 Prayer Book, but not into the 1688. In the 1689, the Collects for Advent 4 to Easter Day are all written in the hand of an Emanuensis (copper-plate); Easter 1-3 by Tenison; Easter 5 to Trinity 9 by the Emanuensis, and Trinity 10 to the end by Tenison. In the Collects written out by the Emanuensis, those between Advent 4 and Easter Eve, have only minor alterations made to them in Tenison's hand, while those from Easter 5 Trinity 9 are almost wholly rejected and replaced with new ones by Tenison. The Sections written by the Emanuensis must have been written out before 11 Nov., for on that day many of the Collects after Trinity were discussed as far as St Philip and St James in Holy-days. All these Collects are written out by Tenison, as is the Service for Rogation day which was discussed on the 15 Nov. The Section from Easter 5 to Trinity which is completely revised, seem to reflect a series of comprehensive and radical discussions on the Trinity Collects, which were undertaken on 15 and 18 Nov. (See Williams quoted above). The first section which is hardly altered was dealt with only briefly on 6 Nov.

Perhaps then, the compilation may be outlined as follows: Patrick compiled a number of Collects in 1688, but did not finish the Revision. In the 1689 Revision, these were copied into the Prayer Book before the Discussions started, by an Emanuensis using a copper-plate hand. The first section was briefly discussed on 6 Nov., and the results of those discussions were written into the text by Tenison, who often altered only a single word. It may well be that the work undertaken in 1688 by Patrick, had been done thoroughly only as far as Easter Eve, and that he completed it at a slightly later date; anyway, the Commission seem to have felt that more alteration was needed to his compilations after Easter Eve, and they proceeded to revise the Collects in detail, Tenison writing in those which were lacking. It will be noticed from the notes on the new Collects, that the method of compilation has changed at this point; from Trinity 1, with the sole exception of Trinity 11, all the Collects are taken from the Epistle for the day, with little material added from elsewhere in the Bible, except where parts are taken from the previous draft by the Emanuensis. It is almost as if the Commission had sat round a table, with the Prayer Book open in front of them, and welded phrases from the Epistle into a coherent Prayer. The Collects before Easter show a much more complicated internal structure. This would account for the fact that Tenison has written them all out. If this is so however, what part did Stillingfleet, Burnet and Tillotson play in this? The answer is, little or none at all; the only person who could have influenced their construction was Burnet, who was present at all the Meetings. Stillingfleet did not attend the Commission after 1 Nov., and so was not present at a single discussion of the Collects; and Tillotson was not present on 11 or 18 Nov. This being the case, if what Nicholls says is based on fact, they must have been concerned with the Collects in the Revision of 1688, and therefore not only been part of the Committee, but aided Patrick in the original composition of those sections in the Emanuensis hand.

The Collects themselves are based almost entirely on the Epistle for the Day, despite Williams' assertion that the principle of composition was that they should be taken out of the " Epistle and Gospel ". They are Scripturally based to an intricate degree, and it is noticeable that when a point raised in the Epistle is better expressed elsewhere in the New Testament, the better phrase is used. The analysis of the Collects shows the extent to which this is done, as well as the extent to which they used Scripture phrases.

The Collects are longer, and contain more than one petition in conformity with the criticisms quoted above. Their literary worth is in the eye of the beholder, and all I will venture to say is that the continual catalogues of virtues to which the faithful should aspire (meekness, patience, kindness, humbleness, long suffering, patient suffering etc), and the emphasis on the Sinfulness of man, would become most tedious if they were actually used. Lacking in the precision of Cranmer's Collects, they have a tendency to ramble, but to many of their contemporaries with notable exceptions (cf. JRC above) they would have commended themselves as an improvement on the lines of those who compiled the Prayer Book in 1662.

## NOTES ON THE COLLECTS, EPISTLES AND GOSPELS

*1.* It is difficult to determine whether the Revisers intended to underline or delete the phrase " that hath a Vigil or Eve ". The " Q " would suggest that it should be underlined, but the omission of the Table of Vigils at the front of the book, implies its deletion. The latter would be in conformity with the Exceptions VI: " That the religious observation of saints-days appointed to be kept as holy-days, and the vigils thereof without any foundation (as we conceive) in Scripture, may be omitted." The difference between a Vigil and an Eve is that a Vigil requires the faithful to fast; the Prayer Book does not seem to differentiate them however. If the phrase were to be deleted, there would be no difference in the practice of anticipating the Collect of the holy-day, as only the word " Vigil " and the word " Fast " from the Kalendar were removed to satisfy the Dissenters. The rubric would still presuppose the anticipation.

2. Black fails to record the alteration of the name " Jesu " to " Jesus ".

3. Emanuensis.

Prev. Reading i. who has given us Cause of great joy . . . . i. set before us, we may through thy help be carefull for nothing, but thankfully. . . .

Analysis.

| | |
|---|---|
| O Lord . . . Saviour among us. | Luke. 2.10 " For behold, I bring you good tidings of great joy, which shall be to all people." (cf. i above). |
| Raise up . . . . (we pray thee). | 1662. " Raise up (we pray thee) thy power." |
| & possess . . . . Love. | Original material. |
| that whereas thro. | 1662. |
| ye Cares of this Life.. | (Cf. Matt. 13.22). |
| we are sore . . . before us. | 1662. |
| we may be carefull . . . nothing. | Phil. 4.6a (Epistle). |
| but thankfully . . . everything. | Abbreviation of Phil. 4.6b. |
| thy bountiful . . . . Mercy. | 1662. |
| The Peace of God . . . . Minds. | Phil. 4.7. |
| thro' the satisfaction. . . . | 1662. |

4. Emanuensis.

Prev. Reading i. take our Nature upon Him & as at this time, to be born of a pure Virgin, yt he might dwell among us, full of Grace & Truth. Grant . . . (based on Gospel; John 1.14).

The omission of " as at this time ".

1549, 1552: " nature upon hym, and this daye to bee borne of . . ."

Exceptions: " We desire that in both collects the word ' this day ' may be left out, it being according to vulgar acceptation a contradiction."

Bishops Reply: " That the words ' this day ', both in the collects and prefaces, be used only upon the day itself; and for the days it be said, " as about this time ".

D. B.: " i. For ' this day ' reading ' at this time '.
ii. this day (or as about this time) ".

S.L.: (St. Stephen's Day) " Then shall follow the Collect of the Nativity, which shall be said every day in the week unto New-Years Day: but instead of the words (and this day to be born) the Presbyter shal say (at this time to be born)."

It was evidently decided that the phrase " as at this time " was subject to the like objections.

Analysis.

| | |
|---|---|
| Almighty God . . . . Son | 1662. |
| ye brightness . . . . Person | Heb. 1.3 (Epistle). |
| to take . . . . Holy Spirit | 1662 omitting " as at this time ". |
| till Christ . . . . formed in us | Gal. 4.19 " . . . . I travail in birth until Christ be formed in you . . .'. |
| And we be . . . . Divine Nature | 2 Pet. 1.4 " precious promises: that by these ye might be partakers of the divine nature, having escaped the corruption that is in the world through lust." |
| thro' ye same. . . . | 1662. |

5. Unaltered because it was one of the new Collects composed for 1662.

6. Emanuensis.
   **Prev. Readings** i. Blessed Apostle & Evangelist St John . . . . i. that we walking in ye light of thy Truth.

   Analysis.

| | |
|---|---|
| Merciful God . . . . at all. | 1 John 1.5b (Epistle). |
| Enlighten . . . . beseech thee. | Cf. notes on Versicles and Responses at Morning Prayer. (note 10 p. 194). |
| with such . . . . John. | 1662, with the omission of " Saint ", and the alteration of " doctrine of " to " Doctrine taught by ". The Gospel is the Doctrine of Christ, not of a man. |
| That we . . . . Holiness of Life. | 1662. " light of thy " omitted as an afterthought. (cf. i above). |
| may have . . . . Jesus Christ, | 1 John 1.3b. |
| by whose blood . . . . or Sins, | 1 John 1.7b. |
| we may . . . . Everlasting Life. | 1662. " Light of " omitted in conformity with its omission above. |
| thro' ye same. . . . | Note: the subject of the collect is changed from " the Church " to " us " so there is a certain amount of difference from the Prayer Book in those places based on 1662. |

   Exceptions: (St John and Innocents). " We desire that these collects may be further considered and abated, as having in them divers things that we judge fit to be altered."

7. Emanuensis (both versions).
   **Prev. Reading** i. O Almighty God, who out of the mouths of babes and sucklings hast ordained strength, and madest infants to glorifie thee by their deaths; Mortify and kill all vices in us, and so strengthen us by thy grace, that by the innocency of our lives, and the constancy of our faith even unto death, we may glorifie thy holy Name, and be found without fault before the Throne of thee our God, thro' Jesus Christ our Lord. Amen.

   (1662, with phrase " and be found without fault before the Throne of thee our God " added. Based on Rev. 14.5 Epistle).

   Analysis.

| | |
|---|---|
| O most . . . . or Nature | Links up with the Christmas Collect. |
| didst preserve . . . . were slain | Paraphrase of Gospel Mt. 2.13-18. |
| Grant yt . . . . Adversities | |
| we . . . . confidence in thee | |
| & do thou . . . . wicked men | 'Rage' of Herod suggested by Mt. 2.16a cf. 1 Pet. 5.10 " But the God of all grace, who hath called us unto his eternal glory by Christ Jesus, after that ye have suffered a while, make you perfect, stablish, strengthen, settle you." (cf. also Jas. 5.10). |
| or strengthen . . . . . sufferings. | |
| to glorify . . . . | 1662. |

   Exceptions: see note 6 above.

8. Emanuensis.
Analysis.

| | |
|---|---|
| Almighty . . . . holy Spirit | 1662, omitting ' as at this time '. |
| which we . . . . towards thee | Simply an extension of the thought of the 1662 Collect. |
| thro' Jesus Christ our Lord. | 1662, but omits ' the same '. |

9. Emanuensis wrote the first draft (i.) and the alterations (ii and Text) were made by Tenison.
Prev. Readings i. Holy will, & thereby obtain ye Blessedness of not having our Sins imputed to us, but of being accounted Righteous in thy sight, thro' ye same thy Son our Saviour Jesus Xt. Amen. ii. Holy will, & thereby obtain ye remission of our sins & be (accounted) Righteous in. . . . (accounted) deleted subsequently. The Text is Tenison's fair copy of ii.

Analysis.

| | |
|---|---|
| i. thereby obtain ye . . . . | |
| thy sight. | Cf. Rom. 4.8-9, but in general a paraphrase of the Epistle. |

Text:

| | |
|---|---|
| & thereby . . . . of our sins | Cf. Rom. 3.25 " Whom God hath set forth to be a propitiation through faith in his blood, to declare his righteousness for the remission of sins that are past . . .". |
| & ye Righteousness . . . . Lord | Rom. 3.22 " Even the righteousness of God which is by faith of Jesus Christ unto all and upon all them that believe." Note: this is the chapter before the Epistle. |

10. Emanuensis.

Previous Readings i. & conduct them to ye very place where he lay. (word " conduct " altered to " guide " by Tenison). ii. govern'd by thy Holy Spirit.

Analysis.

| | |
|---|---|
| O God . . . . Gentiles | 1662. |
| & guide . . . . he lay | Matt. 2.9 (Gospel) |
| Mercifully grant . . . . Gospel | Eph. 3.5 (Epistle) |
| may make . . . . Holyness | |
| & be so entirely . . . . Spirit | Cf. All Conditions of Men; " may be so guided and governed by thy good Spirit . . .". |
| that we may be brought after this life | 1662. |
| into that . . . . now is | |
| and there . . . . Presence | 1662. Word " Godhead " altered to " Presence ". |
| Thro . . . . | 1662. |

11. Emanuensis.

Prev. Reading i. & perfect Will revealed to us by him.

Analysis.

| | |
|---|---|
| O God . . . . incourage us | Original material. |
| to call upon thee | 1662. |

| | |
|---|---|
| we beseech . . . . hear us | |
| & grant . . . . know what | 1662. |
| is thy good . . . . will | Rom. 12.2 (Epistle). |
| revealed to us: | |
| And also . . . . ye same | 1662; " so " added. |
| yt we may . . . . unto thee | Rom. 12.1. |
| thro' . . . . | 1662. |

12. Emanuensis.

Prev. Reading i. Relations wherein thou hast set us.
Analysis.

| | |
|---|---|
| Almighty . . . . thy people, | 1662. |
| & so rule . . . . & Relations | Perhaps paraphrase of Rom. 12.6 (Epistle) cf. also i above. |
| constantly . . . . wch is good | Rom. 12.9. |
| being fervent . . . . Lord | Rom. 12.11. |
| Rejoyceing . . . . Prayer | Rom. 12.12. |
| yt we may . . . . or Life | 1662. |
| thro' . . . . | 1662. |

13. Emanuensis.

Prev. Readings i. & endue us wth such an humble, meek, patient, & fore-bearing Spirit; yt no Evill . . . (Alteration to " spirit of meekness & patience " made by Tenison.)

i. lieth in us, living peaceably with ym. And into whatsoever Dangers & Necessities we may fall by doing our Duty, stretch forth thy right Hand we humbly beseech thee to help & defend us, thro Jesu Xt or Ld. Amen.

The phrase " providing things honest in ye sight of All men " is deleted.

In the margin however there is the word " stet ". Black has interpreted this as referring to the inclusion of " And into . . . . defend us " but not the phrase " providing . . . . men ". It is more probable however, from the positioning of the word stet, that it refers simply to the phrase beginning " providing ". This is the interpretation put forward in the text. The alterations in this last section were made by Tenison.

Analysis.

| | |
|---|---|
| i. living peaceably with ym. | Rom. 12.18 (Epistle). |
| And into . . . . Necessities | 1662. |
| we may . . . . duty | Qualification of 1662. |
| stretch forth . . . . defend us | 1662. |
| Text. | |
| Almighty . . . . infirmities | 1662. |
| & endue . . . . patience | |
| yt no Evill . . . . unto them | Rom. 12.17 (Epistle) seen perhaps in the light of Lk. 6.27. |
| but we . . . . good | Rom. 12.21. |
| providing . . . . all men | Rom. 12.17b. |
| & if it . . . . All men | Rom. 12.18. |
| thro . . . . | 1662. |

14. Emanuensis.

Prev. Readings i. in many things we offend All.
i. that being stedfastly faithfull.
i. accepted by thee.

Analysis.

| | |
|---|---|
| O God . . . . dangers | 1662. "temptatios &" added by Tenison in conformity with its mention later in the Collect. |
| that by . . . . our nature | 1662. |
| in many ways . . . . All | Jas. 3.2: 'For in many things we offend all." Cf. i. above. This phrase was added by Tension. |
| Grant . . . . temptations | 1662. |
| that being . . . . thee | |
| obedient . . . . their due | Rom. 13.1, 7a (Epistle). |
| & doing yt wch is good, we | |
| . . . . of thee | Cf. I Tim 2.2-3: (Pray for) "Kings, and for all that are in authority; that we may lead a quiet and peaceable life in all godliness and honesty. For this is good and acceptable in the sight of God our Saviour." |
| thro' . . . . | 1662. |

*15.* Emanuensis.

Prev. Readings. i. Long-suffering, & such like Vertues: that thus resting Analysis.

| | |
|---|---|
| O Lord . . . . true religion | 1662. |
| And to stirr . . . . Profession | Trinity 25 Collect: " Stir up . . . . the wills of thy faithful people." Heb. 10.23: " Let us hold fast the profession of our faith without wavering; (for he is faithful that promised." Tit. 2.10: " that they may adorn the doctrine of God our Saviour in all things." |
| by putting . . . . Long-suffering | Col. 3.12 (Epistle). |
| that resting . . . . Grace | (Heb. 4.14, 16??). |
| & doing all . . . . Savr | Col. 3.17a. |
| we may . . . . Power | 1662. |
| giving thanks unto thee | Col. 3.17b. |
| thro' . . . . | 1662. |

*16.* Remains unaltered because it was newly composed for 1662.

*17.* Emanuensis.

Prev. Readings i. by thy Grace have entred into ye Christian Course, may be temperate. ii. Course of ye Christian life.

Analysis.

| | |
|---|---|
| O Lord . . . . thy people | 1662. |
| that we . . . . Christian life | Metaphor of the Race; cf. 1 Cor. 9.26b where the Metaphor of fighting also occurs. This link may have suggested, 2 Tim 4.7: " I have fought a good fight, I have finished my course, I have kept the faith: Henceforth there is laid up for me a crown of righteousness . . . and not to me only, but unto all them also that love his appearing." Final alterations by Tenison. |

| | |
|---|---|
| may be . . . . all things;<br>**and so run . . . . before us** | 1 Cor. 9.25 (Epistle).<br>(Cf. Heb 12.1: " Let us run with patience the race that is set before us."). |
| as to obtain . . . . Crown<br>wch thou . . . . Love thee<br>thro' . . . . | 1 Cor. 9.25.<br>2 Tim. 4.8 (see above).<br>1662. |

18. Emanuensis.
Analysis.

| | |
|---|---|
| O Lord God . . . . against all<br>adversities . . . . under them | 1662. |
| but having . . . . Patience<br>thro' . . . . | Lk. 8.15 (Gospel).<br>1662. |

19. Emanuensis.
Prev. Reading i. of all vertues, without wch whosoever liveth is counted dead before thee; Grant (1662).

Analysis.

| | |
|---|---|
| O Lord . . . . charity<br>wch is . . . . & patient | 1662.<br>(Cf. Col. 3.12-14; " Put on therefore, . . . . bowels of mercies, kindness, humbleness of mind, meekness, long-suffering; Forebearing one another . . . And above all these things put on charity, which is the bond of perfectness."). |
| ye very bond . . . . vertues<br>Grant this . . . . | 1662 (cf. i above).<br>1662. |

20. Emanuensis (Collect only).
Prev. Reading i. that we heartily lamenting our sins wth unfeigned sorrow for ym, & abhorence of ym. (Altered by Tenison.)

Analysis.

All 1662, with qualifications added relating to the Exhortation in the Commination Service.

Exceptions: " We desire that these collects may be further considered and abated, as having in them divers things that we judge fit to be altered.'

Epistle; Exceptions XIV: ' That no portions of the Old Testament, or of the Acts of the Apostles, be called " epistles ", and read as such.'

Bishops Reply: " That when any thing is read for an epistle which is not in the epistles, the superscription shall be, ' For the epistle '."

21. The Section from " See the Comination " to the end of the Exhortation is written out by Tenison.

" See the Comination." The Commination service has changed its name to " The latter part of ye Office for Ashwednesday ". The whole office is seen as comprising, Morning Prayer, Sermon (or Homily), Litany and the " Latter Part ". In the Latter part the exhortation expands with similar phraseology, this exhortation which is to be used the Lords Day before Ashwednesday.

Exhortation. For analysis and notes, see under the Commination Service. Previous Readings i. for ye worthy Comunion at Easter.
i. forebearing all Feasting & entertainments.

22. Emanuensis.
Note: ' Receive (The) grace of God." The Emanuensis has written this collect at the bottom of the page. The word " The " is printed there, anticipating the first word overleaf, and it is round this that the Collect has been written. As the word is not deleted, it is presumed that the Emanuensis intended its inclusion.

Analysis.

| | |
|---|---|
| O Lord . . . nights | 1662. |
| & vanquish . . . . Devill | (summary of Gospel). |
| by wch . . . overcome. | |
| Grant that . . . vain, but | 2 Cor. 6.1 (Epistle). |
| use such . . . . Spirit | 1662. |
| no desire . . . . Duty; | (summary of the three temptations). |
| but we may ever . . . . | 1662. |

23. Emanuensis.

Prev. Reading i. received how to walk.
Analysis.

| | |
|---|---|
| Almighty God . . . . soul | 1662. |
| and as we have . . . . & more | 1 Thess. 4.1 (Epistle). |
| thro' or Lord . . . . | New conclusion. |

24. Emanuensis.

Analysis.

| | |
|---|---|
| We beseech . . . . servants. | 1662. |
| and as thou . . . . truth. | 2 Cor. 4.6 " For God, who commanded the light to shine out of darkness, hath shined in our hearts, to give the light of the knowledge of the glory of God in the face of Jesus Christ." |
| so enable . . . . Light. | Eph. 5.8 (Epistle). |
| and to have . . . . Darkness. | Eph. 5.11 (Note the connection of these two verses with 2 Cor. 4.6 above). |
| that bringing . . . . Truth. | Eph. 5.9. |
| we may . . . . Protection. | Cf. 1662: " to be our defence against all our Enemies." |
| thro' . . . . | 1662. |

25. Emanuensis.

Prev. Reading i. worthy of thy holy calling (alteration by Tenison).
Analysis.

| | |
|---|---|
| Allmighty . . . . Jesus. | General summary of Epistle; cf. also 2 Cor. 9.14-5: " And by their prayer for you, which long after you for the exceeding grace of God in you. Thanks be unto God for his unspeakable gift." |
| & conveyed . . . . Commands. | Cf. Col. 3.24: " Knowing that of the Lord ye shall receive the reward of the inheritance; for ye serve the Lord Christ." |
| wch is . . . . Service; | Rom. 12.1: " present your bodies a living sacrifice, holy, acceptable unto God, which is your reasonable service." |

| | |
|---|---|
| Grant that . . . . in thee<br>& walk . . . . calling | (Phil. 4.4).<br>Eph. 4.1: "that ye walk worthy of the vocation wherewith ye are called." |
| thro' . . . . | 1662. |

26. Emanuensis.

Analysis.

| | |
|---|---|
| O Allmighty . . . . to come | Heb. 9.11 (Epistle). |
| & by . . . . for us; | Heb. 9.12b, c. |
| Mercifully . . . . people | 1662. |
| that by ye . . . . God | Heb. 9.14. |
| that we . . . . Inheritance, | Heb. 9.15c. |
| thro' . . . . | 1662. |

27. Emanuensis.

Analysis.

| | |
|---|---|
| Almighty . . . . flesh | 1662. |
| & that in . . . . Cross | Collation of 1662 and Phil. 2.7-8 (Epistle). 1662: "flesh, and to suffer death upon the Cross, that all mankind should follow the example . . ." Phil. 2.7-8: "And took upon him the form of a servant . . . . and became obedient unto death, even the death of the cross:" |
| for our Redemption | Cf. Prayer of Consecration; "to suffer death upon the Cross for our Redemption." |
| that all . . . . Humility | 1662. |
| Patience & Obedience | This addition is in conformity with the virtues listed below, of Obedience and Patient Suffering, and the 1662 reference to "Patience." 1662 reads; ". . . should follow the example of his great humility, mercifully grant, that we may both follow the example of his patience . . ." Obedience is added from Phil. 2.8 to balance the collect. |
| Mercifully grant | 1662. |
| yt this . . . . Jesus | Phil. 2.5. |
| that we . . . . of his | 1662. |
| humble . . . . Suffering | humble (1662 Humility) Obedience (Phil. 2.8) Patient Suffering (1662 Patience, cf. James below).<br>Jas. 5.10: "who have spoken in the name of the Lord, for an example of suffering affliction, and of patience". |
| and also . . . . Resurrection<br>to live . . . . ever | 1662 (adds ' glorious '). |
| Grant this . . . . | New material. |

216

*28.* Emanuensis. (" A Sermon . . ." written in by Tenison.)

Analysis. Collect 1.

| | |
|---|---|
| Allmighty God<br>ye Father of mercies | 1662. |
| we beseech thee graciously | 1662. |
| to hear ye . . . . Church | Collect Trinity 23; " Be ready, we beseech thee, to hear the devout prayers of thy Church." |
| for wch . . . . Cross; | 1662 (word " contented " changed to " content "). |
| & according . . . . blood | General summary of Heb. 9.11-10.29. |
| put thy laws . . . . more; | Heb. 10.16-17 (Epistle). |
| for ye sake . . . . Hand | Heb. 10.12. |
| & now . . . . | 1662. |

*29.* Analysis. Collect 2.

| | |
|---|---|
| Almighty . . . . same | 1662. |
| drawing near . . . . wavering | Heb. 10.22-23 (Epistle). |
| & in their . . . . serve thee | 1662. |
| thro' . . . . | 1662. |

*30.* Collect 3.

Prev. Reading i. Shepherd, Jesus Xt or Lord, who is or High Priest in ye Heavens, expecting till all his Enemies be made his Footstool, To whom with thee & ye Holy Spirit. ii. . . . . footstool, who liveth & reigneth with thee & ye Holy Spirit, One God, world without end. Amen. Black reads " world hast shown "; the correct spelling is " shewn ".

Analysis.

Reading i. above is based on Heb. 4.14 " Seeing then that we have a great high priest that is passed into the heavens " and Heb. 10.13 (Epistle).

| | |
|---|---|
| O Merciful . . . . sinner<br>but by ye . . . . world | 1662. |
| hast shewn . . . . live | 1662. Cf. Ezek. 33.11: " O thou son of man . . . . Say unto them, As I live, saith the Lord God, I have no pleasure in the death of the wicked; but that the wicked turn from his way and live: . . . ." (used in Absolution at Morning and Evening Prayer.) |
| have mercy . . . . Word. | 1662 (adds " Make known . . . . unto ym). |
| Work . . . . home<br>to thy flock . . . . shepherd | 1662. |
| Jesus . . . . | Conclusion of 1662 curtailed. |

Holy Week and Good Friday were normally kept well in the later half of the Seventeenth and early part of the Eighteenth Century, often with fasting and considerable self-denial. Thomas Hearne for example wrote in 1706: " The Queen (Anne) having order'd Good Friday to be kept

217

strictly in London, twas accordingly observ'd in a most decent and Religious Manner by all Friends of the Church, but very negligently and disrespectfully by the Presbyterians and the rest of that Brood." (*Remarks and Collections,* Oxford Historical Society 1885, I, 208). A full description may be found in Wickham Legg p. 211-27.

*31.* Emanuensis.

Analysis.

| | |
|---|---|
| Blessed Lord .... our God | 1 Pet. 3.18 (Epistle). |
| we beseech .... Death | Rom. 6.3. "Know ye not, that so many of us as were baptized into Jesus Christ were baptized into his death?" (cf. 1 Pet. 3.21). |
| so by .... with him; | 1662. |
| & at last .... death | 1662 (with small additions). |
| pass .... | 1662 (omitting ' for us '). |

This 1662 Collect was a new composition in 1661.

*32.* Easter Anthems.

1688: 'Perhaps in ordinary Churches it were better to turn these into metre, that ye people may better both declaim & sing them.'

The development of the Easter Anthems has some interesting points.

1549: 'Christ rising agayne from the dead nowe dieth not. Deathe from hence furth hath no power upon hym. For in that he dyed, he dyed but once to put awaye sinne: but in that he liueth he liueth unto God. And so lykewyse counte youre selves dead unto synne, but lyuyng unto God in Christe Jesus our Lord. Alleluya.

Christ is risen agayne, the fyrste fruytes of them that slepe: for seyng that by man came deathe, by manne also commeth the resurreccion of the dead: For as by Adam all men do dye, so by Christe all menne shalbe restored to lyfe. Alleluya.'

1552: There are no alterations from 1549, except the omission of the word ' Alleluya '.

1559: No alterations, except that the word "counte" is altered to ' accompt ', and after the first section the word "Amen " is added. It is not added after " restored to lyfe ".

S.L.: No Alterations but omits the "Amen " added in 1559.

1662: Retranslated the quotations, and added the Gloria Patri after the second section. Cosin's Particulars of 1660 show a concern however, to balance the two sections: ' At Easter day, it is appointed, yt in stead of ye Venite Exultemus, ye Two Anthemes (Christ Rising, & Christ is Risen) shalbe used. But there is no Gloria Pri sett to follow either of ym, as after ye Venite is ordered before. Therfore ye question is, whether Glory be to ye Father &c should not be here added after either or both of these Anthemes.' (D.B. p. 115). 1662 furthermore added the verse 1 Cor. 5.7, and this move towards the expansion of the Anthems was continued in 1689, with the further addition of Rom. 8.34. The Versicle and Response method is also used in 1689, to secure more congregational participation, without going to the lengths suggested by 1688 above.

Collect.

1688: "This Collect seems too languishing for the great occasion of Easter-day."

Let. Min.: " So are there some-times in the Collects the like obscurity, as that of Easter-Sunday, where the Preface and the Petition (as it seems) want a better connexion." (p. 24)

V. Cleri.: " The Preface and Connexion are thus: That as God by Christ hath opened to us the Gate of everlasting Life, so he would (prepare us for that life) putting into our Hearts good Desires, by his special Grace preventing us, and by his continual help we may bring the same to good effect." (p. 39)

The Collect was written out by the Emanuensis, and altered considerably by Tenison. It is difficult to identify a sequence in the alterations, so the Collect is presented below in full detail.

Allmighty God, who by ye

| | |
|---|---|
| Resurrection of thy Son Jesus Xt. | ' onely begotten ' added. |
| hast overcome Death & opend to us ye Gate of Everlasting Life, We humbly beseech thee yt [as by thy special Grace preventing us, thou dost put into our Minds good Desires] | Deleted in pencil. |
| after those things | Deleted in ink. |
| wch are above, where | Deleted in ink; above this is written ' which are above ', again deleted. |
| Christ sits on thy Right hand; | Deleted in ink. |
| so by thy continuall help we* | Deleted in pencil. |
| may mortify all our* corrupt* affections | Deleted in ink. The word ' stet ' is written above the phrase, and this is again deleted. Inside the deletions, the word ' corrupt ' is altered to ' Earthly ', and this is also deleted. |
| *and* | Deleted in ink, and replaced by the word ' may '. |
| may stedfastly set our Hearts upon* | * Insertion mark, refers to a note in the margin ' Those things wch are above '. |
| Those things above | Deleted in ink. The word ' those ' is replaced by the word ' them ', which in turn is deleted. |
| yt when Christ who is our Life shall appear . . . . (as text) | Note: by the line ' we* may mortify . . . and* ' there is, in the margin, ' q '. |

(* refers to insertion marks in the text)

It is difficult to identify the sequence here, but one might add, that throughout the revision, pencil deletions are invariably later than any other form of alteration. It may therefore be presumed that these two sections were part of a final revision of the text.

Analysis.

Sections deleted;

| | |
|---|---|
| as by thy . . . . Desires | 1662. |
| after those . . . hand | Col. 3.1 (Epistle). |
| so by . . . help | 1662. |
| we may . . . affections | Col. 3.5. |
| & stedfastly . . . above | Col. 3.2. |
| Text. | |
| Allmighty . . . . Life | 1662. |
| We humbly . . . righteousness | 1 Pet. 2.24: ' being dead to sins, should live unto righteousness.' Cf. Collect for Easter 2, where this is part of the Epistle. |
| & stedfastly . . . above | Col. 3.1 (Epistle). |
| yt when . . . in Glory | Col. 3.4. |
| where he now . . . . | 1662. |

33. Prev. Reading i. collect to be the same.

34. Black reads ' Sonn whom Thou hast sent '. The correct spelling is ' whome '.
   Let. Min.: ' . . . Easter-Sunday, where the Preface and the Petition (as it seems) want a better connexion. So also the first Sunday after Easter &c.' (p. 24).
   V. Cleri.: ' The Preface is, Almighty God who hast given thy only Son to die for our Sins, and to rise for our Justification: The Connexion is: Grant us so to die unto sin, (which is the sense of) to put away the leaven of Malice, that we may serve thee in pureness of living and truth (i.e.) we may live unto God.' (p. 39).
   Analysis.

| | |
|---|---|
| Almighty . . . justification | 1662. |
| Increas & . . . sent | Cf. Baptism: ' Almighty and ever-lasting God . . . Increase this know-ledge, and confirm this faith in us evermore.' |
| that so . . . world | |
| & attain . . life | 1 John 5.4-5 (Epistle). |
| through . . . . | 1 John 5.11. |

35. Tenison.
   Prev. Reading i. obtain everlasting life.
   Analysis.

| | |
|---|---|
| Almighty God . . . life | 1662. The word " ensample " is altered to " example " which is the word in 1549, 1552. " our selves " is omitted. |
| that dying . . . . Righteousness | 1 Pet. 2.24 (Epistle). |
| through . . . . | 1662. |

36. Tenison.
   Analysis.

| | |
|---|---|
| Almighty . . . . religion | 1662. |
| ye as . . . . lusts | 1 Pet. 2.11 (Epistle). |
| & follow . . . . Profession | Cf. 1662; " that they may eschew those things that are contrary to their profession, and follow all such things as are agreable to the same." |
| thro . . . . | 1662. |

37. Emanuensis.
Prev. Reading i. O Almighty . . . . people, deleted; with ' stet ' written in the margin.

There was another draft of this collect written on the interleaf, but it has been torn out of the book. The two words which have been added, are in the hand of the Emanuensis.

38. In the next few Collects, the first Collect to be composed was written out by the Emanuensis. These have been deleted, and a new Collect written out by Tenison.

Prev. Reading i. O Lord ye Authour of all Good, grant unto thy humble Servants a right Understanding in Religion, that by thy holy Inspiration they may not onely know, & intend those things, that be Good, but by thy Mercifull Guidence, & Assistance may perform the same; that so not being forgetfull Hearers, but Doers of the Word (ii. Work) they may be all blessed in their Deed, thro' our Lord & onely Saviour Jesus Christ. Amen.

Analysis of i.

| | |
|---|---|
| O Lord . . . . Good | Based on 1662. |
| grant . . . . . . Servants | 1662. |
| a right . . . . Religion | Jas. 1.26 (1662 Epistle). |
| that . . . . . Good | 1662, with "not onely know & intend " added. |
| but . . . . . . same | 1662. |
| that so . . . . . . Word | Jas. 1.22 (Word subsequently altered). |
| they may . . . . . Deed, thro' . . . . . . | Jas. 1.25. |

39. Williams Diary (15 Nov.) " Added a new Service for Rogation-Sunday." Rogation processions were common throughout the Country throughout the Seventeenth and Eighteenth Centuries. Full details of the breadth of the Custom may be found in Wickham Legg p. 228ff and Brightman's *English Rite* II p. 1045ff.

In 1686 Lloyd of St Asaph, one of the Commissioners, had produced " Directions for my Brethren of the Clergy that shall officiate in the Perambulations ", and it is evident that the Recommendations of the Commission, are to be seen within the context of that Directive. The following quotation is therefore transcribed from Wickham Legg p. 249f. (Bodleian MS. Tanner 30. f. 23).

Directions from my Brethren of the Clergy that shall officiate in the Perambulations.

(By William Lord Bishop of S. Asaph. A.D. 1686)

On every day of perambulation, the Incumbent or Curate, and the Church-Wardens and other parishioners, that are to make the perambulation, are to meet together at the Parish Church or Chappel, and there to have the prayers appointed for the day: or in case the perambulation that day will be so large that they cannot well afford time for the full Prayers, yet at least the Minister ought to begin there with the Confession, Absolution and Lord's Prayer; and for all the rest of the office for Morning Prayer, he may bring it in, in parts, at the severall standings in the perambulation, together with the Psalms and Hymns, and Lessons and Prayers that are here recommended for this Purpose.

At every Standing there ought to be used one or more Psalms, or Hymns, a Lesson or Epistle and Gospell, or one of the three Creeds, or the ten Commandments, and one or more of the following Collects or Prayers. There may be fewer or more according to the time.

In one Standing where there is a more remarkable bound to be remembred, it is very fitt that there the Minister should hear one of the Children or of the others there present, say his Catechism, or some part of it; as either the Creed, or Commandements, or the Doctrine of Sacraments, etc.

And in one of the more remarkable Standings it will be fitt to use the Litany; especially if the perambulation should be upon a Wednesday or a Friday, because the Church requires the use of the Litany on those days.

For Psalms to be used in the Perambulation, beside the 95th, 96th, 67th and the 100th, which are used in the office of Common Prayer; I think fitt to recommend these that follow. 1, 8, 15, 19, 23, 24, 33, 34, 37, 65, 103, 104, 107, 133, 144, 145, 147, 148.

For Hymns I recommend the use of the Te Deum, and the Benedicite. For Collect and Epistles and Gospells, those that are appointed in the Church for the 1st and 2d Sunday in Advent; For the 2d, 3d, 4th, 5th or 6th Sunday after Epiphany; For Septuagesima, Sexagesima or Quinquagesima: For the 3d Sunday in Lent or the 5th Sunday after Easter: For the 1st Sunday after Trinity; or for any other Sunday after Trinity, especially the 4th or the 8th.

Of all these Collects, Epistles, and Gospells, there may be used one at a Standing, such as the Minister shall chuse. I also recommend the reading of that part of the Gospell, Math. 6.24, till the end of the Chapter; or the Parable of the sower, Math. 13, from the 1st to the 9th verse; with our Saviour's Interpretation from the 18th till the 23d verse. Other such parts of Scripture the Minister may chuse at his discretion. But whatsoever Lesson he reads it will be fitt to use the Collect of the 2d Sunday in Advent after that which he had read.

For Prayers (beside the Litany as before-mentioned) it will be fitt to use the Prayers, or thanksgivings, for Rain, or for fair weather as there shall be Occasion; also the Collect or Prayer for all Conditions of men, and the generall Thanksgiving; Also the Thanksgiving for Peace and Deliverance from our Enemies, and the Thanksgiving for restoring public peace.

In the end of Every day of perambulation, the Minister ought to bring the People to Church with him, and there to read the Evening Prayer if the time will permitt; or at least to read the last part of it, from the 2d Lord's Prayer to the Blessing. . . .

Analysis.

Collect.

The Collect is a completely new complication, which is not based on either the 1662 or the new Epistle and Gospel. It bears a great deal of resemblance however to the Prayers and Thanksgivings which were suggested by Lloyd as Prayers to be used during the perambulation. There may be some relationship between this collect and the note in the Thanksgivings, in the Prayer for fair Weather; " A new collect was here design'd but not pfected; " perhaps Bishop Lloyd was dealing with the compilation of both collects.

| | |
|---|---|
| Allmighty . . . . fruitful | Cf. Prayer in time of Dearth & Famine. " O God . . . whose gift is it, that the rain doth fall, the earth |

|  |  |
|---|---|
|  | is fruitfull " Gen. 1.22: " And God blessed them, saying, Be fruitful, and multiply." |
| & bring . . . . life of man | Prayer for Rain: " . . . hast promised . . . all things necessary to their bodily sustenance." |
|  | Thanksgiving for Rain: " . . . that it may bring forth fruit for the use of man . . ." |
| & hast . . . . own bread | 2 Thess. 3.12: " Now them that are such we command and exhort by our Lord Jesus Christ, that with quietness they work, and eat their own bread." |
| Bless us . . . . Labours |  |
| & graunt . . . . fruits of the earth. | Thanksgiving for Fair Weather: " and comforted our souls by this seasonable and blessed change of weather." |
|  | Prayer for Fair Weather: " . . . send us such weather, as that we may receive the fruits of the earth in due season." |

& ever rejoyce . . . .

For the Epistle.

There are some inaccuracies in the transcription of the Lesson.

| comand Thee this day, ye Ld thy | (Deut.) this day, that the Lord |
|---|---|
| God |  |
| fruit of ye ground | fruit of thy ground |
| establish Thee a holy people | Thee an holy people. |

Gospel.

This is the section recommended by Lloyd.

Note: " —— " at the beginning of the Gospel, refers to the omission of the word " therefore " from the verse.

Text reads: " body more than raiment " (Matt.) the body than raiment.

40. Prev. Reading i. (Emanuensis) O God, ye blessed & onely Potentate, who only hast Immortality, dwelling in ye Light, wch no man can approach unto, whom no Man hath seen, nor can see; Grant we beseech thee, that like as we believe thy onely begotten Son our Lord Jesus Christ to have ascended into ye Heavens, so we may also in Mind & Heart thither ascend & with him continually dwell: Stedfastly believing yt ye same Jesus who was taken up into Heaven, shall so come in like Manner as ye Apostles saw him go into ye Heavens, where he now liveth & reigneth with thee & ye Holy Ghost One God world without End. Amen.

Analysis of i.

| O God . . . . nor can see | 1 Tim. 6.15-16: ' . . . Jesus Christ: Which in his times he shall shew, who is the blessed and only Potentate, the King of kings, and Lord of lords; Who only hath immortality, dwelling in the light which no man can approach unto; whom no man hath seen, nor can see.' |
|---|---|

| | |
|---|---|
| Grant we . . . . dwell | 1662 (Heart and Mind reversed). |
| Stedfastly . . . . ye Heavens | Acts 1.11 (Epistle). |
| where he now . . . . | |
| Analysis of text. Tenison. | |
| O God . . . . of Heaven | Collect for Ascension I, 1662. |
| graunt . . . . Amen | 1662. (' liveth ' changed to ' livest '). |

41. Prev. Reading i. (Emanuensis) . . . Kingdom in Heaven, and strengthen us in all well doing; that being Sober, & watching unto Prayer, & above all things having fervent Charity among ourselves, & serving thee faithfully wth ye severall Talents, wherewith thou hast intrusted us, we may be exalted at last unto ye same place whither our Saviour Christ is gone before who liveth & reigneth with thee & ye Holy Ghost one God world without End. Amen.

Analysis of i.

| | |
|---|---|
| O God . . . . in Heaven | 1662. |
| and strengthen . . . . doing | Cf. 1 Pet. 2.15: ' For so is the will of God, that with well doing ye may put to silence the ignorance of foolish men.' |
| that being . . . . Prayer | 1 Pet. 4.7 (Epistle). |
| above . . . . ourselves | 1 Pet. 4.8. |
| & serving . . . . us | Cf. 1 Pet. 4.11b, and Matt. 25.15ff (The Parable of the Talents). |
| we may be . . . . | 1662. |

Analysis of text. Tenison.

| | |
|---|---|
| O God . . . . of Heaven | 1662. |
| & yet . . . . Comfortless | 1662 reads, ' leave us not comfortless '. Since the Comforter came down at Pentecost, he is now present. Therefore the phrase is applied to the Apostles. |
| Vouchsafe . . . . comfort us | 1662 (adds ' to guide '). |
| yt being . . . . Prayer | 1 Pet. 4.7 (Epistle). |
| & above . . . . orselves | 1 Pet. 4.8. |
| we may be . . . . | 1662. |

42. Prev. Reading i. (Emanuensis) O eternall God, who according to thy faithfull Promise didst on ye Day of Pentecost, lead thy holy Apostles into all Truth, by sending to them ye Light of thy Holy Spirit; Grant us by ye same Spirit, both to have a right Judgment in all things, & also faithfully to keep thy holy Commandments; that thereby we may know that we love thee, and being beloved by thee, we may ever rejoyce in ye Comfort of thy holy Spirit, through ye merits of Christ Jesus our Saviour who liveth & reigneth with thee, in ye Unity of ye same Spirit One God world without End. Amen.

Analysis of i.

O eternall . . . . Pentecost

| | |
|---|---|
| lead . . . . Truth | John 16.13. " When he, the Spirit of truth, is come, he will guide you into all truth." Cf. John 14.17 (Gospel). |
| by sending . . . . Things, | 1662. |
| & also . . . . beloved by thee | John 14.21. |
| we may ever . . . . | 1662. |

Analysis of text. Tenison.

Prev. Reading i. rejoyce in his holy comfort through. . . .
O etrnall . . . . Pentecost
graunt . . . . in all Things          1662.
& showing . . . . comandments         John 14.21 (Gospel).
may . . . . Him                       1662 (cf. i above).
through . . . .                       1662.

*43.* Munday & Tuesday in Whitsun-week. Additions by the Emanuensis.

*44.* Tenison.

Exceptions: " We desire that these collects may be further considered and abated, as having in them divers things that we judge fit to be altered."

Let. Min. " There are some things obscure, as in . . . . the Collect for Trinity Sunday, Who hast given us grace in the power of the divine Majesty, to worship the Unity." (p. 24).

V. Cleri.: " This is not obscure to any that acknowledgeth the Trinity, which is to be worshipped in the Unity of Divine Majesty: As when in the Litany we pray, O holy blessed and glorious Trinity, three Persons and one God." (p. 38).

See also Notes on the Preface for Trinity Sunday in the Holy Communion Service.

Analysis.

| | |
|---|---|
| Holy . . . . God Almighty | Rev. 4.8.: " Holy, Holy, Holy, Lord God Almighty, which was, and is, and is to come." |
| Thou art . . . . created. | Rev. 4.1 (Epistle). |
| Blessed . . . . majestie | (Cf. Ps. 72.9) |
| who hast . . . . Trinity, | 1662. |
| & to worship . . . . Ghost. | |
| We beseech . . . . Fayth | 1662. |
| & in holiness of Life | |
| & give . . . . Thee | (Cf. 1 Thess. 2.12: " That ye would walk worthy of God, who hath called you unto his kingdom and glory.") |

who livest . . . .

*45.* Prev. Reading i. (Emanuensis) O God most blessed for ever, the Strength of all them that put their trust in thee; Mercifully accept our Prayers; and because thro' ye Weakness of our mortall Nature, we can do no good thing without thee, much less so great a thing as for thy sake to love One another and to have thy Love perfected in us; grant us the Help of thy Grace, that in keeping thy Commandments we may please thee both in Will & Deed, especially in keeping that great Commandment of loving one another as thou hast loved us, whereby we may dwell in thee, & thou in us, thro' Jesus Christ our Lord. Amen.

Analysis of i.

| | |
|---|---|
| O God . . . . ever | |
| the strength . . . . thee | 1662. |
| much less . . . . in us; | 1 John 4.12 (Epistle). |
| grant . . . . & Deed, | 1662. |
| especially . . . . in us | 1 John 4.12-13 (cf. John 15.12). |
| thro' . . . . | 1662. |

Analysis of Text. Tenison.
Prev. Reading i. that we stedfastly . . . . we may please thee . . .

| | |
|---|---|
| O God . . . thy grace | 1662. |
| that stedfastly . . . . commandment | (Epistle *passim*, but) cf. 1 John 3.23. "And this is his commandment, That we should believe on the name of his Son Jesus Christ, and love one another, as he gave us commandment." (Epistle Trinity 2). |
| may please . . . . | 1662. |

46. Emanuensis (both versions).

Prev. Reading i. O Lord, who never failest to help and govern them whom thou dost bring up in thy stedfast fear and love; Keep us, we beseech thee, under the protection of thy good providence, and make us to have a perpetual fear and love of thy holy Name, and a sincere Affection to all our Christian Brethren; that so we may have Confidence towards thee our God, & whatsoever we ask we may receive of thee, because we keep thy Commandments, and do those things that are pleasing in thy Sight through Jesus Christ our Lord. Amen.

Analysis of i.

| | |
|---|---|
| O Lord . . . . holy Name | 1662. |
| and a sincere . . . . Brethren | The phrase "Bowels . . . . Brethren" in the second version is a scriptural rendering of this phrase; this seems to be a phrase 'in the spirit of Comprehension.' |
| that so . . . . God | 1 John 3.21 (Epistle). |
| & whatsoever . . . . Sight | 1 John 3.22. |
| through . . . . | |

Analysis of text.

| | |
|---|---|
| O Lord . . . . govern ym | 1662. |
| who . . . . & Love | 1662 reads; "whom thou dost bring up in thy stedfast fear, and love." |
| keep . . . . Providence | 1662. |
| and give . . . . all things; | (Cf. Collect Trinity 6). |
| and to have . . . . thee | 1 John 3.21 (Epistle). |
| & whatsoever . . . . thee | 1 John 3.22a. |
| thro' . . . . | 1662. |

47. Emanuensis.

Prev. Readings i. the Faith may be defended against the assaults of ye Devill, and comforted in all Dangers & Adversities, thro' Jesus Christ our Lord. Amen. ii. the Faith may resist all ye Temptations of ye Devill and (be) comforted in all Dangers & Adversities, thro' Jesus Christ our Lord. Amen. iii. the Faith, may resist all ye Temptations of ye Devill, & be defended & Comforted by thy mighty aid in all Dangers & Adversities, thro' Jes &c Amen. (Final form written in by Tenison.) Black reads "called us into thy"; this was a previous reading of the word, which was subsequently altered to "unto".

Analysis of text.

| | |
|---|---|
| O God . . . . Jesus | 1 Pet. 5.10 (Epistle). |
| we beseech . . . . unto thee | 1662 reads; "we beseech thee mercifully to hear us; and grant that we to whom thou hast given an hearty desire to pray." |

226

| | |
|---|---|
| and grant . . . . Humility | 1 Pet. 5.5. |
| & casting . . . . thee | 1 Pet. 5.6. |
| may be sober, & vigilant | 1 Pet. 5.8a. |
| & continuing . . . . Faith | 1 Pet. 5.9a. |
| may resist . . . . Devill | |
| & at length . . . . life, | Jas. 1.12: " Blessed is the man that endureth temptation: for when he is tried, he shall receive the crown of life." (connection "Temptation "). |
| through . . . . | 1662. |

48. **Prev. Reading i. (Emanuensis)** O God, the protector of all that trust in thee, without whom nothing is strong nothing is holy; Increase and multiply upon us thy mercy and possess our Hearts with such a strong Belief, that ye Sufferings of this present time are not worthy to be compared with ye Glory, wch shall be revealed in us, that nothing here may ever make us start aside from our Duty but thou being our Ruler & guide we may so pass thro things temporal, yt we finally lose not the things Eternal. Grant this, O Heavenly Father for Jesus Christs sake our Lord. Amen.

Analysis of i.

| | |
|---|---|
| O God . . . . thy mercy | 1662. |
| and possess . . . . Belief | |
| that ye . . . . in us | Rom. 8.18 (Epistle). |
| that . . . . Duty | |
| But thou . . . . | 1662. |

Final form based on Rom. 8.18 (the sections not based on the Epistle being rejected). Written out by Tenison.

49. **Emanuensis.**

Prev. Reading i. . . . seeking Peace & ensueing it: and so to order ye Course of this World by thy wise Governance, that thy Church may joyfully serve thee in all godly quietness, through Jesus Christ our Lord. Amen.

This was deleted and replaced by Tenison.

Analysis.

i. based on 1 Pet. 3.11 (Epistle) and 1662.

| | |
|---|---|
| O Lord . . . . prayers | 1 Pet. 3.12. |
| we most . . . . Courteous | 1 Pet. 3.9. |
| eschewing . . . . all men | 1 Pet. 3.11. |
| yt so we . . . . undrstanding | Phil. 4.7: " And the peace of God, which passeth all understanding." |
| through . . . . | 1662. |

50. **Emanuensis.**

Exceptions: " We desire that these collects may be further considered and abated, as having in them divers things that we judge fit to be altered."

Prev. Reading. i. understanding; Pour into our hearts such love toward thee, that the Body of Sin being destroyed in us, and we loving thee above all things, & walking before thee in Newness of Life, with Christ Jesus: who being raised from the dead, dyeth no more, but liveth for ever, & is become the Author of Eternal Salvation unto all them that

obey him. To whom with ye Father, & ye Holy Ghost be all Honour &
Glory World wthout End. Amen.

Analysis of i.

| | |
|---|---|
| Pour into . . . . thee | 1662. |
| that the . . . . in us | Rom. 6.6 (Epistle). |
| and we . . . . all things | 1662. |
| & walking . . . . Life | Rom. 6.4b. |
| may obtain . . . . Life | 1662. |
| with Christ . . . . ever | Rom. 6.9. |
| & is . . . . obey him | Heb. 5.9: "And being made perfect, he became the author of eternal salvation unto all them that obey him." |

To whom . . . .

Analysis of Text. Final alterations by Tenison.

| | |
|---|---|
| O God . . . . understanding; | 1662. |
| Graunt . . . . all things | 1662. |
| & walking . . . . Life | Rom. 6.4b. |
| may obtain thy promises | 1662. |
| thro . . . . | 1662. |

51. Emanuensis.

Prev. Reading i. and becoming the Servants.

Analysis.

| | |
|---|---|
| Lord of . . . . religion | 1662. |
| that we . . . . Life | Rom. 6.22 (Epistle). |
| thro' . . . . | 1662. |

52. Collect and note in Tenison's hand; an alternative Collect was written
out by the Emanuensis on the interleaf, but this has been cut out of the
text.

"This to be put . . ." Williams Diary (11 Nov.) "Order'd, That the
Collects that are good but not suitable to the Epistle and Gospel be
retained but put into the Number of the voluntary Prayers."

Analysis.

| | |
|---|---|
| Most gracious . . . . Father | Rom. 8.15b (Epistle). |
| Graunt yt . . . . body | Rom. 8.12. |
| & being . . . . Spirit | Rom. 8.14. |
| may live . . . . wth him | Rom. 8.17. |
| who liveth . . . . | |

53. Emanuensis.

Analysis.

| | |
|---|---|
| O God . . . . before us | |
| thy Judgments . . . . Example | Rom. 10.11 (Epistle). |
| Preserve us . . . . them | Cf. Rom. 10.19-21. Ps. 95 (Venite) "as in the provocation . . . unto whom I swear in my wrath ". |
| & never . . . . bear it | Rom. 10.13. |
| through . . . . | 1662. |

54. This, and all the remaining Collects are altered by Tenison only.

Analysis.

| | |
|---|---|
| O God . . . . thy Church; | 1 Cor. 12.4 (Epistle). |
| we beseech . . . . ye same | |

| as may be . . . . body | Cf. 1 Cor. 12.7 and 1 Cor. 14.12: "forasmuch as ye are zealous of spiritual gifts, seek that ye may excel to the edifying of the church." |
| united . . . . Love | (Cf. 1 Cor. 12.25: "that there should be no schism in the body; but that the members should have the same care one for another."). |
| & ye same Spirit | Cf. 1 Cor. 12.11. |
| through . . . . | 1662. |

55. Tenison.

Black reads "Light of ye Gospell", the text here reads "yr". Either may be regarded as a possible reading.

Analysis.

| O God . . . . yr Gospell | 2 Tim. 1.10: "But is now made manifest by the appearing of our Saviour Jesus Christ, who hath abolished death, and hath brought life and immortality to light through the gospel." |
| & hast . . . . dead | 1 Pet. 1.3: "Blessed be the God and Father of our Lord Jesus Christ, which according to his abundant mercy hath begotten us again unto a lively hope by the resurrection of Jesus Christ from the dead." |
| make us . . . . ye Lord | 1 Cor. 15.58: "Therefore, my beloved Brethren, be ye stedfast, unmoveable, always abounding in the work of the Lord, forasmuch as ye know that your labour is not in vain in the Lord." |
| who died . . . . again & now liveth . . . . | Cf. 1 Cor. 15.3-4 (Epistle). |

56. Tenison.

Note: the Collect is not deleted, and there is an indecipherable word in the margin. The Epistle is deleted however, and nothing has been supplied in its place. It was possibly deleted in error, instead of either the collect, or the Epistle for Trinity 13 (see notes below).

Prev. Readings i. Gospell of our Ld & Saviour Jesus Christ.

i. through Jesus Christ thy Son our Ld.

Analysis.

| O Most . . . . ye Spirit | 2 Cor. 3.8 (Epistle). |
| hast given . . . . Sonn | (Cf. 2 Cor. 3.6-7). |
| we beseech . . . . It | Cf. Versicles and Responses at Morning Prayer. |
| & frame . . . . It, to thy . . . . | |

Exceptions: this is another collect objected against; cf. Trinity 6.

57. Tenison.

Analysis.

| O Aetrnall . . . . Christ Jesus | Gal. 3.28 (Epistle). |
| grant . . . . him | Gal. 3.27. |

so faithfully . . . .      1662.
Epistle.

The 1662 Epistle is Gal. 3.16-22, and Black reads "Enlarged by the following addition)".

It would seem however, that the section written out in full on the interleaf, is intended to replace the 1662 Epistle, rather than be added on to it.

(a)  The new construction is headed,

The Epistle.

Gal. 3 from 22 to the End.

This implies that it is a separate entity, rather than an addition to other material. One might add, that perhaps the Epistle for Trinity 12 was deleted in error, the intention being to delete this Epistle.

(b)  The New Epistle begins with v 22, which is the last verse of the 1662 Epistle. Nowhere else in revision is a verse copied out from preceding material to show a connection. The dash, at the beginning of the new Epistle, does not imply a connection with 1662, but shows the omission of the word "But" from the text (cf. e.g. the new Gospel for Easter 5, where it shows the omission of the word "therefore").

(c)  The Collect is based solely on Gal. 3.22-29, and there are no references to the 1662 Epistle.

It is probable therefore that it was intended to replace, rather than add to, the 1662 Collect.

58.  Tenison.

Analysis.

| | |
|---|---|
| **Almighty** . . . . **& Lusts** | Cf. Gal. 5.24 (Epistle). |
| **& to** . . . . temperance | Gal. 5.22. |
| that we . . . pmise | 1662 reads: " and that we may obtain that which thou dost promise, make us to love that which thou dost command." |
| through . . . . | 1662. |

59.  Tenison.
Prev. Readings i. Almighty God who hast called us to be ye Followers of our Lord Jesus Christ, who was made perfect through sufferings; indue us we beseech thee, wth . . . . ii. (altered first to read) Followers of him.

Analysis.

| | |
|---|---|
| Almighty God . . . . sufferings | Heb. 2.10: " to make the captain of their salvation perfect through sufferings." |
| hast called . . . . followers | |
| indue us . . . . in him | " flesh " in Gal. 6.12 (Epistle) perhaps connects with Rom. 8.9: " But ye are not in the flesh, but in the Spirit, if so be that the Spirit of God dwell in you. Now if any man have not the Spirit of Christ, he is none of his." |

| yt we . . . . World<br>may patiently . . . . Cross<br>& being . . . . holiness | Gal. 6.14.<br><br>Eph. 4.23-24: "And be renewed in the spirit of your mind; And that ye put on the new man, which after God is created in righteousness and true holiness." cf. Gal. 6.15c "but a new creature." |
| & walking . . . . upon Us<br>through . . . . | Gal. 6.16.<br>1662. |

60. Tenison.

Prev Reading i. in our inner man.

Analysis.

| O God . . . . named | Eph. 3.15 (Epistle). |
| grant . . . . inner man | Eph. 3.16. |
| yt Christ . . . . Love | Eph. 3.17. |
| may be able . . . . comprehend | Eph. 3.18. |
| thy Love . . . . virtues | Eph. 3.19. |
| through | 1662. |

61. Tenison.

Black leaves " in us all " in the text, when in fact ' us ' is deleted.
Prev. Reading i. through All, & in us All. . . .

Analysis.

| O God . . . . in All | Eph. 4.6 (Epistle). |
| grant . . . . follow us | 1662. |
| yt we . . . . call'd | Eph. 4.1. |
| wth all . . . . in Love | Eph. 4.2. |
| endevouring . . . . Peace | Eph. 4.3. |
| That, being . . . . works | 1662. |
| we may finally . . . . | |

62. Tenison.

Analysis.

| O Lord . . . . Gospell | Epistle generally. |
| grant us . . . . thee | 1662. |
| so to wait . . . . Christ | 1 Cor. 1.7 (Epistle). |
| to judge . . . . righteousness | Cf. Acts 17.18: "Because he hath appointed a day, in which he will judge the world in righteousness." |
| yt we . . . . only God | 1662. |
| yt we may be . . . . Jesus Christ. | 1 Cor. 1.8. |

63. Tenison.

Prev. Readings i. in ye very spirit of our mind: that being perfectly purged from. . . . . ii. perfectly freed from . . .
i. & becoming kind.

Analysis.

| O God . . . . hearts | 1662. |
| and renew . . . . mind; | Eph. 4.23 (Epistle). |
| that putting . . . . malice | Eph. 4.31. |
| & evry . . . . Affection | |

| | |
|---|---|
| & being kind . . . . forgiven us | Eph. 4.32. |
| we may . . . . hope | |
| for ye . . . . Evills | Eph. 4.30. |
| unto etrnall life, | |
| through . . . . | 1662. |

64. Tenison.

Analysis.

| | |
|---|---|
| O Almighty . . . . holy will | Eph. 5.17 (Epistle). |
| we beseech . . . . Grace | |
| to walk . . . . ye time | Eph. 5.15-6. |
| in all . . . . ye Spirit | Eph. 5.18. |
| we may . . . . in Thee | |
| & give . . . . Jesus Christ | Eph. 5.20. |

65. Tenison.

Prev. Reading i. power of thy Might.

Analysis.

| | |
|---|---|
| O mercifull . . . . Godliness | 2 Peter 1.3: " According to his divine power hath given unto us all things that pertain unto life and godliness, through the knowledge of him that hath called us to glory and virtue." |
| make us . . . . Might | Eph. 6.10 (Epistle). |
| That putting . . . . devill | Eph. 6.13. |
| praying to . . . . perserverance | Eph. 6.18. |
| through . . . . | 1662. |

66. Tenison.

Analysis.

| | |
|---|---|
| O Mercifull . . . . in Us | Phil. 1.6 (Epistle). |
| that or . . . . Judgment: | Phil. 1.9. |
| that, . . . . day of Christ; | Phil. 1.10. |
| being filled . . . . or God, | Phil. 1.11. |
| through . . . . | 1662. |

67. Tenison.

Analysis.

| | |
|---|---|
| O God who . . . . Life | Cf. Phil. 3.17 (Epistle). |
| assist . . . . of Christ | Phil. 3.17 cf. also, 1 Cor. 11.1: " Be ye followers of me, even as I also am of Christ." |
| yt we . . . . earthly things | Phil. 3.19c. |
| but having . . . . Christ | Phil. 3.20. |
| to change . . . . glorious body | Phil. 3.21. |
| in wch he . . . . | |

68. Tenison.

Let. Min.: " Such again, are those Collects which too much incline to the Pelagian Phrase of laying the force of temptation, and man's liableness to sin, upon the frailty and not the corruption of our Nature, as in the first and 24th Sundays after Trinity." (p. 25).

V. Cleri: " what they mean by frailty, that first Collect explains, to be such, as that without God we can do no good thing, which is the great corruption of our Nature; and no Doctrine concerning the corruption of Nature is more plain, than that in our Articles." (p. 40).

Analysis.

| | |
|---|---|
| O God . . . . Christ | Col. 1.3 (Epistle). |
| give us . . . . or God | Col. 1.10. |
| & thereby . . . . Light | Col. 1.12. |
| we may allwaies . . . . Church | Litany: " O God, merciful Father . . . . may evermore give thanks unto thee in thy holy Church, through Jesus Christ our Lord." |
| through . . . . | (Conforms with Litany above). |

69. Tenison.

Prev. Reading i. and hasten we pray thee the Kingdom of our Lord.

Analysis.

| | |
|---|---|
| O eternal . . . . True | |
| &, according . . . . pmises | (allusion to prophesy of Jeremiah) |
| hast raised . . . . Righteousness | Jer. 23.6 (Epistle). |
| we beseech . . . . works | 1662. |
| they may . . . . Ld. | Cf. Lk. 1.17: " And he shall do before him in the spirit and power of Elias . . . to make ready a people prepared for the Lord." |
| And we pray . . . . earth | Jer. 23.5. |
| Grant this . . . . | |

70. For omission of " This day " see Notes on the Collect for Christmas Day.

71. Tenison.

Prev. Readings i. commandments & to lay down. i. thy Truth, as he did through Jesus. . . .

72. Insertion of " signs & wonders " is from the Epistle, Acts 5.12.

73. Exceptions: (St Luke and Michaelmas day) " We desire that these collects may be further considered and abated, as having in them divers things that we judge fit to be altered."

Let. Min.: " Lastly, there are some of the Collects that are too fanciful, and savour of the Breviary, as those of St. Luke, St. John, Simon and Jude. Now after all, I do not say these or the like things are not tolerable, or defensible, but that they are not only capable of amendment, but in a sort do need it." (p. 25).

V. Cleri: " Whatever in the Breviaries are taken out of the Scripture, or Authentick and Antient Ecclesiastical History, is not therefore to be rejected; and that St. Luke was that beloved Physitian mentioned Col. 4.14. is the constant assertion of all Interpreters, and the express words of the Scripture; therefore no Legend. Of these he says, ' That in a sort they need amendment: ' And so doth the Judgment of this nice Enquirer, who, I fear, hath lost his Rationale, which he might easily supply from Dr. Comber's, or Bishop Sparow's Discourses. A man would think this

Writer to have been hired to betray the Cause of the Dissenters, by his weak and impertinent Arguments for its defence: and a great conviction it will be to many, that there need no Alterations to be made, when their prime Advocate insists on such Instances as render him vain and ridiculous." (p. 40).

Prev. Readings i. hast inspired.

i. examples wch he hath given us.

Analysis.

| | |
|---|---|
| Almighty . . . . Jesus Christ | Lk. 1.3 "It seemed good to me also, having had perfect understanding of all things from the very first, to write unto thee in order . . ." |
| grant . . . . certainty thereof | Lk. 1.4: "That thou mightest know the certainty of those things, wherein thou hast been instructed." |
| may most . . . . | |

## A NOTE ON THE SHORTENING OF THE SUNDAY SERVICE, AND THE RELATIONSHIP OF THE LITANY TO THE COMMUNION SERVICE

The Services of Morning Prayer, Litany and Holy Communion were originally designed as separate offices; in the Seventeenth and Eighteenth Centuries however, it was normal to read them, with so little gap in between, that they became almost a single office. This had a number of attendant problems, the most important being that there was a great deal of repetition (see p. 186f.) and the service became too long. Even in the Exceptions there is the comment: "(VII) . . . And further, considering the great age of some ministers, and infirmities of others, and the variety of several services oft times concurring upon the same day, whereby it may be inexpedient to require every minister at all times to read the whole; it may be left to the discretion of the minister to omit part of it, as occasion shall require: which liberty we find allowed even in the first Common Prayer Book of Edward VI ".

The Dissenters objected to frequent communions, although providing the Ante-communion was not read at the altar, they were content with it. (see Holy Communion note 1).

The Commission debated the matter at length: "There was a debate about shortning the Service. Bp. of Sarum moved that on Sundays, the Epistle and Gospel shou'd go for the Lesson; but it was answer'd, that that wou'd be offensive, and besides it would not be so proper and beneficial to the People, as to read the Scriptures in Course. It was Answer'd this might be in the Afternoon. It was proposed by other, that rather they would abridge it, by ending the Litany at the Lords Prayer (the latter part seeming now but a botch, and chiefly respecting times of Persecution) and after that read the Commandments and so conclude." (Williams Diary 11 Nov.)

With this should be compared part of the Let. Min, which if as is suggested, was written by Burnet, becomes very important as regards the Commissions findings. The similarity with Williams Diary, is remarkable: " And here it may well be queried, whether it's not better both for Minister and People, to have the Sunday Service shortned, than continued to that length that it has at present . . . (points out that it is impossible for the Clergy to say properly especially when Occasional, and Afternoon Services

and Catechizing were added to it) . . . . But perhaps you will say, how is this to be done? I answer first, think sensibly of it, and you will soon find out a way. But however to prevent any excuse.
1. Reduce things to the former state they were in, and as they were originally several distinct Offices, so let them be used in their proper times and seasons. As for example, let the Communion-Service be for a Communion, and persons not obliged to read it but at that season, or when there is no Sermon.
2. Why may not the Litany be shortned by concluding at the Lord's-Prayer, and leaving out what follows; which (bating the Responsals) seems not so agreable to the Order of a Litany, and was composed also (as we may guess) peculiarly with respect to a state of Persecution. And so may be left to the discretion of the Minister to read or omit it.
3. That at least it be left to his discretion again in short days and extremity of weather; one day to read one part, and another day another, and all in two days. For why may not that be permitted to be done in two days, which in some Cathedrals is divided into several hours of the same day. And for the same reason, especially where the people have cattel to fodder &c that it be permitted in the Afternoon to leave out the first Lesson, or the like; . . . .'
It may be considered further whether in the Weekly Service in the Country Parishes, it's not to be left to the liberty and discretion of the Minister to use the Prayers without the Lessons, and especially the Litany alone on Wednesdays or Fridays . . ." (p. 18-22).

The Evidence of the 1689 Book itself, however, is not so simple. The Litany concludes thus:
We humbly Beseech thee, O Father.
Collect for purity
The Ten Commandments (AV) " Or sometimes the 8 Beatitudes, especially on Comunion daies, See the comunio Service."
Collect for the Day
Epistle & Gospel
" Then (If there be No Comunion) the Nicene Creed "
" Then the Genral Thanksgiving &c "
Prayer of St Chrysostom
Grace

Rubric for Holy days
The Singing Psalm
Prayer for the Whole state of Christ Church " accommodated "
Sermon.
(When there is no communion this should be read in the same place as the rest of the service)

The Holy Communion Service:
Q of another Collect
& then Let yr Light &c
& of those for ye K.
Lords Prayer
Collect for Purity
Ten Commandments (deleted, with note " as in Exodus ")
Beatitudes 1: with a note " to be put at ye End of ye Litany "
Beatitudes 2: with note " This to be used after or instead of the X comandmts upon the Great Festivals "
(a deleted note: The Collects for ye King & ye Day are to be omitted, when the Comunion Service is not alone used)

Two Collects for the King
Collect for the Day
Rubric for the Epistle and Gospel, with a line beside it
Nicene Creed

Rubric for holy days, with a line down the side of the text, and the note " See at ye End of ye Litany ", and a thin line through the text.
Sermon
Offertory.


It will be realised immediately that this is too complicated to be the scheme of one service. What in fact is here, is three separate Schemes for Sunday worship; (a) The Litany without any part of the Communion Service following. (b) The Litany followed by the Communion Service (c) The Communion service by itself—the note " When the Comunion service is not alone used " implies that it was intended to be used alone sometimes. It is this that has provided many of the complications in the text: It was intended that when it was used alone, it should remain as it was in 1662. Hence the Commissioners were unable to delete prayers which had been transferred etc. The Schemes of the other two services in brief are:

| | |
|---|---|
| The Litany Alone | Litany with Communion. |
| We humbly beseech thee | We humbly beseech thee |
| Collect for purity | Collect for purity |
| Ten Commandments or | Ten Commandments or |
| Beatitudes 1 | Beatitudes 1 |
| Collect for the Day | Collect for the Day |
| Epistle and Gospel | Epistle and Gospel |
| Nicene Creed | |
| General Thanksgiving | |
| " &c " | |
| Prayer of S Chrysostom | |
| Grace | |
| | Nicene Creed |
| Holy Day Rubric | Holy Day rubric |
| Singing Psalm | Singing Psalm |
| Whole State accommodated | Whole State accommodated |
| Sermon | Sermon |
| | " A new Collect " |
| | Let your Light &c |
| | Collect for King |
| | Exhortation |
| | Confession and Absolution |

The Litany Alone.
The prayer " We humbly beseech thee " is the final prayer of the Litany, and on to this the Commissioners have tacked the Ante-Communion Service, which concluded with the Sermon and the Whole State of Christs Church. (The Rubric in the Communion Service for the Ante-Communion, has a line down the side of it showing that it is redundant.) Thus the Collect for purity follows " We humbly beseech thee ", and this in turn is followed by the Commandments and their alternatives. These have been transferred from the Communion service, and written out " As in Exodus ", as have the Beatitudes. (There are corresponding notes to this effect in both services.) The Collect for the Day, Epistle, Gospel and Nicene Creed then follow. This Ante-Communion service is enclosed in the Litany, by the addition of the " General Thanksgiving &c ", which is a reversion to the 1552 position of the Prayers and Thanksgivings. These followed " We humbly beseech thee "; and it may well be intended to remove the Ante-Communion service as an entity, by including it within the Litany, as part of it.
The last section of the service was not determined, but it seems to have been intended to use the remaining part of the Ante-Communion service: The

Prayer for the Church accommodated as a prayer before the Sermon, and the Sermon itself.

The Litany with the Communion Service.

The Communion service in this scheme, is the full service, with reception by the people.

A Possible interpretation might be that the Litany, with the Ante-Communion service embodied in it, should, after the Sermon, be followed by " A New Collect ", " Let your Light " and the Collects for the King. But if this was so, why would it be necessary to omit the Nicene Creed from the Litany, for there would be no place for its inclusion in the Holy Communion Service in this Interpretation. Furthermore, the rubric suggesting the omission of the Collects for the Day and King, if any other service was used with the Communion, implies that the Commissioners had considered the above interpretation as a possibility, and had rejected it. In the 1559 and Caroline Prayer Books, a prayer for the Monarch preceded the prayers in the Litany, following " We humbly beseech thee ". To say a similar prayer in the Communion service would be vain repitition. Thus initially a rubric was put in to omit them. But, the Commissioners reconsidered this, and deleted the rubric, reinstating the Collects for the King.

It is more probable that after the Collect for purity, an alternative of the Commandments and the Beatitudes 1 is allowed. On High Festivals when there would be a Communion Service Beatitudes 2 would be permissable as an alternative, and might be printed in the Communion service itself. The Collect, Epistle and Gospel would be said, and then the Communion proper would begin. That the Epistle and Gospel is the place where the Commissioners envisaged moving from the Litany to the Communion Service, is substantiated by the fact that in the Litany, originally they only added " The Nicene Creed, I believe in One God &c " and then altered it to " If there is no Comunion ", because there would be a repitition with that after the Epistle and Gospel; also, the Epistle and Gospel Rubric in the Communion Service, has a line drawn down the side, showing that it is repititious with the Litany.

The Phrase " If there is no Communion " mentioned above, refers to the remaining lines in that section, thus including the Prayers and Thanksgivings, S Chrysostom, and the Grace. This is quite a natural interpretation, because then the Rubric for Holy-days and Fasting Days would follow in sequence after the Creed. Similarly, if the intention as suggested above, of adding the Prayers and Thanksgivings to the Litany was to enclose the Ante-Communion service, it would be quite logical to omit them, when the Communion Service itself followed.

It will be noted that the Psalm, Prayer for the Church and the Sermon have been omitted. This is remedied by the note beside the Rubric for Holy-days and Fasting days in the Communion service, which refers to the revision of it in the Litany. If the Litany version were used, all these would be used with it. The Cryptic comment at the beginning of the Communion service now has some meaning; for the next thing in the Communion Service is the sentences, but after the Sermon and before the Sentences it is fitting that a Collect or Prayer should be said. As the Prayers and Thanksgivings have been omitted, it is also natural that a Prayer for the King should be included as well. This incidentally would also be the easiest way of printing the Service;

Litany: We humbly beseech thee, Collect for purity, Ten Commandments or Beatitudes 1, Collect for the Day, Epistle and Gospel. Rubric (if there be no Communion) Nicene Creed, General thanksgivings &c (Prayer for King, Prayers and Thanksgivings) S Chrysostom, Grace. Rubric for Holy Days, Psalm, Whole State " accommodated " or another prayer, Sermon.

Communion: Rubric with Beatitudes 2, Nicene Creed, Rubric for Holy-days, Whole state accommodated, Sermon, a Collect, Sentences, Collect for the King, Exhortations, Confession and Absolution.

Communion by itself.

One further problem remains. The service, which has nothing deleted except the Ten Commandments, was intended to remain as it was in 1662, with the Holy-day Rubric in the Communion Service version. The remaining problem is that of the Ten Commandments. They were deleted in the Communion Service and transfered to the Litany. Beatitudes 2 has no rubric attached except that it is to be used after or instead of the Ten Commandments on great festivals. One can only presume therefore that while a transference was made to the Litany, the deletion itself does not refer to the Commandments qua Commandments, but to the version. The Prayer Book Version was to be replaced by that of the AV (" as in Exodus "). When the Book came to be printed, the Commandments would be printed out in that version.

## NOTES ON THE COMMUNION SERVICE

*1.* 1688: Qu. Whether any part of ye Communion service, except what is Used before the Sermon, need be read but upon Communion days: and yt wch is read in the congregation, to be read in the Body of the Church; & none at the table but what concerns ye Communion?

Exceptions X: " That the minister be not required to rehearse any part of the Liturgy at the communion table, save only those parts which properly belong to the Lord's supper; and that at such times only when the said holy supper is administered.

Bishops Reply: Prop 10. '. . . The priest standing at the communion table seemeth to give us an invitation to the holy Sacrament, and minds us of our duty, viz. to receive the holy communion, some at least every Sunday; and though we neglect our duty, it is fit the Church should keep her standing.'

(This was the whole point of the Dissenters' objection; they did not approve of frequent communions, and if the Ante-Communion service was read at the Holy Table, it reminded them of this. Hence equally, the argument of the Bishops is propounded by the greater number of commentators, who were defending the practice of the Church.)

V. Populi: ' This we find reckon'd by those great Lights of our Church, formely mention'd, among the Innovations, the reading ' some part of the Morning Prayer at the H. Table when there is no Communion '. Nor can we be satisfied with what is usually said in defence of the Practice, That 'tis ' to put the people in mind that they should celebrate the Communion every Sunday '. In the Name of God, what need is there of such dumb signs to instruct us in our Duty, which are so contrary to Edification, when we have so many Excellent and Learned Men, who can and ought to do it to much better purpose in their frequent, Eloquent and Pious Sermons out of the Pulpit? Must such Motions, as well as Pictures, be Lay-mens Books? (p. 4-5).

V. Cleri: ' But why must the Communion Service be left out, when the Primitive Church did Communicate at their daily Assemblies? And it is the Peoples faults that the Communion is not Administered every Sunday in the Parish Churches, as well as in the Cathedrals; so that the reading that Service minds the People of their backwardness to partake of so great a Blessing, and both minds and prepares them for it.' (p. 36).

(It was a common misconception throughout our period, that in the Primitive Church, the faithful received daily. It is found in Sparrow, Comber, etc.)

2. 1688: 'the day' put in parentheses, and the marginal note 'omitt'.

   1552: "So many as entende to be partakers of thy holye Communion, shall sygnyfye theyr names to the Curate ouer nyghte, or els in the morninge, afore the begynninge or mornynge prayer, or immediately after."

   1662: "So many as intend to be partakers of the holy Communion, shall signifie their Names to the Curate at least sometime the day before."

   Exceptions: "The time here assigned for notice to be given to the Minister is not sufficient."

   The Commissioners obviously considered that the time should be extended still further, the previous day not being a sufficient warning.

3. Prev. Reading i. minister of this sacrament ought allwaies to be a Bishop or Presbyter.

4. 1688: 'See ye Kings Declaration 25 Oct. 1660.'

   Exceptions: (on this same passage) "We desire the ministers' power both to admit and keep from the Lord's table, may be according to his Majesty's declaration, 25 Oct., 1660, in these words, "The Minister shall admit none to the Lord's supper till they have made a creditable profession of their faith, and promised obedience to the will of God, according as is expressed in the considerations of the rubrick before the Catechism; and that all possible diligence be used for the instruction and reformation of scandalous offenders, whom the minister shall not suffer to partake of the Lord's table until they have openly declared themselves to have truly repented and amended their former naughty lives, as is partly expressed in the rubrick, and more fully in the canons."

   The Declaration itself however continues: "more fully in the canons; provided there be place for due appeals to superior powers. But besides the suffragans and their presbytery, every rural dean . . . . together with three or four ministers of that deanery, chosen by the major part of all the ministers within the same, shall meet once in every month, to receive such complaints as shall be presented to them by the ministers or churchwardens of the respective parishes; and also to compose all such differences betwixt party and party as shall be referred unto them by way of arbitration, and to convince offenders, and reform all such things as they find amiss, by their pastoral reproofs and admonitions, if they may be so reformed; and such matters as they cannot by this pastoral and persuasive way compose and reform, are by them to be prepared for, and presented to the Bishop; at which meeting any other ministers of the deanery may, if they please, be present and assist." (Quoted Cardwell Conferences p. 293-4.)

   (To which of these, or both, the note in 1688 refers, is uncertain.)

5. 1688: "Qu. if the standing with ye face to ye people, wth ye Pr. bac to ye East, be not more convenient."

   1549: "The Priest standyng humbly afore the middes of the Altar, shall saye the Lordes prayer, . . . . ."

   1552: "And the Priest standing at the northsyde of the Table, shal saye the Lordes prayer. . . . . . ."

   S.L.: ". . . where the Presbyter, standing at the north side or end thereof . . ."

   1662: "And the Priest standing at the north side of the Table shall say the Lords Prayer. . . . ."

The 1549 position represents the medieval custom, with a celebrant in a position which represents the "sacrificial aspects" of the Eucharist. The

Northside position was really a protest against this. The Basilicon or Westward position, had been favoured by Bishop Jewel who wrote recommending it as of great Antiquity, and Martin Bucer who greatly influenced the English Reformers, placed the holy table well forward in the church in full view of the Congregation, and adopted the Basilican position. See *The Position of the Celebrant at the Eucharist* by R. C. D. Jasper, Alcuin pamphlet XVI, 1959.)

The Churches of this period might well be splendid affairs, with Altar Frontals, crucifixes, Pictures and Candlesticks on or behind the altar, and canopies above it. A full description may be found in Wickham Legg p. 119-60.

6. 1688: " Lords Prayer here not to be used when joyn'd wth another Service."

7. 1688: " inspiration " altered to read " operation ".

8. The Ten Commandments are deleted, but inside the deletions the alterations read: " Then shall the Minister standing with his face towards the people ". In the fourth commandment read, " Sabbath, which is now ye Lords day ". In the margin is the note, " As in Exodus ". It has been argued (p. 234f.) that it was intended in certain circumstances to include the Commandments, but as they are deleted in the text, they have been omitted.
   1688: The words " Sabbath day " are put in parentheses. And at the conclusion of the response is added, " this law: ye morall duty: tho not ye precise line of it."

9. The first form of the Beatitudes covers two pages. Above the first section is " refer to ye Litany " and at the top of the next page the comment " to be put at ye End of ye Litany ". The text has been printed in this form for the convenience of the reader.

10. Black incorrectly reads ' that '.

11. This refers to the beginning of the Rubric " Then shall follow one of these two Collects for the King and Queen. . . ."

12. This form of the Beatitudes is written on a separate piece of paper and stuck into the book. Prev. Readings i. our Lord Jesus Christ going up into a Mountain, there taught his disciples, saying.    ii. Christ spake these words, and said,

13. Black incorrectly reads " make ".

14. Prev. Reading i. strengthen us with might according. . . .

15. Previous Reading i. . . . . joyfullness.

   Blessed are those servants, whom the Lord when he cometh shall find watching.

   Lord have mercy upon us, & give us grace to be sober and watch unto prayer.

   Blessed are they that hear the word of God and keep it.
   Lord have mercy upon us, & give us grace to order our steps according to thy word, that no iniquity may have dominion over us.

In placing the Beatitudes in this position, the Commissioners were following the lead given by Jeremy Taylor (cf. *Anglican Liturgies of the Seventeenth and Eighteenth Centuries,* by Jardine Grisbrooke, 1958. p. 185ff).

Each response in this version is taken from the Scriptures:

| | |
|---|---|
| . . . give us that godly favour . . . | 2 Cor. 7.10. |
| . . . give us grace to shew . . . | Titus 3.2. |
| . . . & fill us with all the . . . | Phil. 1.11. |
| . . . and make us merciful . . . | Lk. 6.36. |

... & clense us from all ...        2 Cor. 7.1.
... and incline us to eschew ...     Ps. 34.14 (BCP version) 1 Pet. 3.11.
... when we are called to ...        Col. 1.11.
(deleted section)
... & give us grace to be sober ...  1 Pet. 4.7.
... & give us grace to order our ... Ps. 119.133 (AV version).

16. Prev. Readings i. The Collects for ye King & ye day are to be omitted, when the Comunion Service is not alone used.

17. 1688: The words " Let us pray " are put in parentheses, and there is the note in the margin: " Qu. if—?— to be omitted." (The prayer refers to " Charles our King and Governour ".)

18. In both prayers by the alterations of the appellations of the King, is the note " Qr " which was subsequently deleted.

19. The rubric for the Epistle and Gospel, has a line drawn beside it in the margin, with an X added. There is no reason given for this, but it is suggested above (p. 234f.) that it refers to its repetition with the new Litany service.

   1688: The word " Priest " is put in parentheses, and altered to " minister "; the words " sung or " are also put in parentheses, with the instruction, " omitt ".

   1549: After the announcement of the Gospel, " The Clearkes and people shall aunswere, Glory be to thee, O Lorde."
   1552: Omits this.

   S. L.: After the announcement of the Gospel, the " People, all standing up, shall say: Glory be to thee, O Lord. At the end of the Gospel. . . . . . And the People shall answer: Thanks be to thee, O Lord."

   D. B.: After the announcement, " the people all standing up shall say, Glory be to thee O Lord. At ye end of the Gospell. . . . . And the people shall answere, Thanks be to thee, O Lord."

While none of these responses by the people, is included in 1662, it was still the custom to use these or something of a similar nature, in many churches. The most common phrase used was that of 1549 before the Gospel was read, " Glory be to thee O Lord ", and very often after the Gospel, " Hallelujah " was sung or said, or " Thanks be to God for his holy Gospel ".

20. 1688: " who proceedeth from the Father and the Son " is underlined. Cf. Notes on the Athanasian Creed.

21. A very thin line is also drawn through the middle of the rubric.
   1688: reads " place (a) . . . ." (sic)

22. 1688: After the word " Offertory " (b) is added. Read " Lay not up . . . . earth (only or principally) where . . . . but (principally) lay. . . ."

23. 1688: 1 Cor. 9.7, 9.11, 9.13-14, Gal. 6.6-7 are deleted, and 1 Cor. 9.7, 1 Cor. 9.13-14 have marks in the margin beside them. Tobit 4.7, 4.8-9 are deleted, as being Apocryphal, but within 4.7 the previous alteration was made: ". . . poor man, (who is a fitt object of your charitie) and then . . . ."

   Exceptions: " Two of the sentences here cited are apocryphal, and four of them more proper to draw out the people's bounty to their ministers, than their charity to the poor ".

   1689 has altered in conformity with this.

24. 1688: " Whilst these Sentences are in reading " is underlined. " Reverently " is ringed round, and " a " added beside it. " Humbly present and " is boxed in; " holy " is also ringed. The word " Priest " is underlined, and replaced by " Min ".

241

25. 1688: The Prayer mentions " Charles our King ". Throughout this Prayer Book, the State Prayers mention James as being the King, except in the Communion Service where both refer to Charles. The word " Indifferently " is ringed, and replaced by " Impartially ". The word " Curates " is altered to " Pastors "; The phrase " set forth thy true and living word and rightly and duly administer thy holy Sacraments " is underlined, and " with meek heart and due reverence hear and receive thy holy word " is underlined and put in parentheses. In the phrase " that with them we " an insertion mark is added after the word " that ".

Note: the alteration in 1689 to " all Bishops, Pastors and Curates " is a reversion to the reading of 1552.

26. Prev. Reading i. that with meek heart and due reverence they may Allwaies hear and receive. . . .

27. Cf. Notes on the Prayers and Thanksgivings where this prayer also occurs; this version contains the previous readings of the prayer in the Prayers, unaltered.

Black reads " for a comunicatio of or Saviour's wonderfull Love " in error, for " comemoratio of ". He also reads " the holy Table " instead of " thy holy Table ".

28. Prev. Reading i. Q. Whether a shorter Form of warning may not be made seeing in many Parishes the Returns of monethly Comunions are comonly known.

29. Prev. Reading i. Greif, that by ye Ministry of Gods holy God, He . . . (sic).

30. Prev. Reading i. " Consequence " deleted. ii: and replaced.

Let Min: The sentence " Because it's requisite that no man should come to the Holy Communion but with a full trust in God's mercy, and with a quiet Conscience " is " liable to misapplication " particularly for " weak minds ". (p. 24).

V. Cleri: " For if St Paul says, we may not partake of common things with a doubting Conscience, Rom. 14.5, much less of spiritual: And when men consult the Lawyers for their Estates, and physitians for their Bodies, why should they not consult the Ministers for their Souls?" (p. 39-40).

31. Prev. Readings i. The whole section " For as the Benefit is great . . . . sundry kinds of death " is deleted. ii. The word " stet " is added beside the lines " For as . . . . Sacrament " and " So is the dangers . . . . unworthily ".

Black takes these marks as referring to the whole deletion.

32. 1688: " then we dwell in Christ, and Christ in us, we are one with Christ, and Christ with us: " is underlined. " Judge therefore . . . . of those holy mysteries " is bracketed in the margin.

33. Prev. Readings i. Humbly falling upon. ii. Deleted and nothing replaced in text.

1688: The whole prayer is put in brackets, with the note, " Quale: of worthy communicant ". The Phrase " intend to lead a new life " is underlined. In the phrase " meekly kneeling upon your knees " the word " meekly " is deleted and replaced by " humbly ", " upon your knees " is deleted, and replaced by " before him " and the whole phrase is underlined.

34. 1688: The word " Priest " is underlined, and replaced by " Min ".

35. 1688: The word " Priest " is underlined, and replaced by " Min ".

36. 1688: The word " Priest " is underlined, and replaced by " Min ".

37. 1688: The words " the company " are underlined.

*38.* 1688: On part of the remaining interleaf, there remain a few letters: y; him-; ous of.

Very tenuously indeed, one might suggest that this was a previous draft of the Good Friday Preface: . . . . friday . . . making him-self . . . zealous of good. . . .

*39.* " at this time " is not altered in the preface, but cf the Collect for Christmas day.

> Exceptions: " First, we cannot peremptorily fix the nativity of our Saviour to this or that day particularly. Secondly, it seems incongruous to affirm the birth of Christ and the descending of the Holy Ghost to be on this day for seven or eight days together."

> 1662 did alter the phrase accordingly; but it was held that their substituted phrase was liable to the same objections.

*40.* In the margin is the following: " (inequality) Q of / substance Q. whether those words (without any difference or inequality) shall be alter'd."

> Let. Min.: " without any difference or inequality " is regarded as being obscure. (p. 24).

> V. Cleri: " In the Preface at the Communion for Trinity Sunday, that which we believe of the Glory of the Father, the same we believe of the Glory of the Son, and of the Holy Ghost, without any difference or inequality, (viz) as to the Godhead, Christ having said, ' I and my Father are one ': And the Church in all Ages hath professed the same belief in the Father, Son, and Holy Ghost, and ascribes the same Glory to each of them in the Tresagion." (p. 38).

*41.* 1688: " the company " is boxed in.

*42.* Prev. Readings i. minister. ii. presbyter. iii. minister. iv. all deleted and text not restored.

*43.* 1688: " that our sinful bodies may be made clean by his body, and our souls washed through his most precious blood " is deleted, with the note (a) added.

> Exceptions: " We desire, that whereas these words seem to give a greater efficacy to the blood than to the body of Christ, they may be altered thus, ' That our sinful souls and bodies may be cleansed through his precious body and blood '."

> Let. Min.: " That our sinful bodies . . . . precious blood " is regarded as obscure. (p. 24).

> V. Cleri: " i.e. that both our Souls and Bodies may receive all the benefits of his Death and Passion." (p. 38).

*44.* Prev. Readings i. When the Minister. ii. When the Presbyter.

*45.* 1688: The indentation, from (c) to the end is bracketed. and an x placed by (e). It may have been considered that these rubrics were not explicit enough, and although 1662 had composed them with the Exceptions in view, they were still inadequate.

Exceptions: ' We conceive that the manner of the consecrating of the elements is not here explicit and distinct enough, and the minister's breaking of the bread is not so much as mentioned.' (in 1552).

*46.* Prev. Readings i. Bishops, Presbyters . . . ii. Bishops, Ministers. iii. Both deleted, and the text not restored.

*47.* 1688: The word ' meekly ' is underlined.

*48.* 1688: The first words of the Administration, " The Body " and " The Bloud " are both underlined, with an x added.

Exceptions: "We desire, that at the distribution of the bread and wine to the communicants, we may use the words of our Saviour as near as may be, and that the minister be not required to deliver the bread and wine into every particular communicant's hand, and to repeat the words to each one in the singular number, but that it may suffice to speak them to divers jointly, according to our Saviour's example."

D.B.: (after life add) "And here each person receiving shall say (Amen) Then shall the Priest adde, Take & Eate &c . . . . everlasting life. And here each person receiving shall say (Amen). Then the Priest shall adde, Drinke this for the remembrance. . . ."

Wren's Advices: "Answer, by the Receiver, Amen. . . . The Church of Rome to gayne some Colour to their fancy of Transubstantiation, next after these words, (The Body of our Lord Jesus Xt) put in (Amen) there: Now though we approve not of that, yet there is no Reason, why it should quite be omitted." (D.B. 173).

S.L.: ". . . . unto everlasting life. Here the party receiving shall say, Amen . . . . The blood . . . . unto everlasting life. Here the party receiving shall say, Amen." (Note, the second part of the words of Administration is omitted in S.L.)

The addition of "Amen" in 1689, was simply making legal a common custom in the Church. Throughout the seventeenth and eighteenth centuries, Books of Devotion suggest, or take from granted, the practice. A number of examples of this may be found in Wickham Legg p.. 61-2. The Durham Book has a suggestion that the Agnus Dei should be included in the Communion Service (p. 176). It played a part in the service of 1549, but had been omitted in 1552. Throughout our period, it was however used, either as a private form of prayer, or sung as an anthem. A full discussion may be found in Wickham Legg p. 57-60.

49. Williams Diary: (24 Oct.) "About the Lords Supper; Debated the Prayer of Consecration; that it was not the words, but the setting it apart by Prayer, that was the Consecration. Ordered than when they Consecrate afresh they begin with the Prayer."

The reconsecration is in fact in a different form from that implied by Williams, although the theology remains the same. The phrase "hear the Prayers of thy Church that have now bin made unto Thee" takes the whole prayer for granted.

50. 1688: The word "petition" is underlined, with xx added.

51. 1688: The word "fulfilled" is half-boxed in, and the words "weighing our merits" are ringed.

52. 1688: In the words "And that we are very members incorporate in the mystical body of thy Son" all the words except "are very" are underlined, and xx is added after "we".

53. Prev. Readings i. Q. It is humbly submitted to ye Convocation whether Thou only art ye eternall Son of God, may not be put in ye place of, Thou only art ye Lord, as seeming a clearer expression. ii. All this is deleted, except the phrase "Thou only art ye eternall Son of God", and a cross is added which refers to its inclusion in the text, by a similar mark.

1688: "onely art the Lord" is underlined, and (a) added.

Williams Diary: (24 Oct.) "In the Trisagion, alter'd it to Thou O Holy

244

One — — — — Thou O Son of God with the Holy Ghost." (There is no record of this alteration.)

54. 1688: In the phrase "collects to be said after the offertory" there is an insertion mark after the word, "collects" and "after the offertory" is ringed.

55. Cf. notes on the Prayers and Thanksgivings.

56. Prev. Reading i. thy cotinuall pity.

57. Black incorrectly reads " power " instead of " succour ".

58. There is a line drawn down the whole rubric relating to the Ante-Communion Service. It has been suggested above (p. 234f.) that this is because the Commissioners intended to dispense with the Ante-Communion service as an entity, by placing it within the body of the Litany.

59. 1688: In "Every Sunday at the least ", " at the least " is ringed, with a marginal note, " omitt ".
Prev. Readings i. And in every Parish there. . . .
i. ye year, yt is to say, on Christmass-day.

60. Exceptions: " Forasmuch as every parishioner is not duly qualified for the Lord's supper, and those habitually prepared are not at all times actually disposed, but may be hindered by the providence of God, and some by the distemper of their own spirits, we desire this rubric may be either wholly omitted, or thus altered: " Every minister shall be bound to administer the sacrament of the Lord's supper at least thrice a year, provided there be a due number of communicants manifesting their desires to receive."

1689 omits the rubric beginning " And note, that every parishioner . . ." as it is provided for by this rubric.

It is interesting to note that a number of the Commissioners were openly in favour of Weekly Communion, including Beveridge, Patrick and Aldrich. There were ten Churches in London which had a weekly celebration, at this time, and most of the Cathedrals throughout the Country had one. In most Churches however, the Communion was celebrated only once a month, and the attendance at these services was very high. Christmas was the primary festival rather than Easter, and on that day it might be estimated that half the population received Communion. (cf. Wickham Legg p. 21-45).

61. 1688, add ". . . . drink the same, for ye abandoning of any Superstitious uses."

It was still the custom in certain places throughout the Country, to reserve the Sacrament for the use of the sick; in this case often the sick person received only in one kind, with the consecrated bread dipped in unconsecrated wine, to ease the swallowing. (Wickham Legg p. 67f).

62. 1688: " ended, or at some Other convenient Season, the mony given at. . . ."

63. Prev. Readings i. minister shall give them ye sacramental bread. ii. shall give them satisfaction.
Black reads " press It " in error, for " persist ".

64. Prev. Reading i. in ye Comunion for ye sick, the Exhortation to kneel may be omitted, if ye person be not satifyd or canot bear kneeling.

Kneeling at the Sacrament.

Those who dissented from kneeling, did so on the grounds that it implied an adoration of the sacramental elements; its defenders pointed to the attitude of reverence with which one approached the king, holding that a similar posture should be adopted when approaching God's altar.

Exceptions XVIII, 3: "That none may receive the Lord's supper that dare not kneel in the act of receiving; but the minister must exclude all such from the communion: although such kneeling not only differs from the practice of Christ and his apostles, but (at least on the Lord's day) is contrary to the practice of the catholick church for many hundred years after, and forbidden by the most venerable councils that ever were in the Christian world. All which impositions are made yet more grievous by that subscription to their lawfulness which the canon exacts, and the heavy punishment upon the non-observance of them which the Act of Uniformity inflicts."

Bishop's Reply 15: "The posture of kneeling best suits at the Communion as the most convenient, and so most decent for us, when we receive as it were from God's hand the greatest of seals of the kingdom of heaven. He that thinks he may do this sitting, let him remember the prophet Mal. Offer this to the prince, to receive his seal from his own hand sitting, see if he will accept it. When the Church did stand at her prayers, the manner of receiving was "more adorantium" (S. Aug. Ps. xcviii. Cyril, Catech. Mystag. 5) rather more than at prayers, since standing at prayer hath been generally left, and kneeling used instead of that (as the Church may vary in such indifferent things). Now to stand at communion, when we kneel at prayers, were not decent, much less to sit, which was never the use of the best times."

Williams Diary: (18 Oct.): "As for the posture of the Sacrament, it was first moved that it might be kneeling or standing at Liberty, but at last it was agreed for those that scrupled kneeling, that it shou'd be in some posture of Reverence, and in some Convenient Pew or Place in the Church so that none but those that kneeled, shou'd come up to the Rails or Table, And that the Persons scrupling shou'd some Week Day before come to the Minister; and declare that they cou'd not kneel with a good Conscience. This was agreed to, and drawn up. Only the B. of Winchester moved that the Names of such Persons might be written down, but this was not approved, and after all He dissented from the whole."

Let. Min.: "Or if kneeling at the Sacrament, that the person so scrupling may have it delivered unto him in another posture, provided it be not at the Table, but in some convenient Pew or Place appointed by the Minister". (p. 9).

Let. Friend: "Kneeling at the Sacrament of the Lord's Supper is a posture so proper to that Holy Ordinance, that . . . . this is the last I should be willing to part with: because I think the highest posture of Devotion is that which is always most natural for us to be in when we are receiving from Christ so great and inestimable Benefits as those which are reached out unto us in that Holy Mystery. But since . . . many . . . have been so far imposed on by several fallacious arguments . . . . as to think it sinfull to receive in this posture, and hereby the Table of the Lord becomes deserted . . . . it is time for us now to abate our rigor in this matter; and when we are not able to bring men up by reason of their weakness to the Constitutions of the Church, be so far indulgent as to descend to them, and give them the Sacrament in their own way, rather than for the sake of a posture onely debar them, of the Benefits which their souls may receive thereby." (p. 11-12).

V. Cleri: "He can, it seems, see a reason, why the scrupulous Person should forbear that blessed Sacrament, for fear of a fit and prescribed Ceremony; but he can see none, why the Sacrament should not be administered to them

246

in their own way. I would ask him, Is it not fit when we pray with the Minister as we ought to do, ' that the Body of our Lord Jesus Christ, which was given for thee, preserve thy Body and Soul to everlasting life ', to kneel . . . . whether the ancient Communicants did stand or kneel, they did in obedience to the Constitutions of the Church; and so ought we. Hear Mr Baxter in this case: ' If it be lawful to take a Pardon from the King upon our knees, I know not what can make it unlawful, to take a sealed Pardon from Christ upon our knees,' see Christian Direct. p. 616. ' And as for kneeling at the Sacrament, since the Rubrick, my Judgment was ever for it: God having made some Gesture necessary, and confined us to none, but left it to humane determination: I shall submit to the Magistrates in their proper work. I am not sure, Christ intended his Example as obligatory; but I am sure he hath commanded me Obedience and Peace. p. 411 of the Five Disputations." (p. 49).

Other Authorities: For the abatement of rigour or alteration: V. Populi p. 8-9. Let. Till. VIII, Conformists Reasons p. 5. Against any alterations: JRC p. 39-40; The Way p. 3; New Survey p. 52; To the Revd & Merry Answerer p. 2; Brief Discourse p. 26-8.

Unlike the surplice, which in practice was not always worn, kneeling to receive Communion was the normal posture, although some exceptions can be found. Churchmen, who were willing to relinquish a great deal for the sake of Unity, often refused to compromise on this position. Anglican Theology of the Real Presence was of course, much " higher " than the dissenter's, and to many it would seem irreverent not to kneel; indeed, in some places it was the custom to prostrate oneself before the altar before receiving, and a number of devotional manuals suggest this.

## NOTES ON THE PUBLICK BAPTISM OF INFANTS

*1.* Prev. Readings i. Children shall be presented to be baptiz'd by God-fathers & Godmothers, wch is still continued. . . .

Exceptions: " Here is not mention of the parents, in whose right the child is baptised, and who are fittest both to dedicate it unto God, and to covenant for it: we do not know that any persons except the parents, or some others appointed by them, have any power to contract for the children, or to enter them into covenant. We desire it may be left free to parents, whether they will have sureties to undertake for their children in baptism or no."

Williams Diary: (18 Oct.) " They considered the Case of Godfathers, and it was propos'd that Parents (comprehending therein Grandfathers &c) might upon occasion be admitted. . . . . (21 Oct.) They then proceeded to the Case of Godfathers. It was pleaded by Dr. Beverige, 1. That it was very Antient. 2. That We should have a Care of going off from the practise of the Universal Church, and that no instance cou'd be given in Antiquity where this was not used. To which it was answered, That it was a very usefull and laudable practice and shou'd be encouraged, but withal it was too often made a matter of Interest. 2. That it was ───── as is publisht by Balurius ─────. 3. That it was hard to find an instance of a Child Baptised before St. Cyprians Time. At last it was agreed that a Rubrick should be drawn up, that if the Parent should say He cou'd not conveniently procure Godfathers, He himself shou'd be admitted to be a Sponsor." (Balurius should read Baluzius, the mistake might be due to an Emanuensis' error.)

Let. Min.: " And the same course may be taken for Godfathers, which if the Parent signifies he cannot procure, or is not satisfied in, it shall be lawful for the Minister to accept of the Sponsion of the Parent." (p. 9).

JRC: In favour of retaining the custom of Godparents p. 35-7.

It was not always easy to find Godparents, because of the Demands made on them by the Prayer Book, that if anything should happen to the parents, they would be responsible for the child's education and living. Many were not prepared to commit themselves to this extent.

There are three words which are used in this discussion, each of which has a different meaning: " Sponsor " is used of someone who responds on behalf of the one who is to be Baptised; " Sureties " is the name given to the one who gives security, that the Baptised will be brought up to lead a Godly and Christian life; " Godparents " are those who undertake the parental obligations in regard to the things of God. Thus when the Commissioners omit the word " Godparents " they are doing so in conformity with the Exceptions quoted above, that the parents right should not be usurped.

2. Exceptions: " We desire that more timely notice may be given ".

3. Exceptions: ' We desire it may be so placed as all the Congregation may best see and hear the whole administration.'

4. Prev. Reading i. if there be any reasonable cause of doubting.
1688: " shall say, if ye minister think the case in the least doubtfull."

5. Prev. Reading i. Q. Whether this may not be the Prface. Dearly Beloved forasmuch as our Saviour Saith that that wch is born of ye flesh is flesh, & yt none can enter &c.

   1688: The words " all men are conceived and born in sin, and that our " are underlined.

6. Prev. Reading i. after ye Institution of Baptism by thy. . . .

7. Exceptions: " It being doubtful whether either the flood Jordan or any other waters were sanctified to a sacramental use by Christ's being baptized, and not necessary to be asserted, we desire this may be otherwise expressed."
   Let. Min.: " By the Baptism of thy well-beloved . . . . sanctifie water " is regarded as being obscure. (p. 24).
   V. Cleri: " i.e. didst appoint and consecrate the Element of Water, to be the outward sign of the Grace conferred in that Sacrament by the Blood and Merits of Christ." (p. 38).

8. 1688: In the section " and being stedfast in faith, joyful through hope, and rooted in Charity, may so pass the waves of . . . . he may come to the land of everlasting ", there is an insertion mark after the word " and ", and the phrases " joyful through ", " and rooted in ", " the waves of " and " the land of " are each put in parentheses.
   Prev. Reading i. . . . . he may come to ye happiness of Everlasting life, there to &c through Jes. Ch. or Ld. Amen.

9. 1688: In the phrase, " remission of his sins ", the words " his sins " are underlined, and the whole phrase put in parentheses.

10. 1688: " outward gesture and deed " underlined, with " Q " in the margin.

11. 1688: The section " doubt ye not therefore, but earnestly believe, that he will likewise . . . . everlasting kingdom " is underlined. The words " that he will " are deleted, and insertions marks placed between " will " and " make ", and between " and " and " make him partaker ". The final readings therefore are: ". . . . Arms of his mercy, that he is ready on his part to give . . . . eternal life, and to make him partaker. . . ."

12. Prev. Readings i. Then shall the Minister speak unto the Sureties on this wise. . . . ii. Then shall ye Minister speak to ye Congregation on this wise. . . . . iii. Then shall ye Minister say to ye Congregation.

13. 1688: "Release him of his sins" is underlined, and put in parentheses.

14. 1688: The word "carnal" is underlined, with "Q" in the margin. Let. Till. X. "Whether the promises of the sureties in the office of Baptism might not be made a little more intelligible to ordinary people?"

15. The last question and its answer was added in 1662. This further addition may reflect an outlook similar to that of the Compilers of the Durham Book, who at first read "I promise & vow by God's grace so to doe."

16. 1688: "Adam" is put in parentheses, and in the margin is the note; "Qu. Man". The words "is here dedicated" are underlined.

17. 1688: The whole section "whose most dearly beloved . . . . of the Holy Ghost" is put in brackets. Inside this the word "teach" is put in parentheses, and altered by a marginal note to "Preach the Gospell". "Sanctifie this Water to the mystical washing away of sin" is deleted, and there is a note in the margin, "Water according to his Institution". And explanation of this may be found in the rather fuller version of the section remaining in the Baptism of those of "Riper Years": "and grant that these persons now to be Baptized with Water according to his Institution, may receive. . . ." The phrase "and elect children" is underlined, and the word "elect", altered to "choice" which is deleted, and "stet" written beside it.

18. Prev. Readings i. And then naming it after them, He shall pour water upon It & use caution according as he shall be certifyd of ye Condition of ye child.

    1688: The phrase "If they shall certifie him that the child may well endure it" is put in parentheses, with "Q" in the margin.
    The next section was first altered: "he shall dip or sprinkle it, in the water discreetly and warily" which was subsequently altered to "he shall dip or sprinkle it or discreetly pour water upon It". The rubric following, which is omitted in 1689, is put in parentheses, and the note added, "Qu. if not to be his head".

    Williams Diary: (24 Oct.) "About Dipping—said it was the Custom to dip in England—Bp. of St. Asaph said, it was so still in some parts of Wales; putting in the head, and letting it run over the Body.—Orderd that both be inserted . . . . (18 Nov.) There were some few Alterations, as particularly that dipping shou'd be continu'd in Baptism. . . . ." (While Williams here is inconsistent with himself, he is accurate as far as the text is concerned.)

19. The Use of the Cross in Baptism. See notes on the rubric at the end of Baptism.

    1688: The phrase "Congregation of Christs flock" is put in parentheses.

20. The prayer book used by the Commissioners was deficient, reading in this section, "child is by Baptism regenerate and grafted." They were quite aware of this error, for in the Private Baptism of Infants, the words "by Baptism" are put in parentheses, and underlined, with the note added in the margin, "Q. Added latelie by ye Printer in K James's time."

    1688: The phrase "regenerate & grafted into the body of Christs Church" is put in parentheses.

21. 1688: The phrase "regenerate this Infant with thy holy Spirit" is put in parentheses.

> Exceptions: XV. " That whereas throughout the several offices, the phrase is such as presumes all persons (within the communion of the church) to be regenerated, converted, and in an actual state of grace (which, had ecclesiastical discipline been truly and vigorously executed, in the exclusion of scandalous and obstinate sinners, might be better supposed. . . .) we desire that this may be reformed."

> " We cannot in faith say, that every child that is baptized is " regenerated by God's Holy Spirit"; at least it is a disputable point, and therefore we desire it may be otherwise expressed."

It is probable that in the discussions on this point, the Commission had the above exception before them, for they discuss the phrase " Regenerated by Thy Holy Spirit", although the word " regenerate" is altered to "regenerated " in the prayer " Seeing now", yet there is no reference to the Holy Spirit there. In the prayer objected to by the Dissenters, the phrase is not exactly as they quote it; instead of " regenerate this infant by thy Holy Spirit " it is " regenerate this Infant with thy Holy Spirit". The Discussions in the Commission would seem to be on the Exception itself.

> Williams Diary: (28 Oct.) " There was a long debate about Baptismal Regeneration, and the phrase in the Office ' Regenerated by Thy Holy Spirit '. It was desired by Dr. T. that either the latter part of it, ' by thy Holy Spirit ' it might be left out, or explain'd, Forasmuch as the Phrase (as now used) implies an actual Change. It was answered, that the Phrase has been antiently apply'd to Baptism, and if there were not more in Baptism that the outward washing it would give away the Cause to the Anabaptists. But it was again reply'd, Not so, because it was a Federal Regeneration; and what gave a Title to the Privileges of that Covenant (of which the Assistance of the H. Spirit was One) according as They were capable of Them. It was Argued further, that this was a Phrase disputed by the Non-Conformists, and by all those that were against falling from Grace—It was said further, Baptism did unite us to the Spirit. . . . (30 Oct.) . . . the Phrase " Regenerated " in the Prayer was objected against. Dr. Goodman, S. and T. said it was fitt to be expunged especially in the Thanksgiving, or moderated because of the Dissenters, & because. . . . (sic) . . . It was answer'd, That this was the Doctrine of all Reformed Churches, and that this could not be without altering the Office of Baptism the Catechism &c. and it was put to the Vote, whether it was now to be done, or left to the Convocation. Carry'd for the latter."

22. 1688: The phrase " in the vulgar tongue " is underlined.

23. 1688: The phrase " in the vulgar tongue " is underlined.

24. 1688: The rubric is deleted, and the note added, " Q. if this is not to be omitted ".

> Brief Discourse: " ' Its certain by God's word, that Children Baptized dying before they commit actual sin, are undoubtedly saved: This ' saith he, ' savours of Pelagianism '. Ans. I don't understand the falseness, or Pelagianism of it. It's certain by God's word, that ' of such is the Kingdom of God ', and so they must be capable of it. If capable of it, it must be upon Gospell terms; but what terms they are capable of but Baptism, I understand not."

25. Prev. Reading i. Mind of ye Obligation.

*26.* The Use of the Cross.

Exceptions: XVIII. 2: "That none may baptise, nor be baptised, without the transient image of the cross, which hath at least the semblance of a sacrament of human institution, being used as an ingaging sign in our first and solemn covenanting with Christ, and the duties whereunto we are really obliged by baptism, being more expressly fixed to that airy sign than to this holy sacrament."

Williams Diary: (18 Oct.) "They proceeded to the Cross. Dr. Bev: said, They might as well object against holding the Child in Arms, and there was no end if We woul'd take away all scruples. It was argued this was a distinct thing from the other Ceremonies, for there must be some Time, Place, Posture, Habit; but this depended wholly upon human Institution, And after a full debate it was agreed, 1. That the Persons indulged were to declare in their Conscience They thought it Sinfull to have it used. 2. That the Children should be Baptized last, that were to be baptised without the Cross. This was drawn up and Assented to . . . (21 Oct.) Went over what was done about the Cross . . . and agreed to leave out that of the Childrens being Baptised last—It was desired that some expedient shou'd be thought of for the ease of Ministers in the Use of the Cross. . . . (18 Nov.) . . . It was proposed by W. that a Rubrick shou'd be drawn up respecting those Ministers that shou'd Scruple the use of the Cross; that being the most material point in question among the Non-conformists, and which they all agreed in their dissent from. It was moved by Dr. G. that however, this should extend to those that were to come in, not to those that were already in the Church. It was agreed, that it should be much after the way taken in the Rubrick about kneeling." (These developments are not reflected in the text, which seems to be a fair copy from separate papers.)

Let. Min.: "As for instance, if the Minister to be admitted, yet scruples the use of the Surplice or Cross, upon application to the Bishop, another may be appointed to do that Service. And if one of the Laity scruples the use of the Cross, the Minister may be permitted in that case to Baptize without it." (p. 9).

Let. Friend: ". . . . I readily assent that the Cross in Baptism had a very good reason for its first institution: For when in the primitive times the Heathens made it a matter of constant reproach to the Christians, that they worshipped a crucified God, they for this reason appointed the Cross after Baptism to be thenceforth put as a Badge upon all whom they received into the Church, to let them know, that they ought not to be ashamed thereof. . . . But now . . . we live in a State which is totally Christian . . . it cannot be denied but that this Ceremony hath now totally lost its use. . . . But in our present circumstances, when it is become not only useless but also mischievous to the cause of Christ by reason of the Dissentions and Schisms which it occasions in his Church . . . I think we have an obligation upon us not to be resisted from the absolute necessity of the thing, either totally to lay this Ceremony aside, or else make such abatements concerning its use, as may allay all these heats of contention, and mischiefs of separation which have been caused in the Church of Christ thereby . . ." (adds that on occasion the Church has attributed to it a sacramental effect which belongs to Baptism only) (p. 9-10).

V. Cleri.: "Sure this Person did never consider, that the Church hath declared that Sacrament sufficiently administered where the Cross is omitted; and had he considered the definition of a Sacrament in the Catechism, he might perceive, that no part of that definition agrees with the Cross to make it Sacramental; and when we see that the Disputes for laying aside the Cross, have been improved to the layin aside of Baptism, let the Author consider where the guilt doth lie. (p. 48-9).

New Survey: "The yielding to the Dissenters may be such, as not utterly to take away any thing, but to leave some things at liberty, as the ceremonies; especially the Sign of the Cross. . . . Where Ministers scruple the use of that sign of the Cross, but the Parents are for it, they may get any Neighbouring Minister that is of the same Opinion to Baptize their Child after their manner. If their Parents be against it, the Minister holding it but a thing indifferent, why may not he forbear the use of it for the satisfaction of the Parents? I do not read of any that lived and dyed Nonconformists, but scrupled the Sign of the Cross, which shows that they are not satisfied in Conscience about it: But our Consciences will bear the yielding of it up for Peace, because we hold ceremonies to be . . . . things Indifferent, in themselves neither good or evil. . . . (p. 32, 60).

Other Authorities: JRC p. 34, is in favour of its retention, and Let. Till. VIIII. wishes more latitude in its use.

## NOTES ON THE PRIVATE BAPTISM OF INFANTS

*1.* While nothing is precisely stated in the Office, it appears that the Commissioners completely rethought its format and content. This can be deduced, from lines which are drawn down the side of the page, and the principle that there should be nothing Repititious.

The Evidence is in brief, as follows: A Line is drawn in the Margin beside these prayers and rubrics:

And let them not doubt . . . .

I certifie you . . . .

But if the child . . . .

By whom was this child . . . .

And if the Minister . . . .

I certifie you . . . .

They brought young Children . . . .

After the Gospel . . . .

Beloved, ye hear in this Gospel . . . .

Our Father . . . .

Almighty and everlasting God . . . .

Then shall the Minister demand . . . .

Dost thou in the name . . . .

Dost thou believe . . . .

At the Rubrick " Then shall the Minister demand " there is a note, subsequently deleted, " Q. of ye Omission of this to Seing now dearly Beloved."

There is a circular line, embracing: ' Wilt thou then obediently ' and ' We receive this child . . .' Another line, continues from " Seeing now " to the end of the office.

It is evident that the omission of " Then shall the Minister demand " to " Seeing now " would be on the grounds of repitition with the promises made at Baptism, in the new form of Service. (Note additions at the Beginning of the text). On the other hand, the word " this " might not refer to " Then shall the Minister ' 'etc. but to the whole of the section marked with a line. This would account for the circular line between, " Wilt thou then " and " We receive this Child "; the straight line was drawn first, and then it was decided to include these two extra prayers in the omission; a mark was then made to show that these two prayers were to be included.

A further addition to the omission was decided upon, and the remaining part of the Office, from 'Seeing now' to the end, has a line drawn beside it in the margin, and the note beside "Then shall the Minister" was deleted, as being no longer applicable. The final form of the Service is simply that of the first section of the text, ending with the prayer "We yield thee". This is in conformity with the objection in the Exceptions: "We desire that baptism may not be administered in a private place at any time, unless by a lawful minister, and in the presence of a competent number: that where it is evident that any child hath been so baptised, no part of the administration may be reiterated in publick, under any limitations: and therefore we see no need of any Liturgy in that case."

This was what the Commissioners had in mind, although the exact content of the Private Baptismal service, was open to debate. The text is printed here as it stands in the Book, for the sake of accuracy. The alterations to Publick Baptism have been copied into the text, and these are reproduced.

2. Prev. Reading i. ye Parent & Sureties are satisfy'd.

3. 1688: The phrase "regenerate this Infant with thy holy Spirit, to receive him for thine own childe by Adoption, and" is put in parentheses, and the word "him" is deleted, in the phrase "incorporate him into thy holy Church".

4. There is a line in the margin, from this point to the end of the Creed.

5. 1688: The section "who being born in original sin, and in the wrath of God" is put in parentheses, and deleted, with the note; "Qu. if not to be omitted".

6. Prev. Reading i. Q of ye. (Probably a mistake of positioning for note 7 below, which was discovered in time.)

7. Prev. Reading i. Q of ye Omission of this to Seing now dearly Beloved.

8. Prev. Readings i. and vanitys of ys wicked world. ii. deleted and the text not replaced.
   Black adds this as if it had not been deleted.

9. The Prayers 'Wilt thou then', and 'we Receive' are enclosed with a semi-circular line.

10. A line is drawn from this point to the end of the Office in the margin.

11. Black states 'the position of this Note is such as to make it possibly applicable to all the remainder of the text, marked with a marginal line'. It, of course, refers only to the words 'by Baptism', which are put in Parentheses and underlined, as being a textual misprint in the Prayer Book.

## NOTES ON BAPTISM OF THOSE OF RIPER YEARS

1. 1688: The phrase "a week before at" is underlined, and the word "persons" has an x beside it.

2. The words "Godfathers and Godmothers" are underlined.

3. Prev. Reading i. Prayer, if it may be, as the Minister. . . .

4. 1688: In the phrase "and they that are in the flesh" the words "are in" are put in parentheses and underlined, and after the word "flesh" the note "(a)" is added.

5. 1688: read, Minister.

6. 1688: read, "Almighty and Everlasting God, whose most dearly . . . . Go preach the Gospell to all Nations and . . . . Congregation: and grant that these persons now to be baptized with Water according to his Institution, may receive. . . ."

7. 1688: The words "Godfathers and Godmothers" are underlined, and replaced in the margin by "witnesses".

8. 1688: read, 'And as for you, who have now by Baptism, taken upon you the Xtian Religion, it is your part and duty also. . . .'

## NOTES ON THE CATECHISM

1. Exceptions: XVII. 5. "The Catechism is defective as to many necessary doctrines of our religion: some even of the essentials of Christianity not mentioned except in the Creed, and there not so explicite as ought to be in a catechism."

"In the general we observe, that the doctrine of the sacraments which was added upon the conference at Hampton-Court, is much more fully and particularly delivered than the other parts of the Catechism, in short answers fitted to the memories of children, and thereupon we offer it to be considered: First, Whether there should not be a more distinct and full explication of the Creed, the Commandments, and the Lord's Prayer. Secondly, Whether it were not convenient to add (what seems to be wanting) somewhat particularly concerning the nature of faith, of repentance, the two covenants, of justification, sanctification, adoption, and regeneration."

It would seem that in a half-hearted way the Commissioners followed the section 'first' above, in that these parts are extended. The reason for simply repeating the comprehensive statements in particular sections, can only be regarded as a help to children; though why the content remains in the same words is mystifying.

Let. Til: X. ". . . . Whether, too, the Church Catechism might not be as useful if some controverted things in the beginning, and some school definitions towards the end of it, were left out? And whether a larger Catechism may not be fitly appointed to be learned after the former? ".

2. 1688: "My Godfathers" has an x placed by it, and the word "Christ" is underlined with (a) beside it. The word "inheritor" is boxed in, with a "B" added; it is altered in the margin to "heir", but there is no indication of what "B" means there.

3. 1688: The word "name" is underlined, and "(c)" placed beside it.

4. 1688: Alteration as 1689. Cf. Baptismal services.

5. "had" is partially deleted, probably by mistake. Note: "& ever", Black incorrectly reads "and ever".

6. Prev. Reading i. What priviledges do Christians receive by being receivd. . . .

7. Prev. Reading i. . . . . Catholic Church?

Answer: They receive these four.
Question: Wch is ye first of Them?
Answer: The First is ye Comunion of Saints or fellowship of all true Christians in Fayth, wp, & charity.
Question: Wch is ye Second priviledge?
Answer: The Second is ye Forgiveness of sins obtained by ye Sacrifice of Christs death, & given to us, upon Fayth in him, & repetance fro dead works.
Question: Wch is ye 3d privilege?
Answer: The Third is, the Resurrection of ye body to a glorious state.
Question: What is ye 4th priviledge?
Answer: The Fourth, Everlasting life in ye Kingdom of Heaven.

8. 1688: After the word "Commandments' 'is the sign "(+)", and after " be? " (a).

9. 1688: After " Ten " is added " (+) ".

10. Exceptions: " We desire that the commandments be inserted according to the new translation of the Bible ".

Note: Within the Ten Commandments there is an asterisk by the words " Sabbath day " and a note, " *wch is now the Lords day ". The new version from Exodus is not written out.

1688: By " Sabbath day. Six " " (b) " is added.

11. 1688: " and to serve him truly all the days of my life " is underlined. Exceptions: " In this answer there seems to be particular respect to the several commandments of the first table, as in the following answer to those of the second. And therefore we desire it may be advised upon, whether to the last word of this answer may not be added, " particularly on the Lord's day ", otherwise there being nothing in all this answer that refers to the fourth commandment."

12. Prev. Reading i. Question. How do you apply this particularly to the 4 first Comandments? & first what is ye duty learn you from ye first Comandment?

13. Prev. Reading i. Wt learn you fro ye. . . .

14. Prev. Reading i. How do you apply this to ye 6 last Comandments? And particularly wt do you learn by ye 5t?

15. 1688: The words " ghostly and bodily " are deleted, and replaced in the margin, by " of Soul & Body ". " From our ghostly enemy " is altered to " from our Spiritual enemy ".

16. Prev. Reading i. How do you apply this to ye several Petitions? particularly Tell me wt you desire of God in ye 1st & 2d petition.

17. Prev. Reading i. I desire my Lord God &c ought to do, that we may. . . .

18. Black adds Question marks which are not present in the text.

19. Exceptions: " That these words may be omitted, and answer thus given; ' Two only, baptism and the Lord's supper '."

20. Black fails to omit " or form " which is deleted in the text.

21. 1688: " And the children of wrath " is deleted.

22. 1688: " (a) " is added before " Repentance ".

23. 1688: After the word " them " adds " (c) ".

24. In the phrase " they promise them both ", " (c) " is added before " they ", and the words " them both " are underlined.

25. 1688: read, " What are the outward (part or) signs. . . ." A ' d ' is placed above " part or ".

26. 1688: After " received ", " (f) " is added.

27. 1688: In the question, " What is the inward part of thing signified ", the words " part or thing signified " are underlined and put in parentheses; above is written " (e) ".

28. 1688: Delete the three questions and Answers beginning " The Body and Bloud ", " What benefits " and " The strengthening ".

Let. Min.: " Of which the Church of Rome has made so great advantage, that it was the matter of a publick Dispute, since printed. To this may be added, the Answer in the Catechism, ' The Body and Blood of Christ, which are Verily and Indeed taken and received by the faithful in the Lord's-Supper ". (p. 24).

V. Cleri: " (i.e.) in a spiritual, but real manner by the faithful Communicants; for there is sufficient caution given against the Doctrine of Transubstantiation." (p. 39).

29. 1662: " So soon as children are come to a competant Age, and can say in their mother Tongue, the Creed, the Lords Prayer, and the ten Commandments, and also can answer to the other questions of this short Catechism. . . .'

Exceptions: "We conceive that it is not a sufficient qualification for confirmation, that children be able to memoriter to repeat the Articles of the Faith, commonly called the Apostles' Creed, the Lord's Prayer, and the Ten Commandments, and to answer to some questions of this short Catechism; for it is often found that children are able to do all this at four or five years old, It crosses what is said in the third reason of the first Rubrick before confirmation, concerning the usage of the Church in times past, ordaining that confirmation should be ministered unto them that were of perfect age, that they being instructed in the Christian religion, should openly profess their own faith, and promise to be obedient to the will of God."

V. Populi: " For our Childrens sake, we could wish that the Order of Confirmation were not made a matter of meer Form and Ceremony; that it were carefully look'd to, not only that they be able to say the Creed, Lord's Prayer, and Ten Commandments, and to answer the Questions in the Catechism, but that they understand them too; to this end that the Rubric, . . . . may be reinforced and observed, that so those that are notoriously scandalous, or grosly ignorant, ' what their Godfathers and Godmother promised for them in Baptism, and which now with their own Mouth and Consent they are openly before the Church to ratifie and confirm ', may not be admitted to it."

## NOTES ON EXHORTATION . . . . BEFORE CONFIRMATION

1. The Title is written in Tenison's hand, but the rest was written out by the Emanuensis.

Williams Diary: (28 Oct.) " They proceeded to the Office of Confirmation, In the first place was read an Exhortation to be used sometime before Confirmation (as there is before the Sacrament) The first thing debated in that was that Hebr. 6 was applyed to it, and so apply'd as if Confirmation was of the Foundation. The B. of S. said it was of the Foundation respecting Government.—B. of A. said that it appear'd to be so, because immediately follows the baptismoi by which the Baptism of Christ was distinguish'd from that of St. John. But B.W. that He thought it was ————— It was agreed to be left out in the Exhortation."

Let. Min.: " In the Office of Confirmation, which if it had notice given of it the Sunday before, by an Exhortation like unto that before the Sacrament; and a Discourse about the Nature, Use, and Obligation of it, immediately before the Bishop Confirms, and a serious Exhortation after it, with some little Enlargements and Alterations of the Collects, it would be a great means to recover the dignity of that excellent Institution, and to form in the minds of youth a greater sense of Religion." (p. 25-6).

V. Cleri: ". . . by all which he provides to bring down the Bishops to more labour than he would have any Country-Minister perform, considering what other Offices they usually perform at the same time, (viz) Administration of the Holy Sacraments, Ordination of Priests and Deacons, &c " (p. 40-41).

2. Prev. Reading i. to remind (Black includes this wrongly in the text).

3. Black makes the paragraphs beginning " Such as " and " Beware " into one rubric, covered by the " Q "; but there is a decided break between them in the text.

These qualifications are added, because some people believed that Confirmation was only a Bishop's blessing, and did not stamp them with any " indelible character ". These people tended to present themselves for Confirmation on more than one occasion, and there is evidence, that some presented themselves to the Bishop whenever he came to town, on the principle that " you cannot have too much of a good thing ".

4. The conclusion of the Exhortation is a catena of quotations, and general biblical phrases.

| | |
|---|---|
| You are to dedicate . . . . Holy Spirit | 1 Cor. 3.16. |
| He will receive . . . . Almighty. | Perhaps based on Jer. 7.23. |
| Having therefore . . . . of God | 2 Cor. 7.1. |
| And ye good God . . . . Amen | Cf. Collect for Easter Day. 1662 version. |

## NOTES ON THE CONFIRMATION SERVICE

1. The following is a paper stuck in the book, in the hand of Tenison. The Text version is that made by the Emanuensis.

" You have been lately informed for what end you ought to come hither. And I hope you are come prepared, according to (the directions in) the exhortation then made to you. With a serious desire, (that is) & resolution, openly to ratify & confirm before the Church, with your own mouth & consent, what your Sureties promised in yr Name, when you were Baptised: and also the promise that, by the grace of God, you will evermore endevour yourselves faithfully to observe such things, as you by your own confession have assented unto."

In this paper, the words I have placed in parentheses, are subsequently deleted, and the words " that is " are placed before the words " With a serious desire ". Note that Tenison reads " promised in your Name ", the Emanuensis, " in your Names ".

2. 1688: The word " vow " is underlined, and the note added; " Here out to be a Repitition of ye things promised in Baptism." Cf. D.B. p. 222, where it is also added.

3. 1688: " your Baptism " is underlined, with the note; " And advice to Godf: &c as to their remaining duty of charitie to such Relations."

4. Exceptions: " This supposeth that all the children who are brought to be confirmed have the Spirit of Christ, and the forgiveness of their sins; whereas a great number of children at that age, having committed many sins since their baptism, do shew no evidence of serious repentance, or of any special saving grace; and therefore this confirmation (if administered to such) would be a perillous and gross abuse."

Williams Diary: (28 Oct.) " The Collect was mended by putting in New Testament Phrases into the place of the old ".

A number of arguments which apply to this, are given in Baptism, note 29, and note 1 of the Exhortation before Confirmation.

5. Exceptions: " We desire that the practice of the apostles may not be alledged as a ground of this imposition of hands for the confirmation of children, both because the apostles did never use it in that case, as also because the Articles of the Church of England declare it to be a " corrupt imitation of the apostles' practice."

6. This Exhortation, like the new Collects is a concatanation of quotations. Analysis.

Dearly Beloved . . . . Christ.
I do therefore . . . . Lord

Matrimony: "I require and charge you both as you will answer at the dreadfull day of Judgment".

yt you observe . . . . Calling
That so . . . . Christ.

(2 Thess. 1.11).

Mortify all . . . . Idolatry
for wch things . . . . disobedience
put away . . . . mouths

Col. 3.5.
Col. 3.6.
Col. 3.8 ("blasphemy" altered to "evill speaking" and "lying, swearing" are added.)

& put on . . . . Long-suffering
Be ye . . . . Christ.
Take his . . . . heart
& be ye . . . . conversation
Be ye obedient . . . . Callings
allways . . . eternall life
He who establisheth . . . . hearts.
And if you . . . . of Life
But if any . . . . in Him
since he . . . . of Grace
for, if after . . . . beginning
Watch ye . . . . weak
And seing . . . . before you
Be you . . . . vain in the Lord
And I pray . . . . Christ

Col. 3.12.

Matt. 12.29.
1 Pet. 1.15.
(Cf. Col. 3.20, 22).
Jude 20, 21.
2 Cor. 1.21, 22.
Rev. 2.10d.
Heb. 10.38.
(Heb. 10.29).
2 Pet. 2.20.
Mt. 26.41.
Heb. 12.1.
1 Cor. 15.58.
1 Thess. 5.23.

## NOTES ON MATRIMONY

1. 1688: The section "to satisfie mens carnal lusts and appetites, like brute beasts that have no understanding" is deleted.

2. 1688: The Phrase "procreation of children" is altered to "procreation of mankind". Then the whole section "procreation of . . . . holy Name" is deleted, and so is the next section, "it was ordained . . . . Christs Body"; the "it was ordained" after "Thirdly" is also deleted.

3. 1688: The word "coupled" is altered to "joyned".

4. 1688: The word "coupled" is altered to "joyned".

5. 1688: read . . . Hand, and the man holding the ring there, and taught (ii directed) by the Pr, shall say. . . .

6. 1688: Delete whole prayer, but inside the word "worship" is altered to "honour", and the phrase "and with all my worldly goods I thee endow" is underlined.

Exceptions: "Seeing this ceremony of the ring in marriage is made necessary to it, and a significant sign of the vow and covenant betwixt the parties; and Romish ritualists give such reasons for the use and institution of the ring, as are either frivolous or superstitious; it is desired that this ceremony of the ring in marriage may be left indifferent, to be used or forborn.

This word 'worship' being much altered in the use of it since this form was first drawn up; we desire some other word may be used instead of it.

258

(Doxology) These words being only used in Baptism, and here in the Solemnization of Matrimony, and in the Absolution of the Sick; we desire it may be considered, whether they should not be here omitted, least they should seem to favour those who count matrimony a sacrament."

Williams Diary: (30 Oct.) "Agreed to make a Rubrick about the Ring; and to leave out 'with my Body' &c and put in other words for it."

Bishop's Reply: "That the words, 'with my body I thee worship', may be altered thus, 'with my body I thee honour.' (Although this was not realized in 1662, the evidence of the Durham Book suggests they were quite prepared to alter it thus, p. 236-7).

Let. Min.: "I take it for granted that the Ring in Marriage is now on all sides accounted a meer civil and not a religious rite." (p. 7). The Author regards "with my body I thee worship" as obscure (p. 24).

V. Cleri: "With my Body I thee worship: Which signifies a civil Respect and Honour, and is more significant than what they would exchange it for, (viz) I give thee Power over my Body." (p. 38-9).

Brief Discourse: "'The putting on the Ring in Marriage, especially the making that Ceremony to be an essential Matter, is Superstition.' A. (1) What Superstition can there be in this, more than in Joyning of Hands, both of which are Civil Rites, and fit Declarations of pledging their Troth to each other? (2) How can that be Essential, which is one of the 'alterable' things meant in the Preface? (3) It's necessary there should be some Rite used, and some actions by which the espousal should be solemnized, and why not a Ring as well as a joyning of hands? . . ." (p. 22).

7. 1688: The following phrases are deleted: "this man and this woman", "That, as Isaac . . . . keep the vow" and "whereof this ring . . . . and may".

8. Prev. Reading i. or going to the Comunion table.

Exceptions: "We conceive this change of place and posture mentioned in these two Rubricks is needless, and therefore desire it may be omitted."

9. There is one alteration in the Psalm; the phrase "O well is thee, and happy shalt thou be" is altered to, "O happy shalt thou be, & it shall be well with Thee."

10. 1688: All the Versicles and responses are deleted, with the marginal note: "It were well if there were here other vesicles. These are used in ye visitation of ye Sick."

11. 1688: In this prayer, the following sections are deleted: "of Abraham . . . . Jacob", "and sow . . . . fulfil the same", "O Lord", and "and bless them". Beside "and sow . . . . fulfil the same" is the note; "This phrase is inexpedient."

12. 1688: read, "we beseech thee to bless these thy servants with Children, if thou in thy Wisdom see it to be convenient for Them: And grant them to live . . . . (sic)".

13. D.B. also originally deleted "amiable", but this was later restored. (p. 240).

14. 1688: Adds note in margin, "Duty of ye Husband".

15. 1688: read, "Now likewise, hear and learn the duties of wives towards . . . .", and the note is written in the margin: "Duty of ye wife."

16. 1688: read, "Let it not be so much that outward adorning . . . .
    apparel; as the hidden man. . . ."

17. 1688: The ending, "For after this manner . . . . any amazement" is
    deleted, with an indecipherable note in the margin, "This is a ———
    ——— against affecting ———————".

18. 1662: "It is convenient that the new married persons should receive
    the holy Communion at the time of their marriage, or at the first
    opportunity after their Marriage."

    1688: The words "Holy Communion" are underlined with an +
    added after them. And a note follows " Conclude with ye Grace of or
    Lord Jesus Christ &c ".

    Exceptions: "This Rubrick doth either enforce all such as are unfit for
    the sacrament to forbear marriage, contrary to Scripture, which approves
    the marriage of all men; or else compels all that marry to come to
    the Lord's table, though ever so unprepared; and therefore we desire
    it may be omitted, the rather because that marriage festivals are too
    often accompanied with such divertisements as are unsuitable to those
    Christian duties, which ought to be before and follow after the receiving
    of that holy Sacrament."

(The matter was somewhat abated by 1662 quoted above, nevertheless
Increase Mather went in head first.)

    Brief Discourse: " 'Ministers are requir'd to give the Holy Communion
    to all new-married Persons, Whereas Marriage-Festivals used to be
    accompanied with such Divertisements as unfit them. By this Doctrine,
    all that may Marry may come to the Lords Supper, whereas Marriage is
    An Ordinance which Men as Men (and not as Christians only), have a
    right unto, So that by this Prescription many will eat and drink
    Damnation to themselves.'

    Ans. (1) If this was required, yet it's not inconsistent with that State,
    which is rightly call'd 'The Holy Estate of Matrimony', and besides,
    those Divertisements do not precede but follow. (2) Surely those Persons
    that are married amongst us, are supposed to be Christians, and not to
    be married merely as Men. (3) If any eat and drink their own
    Damnation, it's their own fault: and the danger of it doth not release
    any of their Duty, or justify their neglect of it. (4) But the Common-
    Prayer-Book doth not compel them; it saith only, That it's 'convenient
    at their Marriage, or at the first opportunity after it '."

## NOTES ON THE VISITATION OF THE SICK

1. Let. Till: "Whether the whole office of Visiting the Sick, also the use
   of Common Prayer by the minister in his own family, may not be left
   indifferent?" (VII).

2. Prev. Reading i. dwell in it, & pticularly to thy afflicted Servt (or
   Servts).
   1688: read, "coming into the sick persons house, may say" The
   section " Peace be . . . . in it " is deleted.

3. 1688: By the word " Remember " the letter (d) is added.

4. 1688: All the Versicles and responses are deleted.

5. 1688: " grieved with sickness " is underlined.

6. 1688: " sense of his weakness " is underlined.

7. Prev. Reading i. blest be thy good. . . .

8. 1688: The word " seriousness " is underlined, and " + " added.

*9.* 1688: "As youth, strength . . . . sickness" is deleted, and there is a marginal note: " Q. This to be put out ".

*10.* 1688: The section, " To try your patience . . . . endless felicity " is deleted.

*11.* 1688: " the eyes of " is deleted.

*12.* 1688: The word " Curate " is altered to " Minister ".

*13.* 1688: The words " Saint Paul " are underlined.

*14.* 1688: The phrase " by suffering patiently . . . . and Sickness " is underlined.

*15.* 1688: " Here with Christ " is altered to " Here as Christ did " and the next line, " our door . . . . life " is deleted.

*16.* Prev Reading i. as to him it shall.

*17.* Note, that the prayer " O Most mercifull God " and the Absolution have been placed in the reverse order from 1662. After the rubric " Here shall the sick person " was the note, " Then ye Min: shall say ye Collect following. O most mercifull God &c as on ye next page ". This was subsequently deleted. The text of the absolution is also deleted, and the new one placed on the next interleaf with the Prayer. It would seem that both the note and Absolution were deleted at the same time, the note being redundant if the Absolution was placed on the following page. This is a more logical order; After confession, the priest prays for absolution, and after the prayer has been heard, pronounced the penitent absolved. The effect is much lessened if after absolution has been given, the priest prays for forgiveness for one " who most earnestly desires pardon and forgiveness."

*18.* Prev. Reading i. Then ye Min: shall say ye Collect following. O Most mercifull God &c as on ye next page.

*19.* Previous Reading i. " Let us pray " deleted. ii. ' stet " marked beside it. iii. Written out again.

*20.* Black omits to record the word " wn ".

Exceptions: " And that the Absolution may only be recommended to the minister to be used or omitted as he shall see occasion. That the form of Absolution be declarative and conditional, as " I pronounce thee absolved " instead of " I absolve thee," " if thou doest truly repent and believe "."

Let. Min: Regards the phrase " by his authority committed to me, I absolve thee " as being " very liable to misapplication ". (p. 24).

V. Cleri: " By his Authority committed to me, I absolve thee; which the Priest having prayed God to do, he applieth in Nomine domini, in the Name of the Father &c. By the Authority committed to me as God's Minister, I absolve thee. . ."(p. 39).

The " Bishop of Worcester's Charge . . . Primary Visitation, 1690 Worcester MDCXCI," (Stillingfleet) points to some of the problems facing the clergy in the use of the absolution: " Where the Power of Absolution is grounded upon the Supposition of true Faith and Repentance . . . . For the Church cannot absolve when God doth not. So that the real comfort of the Absolution depends upon the Satisfaction of the Person's Mind, as to the Sincerity of his Repentence and Faith in Christ " (p. 27-8). In Theophilus Lindsay's copy in Dr. Williams Library (pp. 50) there is the note: " of what service then is the Church's Absolution, but for the sake of our craft, and to advance the Priesthood?".

21. An Analysis of the Hymn.

| | |
|---|---|
| Unto thee do I .... | Ps. 123.1 "Lift I" changed to "do I lift". |
| My help .... | Ps. 121.2 (BCP) "even from the Lord" is altered to "from thee O Ld", and "hath" to "hast". |
| O Ld. rebuke ... | Ps. 6.1 Collation of AV and BCP: (A.V.) O Lord, rebuke me not in thine anger, neither chasten me in thy hot displeasure. (BCP) O Lord, rebuke me not in thine indignation: neither chasten me in thy displeasure. |
| Have mercy .... Look upon my affliction .... | Ps. 6.2a, 4b (AV). Ps. 25.18 (AV) Ps. 25.17 (BCP). (AV) Look upon mine affliction and my pain; and forgive me all my sins. (BCP) Look upon my adversity and misery: and forgive me all my sin. |
| If thou Lord .... But there is .... O Comfort ye Soul .... Whome have I in .... | Ps. 130.3 (BCP). Ps. 130.4 (AV). Ps. 86.4 (BCP). Ps. 73.25 (AV) with the alteration of "Beside" to "Besides". |
| My heart & my flesh ... | Ps. 73.26, with "heart and flesh" in reverse order from text. |
| It is good for me .... | Ps. 73.28 (AV) Ps. 73.27 (BCP). (AV) But it is good for me to draw near to God: I have put my trust in the Lord God, that I may declare all thy works. (BCP) But it is good for me to hold me fast by God, to put my trust in the Lord God: and to speak of all thy works in the gates of the daughter of Sion. |

22. 1688: read, " by thy most precious bloud shed on ye cross hast ".

23. 1688: The following notes remain on the interleaf. They have been deleted, but " stet " placed by the side of them.

" When ye Person is drawing on, & his Agonie continuing (i more than one hour) Long, it were good to assist (ii him or her) with sentences out of SS, & (ii wth) Litanies proper for Comforting ye soul in a mas extremis & helping it to comend it self with zele to God.

Some such are to be foud in the devotions at ye End of ye whole duty of man.

There wants a Prayer of Resignation, & for Cofort of ye grieved friends of ye departed, most seasonable at that time to break ye greatness of their passion."

Sections above marked (i) have been subsequently deleted, (ii) are additions to the first draft.

# NOTES ON THE COMMUNION OF THE SICK

*1.* 1688: On a remaining interleaf is written: " The poor who are sick having no decent Vessells for ye Comunion, it were well if it obtain'd evry where as it does (i. at S.M. ye F. &c) in some places that there were little cups & patins very portable for this purpose, in ye perpetuall Custody of ye Ministers, who canot, of a suddain, comand ye church plate, wch also is less portable ".

The section (i . . .) is subsequently deleted. It is an abbreviation of " Saint Martins (in) the Fields ", Tenison's Church.

*2.* Prev. Readings i. three at the least. ii. one at the least.
i. least, besides ye Minister & sick person (when more canot be had.
1688: " There are divers persons Imprisoned & confined by lameness & weakness &s who can bear a larger Office than this, and to whose circumstances some Collects &s might be fitted, It were good (fo greater solemnitie in a mattr of such momt) to make a form wch a sick man desirous of receiving ye bl: Sacrament, but uncapable (wn not able to swallow, or by such other waies, prvented) might make solemn profession of his readiness upo suppos: that ye Impediments were removed; that it might be sd. to his cofort. God accepteth ye will for ye deed, as also to ye comfort of his Friends: & that ye Exaple of it might be before others ".

*3.* 1688: " Whensoever ": adds " Q. if ". A further note is added. " A Collect Aftr Sacramt relating to ye sick might also be added, & wth relation to his having rec'd his viaticu, if at ye poynt of death."

The word " viaticum " or last communion to thy dying, is not infrequently used throughout this period, and in many cases (e.g. Thorndike) it is linked with a continuous reservation of the Sacrament for this purpose. Sparrow in his Rationale uses the word a great deal in connection with the sick, in all editions. Examples of the word's use, and its connection with reservation may be found in Wickham Legg p. 24, 45-7; and Lowther Clarke p. 592ff.

*4.* 1688: " The Epistle being already mention'd in ye Collect; phaps a new one should be chosen."
" Epistle & Gospell to be longer where ye Case will permit as wth ye Bedrid &c."

*5.* 1688: The word " Priest " is altered to " minister ".
Private Confession was practiced by many at this time, and recommended in many Devotional Manuals and Books; a full description may be found in Wickham Legg p. 263-77.

*6.* 1688: The word " Priest ' 'is altered to " minister ".

*7.* 1688: read, " person, unless he perceivs him ready to expire ".

*8.* 1688: read, " and giving him most hearty thanks for Them, (i he really partaketh of all ye) Almighty God will, in these cases, accept ye will for ye deed, though he do's not actually receive the Elements." The section " he doth eat and drink . . . . with his mouth " is deleted.

*9.* 1688: " sweating-sickness. first (I think) observ'd here in ye time of Hen. 7th ".

*10.* 1688: read, "Minister may only Communicate. . . ."

## NOTES ON THE BURIAL OF THE DEAD

*1.* The rituals surrounding Funerals in this period, were considerable. It was frequently the custom to provide gifts to one's neighbours on the day of burial of a loved one, which would include drink, as well as posies of ever-greens, Laurel, Ivy or Rosemary, which were regarded as symbols of the soul's immortality. Psalms and hymns were sung as the corpse was taken out of the Church, sometimes preceded by the choir. If the deceased was wealthy enough, candles would be placed round the coffin as it stood in the Church, and the choir and clergy would carry tapers or smaller candles (cf. Wickham Legg p. 195ff).

2. 1688: " Qu. It would be convenient besides ye generall office, to have some particular (ones) Collects, for ye Conditions of ye dead.
As (ye order of) for ye buriall of Infants. of Madmen. of executed persons not excomunicated."
Sections in parentheses, subsequently deleted.

3. 1688: " Qu. if the hymns may not be improv'd be leaving out some verses not propr to ye Occasion & supplying them by other Places?"

4. 1688: " In Places where there are many Burialls in one night (as in S.M.F. where we have had 14) one Chapter is not sufficient. Such Repitition of it wears it into disregard.
There may be selected divers chapters wch may sute ye Conditions of those who are to be buried.
This Chapter is full of ye most philosophicall Theologie, & above ye heads of many.
And, in cold & late seasons, it is too long."

5. 1688: " Priest " altered to " Min ".

6. 1688: The section " to take unto himself the soul of our dear brother " is underlined. Read: " dust to dust, firmly believing the resurrection of ye dead through ".

Exceptions: " These words cannot in truth be said of persons living and dying in open and notorious sins."

Bishops Reply: allowed that the words " sure and certain " should be left out, and although this was not done in 1662, the Durham Book suggests a number of alternatives. (D.B. p. 250).

Let. Min: (This) " supposes Discipline; and therefore where Discipline is not exercis'd, it's hard to use it in all cases, without a further Explication ". (p. 24).

V. Populi: " We do not enquire how the Clergy can read this over all Dead men that are not either Excommunicated, Unbaptised, or have not laid violent hands upon themselves. Tho we could wish men that are so charitable to the dead, would be so to the living too. But we too often accompany the Corps of a drunken, debaucht neighbour of ours; who lived all his days in the habitual practice of many deadly sins, and gave no signs of Repentance that we could ever hear of it; it may be the fatal arrow struck through him while he was in the very act of some foul sin. The Grave cannot strike a colder damp on our bodies, than the thoughts of this doth on our Devotions; and we can no more say ' Amen ' on such occasions, than the dead man himself, on whose funeral we attend. 'This true indeed, we are told that these words to suppose the ' strict exercise of Discipline '. But so long as we see no such thing, 'tis an Hypothesis that gives us no relief at all." (p. 6).

V. Cleri : " By which no more is meant, than what, as some understand, the Scripture says: ' The Spirit returns to God that gave it ': or if it supposeth Discipline; so it expresseth Charity, where Discipline hath not excluded them from the Communion of the Church, that we hope they rest with God." (p. 39).

New Survey: "And as the great Dean of St Pauls motioned, whether those expressions, which suppose the strict exercise of Discipline in Burying the Dead, were not better left at liberty in our present case;— (there being a confessed want and neglect of Discipline)" (p. 32-33).

Brief Discourse: "A. (1) The Office of Burial, supposes that of Visitation of the Sick to go before, where the Minister is appointed to examine, "Whether he repent him truly of his Sins &c'. (2) It supposes the Exercise of Discipline; and that such as he speaks of have the censures of the Censures of the Church exercised upon them, which if they be not exercised, we know whom we are to thank for the relaxation of it. (3) However, the Church provides not for extraordinary, but Ordinary cases; and if an extraordinary case happens, and be notorious, no Rule of this nature can then bind. (4) If it be not notorious, it's safer to err on the Charitable side. . . ." (p. 22). (cf. also Let. Till VII).

Throughout this period there is a concern about the Discipline of the church and its neglect, which tends to focalise on the Burial Service, where that neglect was most evident. The revisers of 1688, thought it sufficiently important to add a note in the Commination Service; " Qu. if the Convocation ought not to considr about ye best meas to restore discipline, rather yn to suffer ys to stand as a perpetuall coplaint wtht seeking for redress." And beside the Office for making deacons, listed a number of " Church Forms " for, admonition, silencing, suspension, suspension from the Sacrament, Excommunication, Excommunication of a Clergyman, and Degradation. The other side is suggested by Let. Min., who feels the need of services for Receiving Penitents after Apostacy, or scandal; Receiving those absolved from Excommunication, and an office for Prisons and especially for use at times of execution. This shows a serious concern for the situation, and indeed V. Populi devotes a number of pages to the topic of " Removing scandalous Ministers " (p. 33ff); he dwells little however, on how this should relate to the Laity, and except in the quotation above never refers to it. Further concern is voiced in the Exceptions (XV). Let. Min. p. 16 and Let. Till. XIII.

Discipline was not, however, completely lacking, and the latest evidence we have of people doing public penance in church is as late as 1761. Penance could be done in public for anything from drunkenness to prostitution, and Excommunication for non-repentance of these crimes was well known.

Evidence relating to parts of this question may be found in Wickham Legg p. 252-62.

7. 1688: The word " sung " is underlined.

8. 1688: The word " Priest " is underlined, and altered to " min ".

9. 1688: The word " Priest " is underlined, and altered to " min ".

10. 1688: The phrase " and hasten the coming of thy kingdom " is underlined, with the word " obscure " written in the margin.

11. Exceptions: " These words may harden the wicked, and are inconsistent with the largest rational charity."

12. 1688: " These words cannot be used with respect to those persons who have not by their actual repentance given any ground for the hope of their blessed estate."

## NOTES ON THE THANKSGIVING AFTER CHILDBIRTH

1. Prev. Readings i. " decently apparelled " deleted. ii. " stet " added in the margin.
   1688: " decently apparelled " underlined, with " Qu." beside it.

The phrase was added in 1662. It does not refer to the dress of the woman concerned but to the custom of wearing a veil. In the middle ages a Veil or "kerchief" had been worn, and as late as the reign of James I a woman was excommunicated for not complying with the custom. In the Durham Book the first reading follows this: "The woman a month after her delivery being recovered shall upon some Sunday or other Holyday come decently vayled into the parish Church. . . ."

Wren's Advices of 1660 also suggests that "The woman decently vayled, shall at the beginning of the Communion Service . . ." The absence of any rubric about the dress of a woman, was felt in 1661 (Cosin Particular 90), and although it was in some ways desirable to specify that a veil should be worn, it was decided to make the requirements more general. It may well be that 1688, and the first discussions in 1689, considered the advisability of changing the phrase "decently apparelled" to one specifying the use of a veil. (cf. D.B. p. 252-53).

2. 1688: The word "Priest" is altered to "Min".

3. Prev. Reading i. say this Hymn.
1688: The word "Priest" underlined, and the word "min." added in the margin.

Ps. 116 is deleted, but within the deletion there are two alterations to the text. vs. 3 "pains of hell" altered to "deadly pains"; vs. 10 deleted.

1688: Vs. 3. "the pains of hell" is underlined; vs. 6 "the simple" is underlined; vs. 10 a note in the margin reads: "ys may be omitted."

4. This new hymn is made up of a concatenation of verses from the Psalms, using both the Prayer Book version and the Biblical (A.V.) Psalter, (cf. Psalm in Visitation of Sick).

Analysis.

| | |
|---|---|
| Blessed be ye Lord . . . . | Ps. 66.20 (AV) altering the word "God" to "ye Lord" and the word, "which" to "who". |
| I was in pain . . . . | "I was in pain" is based on Ps. 116.3, and the remainder of the verse is 116.4 (AV) "upon" altered to "on". |
| Gracious . . . . | Ps. 116.5 (AV). |
| I love ye Lord . . . . | Ps. 116.1 (AV) "supplications" altered to "supplication." |
| Because he hath . . . . | Ps. 116.2 (AV). |
| I will pay . . . . | Ps. 116.14 (AV) "I will pay my vows unto the Lord now in the presence of all his people." |
| | Ps. 116.9 (AV) "I will walk before the Lord in the land of the living." |
| Shew me thy waies . . . . | Ps. 25.4 (AV). |
| Lead me . . . . | Ps. 25.5 (AV) "Lead me in thy truth, and teach me: for thou art the God of my salvation." |
| | Ps. 25.4 (BCP) "Lead me forth in thy truth, and learn me: for thou art the God of my salvation." |
| Give me understanding . . . . | Ps. 119.34 (AV). |
| Make me to go . . . . | Ps. 119.35 (AV) but cf. readings; (AV) therein do I delight (BCP) therein is my desire (1689) therein is my delight. |

Prev. Reading (an error in copying out) i. I was in pain & thou called. . . .

5. 1688: "Priest" to be replaced by "Min".

6. 1688: "It were well if other versicles & another collect (wch might relate more to ye pticular deliverance & duty of ye woman) were here added."

7. Exceptions: "It may fall out that a woman may come to give thanks for a child born in adultery or fornication, and therefore we desire that something may be required of her by way of profession of her humiliation, as well as of her thanksgiving."
This was not conceded in 1689, but the phrase "Which putteth her trust in thee" was altered to soften any objections.

8. This is based on Luke 1.75.

9. "Let us Pray" is omitted.
1688: "Let us pray" deleted, with the note:
"The foregoing service being so short needs not this." The note is also added: "Qu. of a collect for a woman miscarrying?"

## NOTES ON THE COMMINATION SERVICE

1. Prev. Reading i. This to be put after ye Gospell for Ashwednesday Part of The office of Ashwednesday.
Brethren this Time of Lent upon wch we are now entred, was, by ye Primitive, observed very religiously & set apart for examining our selves. (present title) i. The Second office.
1688: "Qu. if all this may not be improv'd &c" also, in the second paragraph of the 1662 Exhortation, the words "discipline may be" restored, are underlined, and the note added: "Qu. if the Convocation ought not to considr about ye best meas to restore discipline, rather yn to suffr ys to stand as a perpetuall coplaint wtht redress (ii. seeking for redress)." (see note on Discipline p. 264f.).

2. The Exhortation.
Prev. Readings i. by ye Primitive Church observed very religiously, & set apart for examining their sins. ii. . . . . apart that All men might examine.
i. for true fasting, & for ye duely preparing
i. Penances, were ye things mainly pressd & inisted on
i. & returning to ye Primitive Practice
i. of any Value in ye Sight of God, but as they work in us true Repentance
i. Blessedness to wch our Saviour called us in his Gospel, as also . . . . to flee from ye Wrath to come & lay . . .
Exceptions V: "That there be nothing in the Liturgy which may seem to countenance the observation of Lent as a religious fast; the example of Christ's forty days and nights being no more imitable, nor yet intended for the imitation of a Christian, than any other of his miraculous works were, or than Moses his forty days fast was for the Jews: and the act of parliament, 5 Eliz. forbidding abstinence from flesh to be observed upon any other than a politick consideration, and punishing all those who by preaching, teaching, writing, or open speeches, shall notifie that the forbearing of flesh is of any necessity for the saving of the soul, or that it is the service of God, otherwise than as other politick laws are."

It is evident that the practice of fasting was widely observed in London during this period, when it was the custom to eat only one meal on a fasting day, and as far as possible keep Lent as a time of abstinence from flesh. A number of Cookery books were produced which catered for Lenten fasting, and since these went through a number of editions, it may be presumed that there was a not inconsiderable market for them. Ashwednesday seems to have been well observed, and Horace Walpole takes it for granted that people would understand a jest on the commination service; " The penalty of death came over as often as the curses in the Commination on Ash-Wednesday." A full description of these points may be found in Wickham Legg p. 211-27.

3. Prev Reading i. Min: Blessed &c as in ye Comunion Service.

4. Prev. Readings i. O Ld prserve us fro these Sins. ii. O Ld prserve us fro these & all other heinous Sinns.

   Exceptions: " From all fornication, and all other deadly sin ". In regard that the wages of sin is death; we desire that this clause may be thus altered; " From fornication, and all other heinous, or grevious sins."

5. Prev. Reading i. holy word; and that All they are accursed. . . . .

6. " Let us pray " is omitted.
   1688: " Let us pray " is deleted, with the note added: " Q ".


## NOTES ON THE REVISION OF THE PSALTER

1688: There is only one alteration in the whole Psalter.
" Ps cxxxvj; For his mercy endureth for ever (underlined)
This Chorus should not be put with ye same verse wth ye rest but is 7y, throughout ye Psalm, to be made ye peoples Answer."
The abbreviation 7y, is for " severally ". This alteration would mean that in the alternate reading of the Psalms, the Priest and people would recite only one line each, instead of the whole verse.

Exceptions XII: " Because singing of psalms is a considerable part of publick worship, we desire that the version set forth and allowed to be sung in churches, may be amended; or that we may have leave to make use of a purer version."

Williams Diary: " (3 Oct.) The next point in Debate was the Version of the Psalms in the Common Prayer. It was debated whether keep the Old Translation, or have yt altered, or wholly take in the new.
Here Mr. Kidder was desired to give some account of what He (at the desire of some of the Bps.) had observed. He shewed that the first half was faulty, the latter much better, (and from thence he collected that the Translator by that Time he had gone through the first half grew weary of his Work, and rather chose to Translate it a new, then patch it up as before) and that it differed from the LXX as well as from the Hebrew . . . . (16 Oct.) Before which the Dn. of Peterborough was desired to read his Observations on the Psalms (as He had digested them) which He did, and that matter was again discoursed."

Calamy: " Whether the amendment of the translation of the reading Psalms, (as they are called,) made by the Bishop of St. Asaph and Dr Kidder, or that in the Bible shall be inserted in to Prayer Book, is wholly left to the convocation to consider of and determine." (Conferences p. 432).

Let. Min: " To this I may add the revising of the Psalter added to our Liturgy; which though in its time, and before a better could be had, was of singular use, yet seems now not so defensible, where there is a 'more correct' in our hands. 'A more correct' I call it, after the Bishop of Cork, since those that will take the pains to compare this with the original, cannot but be sensible of the manifold variations from the Hebrew, some while adding phrases and verses; another while leaving out, and frequently mistaking the sense of it; . . . ." (p. 6).

Let. Friend: "must we always be forced to read the old Translation of the Psalms, and impose that on the people for true Scripture, which in so great a number of places quite differs from it?" (p. 15).

V. Cleri: "Though there be Variations in the two Translations, yet they do not contradict one the other; but rather explain and give light to each other; as the divers Commentaries of Learned Men do. 2. The Translation of the Liturgy-Psalter is taken mostly from the Septuagint, or Greek Copies, which that Church still observed; and it is observable, that our Saviour and the Apostles, when they quote the Scripture of the Old Testament, to confirm their Doctrine, do frequently make use of this Translation, though the Hebrew was as well known to them as the Greek. 3. There are Variae Lectiones even in the Hebrew Copies, which the want of Points hath occasioned; concerning which there are yet great Disputes among the Learned Criticks. 4. The best Translations have many Defects and Inconsistancies, occasioned by the various Significations of the Hebrew words; as the word 'Barach' signifies both to Bless and to Curse: So that though the one should be granted to be more correct than the other, yet because the one serves as a short Paraphrase to explain the other, and the People have the Use of both, this Exception is a meer Cavil ". (p. 27).

Other Authorities dealing with this: JRC 26-28, 31. V. Populi p. 5. Let. Till. VI, Brief Discourse p. 17.


## NOTES ON FORMS OF PRAYER TO BE USED AT SEA

There are a number of alterations made in the 1688 revision;

1. Note the Monarch mentioned in " O Eternal Lord God " is Charles.
2. O Eternal Lord God: A note in the margin: " Qu. About a collect propr for Merchantme, ys seeming to be fitted for men of warr in a time of warr."
3. Prayers to be used in Storms: O most powerful. read " quiet about us, we have bin too forgetfull of thee our God ".
4. Rubric before the absolution: The word " Priest " altered to " Min."
5. At the end of the form: " Qu of a collect when they first sett out; & of another when they come into a Port ".


## NOTES ON THE ORDINAL

1. 1688: (written on an interleaf opposite). " There should be a Form for ye Ordination of Schollars of foreign churches. at least the oaths of Alleg: ought to be left of as to them. because that renders them liable to the displeasure of their respective Princes who will look upon them as ill subjects who have sworn fidelitie to another Governour."

(The following is deleted) " For ye promoting union betwixt the Protestant Churches. Episcopacy (is held as an opinion to be judicious by many) should not, however, be urg'd as a poynt necessary to be had by all that take orders. It may suffice that it be looked upon as the Antient (i Practice) Form in ye Churche, & as ye best where it may be had."

269

2. Prev. Reading i. and to come.

3. Prev. Reading i. whether we.

4. There is so much concerning Ordination in William's Diary, that it is not quoted in this section. cf. Appendix 1, where the full text of the Diary is given (Nov. 1ff).

5. See below note 13.

6. 1688: (On the opposite interleaf is written).

" Ch: Censure. There want church forms of

| | |
|---|---|
| Admonition | alone |
| | bef. (i dean &) Chaptr |
| | bef. ye Congreg. |
| Silencing | |
| Suspension | ab officio |
| | beneficio |

suspension fro Sacrament.
(degredation)

| | | |
|---|---|---|
| Excom: | Major | |
| | minor | |

of a Clergyman
degradation.

Habit. It were well if there were some plainr directions about habits, as also some alteration in ye Cano (as far as it goes) already made, about habits. Ye Canonical coat seems to be like a Coachmans, &, by custom, made indecent. Tis pity men should be in all affairs in ye habit in wch they officiate. Wt a figure do's a Presbyter make in a dustie winter Journey, wth his all bespatterd Gown. It seems enough in such cases, if there be any thing wch may distinguish him. for some such badge prvents scandall, & such ills as Monks commit in lay-habit wch they would not do if known to be of ye order. Sometimes respect is gained by ye cloth, sometimes affront."

The Sections in Parentheses are later deleted.

7. 1688: (by the Collect before the Epistle) " S. St. another sort of death ".

8. In the margin. q at home.

9. In the margin. q elsewhere.

10. Prev. Reading i. ye Bishops.

11. Prev. Reading i. Ordinations of Presbyters (or Priests) or Deacons.

12. Prev. Readings i. in the Form used.
    i. Archbp. Bramh.

13. This section in Latin is written in in a different hand, probably Tillotson's.
    Let. Min: " Reordination. This is the case of those that are not now against Episcopal Orders, but having been Ordained by Presbyters, they think it unlawful to renounce them; and to be Reordained, where they have been already Ordained.
    They plead for themselves:

    That though by the late Act of Parliament none are to be admitted to officiate in the Church of England without Episcopal Ordination, yet it was not so before.

For 1. the Ordination by Presbyters was by our Church accounted valid, though not every way perfect, and Foreigners were suffered to enjoy Ecclesiastical Preferments here without Reordination, as was the case of Peter du Moulin &c.

2. It was not only so with Foreigners, but also those that were made Presbyters by Presbyters in Scotland, were made Bishops without any New Ordination.

3. They plead that their case is somewhat different, yet it's so near the same, that the difference cannot (as far as they conceive) make that altogether invalid in them, which was so far valid in the other, as not to require a New Ordination.

4. They plead Quod fieri non debet factum valet; and that were it to do again they would not chuse it, but being done, and sometimes when they could not have Episcopal Ordination, they think some favour is to be allowed for this once. My business is not to enquire into the sufficiency of their Reasons, but what may be done for the composing now of this matter, and the preserving of the Right of Episcopal Ordination (which St. Hierom himself makes the sole Prerogative and distinguishing Character of that Order) and the quieting of the Consciences of those that are herein concerned. Now there are three methods may be taken; either That observed by Archbishop Bramhall, or a Form of hypothatically drawn up, or that of the Bill of Union. I cannot think that of the Primate has escaped you, but yet because I have the Book before me, I shall transcribe it: " Non annihilantes . . . . In cujus rei testimonium &c.

We may here observe how cautiously this great Man proceeded betwixt ratifying and annulling their Orders, that he might not give or take away too much. And withal how far he thought it necessary to go for the peace of the Church, and the taking away the occasion of Schism.

The other method is hypothetical, after the same way that's used in Baptizing such of whose Baptism we have no proof, viz, " If thou art not already Ordained, I Ordain thee, &c.'

The only Objection I can forsee at present, against this, is that the other is matter of Fact that is in question, but here it's matter of Right.

But to that I answer, that is not to the point; for both Cases are hypothetically put, and so the Right is no more determined by the one, than the Fact is by the other. And ' if thou art not already Baptized &c ' doth not declare any thing about the Fact, then, ' If thou art not already Ordained, &c ' doth not declare any thing about matter of Right, but both are left in suspence; and so ' If thou art not already, &c ' is no more than the Bishop's nec validitatem aut invaliditatem determinantes.

The 3rd is that of the Bill of Union (as I have heard) which is that the person to be qualified, shall be by imposition of the Bishops hands, receiv'd with a certain form of words, to signifie his admission into the Church of England, as a Minister therein." (p. 9-11).

This Quotation should be compared with William's Diary, to which there is a surprising likeness. If as has been suggested in the introduction, this was the work of Burnet, one of the Commissioners, it becomes a very important piece of evidence on the thoughts of the Commission in dealing with the problem, and adds more weight to William's Diary.

V. Cleri: ". . . It was ever so in the Church of England, except in some extraordinary Cases, where Ordination by Bishops could not be had; as in the Case of the three Scottish Bishops : but here the Case is altered, there being Bishops ready to give Orders, ever since 1660; wherefore such as have been Ordained by Presbyters since that time, may be said to do it in Contempt of their Authority in that Case; nor were those that were Ordained before that time deprived of an opportunity to take their Orders from the Hands of a Bishop, there being some still ready to confer them; and many in the preceding Years did accept of those Orders from Bishops; which argues, that such as did not refuse it in Contempt, or for their Preferment, which was denied to some, because they had been Episcopally Ordained; but the main Argument may be taken from Dr Beveridge's Text, 1 Cor. 11.16. ' If any Man seem to be contentious, we have no such Custom, neither the Churches of God ': for search all the Ecclesiastical Records, and you will find, that, except in case of great necessity, no Ordination hath ever been accounted valid, but such as hath been administered by the Hands of a Bishop; and if any did contest it, they have been branded as contentious Persons  . . . . But he pleads further, p. 10. Quod fieri non debuit factum valet: Though it ought not to be done, yet being done, it is valid.

This is denied, because both those Presbyters that gave it, and those who received it, were guilty of a Schism, as much then as now (for the Practice is still continued) Episcopal Ordination, being still to be had without any considerable difficulty. And the Author grants, that St. Hierome, (tho' pleading the Cause of Presbyters against Bishops, yet) grants that it was the sole prerogative and distinguishing Character of that Order (viz) of Bishops to Ordain: His words are, Quid enim non faciat Presbyter, quod facit Episcopus excepta Sola Ordinatione: And therefore the Salvo's which he makes for the sake of some particular persons, against the constant practice of the Universal Church, and particularly against the Law of the Land, cannot be excused from being a Plea for the present Schism; and the perpetuating thereof, such Ordinations being still practiced." (p. 29-30).

Other Authorities: There is a rather long, but important assessment of the situation in JRC p. 43-53, and a superficial one in the Healing Attempt p. i-ii.

The Commissioners tried to compromise with the view expressed in Vox Cleri, although the use of the imperative ambiguous formula was not the way to unite Ministries of different denominations; conditional ordination was held to be equivocation by both sides. The two quotations above, and Williams' Diary, show how far apart the two sides were, even within the Church of England. Much of the problem was occasioned by thinking in terms of " the Dissenters " rather than in terms of the individual sects, which comprised the Non-conformist party; this meant that those arguing for relaxation in this matter, had to argue a general case on a broad front, which their opponents had little difficulty in ridiculing. Their opponents' hand was further strengthened by the fact that the Dissenters themselves were unwilling to accept anything which suggested that their former Ordination was imperfect. Comprehension floundered on this rock; No alterations to the Prayer Book would bring men into the Communion of the Church, who believed Prebyterial Orders valid and Episcopal Orders unnecessary; No Churchman, who considered Episcopal Orders vital to the exercise of the Christian Ministry, could accept them. The Debate had begun long before, 1689 provided no conclusive answers; and no one has since. The arguments quoted above, are still re-iterated today.

**Dr P. F. Bradshaw's Book,** *The Anglican Ordinal* (1971) places the 1689 Reforms in their context. His excellent work is my excuse for dealing with this matter so briefly.

In the Commission itself the matter of reforming the Ordinal was never finished. It would seem that so much time was taken up debating the Reordination of Dissenters, that there was no time left for a thorough revision of the remainder of the Text. After the ' Form and Manner ' there is the note " The Commissioners proceeded no further for want of time the Convocation being mett ". What has been added to the text, is the result of the deliberations recorded in Williams' Diary, and this is only a fragment, if an important fragment, of the Ordinal as a whole.

14. 1688: read, " Bp: will you reverently obey your Ordinary and other chief Ministers, unto whom is committed the charge and government over you so far as they urge any thing according to ye Rules & Cannons of ye Church; following with a glad mind and will their godly admonitions, and submitting your selves to their godly judgments so far as con———— with peaceable & huble carriage? "

15. 1688: By the first Veni Creator is written " Qu ".

16. The prayer " Receive the Holy Ghost " is deleted, and this prayer following stands on the interleaf. The quotation from St. Augustine is written in the Margin, beside " Receive ".

17. 1688: read, " thereunto & any where in times & places of necessities (wn ye Eccl. Gov. is not truly Apostolical)."
The section in parentheses has been subsequently deleted, and the note added; " too great power: if every ————— Judges themselves ".

18. There are two alterations to this form in 1688: (1) Oath of due obedience to the Archbishop: concludes, " and to their Successors According to ye Laws of Ch. & state. So help me God, through Jesus Christ." (2) The Archbishop's Question, ' Be you ready . . .". Read, " Are you ready with all faithful diligence, to banish and drive away wth ye sword of ye Spirit, all erroneous . . ."

By the Veni Creator is the note " Qu ".


## OTHER ALTERATIONS AND ADDITIONS IN THE REVISION OF 1688

In the Service for 5 Nov.

(1) In the prayer " O Lord, who didst this day discover " read, " judgment and justice, to humble all such workers . . ."

(2) In the following prayer, " Eternal God ", the words " Three Estates " are underlined.

In the Service for the King's Birth

(1) In the prayer " O Lord God of our Salvation " the word " heirs " is underlined, and " q " written in.

(2) The prayer " O God who by divine providence " is deleted.

(3) In the Prayer " O Lord God ", " and that our Gracious " to the end of the prayer is deleted.

(4) The Prayer " O most gracious God; Grant we beseech thee " is deleted.

(5) In the Prayer " O Lord who upholdest " the word " whole " in the phrase " whole Royal Family " is underlined, and " q " is written in the margin.

There are a number of further alterations, including a revision of the Thirty Nine Articles:

Article 1: "There is but one living . . . . And in unity of this Godhead there be three persons of one essence, power and eternity . . . ."

Article 2: "The Son . . . . who truly suffered, was crucified, dead, and buried, to reconcile his Father to us, and to be a sacrifice, for ye sinns of ye world."

Article 3: " Q. If, being in ye Creed, it may not be here omitted, seeing it is put down without explication?"

Article 4: ". . . . perfection of Man's nature, wherewith ascending bodily into heaven, He there continues until he returns to judge . . . ."

Article 5: ". . . . . is of one essence, majesty and glory . . . ."

Article 6: ". . . . necessary to salvation. By the name of the holy Scripture we do understand those canonical Books of the Old and New Testament, of whose authority was never any general doubt in the Church."
The names of certain books are altered thus:
" The 2 Book of Chronicles, the Book of Ezra, the Book of Nehemiah, the Book of Hester . . . ."

Article 8: Read; "The Three Forms by wch we make Profession of One Fayth, commonly calld ye Apostles (Creed), ye Nicene Creed, (ye Athanasian Creed) as also ye Articles of that comonly called ye C. of S.A. ought to be receiv'd & believ'd for the (substance) articles of them may be proved &c ".
There is a note beside " ought to be receiv'd " reading, " are received in ye Church ".

The sections marked by parentheses are deleted.

Article 9: ". . . . inclined to evil, & thereby become a child of wrath ". (The remainder of the text is deleted.)

Article 11: ". . . justified by faith onely that is, by a trusting to (ye mercies) Gods mercy in Christ (through) upon our (efficacious) assent [in yt] to ye terms of ye Gospell. [And living according to it]."

The sections marked by ( ) are deleted, and those enclosed by [ ], are insertions into the first draft.

Article 12: The phrase " and follow after Justification " is underlined with a " Qu ", and the phrase " by their virtue " is added after " away our sins ".

Article 13: (in the margin) " Qu. conc ye whole ".
(on the interleaf) " Works done by Persons who have not Fayth in Christ, have not a promise of such blessings as the Gospell offers to Believers."

Article 17: Read, ". . . . decreed by his Counsel, upon the Terms of his Gospell, to deliver . . . ."

Article 18: Read, ". . . every man shall undoubtedly be saved . . . . Scripture doth promise Salvation onely unto those who believe in ye name of Christ." (The word " Salvation " is underlined twice.)

274

| Article 20: | Read, ". . . . Rites or ceremonies as matters of decencie & order. And it hath also Authoritie in Controversies of Fayth for ye preserving the Peace of ye Church by keeping ye people to ye Rule of Fayth. But it is not lawful for the Church . . ." |
|---|---|
| Article 21: | Read, ". . . . not be contemptuously gathered . . . ." |
| Article 23: | Read, ". . . and sent, which after due personall Qualification be chosen . . . ." |
| Article 25: | Read, ". . . profession: but also they . . . . sure pledges and Effectual . . . ." |
| Article 27: | The Phrase " faith is confirmed " is underlined, with the note in the margin, " Qu about Infants who as yet have not fayth? " |
| Article 28: | Read, " the bread which we break is a comunion of the Body of Christ, and likewise the Cup of blessing is a communion of the Bloud of Christ . . . ." |
| Article 35: | The phrase " and necessary for these times " is deleted. By the Homilies is the note, " Qu. Abt a new book of Homilies wth more subjects & in method." |
| Article 36: | The phrase " of Edward the Sixth " is underlined with a " Qu ". |

There is a final note added: " Qu. If some of these Articles wch did respect especially ye Controversies in ye times in wch they were formed, are of necessity to be retained? "

Many of these changes are in keeping with the revision in general. The Alteration to Article 20, is however a double-edged sword. On the one hand it favours the dissenters, in that it covers a number of alterations which are envisaged in the Revision, and on the other hand the phrase " decencie & order " could be held to exclude such things as the Cross in Baptism which like the Surplice, was held to be " decent " and also unlike the surplice, " antient ". Article 8 is also altered in conformity with the alterations envisaged to the rubric before the Athanasian Creed. The most important alteration however, is the softening of the Doctrine of Original Sin; the phrase is deleted from Article 2, and much of Article 9 is deleted. There are the following notes on the blank interleaves at the back of the book.

" Additionall Services.

1. A Service fo ye (i night) day o yt of wch ye Supper was instituted. The Sacrament will be ye better udrstood by understanding ye paschale solemnitie, & ye time will help devotion.

2. Service for Passion week.

3. Partic. Litany for Good Friday setting forth ye passion more particularly & amply.
There wants a propr preface for yt day in ye Com: Office.

4. A Cours of Learning for ye Universities both in generall learning & yt wch belongs to the three Faculties. The Prsent Methods are not sufficiet: & there is nothing like a (?scheme) of rationall divinitie. An uniform in all (i Colls) univrs & schos.

Ag. All forr Jurisd.

A Godly & ———

Ag. Exhibits in visitn &c

Ag. Licences & marr &c

Ag. Chu ———

Of Comiss wth prot ———

Homilies.

We want a Body of divin. in 52 sermons for Afternoons. They should not exclude preaching wch extends to all Cases & may be applyd as occasion servs, to ye Condition of ye souls of ye Parish: wch fixed Homilies cannot so well be.

besides wthout preaching idleness would grow upo ye Clergy, & contempt fm ye people who look upon their preaching as their great pains.

Ye 52 Hom. would begett great uniformitie in ye belief of ye people: being read all ovr ye natio.

Catech.

A Set of Religion in method.

Ye 4th Com. &c to be stated in its sense.

Serm.

Psalms."

Note: in 4 above, there is nothing added; nor after " serm " and " Psalms ". The second section " A Cours of Learning " is very difficult to decipher, and the list beginning " Ag. All . . ." is so uncertain as to justify its complete omission.

## NOTES ON THE DIARY OF JOHN WILLIAMS

1. The original of Bishop Williams' Diary is lost, and the Editions we possess are both fourth-hand at least. The one quoted here, is that transcribed also by Black, from the Secker MSS (24/6) in Lambeth Palace Library. This copy is a transcription made for Secker by an emanuensis, from another copy of the Diary belonging to " Mr Sturges, Prebendary of Winchester." Mr Sturges' copy was itself a copy of Gibson's transcription from Bishop Williams' Original papers.

   There is however another manuscript of the Diary, purporting to have a similar history. This is MS 1774 in Lambeth Palace Library. Together with the MS is a letter dated 7 April 1834, part of which reads, " I will further observe that the Manuscript is in the hand of my Grand-father Bishop Terrick being a certified Copy of the original among Bishop Williams papers: & the same may be said of an interleaved common Prayer book containing the suggestions of the Commissioners, as well as of those of the Rev. Samuel Clark . . . ."

   Richard Terrick was Bishop of London in 1764, dying in 1777. There is no information available as to what edition this was copied from. It claims, like the Secker MS, to be copied from Gibson's transcript; but the wording, spelling and sometimes the order is completely different from the Secker MS. There is one thing in its favour; at the beginning of the Secker MS, there is a note " N.B. Before the 2d Sess . . . ." which contains a list of those who never attended the Commission. This cannot have been originally in this position, but would have been placed at the end of the text, when such information could be deduced. This is its position in the Terrick MS. The variations transcribed by Terrick, except differences of spelling, are printed in italics.

2. This note is written in Secker's hand, not as Black suggests, Dr Ducarel's.

3. " *The Tenor of it was in the following Words* ".

4. " *Judgments* ".

5. There are a number of minor differences throughout the text in Terrick, as for example "Meaw" instead of "Mews", "Sarum" instead of "Salisbury", "Winchester" instead of "Winton" in this case. As these make no material difference, they are regarded as different spellings.

6. " *1. Dr Goodman A.D. Middx 2. Dr Beveridge A.D. Colchester 3. Dr Alston A.D. Essex 4. Dr Battley A.D. Canterb.* "

7. This whole section is placed at the end in Terrick's version.

8. " *the first point proper to be considered was . . .* "

9. " *That if not the whole to be read, some parts the most useful might be retained. Dr Jane.* "

10. " *with* ".

11. " *It was debated whether to keep the old Translation, to have that alter'd, or to take wholly the new.* "

12. " *half was very faulty, the latter much better, from whence He collected. . . .* "

13. Omits " *Oct 14* ".

14. Omits " *at 10 o'Clock* ".

15. " *Sprat Bp of Rochester* ".

16. Omit " *and that* ".

17. " *persons concern'd therein* ".

18. " *Who* ".

19. " *given our assent and Consent unto them* ".

20. Omits " *sure* ".

21. " *right or wrong* ".

22. " *who* ".

23. " *if this Commission ended* ".

24. " *their hands* ".

25. " *and in great* ".

26. " *who* ".

27. " *for their acting* ".

28. " *1 oClock* ".

29. " *N.B. Octr. 16th* ". Omits " *Dr Patrick* ".

30. For " *Dean of Peterburrow* " read " *Bishop of Chichester* ".

31. " *Deans of Christ Church (Dr Aldrich) and Glocester (Jane) went out, and came no more* ".

32. " *Posture at the Sacrament* ".

33. " *those who kneel'd, should come to the Table: And* " (adds on left page) " *The Rubrick agreed to by the Commissioners. To take off all pretence of Scruple, if any not being satisfied therewith shall some day in the week before they intend to receive the Holy Communion come to the Minister of their Parish, and declare, that they are verily persuaded in their Conscience, that they cannot receive it kneeling without Sin, then the Minister shall endeavour to give them satisfaction in this*

*matter, after which, if they still persist, then the minister shall give them the Sacramental Bread & Wine in some convenient place or pew without obliging them to kneel."*

34. " They might object as well against ".

35. " argued, that this ".

36. " after a full hearing ".

37. Omits " Oct. 21 at 3 a Clock ".

38. " To this it was ".

39. Black reads ' Baluzius ' which is the correct name of the scholar; the text however reads " Balurius ". Terrick reads " Baluzius ".

40. (adds on the left hand page) " *Rubrick agreed upon. Whereas it is appointed by this office that all Children shall be presented by God fathers and Godmothers to be baptized, which is still continu'd according to the ancient Custom of the Church, that so besides the obligation laid upon the Parents to breed up their Children in ye Xtian Religion, there may be likewise other Sureties to see, that the Parents do their Duty, and to look to the Christian Education of the persons baptiz'd in case of the default or death of the Parents, yet there being some difficulties in observing this good and useful Constitution, It is hereby provided That if any person comes to the Minister and tells him He cannot conveniently procure Godfathers and Godmothers for his Child, and that He desires the Child may be baptiz'd upon the Engagement of the Parents only, In that Case, the Minister, if he persists shall baptize him upon the Suretyship of ye Parent or Parents or some other near Relation."*

41. " now set on foot:"

42. " officiate in the Service: It was desir'd that we should meet the next day ".

43. Omits " Tuesday Oct. 22 Met as Sub . . . . 10 "

44. Omits " that ".

45. Omits " - - - said in that of Ely ".

46. Omits " On Wednesday Oct 23 ".

47. 2dly That it was Receiv'd ".

48. Omits " Thursday Oct. 24 met about 10 ".

49. " It was said it was the Custom ".

50. " run over the other parts of the Body. Order'd ".

51. " Dr Beveridge. He took it so ill, that He was leaving us, But Dr. Beveridge ask'd his Pardon."

52. " Friday 1 o Clock, the Commissioners met. Present 15 ".

53. " Bishop of London, adjourn'd till Monday 3 o Clock ".

54. Omits " On Monday . . . Clock ".

55. For " Dr. T " read " Dr Fowler ".

56. " might either be left out ".

57. " who were . . . . that Baptism ".

58. The word baptismoi is in Secker's hand. Terrick reads baptismos.

59. " the Bishop of Worcester said, that ".

60. Omits " On Wednesday . . . . Clock."

61. " Deans. St Pauls Tillotson, Canterbury Sharp "

62. " Scott and Tenison, it was first to be . . . . Dissenters. It ".

63. Omits " Thursday . . . . Clock ".

64. ". . . . Salisbury, Chichester, Chester, Worcester, Bangor ".

65. Omits " Dr Tillotson ".

66. " office of ye Visitation ".

67. Omits " Met Novr . . . . a Clock ".

68. " Commination office and Considerd ".

69. " That ".

70. " did ".

71. " 3dly That of the . . . . it was alledg'd we had very ".

72. " Whatsoever Sins ye remit &c ".

73. " can never ".

74. " that He did not ".

75. Omits " do ".

76. Omits " therefore ".

77. " 1st As for that of the Foreign ".

78. Omits " (if not Camden) many ". The word " many " is written in the text in Secker's own hand, and this whole phrase would seem to be a gloss.

79. " were Consecrated without being Reordain'd: And that King James the 1st insisted stiffly upon it ".

80. Omits " of such Ordination ".

81. " reply'd, that they had Episcopal Ordination. It was ".

82. " then question'd, How . . . . that were at present in Orders ".

83. Both texts in the heading omit Stillingfleet from the list of people present. Whether this was an oversight or the section beginning " o - - - - " was a flashback, is uncertain.

84. " and a Rubrick was read ".

85. Omits " put ".

86. " Then Dr - - - made another proposal " (sic).

87. " And 2dly The Case of ".

88. " inserted in ye A.Ds. Presentation ".

89. *Omits " On Wednesday . . . . Clock ".*

90. *" Scotland: viz, That ".*

91. *" That He thought ".*

92. *" when their Design . . . . . . the Forms were originally by ".*

93. *" Council at Carthage ".*

94. *" and He insisted ".*

95. *" The Professor (Dr Hall) . . . . preach the Word of God and ".*

96. *Omits " Met Friday . . . . Clock ".*

97. *" the 10 first Collects ".*

98. *" if this is not retain'd ".*

99. *" when that was not us'd ".*

100. *" appears by the Rituals . . . . Ordinationibus ".*

101. *" Ordination defended. See Mason ".*

102. *" non item. L.2. c.2. p. 665,".*

103. *" manus imponebantur, non ipsi eam dabant ".*

104. *" was but to ".*

105. *Omits " Monday . . . . Clock ".*

106. *Omits " &c ".*

107. *" that might ".*

108. *Omits " Wednesday Nov. 12 ".*

109. *Omits " stayd not ".*

110. *" Whole again—made some alterations ".*

111. *"Office at Baptism . . . . Dr Williams . . ."*

112. *" amongst ".*

113. *" who ".*

114. *" Parted till 3 in ye afternoon ".*

115. *" And that was shewn ".*

116. *" by his Comission, so that they could begin nothing, though by the Commission they might debate and object as they ".*

117. *Omits " and 18 Sessions ".*

118. *" Commissioners that never sat were 6. viz. Abp York, Bishops Carlisle, and Exeter, Doctors Beaumont, Mountague and Battley."*

119. In this position is placed the analysis of the Commission in Terrick, which is placed at the beginning in Secker. (Begins, NB. 1 Before the 2d . . . ).

120. This is in the hand of Secker, and not as Black suggests Dr Ducarel.

# SELECT BIBLIOGRAPHY

*MANUSCRIPTS*
Lambeth Palace MSS 886, 1774, 2173, 933-943, 954; Secker Ms 24/6.

*SOME PAMPHLETS 1689-90*
*1688/9*

(Burnet) *A Letter from a Minister in the country, to a member of Convocation* by N.L.

Clarkson, David., *A Discourse concerning Liturgies.*

*Conformists Charity to dissenters, . . . . also several arguments for concessions and alterations in the Common Prayer and in rites and ceremonies.*

*Dialogue between Timothy and Titus, about the articles and some of the Canons of the Church of England.*

*A Glance upon the Ecclesiastical Commission.*

*A Healing attempt; being a representation of the Government of the Church of England according to the judgment of her bishops unto the end of Q. Elizabeth's reign.* (by John Humphreys?)

*A Healing Attempt examined, and submitted.* (by Thomas Long).

Hickeringill, Edmund., *The Ceremony-monger; his Character.*

Jane, William., *Letter to a Friend containing some quaeries about the Commission for making alterations in the Liturgy.*

Mather, Increase., *A Brief Discourse concerning the unlawfulness of Common Prayer worship.*

Owen, John., *A Discourse concerning Liturgies.*

Prideaux, Humphrey., *Letter to a friend relating to the present convocation.*

Shower, John., *An exhortation to repentance and Union among Protestants.*

Tenison, Thomas., *A Discourse concerning the Ecclesiastical Commission opened in the Jerusalem-Chamber Oct 10, 1689.*

*The Way to peace among all Protestants.*

Wake, William., *An exhortation to mutual charity and Union among Protestants.*

Williams, John., *A Brief exposition of the Church Catechism.*

*1690*
*The Church of England and the continuation of ceremonies thereof, vindicated . . . . (against) the ' Vanity, Mischief, and danger '.*

*Conformists Sayings.* (This is the same as *Conformists Charity,* under a new title).

*Conformists Reasons for bearing and joining with the Nonconformists.*

Comber, Thomas. *A Scolastic history of the Primitive and general use of liturgies . . . against Mr David Clarkson's discourse concerning Liturgies.*

*Explanation of the Terms, order and usefulness of the Liturgy of the Church of England.*

*Judgment of the Foreign Reformed Churches concerning the Rites and Offices of the Church of England, shewing there is no necessity of alterations.*

*Just Censure to the Answer of Vox Cleri.*

Long, Thomas., *Vox Cleri; or the Sense of the Clergy concerning the making of alterations in the established liturgy.*

Maurice, Henry., *Remarks from the Country; upon letters relating to the Convocation and alterations in the Liturgy.*

*New Survey of the Book of Common Prayer, humbly proposed to this present parliament.*

Payne, William., *An Answer to Vox Cleri . . . in order to a comprehension.*

*P.M. The Vanity, mischief and danger of continuing ceremonies in the worship of God.* (by Patrick Myddleton?)

*To the Reverend and Merry Answerer of Vox Cleri, to be left at Mr Brabazon Aylmer's . . . with a bundle.*

*Vindication of the two letters concerning the alterations in the Liturgy, in answer to Vox Cleri.*

*Vox Laici; or the Layman's opinion touching the making alteration in our Established Liturgy.*

*Vox Populi; or the sense of the Sober Lay-men of the Church of England, concerning the heads proposed in his Majesty's Commission to the Convocation.*

*Vox Regis et Regni; or a protest against Vox Cleri.*

Williams, John., *Discourse concerning the lawfulness of worshipping God.*

## OTHER PRINTED SOURCES

Abbey C. J. and Overton J. H., *The English Church in the Eighteenth Century.* 2 Vols. 1878.

Baxter R., *Reliquiae Baxterianae,* ed. M. Sylvester. 1696.

Bennet G. V., White Kennet 1660-1728. Bishop of Peterborough. 1957.

Birch T., *The Life of Dr John Tillotson.* 1752.

Bolam, C. G., Goring J., Short H. L. and Thomas R., *The English Presbyterians.* 1968.

Bradshaw P. F., *The Anglican Ordinal.* 1971.

Bosher R. S., *The Making of the Restoration Settlement.* 1951.

Brightman F. E., *The English Rite.* 2 vols. 2nd edn, 1921.

Brokesby F., *The Life of Mr Henry Dodwell with an account of his works.* 2 vols. 1718.

Burnet G., *History of his own time.* 1724, 1734.

Calamy E., *Abridgment of Mr Baxter's History.* 1713.

———————— *An Historical account of my own Life.* ed J. T. Rutt. 1829.

Cardwell E., *Documentary Annals of the Reformed Church of England.* 2 vols. 1839.

———————— *History of Conferences and other proceedings.* 1841.

Carpenter E., *The Protestant Bishop (Aberdeen).* 1956.

———————— *Thomas Sherlock 1678-1761.* 1936.

———————— *Thomas Tenison, Archbishop of Canterbury.* 1948.

Clarke Lowther., *Liturgy and Worship.* 1964.

Cragg G. R., *From Puritanism to the Age of Reason.* Cambridge, 1966.

———————— *Reason and Authority in the Eighteenth Century* Cambridge. 1964.

Cuming G. J., *The Durham Book.* 1961.

———————— *A History of the Anglican Liturgy.* 1969.

Davies, H., *The Worship of the English Puritans*. 1948.

Donaldson G., *The Making of the Scottish Prayer Book*. Edin. 1954.

D'Oyly G., *Life of William Sancroft*. 2 vols. 1721.

Dugmore C. W., *Eucharistic Doctrine in England from Hooker to Waterland*. 1942.

Every G., *The High Church Party 1688-1718*. 1956.

Grisbrooke W. J., *Anglican Liturgies of the Seventeenth and Eighteenth Centuries*. 1958.

Hart A. T., *William Lloyd 1627-1717*. 1952.

───────── *Life and Times of John Sharp, Archbishop of York*. 1949.

Hageman H. G., *Pulpit and Table*. 1922.

Jasper R. C. D., *Position of the Celebrant at the Eucharist*. 1959.

Kennet White, *History of England*. (vol 3). 1706.

L'Estrange H., *The Alliance of the Divine Offices* (1st edn, 1659), 1689.

Legg J. Wickham., *English Church Life from the Restoration to the Tractarian Movement*. 1914.

Lee F., *Memoirs of the life of Mr John Kettlewell*. 1718.

Nuttall G. F. and Chadwick O., ed., *From Uniformity to Unity 1662-1962*. 1962.

Overton J. H., *Church Life in England 1660-1714*. 1885.

Owen D., *English Philanthropy 1660-1960*. 1965.

Peaston A. E., *The Prayer Book Tradition in the Free Churches*. 1964.

Patrick Symon., *The Autobiography of Symon Patrick, Bishop of Ely*. Oxford, 1839.

*The First and Second Prayer Books of King Edward VI*. Everyman edn. No. 448. 1964.

*The Prayer Book of Queen Elizabeth*. Ancient and Mod. Lib. of Theol. lit. (1890?).

Prideaux H., *The Validity of the Orders of the Church of England*. 1688.

Proctor F. and Frere W., *A New History of the Book of Common Prayer*. 1961.

Rouse R. and Neill S., *A History of the Ecumenical Movement*. 2nd edn. 1967.

Rice H., *Thomas Ken, Bishop and non-juror*. 1964.

Singer S. W., *Correspondence of Henry Hyde, Earl of Clarendon*. 2 vols. 1828.

Stephens L., *History of English Thought in the Eighteenth Century*. 1876.

Sykes N., *Church and State in England in the XVIIIth Century*. Cambridge 1934.

───────── *Edmund Gibson Bishop of London 1669–1748*. Oxford, 1926.

───────── *William Wake Archbishop of Canterbury 1657-1737*. 2 Vols, Cambridge, 1957.

───────── *Old Priest new Presbyter*, 1956.

───────── *From Sheldon to Secker*. Cambridge, 1959.

Stromberg K. N., *Religious Liberalism in Eighteenth Century England*. Oxford, 1954.

Wood A. H., *Church Unity without Uniformity*. 1963.

COMBER, Thomas, 183f; 201 n31; 234
COMPTON, Henry, 12; 14; 17; 27-30; 45; 160-9; 171-6; 180 n10
COSIN, John, 180 n2; 191 n1; 192; 193 n7; 218; 266
CUMING, Geoffrey J, 198; 205
DAVIES, Richard, 16
DERING, Sir Edward, 9
DUCAREL, Dr, 277 n2; 280 n120
ELLIS, John, 18
EVERY, George, 18; 24; 204
FINCH, Daniel, 9
FLOYD : an alternative spelling of Lloyd
FOWLER, Edward, 27f; 30; 161; 167-171; 173-5
GARNETT, John, 177
GIBSON, Edmund, 46f; 177; 183 n1; 267f
GOODMAN, John, 27; 30; 161; 167f; 171
GRISBROOKE, Jardine, 240 n15
GROVE, Robert, 14-16; 27f; 30; 161-9; 171-3; 175f; 181 n19
GUNNING, Peter, 180 n2
HALE, Sir Matthew, 7; 190
HALES, John, 185
HALL, Henry, 48
HALL, John, 27; 29f; 161; 164-167; 172f
HEARNE, Thomas, 217f
HENRY, Philip, 16
HERBERT, Sir Arthur, 17
HERRING, Thomas, 47; 183 n2
HICKERINGILL, Edmund, 193
HOOKER, Richard, 185 n2
HOWE, John, 9
HUMPHREYS, Humphrey, 27; 30; 160; 169; 171; 174-6
JACOMBE, Thomas, 180 n2
JAMES II, 10-23; 36
JANE, William, 27; 29f; 33ff; 45; 161-4; 176
JASPER, Ronald C D, 240
JEFFREYS, Lord George, 17
JEWEL, John, 240

JONES, John, 46

KEN, Thomas, 13ff

KIDDER, Richard, 22; 27f; 30f; 155; 161-167; 171; 175; 177

KNOX, John, 185

LAKE, John, 14f

LAMPLUGH, Thomas, 27; 30; 160f; 176

LANGLEY, Sir Robert, 17

LEE, Francis, 18

LEGG, Wickham, 190; 192; 218; 221f; 240; 244f; 263-5; 268

L'ESTRANGE, Hamon, 36

LIGHTFOOT, Dr, 180 n2

LINDSAY, Theophilus, 261

LLOYD (Floyd), William (S Asaph), 9; 13-17; 22; 24; 27f; 30f; 160-8; 171-6; 181 n19; 221f

LLOYD, William (Norwich), 17

LOBB, Stephen, 12

LONG, Thomas, 35; 37

MANTON, Thomas, 1; 7

MACKENSIE, George, 12

MASON, Francis, 171-3

MATHER, Increase, 187

MAURICE, Henry, 32, 40f

MEGGOT, Richard, 12f; 30; 160-4; 176

MEW(S), Peter, 27; 30; 160; 162; 164

MONTAGUE, John, 27; 29f; 161; 176

MOORE, John, 20; 207

MORLEY, George, 9

NICHOLLS, William, 46; 177; 207f

NOTTINGHAM, 1st Earl (Heneage Finch), 24; 28

OWEN, John, 7; 36

PATRICK, Symon, 12-16; 20; 22; 24; 27-31; 66; 69; 107; 160-9; 171-5; 177; 181 n19; 199 n7; 207f

PAYNE, William, 38f

PEARSON, John, 180 n2

PEPYS, Samuel, 6

PENN, William, 12

PETRE, Fr, 11

PRICE, I J, 183f
PRIDEAUX, Humphrey, 23; 36; 41f; 44
REYNOLDS, Edward, 1; 180 n2
SANCROFT, William, 11-17; 19; 22-4; 113; 180 n12; 204f; 207f
SANDERSON, Robert, 180 n2
SCOTT, John, 27f; 30; 161-9; 171-5
SECKER, Thomas, 276; 280 n120
SHARP, Thomas, 20; 24; 27f; 30; 160-75; 180 n10; 207
SHELDON, Gilbert, 9; 180 n2
SHERLOCK, Thomas, 12f
SMITH, Thomas, 27; 29f; 160f; 176
SPARROW, Anthony, 4; 180 n2; 187; 234
SPRAT, Thomas, 17; 27; 29f; 160-3; 176
STILLINGFLEET, Edward, 9f; 14f; 20; 24; 27f; 30; 160-70; 177; 181 n19; 207f; 261; 279 n83
STRATFORD, Nicholas, 27; 30; 160; 167-9; 172-6
STURGES, Mr, 177; 276
SUNDERLAND, 3rd Earl (Spencer Charles), 17
TAYLOR, Jeremy, 240 n15
TAYLOR, John, 46
TENISON, Thomas, 12-16; 20f; 24; 27f; 30-5; 46; 47; 161-9; 171-6; 177; 180 n16 and notes *passim*
TERRICK, Richard, 276-80
TILLOTSON, John, 9; 14f; 20; 24-8; 30f; 35; 45; 160-2; 164-6; 168f; 171-5; 177; 181 n19; 207f; 270 n13
TRELAWNEY, Jonathan, 13f; 27; 29f; 160f; 176
TUCKNEY, Anthony, 180 n2
TURNER, Francis, 12-15; 17; 22f
WAKE, William, 19; 207
WALPOLE, Horace, 268
WALTON, Izaak, 180 n2
WATSON, Thomas, 12f
WHARTON, Henry, 17
WHISTON, William, 194 n14
WHITE, Francis, 12-15
WHITTINGHAM, William, 185
WILKINS, John, 7
WILLIAM OF ORANGE, 16; 17; 22; 23-8
WILLIAMS, John, 27f; 30; 125; 160-77 *passim*, and notes *passim*
WORTH, Mr, 1
WREN, Matthew, 194 n14; 199 n8; 243 n48; 266

THE ALCUIN CLUB—of which Dr Walter Howard Frere was for many years the President—exists for the object of promoting liturgical studies in general, and in particular a knowledge of the history and use of the Book of Common Prayer. Since its foundation in 1897 it has published over one hundred and twenty books and pamphlets.

The annual subscription is £2 and members of the Club are entitled to the publications of the current year *gratis*. Subscriptions, applications for membership and for the list of publications, should be sent to the Assistant Secretary.